PSYCHEDELIC
MEDICINE

PSYCHEDELIC MEDICINE

NEW EVIDENCE FOR HALLUCINOGENIC SUBSTANCES AS TREATMENTS

VOLUME 1

Edited by Michael J. Winkelman and Thomas B. Roberts

PRAEGER PERSPECTIVES

Westport, Connecticut
London

Library of Congress Cataloging-in-Publication Data

Psychedelic medicine : new evidence for hallucinogenic substances as treatments / edited by Michael J. Winkelman and Thomas B. Roberts

    p. cm.

    Includes bibliographical references and index.

    ISBN 978–0–275–99023–7 (set : alk. paper) — ISBN 978–0–275–99024–4 (v. 1 : alk. paper) — ISBN 978–0–275–99025–1 (v. 2 : alk. paper)

    1. Mental illness—Drug therapy. 2. Hallucinogenic drugs—Therapeutic use. 3. Psychotherapy. I. Winkelman, Michael. II. Roberts, Thomas B. [DNLM: 1. Mental Disorders—drug therapy. 2. Hallucinogens—contraindications. 3. Hallucinogens—therapeutic use. WM 402 P9725 2007] RM315.P7599 2007

615'.7883—dc22   2007008459

British Library Cataloguing in Publication Data is available.

Library of Congress Catalog Card Number: 2007008459

ISBN-10: 0–275–99023–0 (set code)   ISBN-13: 978–0–275–99023–7 (set code)
        0–275–99024–9 (Vol. 1)   978–0–275–99024–4 (Vol. 1)
        0–275–99025–7 (Vol. 2)   978–0–275–99025–1 (Vol. 2)

First published in 2007

Praeger Publishers, 88 Post Road West, Westport, CT 06881
An imprint of Greenwood Publishing Group, Inc.
www.praeger.com

Printed in the United States of America

The paper used in this book complies with the Permanent Paper Standard issued by the National Information Standards Organization (Z39.48–1984).

10 9 8 7 6 5 4 3 2 1

CONTENTS

Part II: Medical Applications

Part III: Legal Aspects of the Medical Use

PREFACE: WARNING

THOMAS B. ROBERTS

If a visitor from Mars were to drop by Earth, he might be curious about what we call marriage, so he might look in the Yellow Pages to see who knows about this strange earth-custom. He would find "Marriage Counselors," "Divorce Lawyers," and maybe "Domestic Abuse Courts." The information he'd obtain from interviewing these experts would be accurate but skewed toward problems. He would find very little about the benefits of marriage. A similar situation exists with psychedelic drugs. If he interviewed mental health professionals, emergency room personnel, and law enforcement officers, he would learn about psychedelics' harmful effects, but little about their possible beneficial ones.

In this book, we try to partially rebalance this skewed information and sampling error. The leads that these chapters present are just that—leads, and as you read this book, we hope you'll realize that the possible medical uses our authors present are just that—possible. These chapters offer directions for more advanced and carefully designed research to be accomplished in the future; they aren't the final word by any stretch of the imagination, and we are not recommending their general medical uses until all the necessary research and approval are accomplished, and we hope these books will speed up that process.

With that in mind, remember there are real dangers. Self medication is one of them. What are the others?

- The drugs you buy from a dealer may not actually be the drug you want, and some dealers will sell you anything and tell you it's what you want. Also, its dose is unknown, and it may be contaminated with other drugs or who-knows-what. Unfortunately, this danger is largely a result of our current drug policies.
- Psychedelics can activate parts of your unconscious mind that cause great anxiety and should be faced only in the company of a qualified therapist. These might include traumatic experiences, for example, or childhood fears. Stan Grof's work gives examples of this; fortunately, his patients were undergoing psychedelic psychotherapy not taking the drug on their own. For someone who is pre-psychotic, this could cause a bad trip or even tip the balance into psychosis. Normal people can still bring up irrational fears and thoughts that can continue to interfere with their lives after the drug is gone.
- People have idiosyncratic and genetic-based reactions to drugs. Some people are allergic to aspirin, others to antibiotics. This is also true of psychedelics.
- Genetic differences probably play a role too. For example, Ecstasy (MDMA) works by flooding the space between cells (the synapse) with serotonin. Serotonin is then carried back to the cells by "transporter proteins" to be reused. Some Ecstasy users are prone to depression because they have a short version of the gene that produces a less-efficient transporter. People with two short genes are even more susceptible to depression after MDMA. As the field of pharmacogenomics—the study of the interactions between genes and drugs—grows, it's likely that other gene-based drug effects will be discovered. You don't know about your possible reactions to an unknown drug.
- If you are pregnant, psychedelics can instigate a miscarriage by causing uterine contractions. According to Grof's work, if a woman reexperiences her own birth during the perinatal stage, this sometimes includes uterine contractions.
- Grof makes a sensitive psychiatric point: Although the myth of psychedelics causing birth defects is fading away, a certain number of babies are born with defects even to mothers who have had excellent prenatal care. If this happens to a mother who had psychedelics when she was pregnant—even though she knows the birth defect rumor is a myth—she doesn't need to think everyday for the rest of her life, "What if I hadn't?"
- Should you slip a dose into your friend's coffee? If you believe, as we do, that each person has the right to determine what goes on in his or her own mind, then putting a drug in your friend's coffee destroys this freedom. You are infringing this right to mental self-control.

Psychedelic Warning Label (A former student labeled it this way.)

From my own experiences and through readings, I have become increasingly respectful of the power of LSD and other psychedelic drugs. Like any powerful thing, they can be destructive or constructive depending on how skillfully they are used. Among other things, they can concentrate your attention on the most vulnerable, most unpleasant parts of your mind. Therefore, psychedelic drugs should be explored only under the guidance of a qualified therapist, one who has extensive psychedelic training. If you need assistance, most mental health professionals, as they are currently mistrained concerning psychedelics, may be of little help; some could even worsen your state. Furthermore, street dosages are of unknown strength and questionable purity. Until the time you can explore your mind using psychedelics of known strength and purity under qualified guidance, within the law, I urge you to limit yourself to studying the literature and working within professional and other organizations for the resumption of legal, scientific, religious, or academic research.

—Syllabus "Social Foundations of Psychedelic Studies"
Northern Illinois University

EDITOR'S OVERVIEW OF VOLUME 1

MICHAEL J. WINKELMAN

Our considerations of these ancient—and future—medicines are organized into two volumes. The first addresses the substances from their historical, cultural, clinical, physical health, and legal perspectives; the second focuses on applications to addictions medicine, mental health, and transpersonal and spiritual growth. Together they provide an understanding of why psychedelic medicines are important and provide guidelines regarding how they can better serve humanity in the future.

This first volume provides three major perspectives. The first part addresses the general social, clinical, and epidemiological context for understanding the social dimensions affecting these medicines, their traditional and modern patterns of use, and their safety and efficacy. The second part describes various physical medicine applications of these substances, especially to resistant conditions such as cluster headaches, OCD (obsessive-compulsive disorder), and post-traumatic stress disorder, as well as to other conditions such as depression, anxiety, and the AIDS wasting syndrome. The third part addresses the constitutional and legislative contexts of these still largely illegal psychedelic medicines, examining the legal contexts that have both permitted and prohibited their use in our society. Together these chapters provide a broad framework for understanding the

important applications of these substances and the legal apparatus that inhibits—
and may ultimately permit—their use.

PART I

Winkelman's introductory chapter addresses psychedelic medicine in cross-
cultural perspective, illustrating the therapeutic and spiritual interpretations of
their uses in many societies. The cross-cultural similarities in their use and interpretation reflect a biological foundation for their uses and effects. Winkelman's
chapter addresses some of the standard interpretations of these substances' mechanisms of action in the serotonergic neurotransmitter system. His analyses of the
systemic effects of serotonergic transmission, and the interaction of the psychedelic medicines with serotonergic mechanisms, provide the basis for characterizing their effects as *psychointegrative*. Psychedelics produce a disinhibition of
informational, emotional, and visual processes and stimulation of the integration
of limbic system processes within the neocortex. This in effect integrates behavioral and emotional dynamics with the rational processes of the symbolic brain.

McKenna's chapter on ayahuasca places psychedelic medicines in the
broader historical context, beginning with the Western exposure to these substances in other cultures and continuing through their current prohibition derived
from political reactions to social movements of the 1960s. McKenna's chapter
describes the historical social contexts crucial for understanding our current
political engagement with psychedelic medicines. Here we see how politics
rather than science has come to dominate an arena which should properly be of
medicine, not administrative law. He describes the story of ayahuasca, the most
important and extensive psychedelic medicine traditions on the planet. He recognizes ayahuasca as a quinsentential shamanic medicine; it was used by hundreds
of cultural groups in the past, and survives today among dozens of cultures, in
several Brazilian Ayahuasca churches, and in a variety of healing practices. The
traditions associated with this brew—a combination of several plants—reflect
an astute knowledge of both plant biochemicals and psychotherapeutic management of natural substances. A variety of studies indicates its safety and suggests
numerous medical applications. For many reasons, ayahuasca represents one of
the most potent forces in the psychedelic medicine traditions of the planet.

Passie's chapter provides an overview of how a range of psychedelic medicines have been used in Western therapies, largely based on research carried
out before the 1969 prohibition and practices continuing in Europe. These early
engagements with psychedelic medicine have provided knowledge of a variety
of aspects of the "best uses," both in terms of different therapeutic processes
and with respect to the conditions most effectively treated. The effective treatment of a range of psychological conditions, especially diagnoses resistant to
ordinary psychotherapeutic interventions, points to important applications of psychedelic medicines.

Frecska's chapter addresses the concerns about the safety of psychedelic medicines, examining the epidemiological evidence regarding their risks. His considerations point to both the relative safety of psychedelic medicines and a range of potential acute and long-term psychological side effects. Research also indicates particular groups of people face increased risks from the use of psychedelic medicines. His chapter points to both the strategies for managing these crises and the need for better-controlled studies of these substances and their effectiveness.

PART II

The second part of this volume focuses on a range of uses that has emerged in the public and on clinical applications of psychedelic medicines. Because of federal restrictions and limited funding bases, the studies available generally fall short of the double-blind clinical controls that are the ideal method of evaluation. This lack of clinical studies makes ethnographic studies even more significant.

The important medical knowledge that can emerge from public use of psychedelic medicines is illustrated in Sewell and Halpern's chapter on the notorious cluster headaches. These conditions are also known as "suicide headaches" because of their virtually untreatable nature and the desperate ends to which they occasionally drive their victims. Here we see how medicine is following culture, where the lay discovery of the effectiveness of psychedelic medicines in the treatment of these headaches has finally come to the attention of modern medicine. Sewell and Halpern review a range of evidence regarding the effectiveness of psychedelic medicines in addressing cluster headaches. The near-universal positive responses of cluster headache sufferers and their personal experiences override the necessity of statistical analyses or the customary double-blind clinical trials to establish their efficacy.

Moreno and Delgado's chapter illustrates the use of psilocybin in the treatment of OCD, a chronic and common psychiatric condition that is resistant to conventional treatment. Their studies reflect the combined applications of insights obtained from anecdotal reports with an understanding of the serotonin–psychointegrator interactions to develop hypotheses regarding the clinically efficacy of psilocybin in treating OCD. The clinical data indicated a reduction of OCD symptoms in all patients, including complete remission in some. They speculate on the importance of psychedelics in facilitating developmental psychosocial insights.

Greer and Tolbert's chapter points to some of the specific effects of MDMA in psychotherapy, particularly its role in addressing unresolved emotional conflicts associated with fear responses. MDMA reduces the conditioned fear responses and avoidance of associated feelings, enhancing access to the information contained in these thoughts, feelings and memories. The MDMA effects reduce fear and induce a spontaneous state of loving and forgiving, enhancing awareness about the source of anxiety-provoking feelings. With their reduction, patients find it easier to trust the validity of their own feelings and those of others without fear, and to release the associated emotional blockages.

Mithoefer's consideration of the use of MDMA in treatment of the notoriously resistant PTSD (Post-Traumatic Stress Disorder) illustrates an important reason for opening up clinical research and applications of psychedelic medicines. His chapter emphasizes a point repeated in these volumes, the importance of screening and preparing patients, arrangement of the physical and social setting of therapy, and assuring the adequate preparation of therapeutic team as well. He also illustrates the particular advantages of MDMA in addressing PTSD patients' vigilant, avoidant, and hyperaroused conditions that make them resistant to therapy. MDMA's ability to reduce fear and anxiety, enhance openness, and increase trust in the therapeutic alliance makes it an excellent treatment adjunct.

Montagne points out the early recognition of the value of hallucinogenic drugs in the treatment of depression. He points out that a broad range of psychedelics have effects on neurotransmitters and receptors that influence many psychological conditions, including mood and anxiety. While MDMA may be the most promising of these agents in regard to the treatment of depression, the serotonin-based psychedelics also have promising applications. His conclusions are that current utility of psychedelics in the treatment of major depressive disorders is primarily for those conditions produced by traumatic events (e.g., PTSD) and advanced stages of illnesses such as cancer and AIDS. However, identifying the real potential of the psychedelics in the treatment of depression will have to await the reinitiation of pharmaceutical discovery and development that largely has been on hold since the late 1960s.

Abrams reviews the use of marijuana and cannabanoids in the treatment of the AIDS wasting syndrome, illustrating another application of community-based knowledge in the formulation of clinical hypotheses and experimental treatments. The wasting syndrome involves anorexia and extreme weight loss; frequently fever and diarrhea has been an accelerating factor in precipitating death among AIDS patients, who discovered marijuana as an effective antidote that allowed them to return to eating. Although marijuana was available under the Compassionate Use Investigational New Drug, it was removed in 1992 when delta-9-tetrahydrocannabinol (Marinol) was approved for treatment of anorexia associated with the AIDS wasting syndrome. His research reported here also indicates that smoked marijuana has a potential efficacy in the treatment of painful peripheral neuropathy, another difficult to treat HIV-related condition. Since cannabinoids appear to have role in natural pain modulation as well as the immune systems, their potentials are multifaceted and likely to affect many conditions.

Grob's chapter points to the important applications of hallucinogens in treating problems associated with the management of terminal cancer, such as existential anxiety, despair, and fear. A range of anecdotal evidence indicates their important role in addressing the psychological and existential crises often encountered by both the dying patients and their families. The psychedelic medicines and their spirituality-inducing effects are powerful medicines that go beyond the effects of conventional psychotherapies and psychotropic medication regimens to address the core psychological processes afflicting individuals addressing end of life issues. As Grob points out: "Given the universality of the essential existential dilemma, and the potential for the optimally conducted hallucinogen treatment model to significantly enhance the quality of the end of life period, there is clearly a need to develop further research that will demonstrate the utility of this field of hallucinogen medicine."

PART III

The chapter by Boire places the prohibitions on psychedelic medicines in the broader context of the federal control of drugs. The lack of constitutional authority for the federal government to control what we place in our bodies has led to development of control through administrative law. The process of classifying substances as Schedule I—substances without medical use and with a high risk for abuse—makes them unavailable for all therapeutic uses. Boire shows how these classifications have been achieved through political actions without an impartial consideration of the scientific evidence. His chapter also provides guidelines for adapting to the legal constraints on the psychotherapeutic use of these substances, a limited range of opportunities given the current legal climate. Boire outlines a "medical necessity defense" in the case that one is detained by law enforcement for using a substance as alternative to other ineffective medical treatments. He contends that it should be a valid defense if the treatment (although a Schedule I psychedelic) reduces the patient's severe suffering without causing disproportionate harm to others (patient, other people, or to the State's interest).

Feeney's chapter expands our understanding of the current—and possible—permissible uses of these substances. He examines how the constitutional and legislative provisions relating to protection of religious freedoms, combined with the federal government's special relations with the Native American tribes, have produced a variety of legal contexts affecting the use of peyote and other psychoactive sacramentals. While the deliberations of the federal courts regarding the right to use peyote have focused on the special protections afforded to the members of federally recognized tribes, Feeney points to inconsistencies with other rulings. The existing rulings would not justify denying the right to the use of peyote to nonrecognized Native American groups. This leads Feeney to the conclusion that non-Indians would also be protected if they are practicing traditional Indian peyote religions. By extension, other psychoactive sacramentals cannot be restricted to specific groups, Native American or otherwise, and their use may be protected under federal (but not state) laws.

Groisman and de Rios examine the defensible legal contexts for use of psychedelic medicines within current U.S. law by a consideration of the cultural background of the ayahuasca churches. The lack of dispute regarding the religious status of the ayahuasca churches reflects their deep history in Brazilian society and their broad acceptance as part of the societal religious milieu. In the deliberations of the U.S. Supreme Court justices, specific traditions of American jurisprudence and Congressional laws made particular concerns the focus of attention, namely the potential harm to users and society. These considerations, rather than the religious use of these substances, made the government's case unconvincing and provided the ground-breaking legal victory for the ayahuasca churches.

CONCLUSIONS

We here preface our own conclusions, that the legitimate use of humanity's most important and ancient plant medicines should not be restricted by politics, but instead guided by science. We believe that the free exercise of science is a political right, one that informed citizens need to act on in order to protect its free exercise. As our contributors lay out the scientific evidence in the following chapters, we hope that you too will be convinced that the weight of science rather than the arbitrary prerogatives of administrative law should govern our health care.

PART I

THE SOCIAL AND CLINICAL CONTEXT

1

THERAPEUTIC BASES OF PSYCHEDELIC MEDICINES: PSYCHOINTEGRATIVE EFFECTS

MICHAEL J. WINKELMAN

INTRODUCTION

For thousands of years, human beings have used medicinal plants to enhance their health and well-being. In cultures around the world, plants commonly referred to as psychedelic, hallucinogens, and entheogens have played central roles in their healing practices. These vision-inducing plants have also played important roles in the religious and spiritual practices of many societies, evoking powerful emotional, cognitive, and therapeutic reactions. These plants that were central to concepts of health, spirituality, and well-being were, however, demonized and rejected by European cultural institutions in the process of the development of the modern world. Their legacy was largely lost to Western civilization until anthropology recovered this knowledge, and it was re-embraced by some in the context of the social revolutions of the 1960s. This convergence of politics and foreign ethnomedicines provoked oppressive reactions, leading to a virtual ban on the use of these powerful medicines in research and therapy.

This introduction has several purposes:

1. to situate these plants in a social context that explains the divergent perspectives on these substances;

2. to provide a general understanding of the premodern perspectives regarding the uses of these substances as medicines;

3. to explain our use of *psychedelic,* as opposed to *hallucinogen* and other terms, to refer to these substances and their effects; and

4. to illustrate the neurological bases of the effects of psychedelic substances as *psychointegrators* (as discussed below).

Psychedelic plants constitute part of humanity's ethnobotanical knowledge of substances of great medicinal and therapeutic importance cross-culturally and throughout history. Where used, these substances generally have been viewed as central sources of spiritual experience and religious participation, providing inspiration for the institutionalization of religious sentiments and activities (e.g., see La Barre 1972; Schultes and Hofmann 1979; Dobkin de Rios 1984; Winkelman and Andritzky 1996; Schultes and Winkelman 1996; Rätsch 2005). These plants are also considered the most powerful of medicines, central to the cultures' healing traditions. These plants are important in understanding cultural and religious development as well as, perhaps, the evolution of humans' "wet ware"—the neurochemical transmitter systems of our brains.

Societal Differences in the Use of Psychedelic Plants

Cultural use of psychedelic plants is not universal but varies as a function of social conditions. Different types of societies make different assessments of their value and potentials. These differences in their use are reflected in the dramatically larger number of psychedelic plants used in the New World in comparison to the Old World cultures (La Barre 1970). These differences have been attributed to cultural factors because there are psychedelic plants present but not used for religious purposes in the Old World (e.g., Europe) (La Barre 1970; Furst 1972; Schultes and Hofmann 1979), where they were often associated with witchcraft (Harner 1973). Institutional political factors are also responsible for the lack of use of these psychointegrator plants. Hallucinogenic plant use is not typically institutionalized in complex societies (Dobkin de Rios and Smith 1977; Winkelman 1991). Cross-cultural analyses reveal that increasing social and political complexity, particularly political integration, leads to reduction in the use of psychointegrator plants (Winkelman 1991). This negative relation to political integration reflects the dynamics of their psychocognitive effects and their inherent conflicts with the psychosocial needs of hierarchical societies.

The repression of and restrictions on use of psychedelics as a function of increasing political integration reflect their typical patterns of use and their effects on social relations and personal interpretations of the world. Dobkin de Rios and Smith (1977) suggest that these plants are typically repressed in state-level societies because they constitute a potential threat to the religious interpretations of those who hold social and religious power. Psychedelic medicines are typically employed in social settings where local idiosyncratic interpretations derived from the set and setting (personal expectations and the local situational influences) play powerful roles in shaping the experiences. Local interpretation of the experiences could pose a threat to the centralized hierarchical control of religious consciousness and political authority, thus undermining social control. Such conflicts could be expected, given the typical cross-cultural patterns of use of these plants in small group community settings, where they enhance group cohesion and reaffirm traditional value orientations and cosmological beliefs. They consequently reinforce a traditional community-based mythos and social order rather than interpretations of hierarchical political orders and their ideologies of control.

The social contexts associated with the use of psychedelics illustrate their applications to facilitate adaptations to social change. Under conditions of rapid social change, they facilitate adjustments to changing circumstances by enhancing the mediation between conceptual systems (e.g., see Andritzky 1989). The widespread use of the *Banisteriopsis* genus (*ayahuasca*) in Amazonia in collective rituals assists group identity formation and management of acculturation problems by mediating between the indigenous world view and the European-derived systems (Andritzky 1989). The symbolic synthesis of traditional and new beliefs provoked by the use of these plants facilitates psychosocial adjustment. A similar dynamics of psychosocial adjustment was noted in the selective adoption of the Peyote Religion (Native American Church) among the Navajo (Aberle 1966). The early Navajo adherents were primarily those who experienced the greatest relative loss from federally imposed livestock reduction programs. The Native American Church provided a community ethos that reinforced orientations to traditional values of community solidarity and facilitated an adjustment of the Navajo values of collectivism to the broader society's emphasis on individualism. The burgeoning use of psychedelics in American culture was also associated with periods of rapid social change in the United States (i.e., 1960s and 1990s). There is, however, a more primordial pattern of use of psychedelic medicines.

Cross-Cultural Uses of Psychointegrators

In cultures around the world that use psychedelic plants, they are consistently associated with the fundamental principles reflected in the etymology of the term *entheogens*—generating the experience of the god within—reflecting the belief that these plants are powerful spiritual sacraments that provide access to sacred worlds. These sacred substances also have simultaneous therapeutic applications (see Embodden 1972; Furst 1972, 1976; Schultes and Hofmann 1979; Wasson et al. 1986; Dobkin de Rios 1984; Schultes and Winkelman 1996; Winkelman and Andritzky 1996; Rätsch 2005). As the authors in the present volumes show, these uses are dramatically expanded as their medical potentials are discovered in the context of the diseases and illness of the modern world.

In the premodern world, psychedelics were revered for their ability to dramatically alter experience, shifting self-awareness to an "other-worldly" sacred or spiritual domain. This spiritual encounter was seen as having important applications as a therapeutic event. Indeed, the plants themselves were viewed as animistic agents, providing the basis for personal relations with an animistic world, especially power animals. The experiences they induced provided the opportunity for participation in a mythical time which was the origins of cultural values and religious beliefs. This direct contact with a spiritual source of power was related to self-identification and ego transformation. The use of these substances was focused on healing and divination, and for enhancement of social solidarity and interpersonal and community relations and for strengthening social identity and group cohesion (Dobkin de Rios 1984; Winkelman 1996a).

The worldwide interpretations of these substances emphasize their simultaneous religious, spiritual, and medicinal roles. McKenna (1992) documents the worldwide prehistoric practices of using mushrooms as a central part of a cultural ethos relating to the earth and mysteries of nature. He contends that the mushrooms enhanced self-awareness and a sense of contact with a "Transcendent Other." This reflected an experience of the sentience and intelligence of nature, an intimate awareness of our interconnectedness with nature, the earth, and the universe. McKenna proposed that entheogenic substances played an important role in the evolution of human consciousness, producing a sense of interconnectedness and balance with nature.

Psychedelic medicines were central to many shamanic practices, raising the question of whether they were the progenitors of humanity's original spiritual practices. The prehistorical role of vision-inducing plants as progenitors of religion was suggested by La Barre (1972), who called attention to their potentials to stimulate the visionary and supernatural experiences which often give rise to religious traditions. He suggested that these substances stimulate aspects of the subconscious mind, represented as supernatural beings and spiritual beliefs, reflecting the subjective world of human experience, perception, and consciousness. In essence, the cross-cultural patterns of the use of psychedelics indicate that they are functionally related to the origins of religion, consciousness, and perhaps ultimately modern human consciousness. Why should these plants have such central roles in human consciousness and culture? The answer lies in their neurological effects that produce an integration of various psychophysiological processes, a biologically driven psychointegration.

Neurophenomenological Approaches: Psychedelics as "Psychointegrators"

Explaining the institutionalized use of psychedelic plants requires integration of interdisciplinary, cross-cultural, and neurophenomenological[1] perspectives to provide understandings of: 1) their cross-cultural similarities in terms of biochemical mechanisms and 2) their psychodynamic effects on human experience.

The cross-cultural similarities in the experiences and interpretations of these substances suggest similar psychophysiological properties of the diverse psychedelic plants. Neurophysiological studies illustrate their common physiological effects produced through intervention in the serotonergic neurotransmitter systems. An interdisciplinary synthesis (Winkelman 1996a, 2001) provides the rationale for the term "psychointegrator" to refer to the central effects of these substances, explaining their cross-cultural social and therapeutic uses in terms of effects on the serotonergic neurotransmitter systems.

The role of serotonin as a "neuromodulator," the structural similarity of psychedelics and serotonin, and the specific effects of the psychedelics on serotonergic transmission are the bases for their characterizations as "psychointegrators." Psychointegrators enhance integration of information through stimulating areas of the brain central to managing processes related to fundamental aspects of self, emotions, memories, and attachments. These processes are necessary for the overall integration of information in the brain. This psychointegrative effect is manifested physiologically in the typical effects on brain waves produced by these substances, the stimulation of coherent theta wave synchronization along the neuraxis, the nerve bundle linking the structural levels of the brain. It is manifested psychologically in the experiences of healing, wholeness, interconnectedness, cosmic consciousness, and other transpersonal experiences which these substances regularly produce (e.g., see Grof 1975, 1980, 1989, 1992; also Volume 2).

Psychointegration underlies the psychedelics' cross-cultural use as sacred and therapeutic agents. The effects of psychointegrators upon neural, sensory, emotional, and cognitive processes illustrate their adaptive advantages produced by the stimulation of the serotonergic systems. This involves an enhancement of consciousness provoked by increasing the integrative information processing, achieved by activation of the serotonergic circuitry between the lower structures of the brain (R-complex and paleomammalian brain; MacLean 1990). Psychointegrative effects derive from the disinhibition of emotional and social processes and the stimulation of systemic integration of brain functions, particularly the integration of limbic system emotional processes with the neocortical processes. Psychointegrators couple nonlinguistic behavioral and social–emotional dynamics with rational processes and functionally integrate different systems of the brain. Psychointegration produces spiritual and transcendent experiences by enhancing operations of basic structures and functions of consciousness (self, other, and affect/attachment) (Winkelman 2003).

These neurological foundations help explain the widespread common patterns of use of these plant substances in religious and therapeutic practices. Psychedelic plants are generally used along with other means of inducing ASC (altered states of consciousness) in shamanistic healing practices that reflect the nearly universal institutionalization of the psychobiological potentials of ASC (Winkelman 1986a,b, 1990, 1992). Through a number of physiological and psychological mechanisms, the ASCs they produce result in physiological changes that facilitate healing and cognition (Winkelman 1992, 2000).

These psychedelic-induced alterations of consciousness are a quintessential spiritual experience of "ecstasy," providing a neurological basis for the role of chemical agents as sources of spiritual experience and personal transformations.

Why *Psychedelic* Medicines? Hallucinogens, Entheogens, and Psychointegrators

The use of the term *psychedelic* to refer to these medicines and their effects reflects a careful consideration of many perspectives, including botanical, medical, and social. Other frequently employed terms which are similar, but not synonymous, include *psychotomimetic, hallucinogen, holotropic, entheogen,* and more recently, *psychointegrator.* All of these, including *psychedelic,* have limitations. We have chosen to use *psychedelic* for its currency, but not without reservations.

HALLUCINOGENS

Cross-cultural commonalities in the experiences induced by the diverse substances called hallucinogens do not derive from a common botanical family; the diverse plants and substances that produce these effects occur in nearly 100 species and a wide range of genera and families (Schultes and Hofmann 1979; Rätsch 2005). The classic characterization of these substances as hallucinogens was based on subjective criteria, their ability to produce visions, voices, thoughts, and alterations of perceptions and mood in nontoxic doses (Siegel 1984). This subjective basis for the classification of these substances as *hallucinogens* therefore reflected cultural interpretations emphasizing a medical definition of hallucinations as false and disturbances of thought and/or experiences without a real basis. Similarly, the early psychiatric term psychomimetic—psychosis mimicking—implies a psychotic and delusional basis for the experiences, ignoring their central phenomenological aspects of these experiences as representing transcendental truths, realities with greater veridicality than our ordinary real reality experiences. Cross-culturally, these substances are interpreted as invoking perceptions of a spiritual realm, an important source of valid information, in direct contrast with the implications of delusions emphasized by these other terms.

Recognition of the shortcomings of these medical terms prompted the development of new terminology. The term psychedelic, referring to the extraordinary conceptual (mind-manifesting) impact upon human experience and understandings, was developed in the context of LSD (lysergic acid diethylamide) experiences and the social movements with which they were associated. Consequently, there are general connotations associated with the term psychedelic derived from these counter-cultural social movements. This has politicized the term psychedelic and consequently made it undesirable to many. The focus on the mental also fails to capture the significant emotional and therapeutic experiences associated with these substances.

ENTHEOGENS

Schultes and Hofmann (1979) referred to these substances as "plants of the gods," reflecting the indigenous terms for these plants found around the world and the perceptions of these plants as having indwelling spiritual influences. In light of these widespread characterizations, Ruck et al. (1979) coined the term entheogens from the Greek *entheos,* referring to "the god within," and *gen,* "action of becoming." While reflecting many cultural perceptions of these substances, the concept of entheogen does not reflect other personal and cognitive dynamics of these plants' effects. Furthermore, entheogen implies a spiritual basis that may alienate a more scientific approach to the study of these substances.

PSYCHOINTEGRATORS

Winkelman (1996a, 2001) introduced the term psychointegrators as reflecting both neurological and experiential effects of these substances. The cross-cultural perceptions regarding the effects of these substances coincide with the principles of their action based on neurobiological research, providing a neuro-phenomenological perspective that integrates neurological and experiential effects (Winkelman 1996b). Psyche reflects not only the mind but also the soul and spirit, the broader bases to which psyche once referred. Psychointegrator implies the stimulation of the mind, emotions, body soul, and spirit to integrative development. Psychointegration involves a stimulation of both mental and emotional processes through a physiological dynamic that forces the organism toward an integrative holistic growth state in the integration of the soul, mind, and spirit for growth and development. This model of psychointegration is extended in Vollenweider's (1998) research of their effects on the cortico-strato-thalamocortical loops linking the sensory gating systems of the lower brain and the receptor areas of the frontal brain. These same meanings are inherent in the term holotropic proposed by Grof (1975, 1989; also see Volume 2) to describe the psychodynamic actions of these substances in promoting an orientation toward wholeness.

The neurotransmitter effects of psychointegrators on the serotonergic neurotransmitter system involve a number of psychointegrative effects. These begin with neurotransmitter processes, and continue through effects on neural circuitry, functional systems of the brain, and consequently emotional, cognitive, and psychological processes. These together produce systemic macro-level integrative effects across hierarchical levels of the brain (e.g., the enhanced connections between the R-complex and limbic brain) (Winkelman 1996a) and across functional systems (Vollenweider 1998). These psychointegrative effects are epitomized by their stimulation of the functions of the serotonergic neurotransmitter system, a "neuromodulatory" system which integrates diverse forms of information and systemic demands of the body, modulating the activities of dozens of bodily and brain processes, including the other neurotransmitter systems.

The psychointegrators are by necessity also "disintegrators"—the connection with all comes as a consequence of disintegration of the ego. Some of these effects result from their powerful "de-conditioning" influences, where they inhibit conditional responses and block habitual neurotransmitter pathways. Their effects are also extremely dissociative, engaging in some systems to the exclusion of others—such as the external environment. Their dissociation reflects the extreme activation of other kinds of connections that totally occupy consciousness.

In spite of the greater accuracy of the term psychointegrator, we have nonetheless decided to use the term psychedelic for the title to these volumes and accept our authors' use of other terms such as hallucinogen and entheogen. The use of psychedelic is in part practical, given its greater acceptance, currency, and widespread recognition. Psychedelic (mind-manifesting) is also political, a reminder to use our minds, in response to the stifling political climate which has until recently precluded the effective investigation and therapeutic use of these important medicines. Psychedelic was coined in a context in which its political dimensions soon became obvious to supporters and detractors. As our conclusions to this volume indicate, we think that in addition to scientific, religious, and even business approaches, political approaches are also necessary to reform well-intentioned but misguided governmental policies and administrative decisions that precluded access to these substances for research and therapeutic purposes for too many years. These two volumes indicate that a realistic, evidence-based approach is making headway.

NEUROLOGICAL PERSPECTIVES ON PSYCHOINTEGRATORS

The effects of psychedelics on neurotransmission are responsible for the principal aspects of the associated physical, emotional, cognitive, and sacred experiences and their therapeutic applications. The model of psychointegration presented here is not the finding of a single study but represents an integration of many studies and the generalizations regarding the effects of psychedelics that have developed over decades of research. The effects of the psychedelics on neurotransmission are among the best understood effects of drugs on neurotransmission (Mandell 1985). Since the 1960s, it has been recognized that the major substances labeled as psychedelics (hallucinogens such as LSD, mescaline, and psilocybin) have common effects on the serotonergic neurotransmitters.[2] Laboratory studies of LSD effects provide diverse findings as a consequence of differences derived from varying procedures and dosages, as well as distinct phase effects and the consequences of set and setting (Freedman 1984). Most psychedelics (e.g., indoleamines, such as psilocybin and LSD, and the phenethylamines, such as mescaline and tetrahydrocannabinols) have effects that generalize to one another, reflecting similar neurochemical mechanisms of action and global properties involving effects upon serotonin pathways and mechanisms (Aghajanian 1994; also see Vollenweider 1998).

Similar effects on serotonin mechanisms are produced by LSD and lysergic acid amide (found naturally in morning glories), psilocybin (from mushrooms of the genera *Psilocybe, Conobybe, Paneolis,* and *Stropharia*), harmine and harmaline of the genus *Banisteriopsis,* and DMT (dimethyltryptamine) and similar substances from the *Virola* genus and species of *Anadenanthera.* Mescaline (from peyote) and similar synthetic drugs (STP, DMA, MDA, and MMDA) and myristicin and elemicin from the genus *Myristica* (e.g., nutmeg) more resemble norepinephrine but have end effects similar to those of the LSD-like substances [but see Passie's Chapter 3, this volume, and Frei et al. (2001) for distinct mechanisms and EEG effects of MDMA]. These substances' effects on sensory, behavioral, emotional, cognitive, and psychodynamic experiences and processing involve integrative effects on information processing, providing the rationale for their characterization as psychointegrators (Winkelman 1996a, 2001).

A basic systemic effect of psychointegrators involves induction of serotonergic-mediated discharge patterns from the limbic or paleomammalian brain that result in enhanced connections and coordination across the levels of the brain. This is reflected in a general increase in the coherence of the brain waves, their limbic-frontal cortex integration, and the interhemispheric synchronization of the two cerebral hemispheres (left brain–right brain) of the frontal cortex (Mandell 1980, 1985; Winkelman 1996a). The serotonergic action of the LSD-like psychedelics integrates brain functioning from neurophysiological through cognitive levels, stimulating an integration of pre-linguistic social, emotional, and behavioral processes with the frontal cortex's linguistic and egoic functions.

The therapeutic effects of psychointegrators derive from the activation of emotional and personal processes coordinated in the limbic system and paleomammalian brain, which underlie personal identity, attachment and social bonding, emotion, and conviction in beliefs. Psychointegrators stimulate the integration of the brain's behavioral and social–emotional processing output into the frontal cortex's language-based ratiomentation, egoic representations, and personal identity. These biochemically based physiological effects may produce awareness of repressed memories, integration of emotional and rational processes, and resolution of conflicts through integration of the processes of the different functional systems of the brain. The systemic integrative effects of these substances begin with their action at neurotransmitter levels, providing a rationale for using the term *psychointegrator* to refer to their effects.

Psychointegrators and Neurotransmitter Functions and the Brain

Neurotransmitters act through a number of mechanisms, exercising both inhibitory and excitatory effects (blocking and facilitating) in modulating the effects of other neurotransmitters. Psychedelics have these roles in the serotonergic system's receptor sites sometimes as agonists, and in other sites as antagonists (or blockers) thus preventing the normal responses of a receptor. These effects on neurotransmission mediate their profound effects on human consciousness (for sources, see note 2). Psychointegration derives from a range of effects on brain transmission. Because of the diverse types and functions of serotonin and the diverse actions of the psychointegrators, there are various kinds of interactions between the two, including interference with serotonin reuptake, activating serotonin receptor sites, and blocking the action of serotonin on its usual neurotransmitters sites.

Mandell (1980) first proposed that common neurobiochemical pathways of psychedelic and other transcendental experiences involve a biogenic amine–temporal lobe interaction manifested in high-voltage slow wave EEG activity originating in the hippocampal–septal area of the limbic system. This limbic system discharge pattern reflects the activation of serotonergic connections with lower brain structures, engaging a circuitry that produces strong theta wave discharges. These discharges ascend the neuraxis, the major ascending nerve bundles of brain, producing an integration of limbic processes in the frontal cortex and an interhemispheric synchronization and coherence between the two frontal hemispheres. This promotes a physiological synthesis or integration of the behavioral, emotional, and cognitive levels of the brain. These constitute psychointegration effects—increases in the coherence of brain discharges; an integration of behavior, feelings, and thoughts; and enhanced integration resulting in insight.

The LSD-like psychointegrators interact with serotonergic neurotransmitters across all major levels of the brain, generally augmenting normal processes in activities regulated by serotonergic processes and the structures on which they have effects. Psychointegrators' effects on neurotransmission reduce habitual repressions, consequently enhancing brain activity and simultaneously stimulating processes that are normally dissociated. Psychointegrators result in the increases in activity of several key areas of the brain:

1. the raphe and reticular formations of the brain stem area that control the amount of information the higher levels of the brain receive;
2. the limbic system, particularly the hippocampus and amygdala, that provides emotional information and personal memories and sense of self; and
3. the visual and auditory areas of the frontal cortex.

SEROTONERGIC AND MACRO-LEVEL EFFECTS OF PSYCHOINTEGRATORS

Serotonin inhibits firing in the raphe area, depressing neuronal firing in lower areas of the brain. LSD-like psychointegrators act on the serotonergic neurons in the locus coeruleus to counteract this inhibition. The locus coeruleus, which serves as a nodal point for convergence of somatosensory and visceral information, has projections which innervate most areas of the neuraxis, principally the thalamus, hypothalamus, cerebellum, basal forebrain, hippocampus, and neocortex. LSD-like psychointegrators also effect serotonin autoreceptors in the raphe, resulting in a disinhibition of forebrain targets. The release of the tonic inhibitory serotonin effects increases activity in the lateral geniculate nucleus and amygdala, enhancing a key emotional processing center of the brain. LSD-like psychointegrators potentiate serotonin's excitatory effects on brain stem and spinal cord areas where serotonergic input results in excitatory effects on the cerebral cortex and brain stem.

A basic commonality in the effects of psychointegrators involves disinhibiting the mesolimbic temporal lobe structures. The habitual effect of serotonin in depressing the action of target neurons in the forebrain is blocked by the effects of LSD on serotonin neurons, resulting in the disinhibition of their typical repression, releasing the visual representation processes manifested as visions. The most intense disinhibition and therefore greatest release of activity is on the limbic system's emotional processing areas and the visual areas of the cortex, resulting in intense visual and emotional experiences. This disinhibition of the mesolimbic temporal lobe structures is manifested in high-voltage synchronous activity in the hippocampus and synchronous discharges in the temporal lobe limbic structures. It results in synchronous theta range (3–6 cps) brain wave patterns which drive impulses into the frontal cortex. These discharges replace the typical desynchronized fast wave activity characteristic of the frontal cortex with slower more coherent wave patterns. These coherent discharges produce synchronous slow wave patterns in the frontal lobes, reflecting the discharge patterns of the lower brain structures and causing synchronization of the two sides (hemispheres) of the frontal cortex. These synchronizing effects in the brain are the neurological causes of the integrative experiences of psychointegrators, their potential to produce experience of connection, understanding, and oneness. Psychointegrators stimulate the brain to process information in this integrated fashion.

These combined effects of psychointegrators on the various serotonergic regions of the brain result in the increase in information from the environment, body, and memory; the enhanced experience and recall of emotions, motivations, and cognitive processes; and increases in awareness and internal attention. These diverse effects result in a synthesis of information from the entire brain, enhancing regulation of the autonomic nervous system and integration of emotions and visual–cognitive representations (Winkelman 1996a). Elevation of repressed memories into consciousness permits catharsis and abreaction, allowing conflicts to be integrated and resolved. The tendency of these substances to elicit distressing personal material, unresolved conflicts, repressed experiences, and unintegrated aspects of self suggests that it is their stimulation of the limbic system that provokes the release of distressing material related to the sense of self and social attachments. In addition to their internal effects, the psychointegrators can also increase arousal, heightening sensory receptivity and responsivity to the environment, particularly at low dosages. This, combined with their blockage of some circuitry, contributes to reduced or reversed habituation of typical response patterns, and leads to new patterns of behavior and perspectives.

The limbic-frontal driving elevates information from the behavioral and emotional brains, forcing what is ordinarily unconscious material into the cerebral cortex. This forms the biological process for integrating feelings with thoughts, enhancing integration and insight. Enhanced awareness of repressed memories, combined with increased emotional activation and lability and disruption of habitual behavior patterns, can result in dissolution of egocentric fixations. Psychointegration permits aspects of the self to become reprogrammed into new patterns of thinking and feeling.

Psychointegrators and the Triune Brain Systems

Psychointegrators primarily enhance activation of the lower levels of the brain that MacLean (1990, 1993) refers to as the R-complex and the paleomammalian brain, or limbic system. The paleomammalian brain is primarily concerned with self-identity, species survival, family and social relations, as well as learning and memory, and sexual and aggressive emotions and their integration in human behavior. The activation of the paleomammalian brain and its functions by the psychointegrators (and ASCs in general) enhances systemic integration of the psyche. The stimulation of the R-complex by psychointegrators provides an enhanced integration of all areas of the brain; they are responsible for the heightened arousal and awareness, and interference with habituated behavioral routines which the reptilian brain manages. The paleomammalian brain and limbic system provide the social and emotional influences on mentation and behavior.

These primary cognitive processes are based upon nonverbal communication forms of mental and social representation which manage processes and interpretations of emotional and social life. These experiences of lower structures of the brain and consciousness that are elicited by the psychointegrators are discussed by Grof (1975, 1980, 1992) as transbiological realms: the perinatal domain of experiences and the transpersonal domain. The transpersonal domain of the archetypal and mystical structures reveals dimensions of human consciousness and identity beyond (or perhaps better characterized as "below") egoic identity. Naranjo (1996) suggests that psychedelics activate "Kundalini phenomena" involving levels of organismic self-regulation that emerge as a consequence of the activation of mental structures.

PSYCHOINTEGRATORS AND CORTICO-STRIATO-THALAMO-CORTICAL
FEEDBACK LOOPS

The effects of the psychointegrators on the brain are complex, reflective of not only the many compounds found in a single plant but also the diverse neurotransmitter system affected in various ways by the plant compounds. For instance, the differences among the psychointegrators include the distinctive empathic qualities of MDMA as opposed to psilocybin. Vollenweider uses advanced imaging and assessment technologies to show that the effects of psychedelics differ and derive from the interactions among different neurotransmitter systems and areas of the brain. These involve not just serotonin but also its interactions with the dopamine neurons, GABAergic neurons, and the dopamine–glutamatergic neurotransmitter systems.

The research of Vollenweider (1998) expands this model of the psychointegrative mechanisms of action of psychedelics, emphasizing their selective effects on the brain's CSTC (cortico-striato-thalamo-cortical) feedback loops. These loops are the principal organizational networks of the brain.[3] These involve parallel and segregated loops that link the information gating systems of lower levels of the brain (specifically the basal ganglia, substantia nigra, and thalamus) with specific regions of the frontal cortex of the brain. These loops are regulated at lower levels of the brain in the thalamus, which limits the ascending information. Vollenweider characterizes the hallucinogens' effects as involving complex disturbances caused by deficits in the CSTC loops. The psychointegrators disinhibition of these systems floods the frontal cortex with information, leading to breakdown of the integrative capacity of the ego. The limbic loop originates in the hippocampal area and the temporal lobe and projects to ventral striatum, nucleus accumbens, and caudate nucleus, with feedback to the orbitofrontal cortex. These areas exert an inhibitory influence on the thalamus, functioning as "gatekeepers" or filters for the level of the frontal cortex, the basic filtering node for information from the environment and body. Psychointegrators disable this disinhibition process; this increases access to the information capacities. By increasing the flow of information that is ordinarily inhibited, psychedelics permit an overload of information that can overwhelm the frontal cortex.

Vollenweider (1998) reports research that indicates the subcortical loops have an internal functional integrity in their linkages among brain regions and that these are not disrupted by ASCs. ASCs selectively activate different systems. A principal effect of the psychointegrators is on the ego structuring processes. The overload of sensory information produced by the disinhibition overwhelms the cognitive processing capacities and frameworks of the frontal cortex, resulting in fragmentation and dissolution of the inadequate ego structures. This dissolution may be necessary for and contributory to the classic extrovertive mystical experiences of oceanic oneness, connection with the universe made possible by the dissolution of the self-boundary mechanisms.

Setting Effects and Unique Dynamics as Intrinsic Properties of Psychointegrators[4]

The effects of psychedelic medicines on psychology include the setting—and these may constitute some of their most important applications in enhancing the context effects, in particular the dynamics of intensive small group interactions. These settings generally develop high degrees of relaxed intimacy, and social cohesion rapidly develops within the groups under the "prosocial" action of DMT. Consequently, psychointegrators can be seen as having adaptive consequences in terms of reducing, preventing, and interpersonally managing aggressive behavior that can quickly develop in closed, isolated groups (e.g., prisoners, drilling platform workers, remote research groups, and space station teams). Minimizing the inherent dynamic of internal conflict found among humans and other mammalian groups is achieved by ritual processes in the animal world. Among humans these were incorporated into shamanic rituals that used these psychoactive plants as adjuncts to these natural neurochemical processes. A recognized behavioral syndrome caused by chronic, depleted levels of brain serotonin (a tryptamine neurotransmitter) involves poor impulse control, dysphoric-anxious mood, irritability, recklessness, and social ineptitude. These increases in interpersonal discord and aggression are exacerbated by the release of testosterone caused by low levels of brain serotonin, resulting in increased self-detrimental aggression.

The tryptamines methyl analogues such as DMT have an active transport into the brain, enabling it to have the potential to resolve the serotonin depletion syndrome in the fastest way. These substances act much more immediately and effectively in improving serotonin depletion than does the clinical administration of SSRIs (selective-serotonin reuptake inhibitors), which because of autoreceptor self-regulation prevent increased availability of synaptic serotonin during the first two to three weeks of SSRI treatment.[5]

PSYCHOINTEGRATORS AND THE INTEGRATIVE MODE OF CONSCIOUSNESS

The disinhibition of the serotonergic neurotransmitters systems and the resulting loss of their inhibitory effects upon the mesolimbic temporal lobe structures underlies the common effects of psychointegrators in producing ASC and the widely reported transcendental or transpersonal experience. These systematic changes in brain functioning are common to many means of inducing ASC (Winkelman 1986a, 1992, 2000) or as Mandell (1980, 1985) refers to, the "transcendent states." This underlying mode of consciousness (Winkelman 2000) is the basis for the universal distribution of shamanistic healing practices (Winkelman 1986b, 1990, 1992).

The overall brain effects of psychedelic medicines are common to diverse means of inducing ASCs, where high-voltage discharges originating in the limbic system replace the normal waking desynchronized fast wave brain patterns with slow wave (theta) cortical synchronization. ASCs in general reflect this pattern of limbic-driven cortical synchronization, reflecting a basic mode of consciousness (Winkelman 2000). The integrative mode of consciousness represents an optimized homeostatic balance among different functional systems of the brain that permits the emergence of integrative or holistic operations of the brain. This *integrative mode of consciousness* is as fundamental to human psychobiology as the dream, deep sleep, and waking modes of consciousness (see Winkelman 2000).

The psychedelic medicines are the primary exogenous technology humans have to elicit the healing processes produced within the integrating mode of consciousness. The roles and effects of psychedelic plants in human cultures point to their important psychointegrator functions in meeting human needs by the activation of innate structures that meet basic biological needs; psychedelic medicines enhance the endogenous processes of the brain by augmenting the levels of critical but scarce neurotransmitter effects. Siegal (1990) suggests that humans have an innate drive to alter consciousness, which raises the question of the consequences for a society which views such behavior as aberrant, atavistic, and pathological and criminalizes the very substances which are humanity's most important technologies for achieving those conditions. The recurrent societal "rediscovery" of ASCs, particularly those associated with current "drug problems," illustrates the persistent need to seek these states and for societies to adaptively address these issues. Typical cross-cultural patterns of use in regular community ceremonials reflect an adaptation to the episodic psychological needs for their use as psychointegrators. Psychointegrators play a role in managing needs for developmental change or crises-induced problems which require an integration of conscious, preconscious, and unconscious processes, particularly behavioral routines and socioemotional dynamics into a new gestalt or understanding.

CONCLUSIONS

This conjunction of physical medicines—the psychedelics—with the ancient spiritual dynamics of healing reflects neurological concordances, an integration of psychophysiological and psychocultural dynamics. This is reflected in a fundamental adaptation found in all human societies in the form of shamanistic healing practices (Winkelman 1990, 1992, 2000). The particular emphasis on psychedelics as a means of achieving this adaptation reflects the needs for cultures to reorient their psychocultural dynamics to the changes that have occurred in social and cosmological relations, producing new patterns of integration. This suggests that the use of psychedelics will continue in the rapidly changing world and requires that societies take informed approaches to their managed use. Our contributors take great strides in illustrating the scientific bases for the application of these psychedelic medicines to address crucial health problems, including some of the most vexing problems of our times, those associated with addictions.

NOTES

Thanks to Tom Roberts, Ede Frecska, and John Reisenman for their constructive comments on this chapter.

1. See Laughlin et al. (1992) and Winkelman (1996b, 2000) on neurophenomonology approach as a method for linking biological process with cross-cultural reports of phenomenology of religious experiences.

2. These linking nerve systems have basic functions of motor response and co-ordination, body coordination with eye movements, emotions, motivations, and executive functions. They manage the body's orientation to external cues, their relationships to internal information (memory and emotion), and their integration into behavior. These cortico-striato-thalamo-cortical linkages are central to the organized coordination of the organism, engaging brain–behavior relationships in coordinating executive decision-making functions with behavioral motivations and social demands. These subcortical pathways have important functions in linking the limbic system with the neocortex and mediating mood and motivations into behavioral responses.

3. The general mechanisms of psychointegrators effects on the brain are described in many sources; I relied primarily on Aghajanian (1984, 1994), Glennon (1990), Jacobs (1984), Jacobs and Gelperin (1981), Kruk and Pycock (1991), Mandell (1980, 1985), McKim (1991), Miller and Gold (1993), Ribeiro (1991), Ryall (1989), and Schmidt and Peroutka (1989). Vollenweider (1998) provides an updated and extended perspective.

It is generally accepted that the primary effects of the psychedelic medicines is through their action on the 5-HT_{1A} and 5-H_{T2} serotonergic neurons; there is also binding with the 5-HT_5 and 5-HT_7 receptors (Vollenweider 1998).

Serotonin 5-HT_{1A} receptors in the raphe system mediate responses of the serotonergic neurons with respect to their own transmitters; these receptors show a strong sensitivity to LSD-like substances (Aghajanian 1994, p. 140), inhibiting their firing in the raphe area and depressing neuronal firing in lower areas of the brain (the dorsal hippocampus, hypothalamic suprachiasmatic nucleus, amygdaloid cell, caudate-putamen, substantia nigra, trigeminal nucleus, spinal cord interneurons, spinothalamic-tract neurons, and the mesencephalic reticular formation). LSD effects the hippocampus by blocking or suppressing the typical depressant functions of serotonin, permitting the release of responses similar to dreaming, and contributing to production of the typical visual experiences by disinhibiting postsynaptic neurons in the limbic and visual areas.

Indoleamines and phenethylamines cause greater activation of 5-HT_2 serotonin receptors relative to other serotonin receptors (Aghajanian 1994). Primary effects of LSD-like psychointegrators are through the action on the 5-HT_2 serotonergic neurons (Glennon 1990, p. 43). Large concentrations of serotonin 5-HT_2 receptors are in the limbic system in the hypothalamus and basal ganglia; these sensory processing functions are antagonized by LSD (Kruk and Pycock 1991). LSD-like psychointegrators also affect the cerebral cortex and the locus coeruleus 5-HT_2 receptors (Aghajanian 1994). LSD affinity for 5-HT_{2A} and 5-HT_{2C} receptors facilitates the functioning of the locus coeruleus, which receives numerous somatosensory and visceral inputs and projects diffusely to most of the brain (Miller and Gold 1993).

4. This section is based on personal communication from Ede Frecska.

5. While SSRIs provoke an increase in serotonin in the synaptic cleft as a consequence of presynaptic reuptake blockade in the first two to three weeks of treatment, the brain has multiple feedback mechanism to counterbalance that effect. The normal function of the reuptake pump clears out the synaptic cleft of serotonin and thereby diminishes nerve transmission. The results of blocking this pump are excess synaptic serotonin and postsynaptic receptor stimulation, leading to the accompanying psychomotor activation or agitation that occurs during the initial two to three weeks. The presynaptic autoreceptors provide homeostatic mechanisms, decreasing presynaptic firing when transmitter levels are high in the synaptic cleft. When synaptic serotonin levels are high because of SSRI, presynaptic 5HT receptors decrease the firing of the serotonergic

neuron, and the release of serotonin will decrease. The net sum is that synaptic serotonin will not change significantly for at least two to three weeks. Then as these autoreceptors fatigue, their homeostatic mechanism breaks down, the serotonin level starts to increase, and the antidepressive effect manifests clinically, producing the well-known two to three weeks lag of the antidepressant effect.

REFERENCES

Aberle, D. 1966. *The peyote religion among the Navaho.* Chicago: Aldine Publishing.

Aghajanian, G. 1982. Neurophysiologic properties of psychotomimetics. In *Psychotropic agents III,* ed. F. Hoffmeister and G. Stille, 89–109. New York: Springer-Verlag.

Aghajanian, G. 1984. LSD and serotonergic dorsal raphe neurons: Intracellular studies in vivo and in vitro. In *Hallucinogens: Neurochemical, behavioral and clinical perspectives,* ed. J. Barry, 171–81. New York: Raven Press.

Aghajanian, G. 1994. Serotonin and the action of LSD in the brain. *Psychiatric Annals* 24 (3):137–41.

Andritzky, W. 1989. Sociopsychotherapeutic functions of ayahuasca healing in Amazonia. *Journal of Psychoactive Drugs* 21 (1):77–89.

Dobkin de Rios, M. 1984. *Hallucinogens: Cross-cultural perspectives.* Albuquerque: University of New Mexico Press.

Dobkin de Rios, M., and D. Smith. 1977. Drug use and abuse in cross-cultural perspective. *Human Organization* 36 (1):14–21.

Embodden, W. 1972. *Narcotic plants.* New York: Macmillan.

Freedman, D. 1984. LSD: The bridge from human to animal. In *Hallucinogens: Neurochemical, behavioral and clinical perspectives,* ed. J. Barry, 203–26. New York: Raven Press.

Frei, E., A. Gamma, R. Pascual-Marqui, D. Lehman, D. Hell, and F. Vollenweider. 2001. Localization of MDMA-induced brain activity in healthy volunteers using low resolution brain electromagnetic tomography (LORETA). *Human Brain Mapping* 14:152–65.

Furst, P., ed. 1972. *Flesh of the gods.* New York: Praeger.

Furst, P., ed. 1976. *Hallucinogens and culture.* San Francisco: Chandler and Sharp.

Glennon, R. 1990. Serotonin receptors: Clinical implications. *Neuroscience and Biobehavioral Reviews* 14:35–47.

Grof, S. 1975. *Realms of the unconscious: Observations from LSD research.* New York: Viking Press.

Grof, S. 1980. *LSD psychotherapy.* Pomona, CA: Hunter House.

Grof, S. 1989. Beyond the brain: New dimensions in psychology and psychotherapy. In *Gateways to inner space,* ed. C. Ratsch, 55–71. Bridport, Dorset: Prism Press.

Grof, S. 1992. *The holotropic mind.* San Francisco: HarperCollins.

Harner, M., ed. 1973. *Hallucinogens and shamanism.* New York: Oxford University Press.

Jacobs, B., ed. 1984. *Hallucinogens: Neurochemical, behavioral and clinical perspectives.* New York: Raven Press.

Jacobs, B., and A. Gelperin, eds. 1981. *Serotonin neurotransmission and behavior.* Cambridge, MA: MIT Press.

Kruk, Z., and C. Pycock. 1991. *Neurotransmitters and drugs.* London: Chapman and Hall.

La Barre, W. 1970. Old and New World narcotics: A statistical question. *Economic Botany* 24:368–73.

La Barre, W. 1972. Hallucinogens and the shamanic origins of religion. In *Flesh of the gods*, ed. P. Furst, 261–278. New York: Praeger.

Laughlin, C., J. McManus, and E. d'Aquili. 1992. *Brain, symbol and experience toward a neurophenomenology of consciousness.* Boston and Shaftesbury: Shambhala. Repr., Columbia University Press.

MacLean, P. 1990. *The triune brain in evolution.* New York: Plenum.

MacLean, P. 1993. On the evolution of three mentalities. In *Brain, culture and the human spirit: Essays from an emergent evolutionary perspective*, ed. J.B. Ashbrook, 15–44. Lanham, MD: University Press of America.

Mandell, A. 1980. Toward a psychobiology of transcendence: God in the brain. In *The psychobiology of consciousness*, ed. D. Davidson and R. Davidson. New York: Plenum.

Mandell, A. 1985. Interhemispheric fusion. *Journal of Psychoactive Drugs* 17 (4): 257–66.

McKenna, T. 1992. *Food of the gods: The search for the original tree of knowledge: A radical history of plants, drugs, and human evolution.* New York: Bantam Books.

McKim, W. 1991. *Drugs and behavior: An introduction to behavioral pharmacology.* Englewood Cliffs, NJ: Prentice-Hall.

Miller, N., and M. Gold. 1993. LSD and Ecstacy: Pharmacology, phenomonology and treatment. *Psychiatric Annals* 24 (3):131–34.

Naranjo, C. 1996. The interpretation of psychedelic experience in light of the psychology of meditation. In *Sacred plants, consciousness and healing, yearbook of cross-cultural medicine and psychotherapy*, ed. M. Winkelman and W. Andritzky, 75–90. Berlin: VWB-Verlag.

Rätsch, C. 2005. *The encyclopedia of psychoactive plants*, trans. J. Baker. Rochester, VT: Park Street Press.

Ribeiro, C. 1991. Pharmacology of serotonin neuronal systems. *Human Psychopharacology* 6:37–51.

Ruck, C., J. Bigwood, B. Staples, J. Ott, and R. Wasson. 1979. Entheogens. *Journal of Psychoactive Drugs* 11(1–2 Jan–Jun):145–46.

Ryall, R. 1989. *Mechanisms of drug action on the nervous system.* Cambridge: Cambridge University Press.

Schmidt, A., and S. Peroutka. 1989. 5-Hydroxytryptamine receptor "families." *Neuropsychopharmacology* 3:2242–49.

Schultes, R., and A. Hofmann. 1979. *Plants of the gods.* New York: McGraw Hill. Repr., Rochester, VT: Healing Arts Press, 1992.

Schultes, R., and M. Winkelman. 1996. The principal American hallucinogenic plants and their bioactive and therapeutic properties. In *Sacred plants, consciousness and healing, yearbook of cross-cultural medicine and psychotherapy*, ed. M. Winkelman and W. Andritzky, 205–39. Berlin: VWB-Verlag.

Siegel, R. 1984. The natural history of hallucinogens. In *Hallucinogens: Neurochemical, behavioral and clinical perspectives*, ed. J. Barry, 1–18. New York: Raven Press.

Siegel, R. 1990. *Intoxication: Life in pursuit of artificial paradise.* New York: Dutton.

Vollenweider, F. 1998. Recent advances and concepts in the search for biological correlates of hallucinogen-induced altered states of consciousness. *The Heffter Review of Psychedelic Research* 1:21–32.

Wasson, R.G., S. Kramrisch, J. Ott, and C. Ruck. 1986. *Persephone's quest: Entheogens and the origins of religion.* New Haven: Yale University Press.

Winkelman, M. 1986a. Magico-religious practitioner types and socioeconomic conditions. *Behavior Science Research* 20(1–4):17–46.

Winkelman, M. 1986b. Trance states: A theoretical model and cross-cultural analysis. *Ethos* 14 (2):174–203.

Winkelman, M. 1990. Shaman and other "magico-religious" healers: A cross-cultural study of their origins, nature and social transformations. *Ethos* 18 (3):308–52.

Winkelman, M. 1991. Physiological, social and functional aspects of drug and non-drug altered states of consciousness. In *Yearbook of cross-cultural medicine and psychotherapy,* ed. W. Andritzky, 183–98. Berlin: VWB-Verlag.

Winkelman, M. 1992. Shamans, priests and witches: A cross-cultural study of magico-religious practitioners. *Anthropological Research Papers* No. 44. Tempe: Arizona State University.

Winkelman, M. 1996a. Psychointegrator plants: Their roles in human culture and health. In *Sacred plants, consciousness and healing, yearbook of cross-cultural medicine and psychotherapy,* ed. M. Winkelman and W. Andritzky, 9–53. Berlin: VWB-Verlag.

Winkelman, M. 1996b. Neurophenomenology and genetic epistemology as a basis for the study of consciousness. *Journal of Social and Evolutionary Systems* 19 (3):217–36.

Winkelman, M. 2000. *Shamanism: The neural ecology of consciousness and healing.* Westport, CT: Bergin and Garvey.

Winkelman, M. 2001. Psychointegrators: Multidisciplinary perspectives on the therapeutic effects of hallucinogens. *Complementary Health Practice Review* 6 (3):219–37.

Winkelman, M. 2003. Psychointegration: The physiological effects of entheogens. *Entheos* 2 (1):51–61.

Winkelman, M., and W. Andritzky, eds. 1996. *Sacred plants, consciousness and healing, yearbook of cross-cultural medicine and psychotherapy.* Vol. 5. Berlin: VWB-Verlag.

2

THE HEALING VINE: AYAHUASCA AS MEDICINE IN THE 21ST CENTURY

DENNIS J. MCKENNA

INTRODUCTION AND HISTORICAL PERSPECTIVE

Over 40 years ago, Western society was jolted—and forever transformed—by the emergence of psychedelic drugs onto the psychic radar screen of collective consciousness. There was nothing new about psychedelics; after all, the use of psychedelic plants in shamanic practices within many indigenous cultures has roots in the mists of Paleolithic time. Shamanism, a set of "archaic techniques of ecstasy" (Eliade 1964) deliberately aimed at accessing supernatural realms through the induction of altered states of consciousness, was more often than not fueled by the ingestion of psychedelic plants. Shamanism, in its various manifestations throughout the world, constitutes the prehistoric bedrock from which magic, religion, science, and medicine—and to some degree music, poetry, and literature—sprang forth and manifested within human cultures. Within indigenous societies in which shamanism was or is practiced, psychedelic plants and their remarkable properties have been accepted, respected, and utilized for thousands of years. Nor were they unknown to Western civilization prior to the 1960s; there is plenty of evidence, for example, that psychedelic mushrooms may have played a role in certain Christian cults (Heinrich 2002), and during the 19th and early 20th centuries, the peyote cactus and its recently isolated alkaloid, mescaline, was an object of curiosity among the scientific and literary avant-garde in the United States and Europe (McKenna 2006a). But by and large, these substances remained "hidden"; known only to a few cognoscenti, rarely spoken of or discussed openly, they abided on the margins of society.

All of that changed in the 1960s, and in the decade leading up to it. Albert Hofmann's profound and (allegedly) accidental discovery of the remarkable properties of the ergot derivative LSD (lysergic acid diethylamide) in 1943 marked a turning point. LSD began to attract the attention of the medical and psychiatric communities in the early 1950s. There was great excitement among psychiatrists and others that the LSD experience could be regarded as a "model psychosis" from which the biochemical mechanisms of mental illnesses could be studied and understood (Grof 1994). Other practitioners saw great therapeutic potential in the new substance. LSD, they asserted, was capable of "dissolving the ego," and "loosening the boundaries of the self," and under the right circumstances, these properties could be used to facilitate psychotherapeutic processes. Even the Central Intelligence Agency got into the act, and started to investigate LSD's potential for brainwashing and mind control (Lee and Shlain 1985). At the same time, neuroscientists became intrigued by its structural similarities to the neurotransmitter serotonin. At the time, the structure of serotonin had been recently characterized, and the discovery that not only was LSD a member of the same chemical family but also had potent effects on serotonin-mediated processes in animals caused great excitement in the neuroscientific community. Some speculated that these discoveries surely pointed to imminent breakthroughs in the scientific understanding of the neurochemistry of consciousness.

Along with this LSD-triggered ferment in the scientific community, similar rumblings were taking place on the cultural front. Aldous Huxley (1954) published his famous book, *The Doors of Perception,* and this recounting of the author's experience with mescaline quickly attracted widespread notice and acclaim at least among the intelligentsia and literati. One of the most significant events of the 1950s, in terms of bringing psychedelic drugs to the attention of the masses, had to be the publication of *LIFE* magazine on May 13th, 1957 (Wasson 1957). That issue chronicled the adventures of amateur ethnomycologists Gordon and Valentina Wasson in their rediscovery of the shamanic practices involving the use of psilocybin-containing "magic mushrooms" in the mountains of Oaxaca, Mexico. There, in an article enthusiastically headlined "The Discovery of Mushrooms that Cause Strange Visions," the existence of a centuries-old secret cult of psychedelic mycolatry was thrown right into the face of Middle America. Not that there were any pejorative allusions to the practice at the time; it was reported, National Geographic–style, as simply an interesting adventure by a couple of eccentric travelers. The ancient, and in the eyes of the Spanish Inquisition, blasphemous, practice had been forced underground nearly 400 years previously following savage but ultimately unsuccessful attempts at eradication. Suddenly, there it was in the pages of *LIFE* magazine for all to see, complete with color photos and beautiful watercolor renderings of the mushrooms in question. Thus did psychedelic drugs make their dramatic debut in the collective consciousness of America; it may not be much of an exaggeration to state that the "psychedelic sixties" really began with the publication of this article.

At about the same time as Gordon and Valentina Wasson were rambling through the mountains of Oaxaca, in hot pursuit of their momentous rediscovery of the magic mushroom cults of Mexico that brought the psychedelic age into full flower with the publication of their account in *LIFE* magazine in 1957, two icons of the Beat Generation, William Burroughs and Alan Ginsberg, were pursuing a similar but much less noticed quest in the jungles of Ecuador, Colombia, and Peru. Burroughs, Beat poet, famous junkie and homosexual, roustabout, and cultural iconoclast, had long been ahead of his time when it came to the investigation of bizarre drug experiences. In 1953, Burroughs, having gotten wind of an obscure hallucinogen known as *yajé*,[1] set out for South America to find and experience for himself what he was convinced might well be "the final fix." In a tiny volume, first issued in 1963 by City Lights Books of San Francisco under the title *The Yage [sic] Letters,* Burroughs (1963) published an account of his adventures (and misadventures). The book took the form of a series of letters between Burroughs and his friend, fellow poet and countercultural mischief-maker Alan Ginsberg, exchanged as Burroughs wandered from one bizarre scene to another in search of the legendary hallucinogen. Not to be outdone, Ginsberg followed his friend down to South America in 1960 and had his own encounters with the Vine of the Souls; his much shorter account was included in *The Yage Letters* when it was published.[2]

Burroughs and Ginsberg's book evolved over nearly a decade. It may truly be said that its publication marked the first irruption of knowledge of this obscure psychedelic decoction into mass consciousness, although it never penetrated very far and remained known only to a few psychedelic cognoscenti until nearly 40 years later. Of course, what was terra incognita to Burroughs and Ginsberg had been known to science since 19th century botanist and explorer Richard Spruce first reported it in 1851 (McKenna 2006b). Following Spruce's discovery, *ayahuasca* (as the decoction is more commonly known throughout most of the Amazon Basin) became an object of curiosity to pharmacologists and chemists, and a number of investigations ensued that were to stretch over the next 150 years and that continue to the present day (McKenna 2006b).[3] It is not entirely clear where Burroughs first learned about *ayahuasca* (or *yajé,* as it is more commonly known in Colombia and Ecuador), but it seems likely he may have stumbled across it in Lewis Lewin's book, *Phantastica: Narcotic and Stimulating Drugs* (Lewin 1931), during the period of his brief studies at Harvard. It is also possible that while at Harvard, he may have had a chance encounter with legendary ethnobotanist Richard Evans Schultes, the so-called "father of ethnopsychopharmacology," Spruce's scientific heir-apparent and for many years the Director of the Harvard Botanical Museum. As stated by *The Yage Letters,* Burroughs and Schultes did not cross paths until 1953 in Mocoa, Colombia; in fact, it seems likely that the most famous picture of Burroughs on his South American travels was taken by Schultes in 1953 (Davis 1996; Harris 2006). If they ever did meet or discuss *yajé* at Harvard in the preceding years, there is no record of the encounter.

In any case, by the time Burroughs became interested in *ayahuasca/yajé* and set out to find it in 1952–53, it was already old news to Schultes. By then, Schultes was coming to the end of more than 12 continuous years of travel and research in South America, and was headed back to his post at Harvard, where he remained as Director of the Botanical Museum until the late 1990s, when encroaching Alzheimer's disease forced him into retirement (Davis 1996). Following Schultes' return from the field in the early 1950s, he remained active in the field of ethnopsychopharmacology and eventually evolved into a bit of a countercultural icon himself, as he became more widely known as the world's expert on hallucinogenic plants. Throughout the 1950s, 1960s, and beyond, Schultes continued his research on ayahuasca and other psychedelic plants, and spawned several generations of eager graduate students who were devoted to their mentor and who continued to investigate the botany, ethnopharmacology, and chemistry of this fascinating Amazonian hallucinogen. To this day, Schultes' lengthy monograph on the botany and ethnobotany of *ayahuasca* and its admixture plants, published in the Harvard Museum Botanical Leaflets in 1957 (Schultes 1957), remains a landmark publication on the subject. Subsequent efforts by his graduate students, such as Homer Pinkley and Ara der Marderosian (Der Marderosian et al. 1968; Schultes 1972), built on the foundation of Schultes' work and further elucidated much of what we now know about the ethnopharmacology of *ayahuasca*.

Once these shamanic substances had been reintroduced to Western societies, events and cultural dynamics quickly took over. Within a few short years, Timothy Leary emerged on the scene as the self-appointed messiah of psychedelics, especially LSD (even though his initial revelation had come through a chance encounter with mushrooms in Mexico). His slogan, "Turn on, tune in, and drop out," as slickly crafted as any Madison Avenue ad campaign, quickly became the rallying cry of a new, young, bored generation, disenchanted with the corruption and hypocrisies of postwar institutions and mores, yearning for novel experiences, and more than ready to grab just about any bootstrap that might help lever them up out of the box of conventionality and conformity that had been the defining paradigm of the 1950s (cf. Stevens 1987). Of course, the very same anti-authoritarian slogan that held such appeal for so many young people was equally ominous and frightening to the ossified power structures of the "Establishment," which was already starting to feel besieged by the sense that things were spiraling out of control as the zeitgeist gathered momentum for its hell-bent gallop toward the unimaginable Millennium, just a few short decades ahead. The Establishment reacted to these accelerating changes, as establishments always have, through brutal repression and persecution, desperate but inevitably doomed attempts to stave off the tsunami of cultural upheaval. Leary and the other advocates of psychedelic substances were denounced, shouted down, and persecuted; the substances themselves, of course, were demonized. As a result, by the end of the

1960s, the hysteria over psychedelics that had swept the country resulted in the ramming through of a number of legislative measures in Congress and local statehouses. Just about any substance that could conceivably be classified as a "psychedelic" (whatever that meant, and even to this day the term is fraught with ambiguity) became prohibited under regulatory schedules that equated them to the most harmful drugs of abuse. The fact that almost nothing was known about their pharmacology, their dangers or possible uses, or even exactly which substances were to be included under the new laws (U.S. Controlled Substances Act of 1970) did not seem to matter. They were classified as "drugs with no medical utility, and a high potential for abuse," and placed in Schedule I, the most restrictive schedule.

At least, these measures helped "protect" the youth of the nation from this burgeoning threat, or so the legislators and politicians choose to see it. The genie had been put back in the bottle, though of course, not really. What became lost during this period of collective paranoia and ill-considered legislation was the timid, nearly inaudible voice of a few foolhardy souls in the medical and scientific communities who dared to question the wisdom of these actions, who were brave enough to suggest that these substances might have some value or intrinsic interest after all, and who wondered whether, through overreaction, society had lost the opportunity to learn something from them that might ultimately benefit humanity. Of course, given the national mood at the time, these questioners were about as welcome as a drag queen at an American Family Council rally, and so the grumbling of the skeptical few quickly faded from the national dialog. What followed over the next 20 years was the nearly complete suppression of human research with psychedelic substances, although, of course, the substances themselves continued to proliferate throughout society and became ever more widely used. But while "legitimate" clinical research with psychedelics continued at low levels in a few enlightened enclaves in Europe, in the United States the entire field of research became stigmatized and "forbidden." For a young psychiatrist or neuroscientist of the day to choose psychedelics as his or her primary field of study became about as suicidal a career move as a physicist suddenly opting to study UFO propulsion systems as a primary research specialty.

The blanket prohibition on psychedelic substances that was initiated by the passage of draconian and ill-considered laws at the end of the 1960s served to marginalize and effectively inhibit any clinical investigations with human subjects throughout the 1970s and 1980s. During these decades, the focus of research shifted largely from human studies to animal models and in vitro studies of structure–activity relationships, receptor interactions, and basic research on neurochemistry and neuropharmacology. LSD and many other psychedelic substances evolved into valuable research tools in the hands of neuroscientists, a role which continues to the present day. During this period, this basic research made invaluable contributions to neuroscience, but the disconnection between the findings of basic research and any possible clinical or therapeutic application persisted, primarily due to the discouraging and daunting bureaucratic hurdles that confronted any legitimate investigator who might wish to expand the scope of their research into the arena of human psychopharmacology. A notable exception to this existed in the person of Dr. Alexander Shulgin, a medicinal chemist and maverick scientist. As a result of several patents arising out of discoveries made during his brief sojourn as a research chemist working for Dow Chemical Company, Shulgin enjoyed a modest income and the freedom to pursue his own independent research while disdaining government funding and all but the most casual institutional affiliations. Working out of his own small lab, "primitive" by any standards, Shulgin synthesized hundreds of psychedelic analogs (which were technically not illegal as they were included on no list of controlled substances) (cf. Shulgin and Shulgin 1991, 1997) and quietly pursued explorations of their psychoactive properties using volunteer test subjects that included Shulgin himself and a small coterie of trip-savvy friends and colleagues. All of this he accomplished with the uneasy permission of various regulatory authorities, who although they frowned on this "forbidden science" could find no means of prohibiting it, since virtually all of the substances investigated were novel compounds not covered under any statutes. Eventually, decades later, the authorities grew tired of Shulgin's work and concocted an excuse to shut him down, but that is another story (Shulgin and Shulgin 1997). While Shulgin continued to explore the outer fringes of psychedelic psychopharmacology throughout the 1970s and 1980s, he was able to do so because of his unique circumstances. It was not an option available to most young researchers, looking to gain recognition in the competitive world of government-funded Big Science.

That situation only began to turn around, slowly, in 1990, when a young psychiatrist and pineal researcher at the University of New Mexico, Dr. Rick Strassman, decided to tackle the regulatory nightmare head on and filed an Investigational New Drug application with the FDA seeking permission to conduct a small clinical study with DMT (*N,N*-dimethyltryptamine), a synthetic alkaloid that was also known to occur naturally in many plants used in shamanic practices in indigenous cultures. DMT was first synthesized by Manske (1931) in the 1930s, but its hallucinogenic properties did not come to light until the 1950s when a researcher at NIMH, Stephen Szara (1956), published the first reports on its bizarre but extremely short-lived effects. At about the same time as Szara's publications issued, phytochemists were starting to report (sometimes erroneously, cf. Schultes and Raffauf 1960) its occurrence in a number of South American plants used in shamanic practices (Schultes and Hofmann 1980). Several decades later, other researchers reported that not only was DMT widespread in plants but also was a natural constituent of the human brain and pineal gland (Barker et al. 1981). Strassman's previous work on pineal neurochemistry and particularly the pineal hormone melatonin, also a tryptamine and a close chemical cousin of DMT, led him to apply for permission to investigate its effects in human volunteers. Strassman hypothesized that under some circumstances DMT could be synthesized by the pineal gland and released into the circulation, possibly triggering profound altered states of consciousness such as near-death experiences. He proposed to investigate this by exploring the psychological and physiological parameters of intravenously administered DMT in a small sample of human subjects with previous experience with hallucinogens. The story of Strassman's efforts to secure government permission to pursue this research, and its subsequent unanticipated outcome that led him to abandon the field for a number of years, has been marvelously described by the researcher in his compelling book, *DMT: The Spirit Molecule* (Strassman 2001). Although remarkable in itself, Strassman's research was also a milestone in another respect, in that it forced the door barring clinical investigations on psychedelics slightly ajar. His DMT project did not open a floodgate of new research proposals or trigger a torrent of funding; but his work did have the salutary effect of setting a precedent, and making it somewhat easier for subsequent researchers to obtain permission for clinical studies with psychedelics.

What might be called the modern era of research on *ayahuasca*[4] did not really begin until 1972, when European researchers Rivier and Lindgren (1972) published one of the first interdisciplinary papers on *ayahuasca,* reporting on the alkaloid profiles of *ayahuasca* brews and source plants collected among the Shuar people of the upper Rio Purús in Peru. At the time, their paper was one of the most thorough chemical investigations of the composition of *ayahuasca* brews and source plants that referenced vouchered botanical collections. It also discussed numerous admixture plants other than the most commonly employed species, *Psychotria viridis* and *Diplopteris cabrerana,* and for the first time provided evidence indicating that *ayahuasca* admixture technology was complex and that many species were on occasion used as admixtures. In many respects, my own graduate doctoral research on *ayahuasca* (McKenna et al. 1984) was a follow-up to this paper and an attempt to discover answers to some of the unresolved questions raised by the work of Rivier and Lindgren (1972), although my fieldwork was conducted primarily among Mestizo curanderos in Amazonian Peru and not among indigenous groups. Like their work, my investigations included extensive phytochemical analyses of the source plants used in the preparation of *ayahuasca* but had somewhat differing results.

However, this narrative is getting ahead of itself. We must first discuss, for those unfamiliar with the topic, 1) What is *ayahuasca* and what is DMT? and 2) What is the basis of its chemistry and pharmacology? With this as a foundation, we will continue to discuss its potential therapeutic applications.

WHAT IS AYAHUASCA?

Ayahuasca is a hallucinogenic decoction that is widely used in shamanic practices throughout the Amazon basin. *Ayahuasca* is a Quechua term meaning "vine of the souls," which is applied both to the beverage itself and to one of the source plants used in its preparation, a large jungle liana (woody vine), *Banisteriopsis caapi* (Spruce ex Griseb.) Morton, in the family Malpighiaceae

(Schultes 1957). While *ayahuasca* is the most widespread term for the beverage, it is also known by other names, including caapi, natema, yajé, and others, in different regions of the Amazon or in different indigenous groups. In Brazil, transliteration of this Quechua word into Portuguese results in the name, *hoasca*. *Ayahuasca* occupies a central position in Amazonian ethnomedicine, and the chemical nature of its active constituents and the manner of its use make its study relevant to contemporary issues in neuropharmacology, neurophysiology, and psychiatry.

In a traditional context, *ayahuasca* is a beverage prepared by boiling—or soaking—the bark and stems of *B. caapi* together with various admixture plants. The admixture employed most commonly is a member of the coffee family (Rubiaceae), *Psychotria viridis* Ruiz & Pavón. The leaves of *P. viridis* contain DMT, an alkaloid that is necessary for the hallucinogenic effect. *Ayahuasca* is unique in that its pharmacological activity is dependent on a synergistic interaction between the active alkaloids in the plant admixtures. The bark of *B. caapi,* one of the components, contains β-carboline alkaloids, which are potent MAO (monoamine oxidase) inhibitors; the other component, the leaves of *P. viridis* or related species, contains the potent short-acting psychoactive agent DMT. DMT is not active when orally ingested, because it is destroyed by MAO in the liver and gut, but it can be rendered orally active if the peripheral MAO is inhibited—and this interaction is the basis of the psychotropic action of *ayahuasca* (McKenna et al. 1984). Other *Psychotria* species reported to be used as admixtures in lieu of *P. viridis* include *P. leiocarpa, P. nervosa, P. carthaginensis,* and *P. poeppigiana.* There is little chemical data to confirm the presence of DMT in these other species, but the fact that they are employed provides at least anecdotal evidence that they also contain the active principle.

In the Northwest Amazon, particularly in the Colombian Putumayo and Ecuador, the leaves of *Diplopterys cabrerana* (Cuatr.) Gates are added to the brew instead of the leaves of *P. viridis*. This woody vine is in the same family as *Banisteriopsis* and morphologically resembles it. The chief alkaloid present in *Diplopterys,* however, is DMT, the same compound as in the *Psychotria* admixtures, and pharmacologically, the effects are similar. In Peru, various admixtures in addition to *Psychotria* or *Dipoloterys* are frequently added, depending on the magical, medical, or religious purposes for which the drug is being consumed. Although a virtual pharmacopoeia of admixtures (McKenna et al. 1995) is occasionally added, the most commonly employed admixtures (other than *Psychotria,* which is a constant component of the preparation) are various members of the nightshade family (Solanaceae), including tobacco (*Nicotiana* sp.), *Brugmansia* sp., and *Brunfelsia* sp. (Schultes 1972; McKenna et al. 1995). These solanaceous genera are known to contain alkaloids, such as nicotine, scopalamine, and atropine, which effect both central and peripheral adrenergic and cholinergic neurotransmission. "Nightshade" alkaloids (tropanes) such as scopolamine, and *ayahuasca* preparations containing nightshades, can be more dangerous than psychedelics, such as DMT, or brews lacking these additives, as nightshades can cause a profound state of disorientation and delirium, often accompanied by amnesia. In practice, however, these additives are rarely added to the *ayahuasca* preparation, and often, when they are added, only a "symbolic" small amount is added, insufficient to produce a full pharmacological effect.

Active Constituents of Ayahuasca and Its Source Plants

The chemical constituents of *ayahuasca* and the source plants used in its preparation have been well characterized (Rivier and Lindgren 1972; McKenna et al. 1984; Callaway et al. 2005). *B. caapi* contains the β-carboline derivatives harmine, THH (tetrahydroharmine), and harmaline as the major alkaloids.[5] The admixture plant, *Psychotria viridis,* contains a single major alkaloid, DMT[6] (Rivier and Lindgren 1972; McKenna et al. 1984). The concentrations of alkaloids in the *ayahuasca* beverages are, not surprisingly, several times greater than in the source plants from which they are prepared, based on a quantitative analysis of the major alkaloids in several samples of *ayahuasca* collected on the upper Rio Purús.[7]

McKenna et al. (1984) reported somewhat higher values for the alkaloid content of several samples of Peruvian ayahuasca,[8] well within the range of activity for DMT administered i.m. (Szara 1956) or i.v. (Strassman and Qualls 1994) and also for harmine to act effectively as a MAOI (monoamine oxidase inhibitor).[9] A recent study by Callaway et al. (2005) examined the variations in alkaloid profiles of DMT, harmine, harmaline, and THH in 29 *ayahuasca* decoctions obtained from the UDV (Uñiao do Vegetal) church, the Santo Daime church, the Shuar tribe, and the Barquinha church.[10] There are obviously considerable variations in alkaloid content of *ayahuasca* decoctions, and this is readily explained by differences in the methods of preparation, as well as in the natural variations to be expected in the source plants. This conclusion is now well supported and documented in the recent papers by Callaway et al. (2005) and Callaway (2005).

Pharmacological Actions of *Ayahuasca* and Its Active Alkaloids

The oral activity of *ayahuasca* is a function of the peripheral inactivation of MAO by the β-carboline alkaloids in the mixture. This action prevents the peripheral oxidative degradation of the DMT, which is the primary hallucinogenic component, rendering it orally active and enabling it to penetrate the blood/ brain barrier and reach its site of action in the central nervous system in an intact form (Schultes 1972; McKenna et al. 1984). DMT alone is inactive following oral administration at doses up to 1,000mg (Shulgin 1982; Nichols et al. 1991). DMT is active by itself following parenteral administration (a route of administration other than oral ingestion, e.g., by smoking the free base or by injection) at around

25 mg (Szara 1956; Strassman and Qualls 1994). Because of its oral inactivity, users employ various methods of parenteral administration. For example, drug abusers using synthetic DMT commonly smoke the free base; in this form, the alkaloid volatilizes readily and produces an immediate, intense psychedelic episode of short duration (5–15 min), usually characterized by multicolored, rapidly moving hypnagogic hallucinations (Stafford 1977). The Yanomamo Indians and other Amazonian tribes prepare a snuff from the sap of various species in the genus *Virola* that contains large amounts of DMT and the related compound, 5-methoxy-DMT, which is also orally inactive (Schultes and Hofmann 1980; McKenna et al. 1985). The effects of the botanical snuffs containing DMT, while not as intense as smoking DMT freebase, are similarly rapid in onset and of limited duration. The *ayahuasca* beverage is unique in that it is the only traditionally used psychedelic where the peripheral inactivation of DMT present in one plant is prevented by combining it with another plant containing potent and selective MAO-A inhibitors. The psychedelic experience that follows ingestion of *ayahuasca* differs markedly from the effects of parenterally ingested DMT; the time of onset is approximately one hour after ingestion, and the effects last approximately four hours. Usually the subjective effects are less intense than those of parenterally administered synthetic DMT. The subjective effects of *ayahuasca* include hypnagogic hallucinations, dream-like reveries, and a feeling of alertness and stimulation. Peripheral autonomic changes in blood pressure, heart rate, etc. are also less pronounced in *ayahuasca* than parenteral DMT. In some individuals, transient nausea and episodes of vomiting occur, while others are rarely affected in this respect. When *ayahuasca* is taken in a group setting, vomiting is considered a normal part of the experience and allowances are made to accommodate this behavior (Callaway et al. 1999).

The amounts of β-carbolines present in a typical dose of *ayahuasca* are well above the threshold for activity as MAOI. It is likely that the main contribution of the β-carbolines to the acute effects of *ayahuasca* results from their oral activation of DMT, through their action as peripheral MAOI. It is worthy of note that β-carbolines are highly selective inhibitors of MAO-A, the form of the enzyme for which serotonin and presumably other tryptamines, including DMT, are the preferred substrates (Yasuhara et al. 1972; Yasuhara 1974). This selectivity of β-carbolines for MAO-A over MAO-B, combined with their relatively low affinity for liver MAO compared to brain MAO, may explain why reports of hypertensive crises following the ingestion of *ayahuasca* are rare or nonexistent.

β-Carbolines, by themselves, may have some psychoactivity and thus may contribute to the overall psychotropic activity of the *ayahuasca* beverage; however, it is probably inaccurate to characterize the psychotropic properties of β-carbolines as "hallucinogenic" or "psychedelic" (Shulgin and Shulgin 1997). As MAO inhibitors, β-carbolines can increase brain levels of serotonin, and the primarily sedative effects of high doses of β-carbolines are thought to result from their blockade of serotonin deamination. The primary action of β-carbolines in the *ayahuasca* beverage is their inhibition of peripheral MAO, which protects the DMT in the brew from peripheral degradation and thus renders it orally active. There is evidence, however, that THH, the second most abundant β-carboline in the beverage, acts as a weak 5-HT uptake inhibitor and MAOI (Buckholtz and Boggan 1976, 1977). Thus, THH may prolong the half-life of DMT by blocking its intraneuronal uptake, and consequently, its inactivation by MAO. On the other hand, THH may also block serotonin uptake into the neuron, resulting in higher levels of 5-HT in the synaptic cleft; this 5-HT, in turn, may attenuate the subjective effects of orally ingested DMT by competing with it at postsynaptic receptor sites (Callaway et al. 1999).

DMT and its derivatives and the β-carboline derivatives are widespread in the plant kingdom (Smith 1977; Allen and Holmstedt 1980), and both classes of alkaloids have been detected as endogenous metabolites in mammals, including humans (Airaksinen and Kari 1981; Barker et al. 1981; Bloom et al. 1982). Methyl transferases which catalyze the synthesis of DMT, 5-methoxy-DMT, and bufotenine have been found to occur naturally in human lung, brain, blood, cerebrospinal fluid, liver, and heart, and also in rabbit lung, toad, mouse, steer, guinea pig, and baboon brains, as well as in other tissues in these species (McKenna and Towers 1985). Although the occurrence, synthesis, and degradative metabolism of DMT in mammalian systems have been the focus of scientific investigations (Barker et al. 1980, 1981), the possible neuroregulatory functions of this psychotomimetic compound are incompletely understood. Endogenous psychotogens have been suggested as possible etiological factors in schizophrenia and other mental disorders, but the evidence remains equivocal (Fischman 1983).

β-Carbolines are tricyclic indole alkaloids that are closely related to tryptamines, both biosynthetically and pharmacologically. They are readily synthesized via the condensation of indoleamines with aldehydes or alpha-keto acids, and their biosynthesis probably also proceeds via similar reactions (Melchior and Collins 1982). 6-Methoxy-tetrahydro-β-carboline has been identified as a major constituent of human pineal gland (Langer et al. 1984). This compound inhibits the high-affinity binding of [^{3}H]-citalopram to 5-HT transporters in rat brain (Pahkla et al. 1997), and also significantly inhibits 5-HT binding to type 1 receptors in rat brain; the compound has a low affinity to type 2 receptors, however (Taylor et al. 1984).[11] There are implications for this action of tetrahydro-β-carbolines for the pharmacology of ayahuasca. Inhibition of 5-HT uptake by THH, present in significant amounts in ayahuasca, may elevate the concentrations of 5-HT at receptor sites, thus attenuating the hallucinogenic effects of DMT by competitive inhibition at the receptor sites. Additionally, elevated synaptic levels of DMT and 5-HT, both 5-HT agonists, could potentially trigger "serotonin syndrome" if also combined with SSRI (selective serotonin reuptake inhibitors)-type antidepressants. 2-Methyl-tetrahydro-β-carboline and harman have been detected in human urine following ethanol loading (Rommelspacher et al. 1980). It has been suggested that endogenous β-carbolines and other amine–aldehyde condensation products may be related to the etiology of alcoholism (Rahwan 1974). β-Carbolines also exhibit other biological activities in addition to their effects on neurophysiological systems. For instance, Hopp et al. (1976) found that harmine exhibited significant antitrypanosomal activity against *Trypanosoma lewisii*. This finding may explain the use of *ayahuasca* in mestizo ethnomedicine as a prophylactic against malaria and internal parasites (Rodriguez et al. 1982).

CLINICAL INVESTIGATIONS AND LABORATORY STUDIES

Ayahuasca has been the lynch pin of shamanic healing practices in Amazonian shamanism for centuries. In that context, it fulfills multiple roles. It is given as medicine to patients who suffer from psychological and/or physical ailments. It is consumed by *ayahuasqueros* (shamans) themselves as a diagnostic tool to identify the causes of illness and misfortune (and often, these are not distinguished) and to implement appropriate remedies. Such remedies may range from treatment with medicinal plants to the use of songs (icaros), purgation, fumigation with tobacco smoke, massage, and other techniques intended to ameliorate or eliminate the causes of illness or distress, whether of physical or psychological origin. The therapeutic use of *ayahuasca* in its traditional context is not within the scope of the present chapter but has been discussed by numerous other scholars [among them see Luna (1984)]. There is much that may be learned through the study of shamanic healing practices that could be usefully adapted into psychotherapeutic practices, and this question begs for further investigation. In this chapter, however, my focus is restricted to a consideration of some potential therapeutic applications that have been suggested by a previous biomedical investigation of *ayahuasca* use in Brazil, in which I was privileged to participate.

In addition to its continuing use in traditional Amazonian shamanism, starting in the early 1930s, *ayahuasca* became integrated into the religious practices of several syncretic religions in Brazil, where it is consumed as a sacrament in group rituals, sometimes involving up to several hundred people. There are three primary Brazilian religions that employ *ayahuasca* as a sacrament: the UDV, the Santo Diame, and the Barquinha. The first two groups include about 10,000 members each throughout Brazil. The Barquinha is a smaller group, consisting of only a few hundred members, primarily in the Rio Branco area of the Amazon. The religious practices of these groups and their sacramental use of *ayahuasca* is sanctioned and legally permitted by CONFEN, the Brazilian regulatory agency that fulfills a role similar to the FDA and DEA in the United States. Earlier this year (2006), the U.S. Supreme Court rendered a unanimous decision granting a U.S.-based chapter of the UDV the right to use their version of *ayahuasca* (which they term "*hoasca*") in religious practices under the provisions of the Religious Freedom Restoration Act (Supreme Court of the United States 2006).

Owing to a fortunate concatenation of circumstances, in 1991 my colleagues and I were invited to collaborate with Brazilian clinicians to conduct a biomedical investigation of the short- and long-term effects of *hoasca* in members of the UDV. We were able to secure modest funding for the study through private donations, and conducted the field phase of the study in Manaus, Brazil, in the summer of 1993. This project was a truly international and interdisciplinary collaboration, involving the participation of scientists from two U.S. universities (UCLA and University of Miami), three Brazilian institutions (University of Rio de Janeiro, Hospital Amazonico in Manaus, and the Instituto Nacional Pesquisas da Amazonia "INPA" in Manaus, a Brazilian Amazonian research institute), and the University of Kuopio in Finland. The scientific expertise of the investigators was similarly broad, and included psychiatrists, neurochemists, anthropologists, physiologists, and ethnopharmacologists. The major findings of the study have subsequently appeared in peer-reviewed scientific journals.[12]

The project was initiated as a pilot study. Because there had been no previous investigations of the human pharmacology of *hoasca,* the main objective was to gather data, to examine the acute physiological and psychological effects of *hoasca,* and to measure and quantify the pharmacokinetics of the *hoasca* alkaloids in humans (Callaway et al. 1999). A further objective was to determine whether *hoasca* use has any long-term effects. Was there some biochemical or metabolic "marker" that could distinguish long-term, regular users of *hoasca* from members of the general population (without making a judgment as to whether the detection of such a marker was "good" or "bad")? Moreover, what was the impact of regular *hoasca* use, within the ritual context of the UDV church? Did members experience *hoasca* and UDV membership as a positive influence on their lives, and if so, in what ways?

These initial study objectives were relatively modest. The results exceeded expectations in several significant ways (Grob et al. 1996).

Psychological evaluations and psychological screening tests found no evidence of long-term mental or cognitive impairment in long-term *hoasca* drinkers. In fact, most members performed slightly better than control subjects on measures of cognitive functions, verbal facility and recall, mathematical ability, motivation, and emotional well-being and personality adjustment.

There was no evidence of acute toxicity during the sessions or of long-term toxicity or other adverse health effects. *Hoasca,* in the context of the UDV, is consumed regularly by a wide variety of men and women ranging in ages from 13 to 90, and appears to be extremely safe. Many of the older members of the UDV, who are now well into their 80s, have used *hoasca* regularly since their teenage years, and are remarkable for their mental acuity, lack of serious disease history, and physical vigor.

In depth, structured psychiatric interviews of the UDV volunteers revealed remarkable similarities in their life stories that indicated that *hoasca* (and UDV membership) had been a very positive influence in their lives. Almost all the volunteers related that before joining the church and taking *hoasca,* they had been dysfunctional and out of control in a variety of ways. Alcoholism, drug abuse, a tendency to violent behavior, spousal abuse, marital infidelity, dishonesty in business affairs, and other maladaptive behaviors were the norm. Most members related that after joining the UDV, their initial experiences with *hoasca* were horrific, but life changing in profound, positive ways. Most also related having visions in which they saw the future fate that would befall them if they continued on their self-destructive course. They determined to change their lives for the better, and many were rewarded with a vision of Mestre Gabriel, the founder and patron saint of the UDV (or of Jesus or the Virgin Mary). These entities reassured them and confirmed the validity of their decision to change their lives. All of the volunteers affirmed that they had taken these lessons to heart, that they had changed their lives for the better, and were as a result much happier and better-adjusted. Although difficult to measure objectively, casual observations of the social interactions among the UDV members, with each other and between spouses and parents and children, seemed to the investigators to confirm this assertion. More recent studies (Dobkin de Rios et al. 2005) have provided both qualitative and quantitative data that provide support for this supposition.

In the light of these reports of positive life changes, one of the results of the biochemical investigations emerged as particularly intriguing. The neurochemist on the team, Dr. Jace Callaway of the University of Kuopio, Finland, reported that UDV members had a persistent, long-term elevation in the number of serotonin reuptake transporters in their blood platelets (Callaway et al. 1994) compared to age-matched controls that had never consumed the beverage. He subsequently demonstrated that this elevation in serotonin transporters is correlated with a similar long-term upregulation of brain serotonin transporters (Callaway, pers. comm.). This finding became especially significant when viewed in the light of medical literature, indicating that certain maladaptive psychological and behavioral syndromes have been associated with marked deficits in the neuronal densities of serotonin transporters (Tiihonen et al. 1997; Hallikainen et al. 1999; Mantere et al. 2002). These syndromes include severe alcoholism with tendencies toward violence, suicidal behaviors, and severe depression. Thus it appears that regular ingestion of *hoasca* may actually *reverse* a biochemical deficit that has been associated with self-destructive and violent behavior.

In addition to the reports of our UDV study, there exist other indications that *hoasca* may have therapeutic benefits. The "life-story" interviews with the UDV subjects revealed that many had struggled with alcoholism until their experiences with *hoasca,* in the context of the ritual setting, enabled them to confront and ultimately overcome their addictions. In this light, it is not surprising that *ayahuasca* has been used outside the UDV as a treatment for alcoholism and other types of substance-abuse problems. Several South American groups are utilizing *ayahuasca* for the treatment of addiction. Dr. Jacques Mabit, in this volume, describes in detail his own experiences using *ayahuasca* in addiction treatments at his clinic in Tarapoto, Peru. For more on his work, see Mabit et al. (1996).

A number of anecdotal reports have emerged indicating that some users of *ayahuasca* have experienced remissions of cancer (Topping 1998) and other serious illnesses in conjunction with regular use of the tea. Additionally, the longevity, physical vigor, and mental acuity evidenced by many *ayahuasqueros* in

Peru have long been noted as remarkable. Although the evidence is anecdotal, it is indicative that no serious long-term adverse effects appear to be associated with *ayahuasca* consumption, and in some cases, significant long-term benefits may result from its use. The psychological measures applied to the subjects in our UDV study also lend support to this perception; as a group, the UDV subjects performed slightly but significantly better than control subjects on measurements of cognitive functions, verbal and numerical ability, and recall (Grob et al. 1996).

To summarize, the putative therapeutic applications of *ayahuasca* are posited on several kinds of evidence: Its uses in shamanic healing practices in Mestizo and indigenous shamanism; the "*Hoasca* Project," the name under which our biomedical study of UDV volunteers in the 1990s has come to be known; and anecdotal reports or observations regarding such events as spontaneous remissions from cancer or other types of physical or psychological healing. It is a mishmash of data; none of it rises to the level of a well-designed clinical study. Of the three types of evidence, the "*Hoasca* Project" comes the closest to being a scientific study, but even this was an observational study and was not in any sense a clinical trial, nor was it intended as such. In addition to this, we have the fact that *ayahuasca* is being used therapeutically in various venues in South America and elsewhere, e.g., for the treatment of addictions and alcoholism. These uses are not based on the outcomes of controlled clinical trials; rather, they are based on the clinical judgments and empirical experiences of practitioners that *ayahuasca* can be useful in some cases for treating such conditions.

POSSIBLE MECHANISMS OF THERAPEUTIC ACTION

Although the evidence for *ayahuasca*'s healing properties may fall far short of a controlled clinical study, nevertheless the observations of experienced clinicians and psychotherapists, coupled with the results of the *Hoasca* Project, indicate that the preparation can facilitate mind/body healing through a number of complementary mechanisms.

Psychotherapeutic/Shamanic

When LSD was first introduced into psychiatry in the early 1950s, there was great optimism that it would trigger a revolution in psychotherapeutic practice. Because of its ability to loosen the boundaries of the self, to "dissolve the ego," as some characterized it, and to promote introspection, it was considered a useful tool, in conjunction with appropriate psychiatric intervention, for facilitating psychotherapy and the resolution of mood disorders, neuroses, and other kinds of psychological dysfunctions. Similar claims have been made over the years for other types of psychedelics, including *ayahuasca*. Most of the claims are supported by the testimony of patients who have undergone the therapy, or the practitioners who have administered the medicine in a psychotherapeutic context.

There are no rigorous studies "proving" the efficacy of these agents for psycho-therapy, just as there are indeed no rigorous studies proving the efficacy of *any* psychotherapeutic regimen (Leichsenring 2005). Nevertheless, anecdotal and subjective reports are not without weight, especially when the criteria for efficacy are based on subjective experience. On that measure, based on the abundance of anecdotal reports (cf. Metzner 2006), there seems little doubt that *ayahuasca* can have profoundly psychotherapeutic benefits when administered in the right context and under appropriate supervision. The nontraditional use of *ayahuasca* (and other hallucinogenic plants that may be used psychotherapeutically) frequently combines traditional shamanic practices with contemporary psycho-therapeutic techniques. The result is frequently a kind of hybrid therapy, in which the psychotherapist may fulfill many of the functions of a shaman or vice versa (Metzner 1998). It does not seem to matter. The point is that many people have claimed benefit from such psychotherapeutic/shamanic treatments. The fact that these practices have not been investigated more thoroughly and more rigorously is an indictment of a regulatory system that makes such investigations nearly impossible but does not invalidate the experiences of patients who have received it nor their perceived benefits from such treatments.

Long-Term Neurochemical Modulation

Contemporary psychiatry is far more comfortable with a psychopharmaco-logical approach to the treatment of mental disorders than it is with cognitive therapies. This is partly a result of the current paradigm under which much of medicine is forced to practice, in which health maintenance organizations and insurance providers will more readily provide coverage for medications than for any sort of prolonged (and potentially more expensive) cognitive therapy. Even given this "pill for every ill" bias, *ayahuasca* may have something to teach us. Callaway et al. (1994) found evidence for a long-term upregulation of serotonin transporters in the platelets of long-time members of the UDV. This was not an acute effect of MAO inhibition, as the parameter was measured after a two-week washout period in which the subjects refrained from ingesting *hoasca*. This is an intriguing finding. Is the effect therapeutic? It is impossible to know without more rigorous clinical studies. The fact that it was observed in a cohort of subjects who claimed that *hoasca* (in the context of a supportive social environment, viz, the UDV sect) enabled them to implement lifelong behavioral changes that ameliorated or eliminated various destructive behaviors (e.g., alcoholism and drug addiction) indicates that it may be. While correlation is not a cause, these findings suggest that alternative approaches to long-term serotonergic modulation may exist that differ from the current tendency to initiate treatment with SSRIs. It is known that over time, SSRIs will downregulate the serotonin transporters (Huether 1999). *Ayahuasca* apparently has the opposite effect. Is it therapeutic? The answer at this time is that we don't know, but it appears (on the basis of the results of the "*Hoasca* Project") that it may be.

Immune Modulation

Anecdotal reports have recounted individual experiences in which *ayahuasca* is claimed to have "cured" major diseases such as cancer (Topping 1998). I have personally observed one instance where repeated *ayahuasca* sessions appeared to markedly accelerate healing of a badly injured knee suffered by a friend in a skiing accident. In traditional shamanic practice, *ayahuasca* is used to treat physical as well as psychological disorders, and presumably, clients who approach *ayahuasqueros* for such treatments experience some relief; at least some do, some of the time. This raises a question; could the underlying mechanism of *ayahuasca*'s ameliorative effect on physical illnesses, assuming it does occur, be related to immune potentiation? This hypothesis is tempting when it comes to consideration of the spontaneous remission of cancer. In some sense, cancer represents a failure of the immune system. One of the most important protective functions of the immune system is its internal monitoring function in identifying and eliminating precancerous cells before they have the opportunity to proliferate. Similarly, the immune response protects us from external infections as well, and also is deeply involved in inflammatory responses. An abundance of evidence from the relatively young field of psychoneuroimmunology has demonstrated that an intimate link exists between stress, immune functions, and physical and mental health (cf. Vittetta et al. 2005). The possibility that powerful cathartic and/or mystical experiences induced by psychedelics may result in an enhanced immune response that in turn could be the mechanism responsible for spontaneous remissions of cancer and other self-healing responses would appear to be an obvious question for psychoneuroimmunologists to address. Oddly (or perhaps not, considering the "shadow" in which psychedelic research of all types seems to abide), a search of PubMed produced a reference to only one paper (Roberts 1999) in which this subject was addressed (out of a total of 815 references retrieved for the term "psychoneuroimmunology"). The paper was a speculative review proposing the hypothesis; apparently, no empirical investigator has seen fit to follow up the suggestion in the seven years since this paper was published. In a recent paper, Riba and Barbanoj (2005) allude to the fact that current clinical investigations with lyophilized *ayahuasca* preparations have included an assessment of the acute effects of *ayahuasca* administration on neuroendocrine and immune parameters. These results remain unpublished. Although the authors point out that these initial studies will not provide information on the long-term immune-modulating effects of *ayahuasca,* the results are eagerly awaited by those who postulate that activation of immune functions could provide a mechanism for healing of physical illnesses by *ayahuasca,* and possibly other psychedelic substances.

Psychointegration

Healing modalities associated with *ayahuasca* may have their basis in shamanic/psychotherapeutic dynamics, in long-term neuromodulation of serotonergic functions, and in neuroimmunomodulatory processes. In this connection, it is relevant to mention Winkelman's (2001) concept that *ayahuasca* and other shamanic plants and substances are "psychointegrators." Winkelman postulates that *ayahuasca* and other psychedelic plants, whether used in a shamanic or psychotherapeutic context, force a holistic reintegration of basic neurological, emotional, behavioral, and cognitive processes, primarily through long-term modulation of serotonergic systems. The result is that through the activation of higher cortical processes, and the disinhibition of lower brain systems and the visual cortex, more information is made available to the brain and it is stimulated in the direction of more integrative functioning. There are undoubtedly empirical approaches to testing this hypothesis, were it possible to conduct this work under current regulatory paradigms; the EEG work by Stuckey et al. (2005) in Brazil seems to point in this direction. At least it does provide a rationale to support claims for potential beneficial effects of psychedelics for individuals who are neither mentally dysfunctional nor practitioners of psychedelic religions.

FUTURE DIRECTIONS

Ayahuasca has a long and venerable history as the quintessential shamanic medicine. Its reputation as a healing medicine is based partly on its well-documented role in indigenous ethnomedical practices, partly on the testimony of Westerners who have experienced it, and partly on the results of scientific studies such as the "*Hoasca* Project," and more recently, the work of Jordi Riba and his colleagues in Spain. Given current regulatory challenges, the inbuilt biases of mainstream medicine against the use of plant medicines, and especially hallucinogenic plant medicines, it is unlikely that *ayahuasca* is going to find its way into a clinic near you anytime soon (McKenna 2004). One only has to look at the current controversies surrounding the issue of medical marijuana to gain an appreciation for the difficulties involved. Although there is an abundance of evidence from numerous reputable scientific reports and publications that *Cannabis* has therapeutic efficacy (or at least potential) for treating a variety of serious conditions, the recent pronouncement by the FDA (Food and Drug Administration 2006) that "there is no evidence that marijuana has any value as medicine," is indicative of the regulatory and policy climate in which such judgments are made. The statement, profound in its ignorance (Harris 2006), flies in the face of the accepted consensus of a large segment of the scientific community and simply demonstrates, if further proof were needed, that regulatory decisions about the therapeutic use of controlled substances are based on politics, and not science. If these daunting regulatory hurdles block efforts to investigate marijuana as medicine, then it is highly unlikely that *ayahuasca,* which has no popular constituency at all, will ever be employed within the context of mainstream Western medicine. This is not necessarily a bad thing. In shamanic traditions, *ayahuasca* is a mystery, and a medicine; for the syncretic religions of Brazil such as the UDV, *hoasca* is a sacrament. Perhaps, in viewing the respect and reverence with which it is regarded in these traditions, there is a message; perhaps the message is that *ayahuasca* should *not* be made into a pharmaceutical medicine, something to be patented and owned by Merck or Pfizer or some other soulless pharmaceutical conglomerate. That pattern resembles too much the pattern of the past, under which Western science and capitalism investigates and steals the medicines and knowledge of indigenous peoples, while rarely, if ever, giving anything back or even acknowledging the debt that is owed. That has been the pattern for far too long, and perhaps it is time to stop. The social phenomenon of "drug tourism," the recent approval of sacramental use of *hoasca* by the Supreme Court, the proliferation of conferences, and the explosion of knowledge on the Internet, all are hopeful indicators that *ayahuasca* is finding its way to those it needs to find. And those who want to find it, if they pursue their quest in a spirit of humility and respect, will find their way to it. Indeed, this is the way that humanity has always formed alliances with sacred plants, and there may be good reasons for this. This process has expressed itself again and again, throughout the long millennia of humanity's coevolutionary relationships with plants, and it has done so without the need for the intervention of regulatory agencies, capitalism, the pharmaceutical industry, science, or "mainstream" medicine. That sustained alliance will continue, if we can resist the impulse to intervene, and instead learn to "trust the medicine."

NOTES

1. There are several spellings of this word that are commonly employed, most of which are incorrect. Burroughs used the term "yage" in his book, which is both misspelled and lacked the accent on the final "e." In his new book (see note 2, below) Oliver Harris corrects this error but fails to spell the word correctly. In this chapter, I will follow the example set by Schultes (Schultes and Hofmann 1980) and spell the word '*yajé*" except when specifically citing Burrough's title.

2. A wonderful reissue of this work has just been published by City Lights Books under the title *The Yage Letters Redux,* with a lengthy introduction and extensive commentary by Burroughs scholar Oliver Harris.

3. For a detailed discussion of the 19th- and 20th-century history of *ayahuasca,* see my essay, *Ayahuasca: An Ethnopharmacologic History* in Ralph Metzer (ed.) *Ayahuasca: Sacred Vine of Spirits* (2006). Park Street Press, Rochester, VT.

4. Although *ayahuasca,* Quechua for "vine of the souls" is also known as yajé, natema, pilde, hoasca, vegetal, and many other names, *ayahuasca* is the most commonly employed name in the Amazon basin, and this term will be employed henceforth in this chapter, and understood to also represent these many other indigenous names. When specifically referring to the version of *ayahuasca* used by the UDV church in Brazil, we will use the term *hoasca.*

5. Trace amounts of other β-carboline and pyrrolidine alkaloids have also been reported (Rivier and Lindgren 1972; Hashimoto and Kawanishi 1975, 1976; Kawanishi et al. 1982; McKenna et al. 1984).

6. *N*-Methyl tryptamine and methyl-tetrahydro-β-carboline have also been reported as trace constituents.

7. Rivier and Lindgren (1972) calculated that a 200 ml dose of ayahuasca contained an average of 30 mg of harmine, 10 mg of tetrahydroharmine, and 25 mg of DMT. Interestingly, this concentration is above the threshold of activity for i.v. administration of DMT (Strassman and Qualls 1994).

8. These investigators calculated that a 100 ml dose of these preparations contained a total of 728 mg total alkaloid, of which 467 mg is harmine, 160 mg is tetrahydroharmine, 41 mg is harmaline, and 60 mg is DMT.

9. In vitro, these β-carbolines function as MAOI at approximately 10 nM. In mice, harmaline administered i.p. (5 mg/kg) causes 100% inhibition by two hours postinjection, the activity falling off rapidly thereafter (Udenfriend et al. 1958). This dose corresponds to approximately 375 mg in a 75 kg adult, but based on the measured concentration of harmine in the liver, it is likely that one half this dose or less would also be effective.

10. In this study, Callaway and coworkers reported DMT concentration ranged from 0 to 14.15 mg/ml; THH, from 0.48 to 23.8 mg/ml; harmaline, from <0.01 to 0.9 mg/ml; and harmine, from 0.45 to 22.85 mg/ml.

11. The relatively low affinity of tetrahydro-β-carbolines for 5HT2a receptors, however, suggests that DMT, and not THH, is the primary mediator of the hallucinogenic action of ayahuasca (Callaway and Grob 1998; Callaway 1999b).

12. For instance, see Callaway et al. (1999) for the pharmacokinetics of Hoasca alkaloids in healthy humans; Callaway et al. (1996) for quantitation of *N,N*-dimethyltryptamine and harmala alkaloids; Grob et al. (1996) on the human pharmacology of hoasca; and Callaway et al. (1994) regarding platelet serotonin uptake increases.

REFERENCES

Airaksinen, M.M., and I. Kari. 1981. β-Carbolines, psychoactive compounds in the mammalian body. *Medical Biology* 59:21–34.

Allen, J.R.F., and B. Holmstedt. 1980. The simple β-carboline alkaloids. *Phytochemistry* 19:1573–82.

Barker, S.A., J.A. Monti, and S.T. Christian. 1980. Metabolism of the hallucinogen N,N-dimethyltryptamine in rat brain homogenates. *Biochemical Pharmacology* 29:1049–57.

Barker, S.A., J.A. Monti, and S.T. Christian. 1981. N,N-dimethyltryptamine: An endogenous hallucinogen. *International Reviews of Neurobiology* 22:83–110.

Bloom, F., J. Barchus, M. Sandler, and E. Usdin, eds. 1982. β-*carbolines and tetrahydroisoquinolines*. New York: Alan R. Liss.

Buckholtz, N.S., and W.O. Boggan. 1976. Effects of tetrahydro-β-carbolines on monoamine oxidase and serotonin uptake in mouse brain. *Biochemical Pharmacology* 25:2319–21.

Buckholtz, N.S., and W.O. Boggan. 1977. Monoamine oxidase inhibition in brain and liver produced by β-carbolines: Structure-activity relationships and substrate specificity. *Biochemical Pharmacology* 26:1991–96.

Burroughs, W.S. 1963. *The yage letters*. San Francisco: City Lights Books.

Callaway, J.C. 1999. Phytochemistry and neuropharmacology of ayahuasca. In *Ayahuasca: Human consciousness and the spirits of nature,* ed. Ralph Metzner, 50–75. New York: Thunder's Mouth Press.

Callaway, J.C. 2005. Various alkaloid profiles in decoctions of *Banisteriopsis caapi. Journal of Psychoactive Drugs* 37:151–56.

Callaway, J.C., and C.S. Grob. 1998. Ayahuasca preparations and serotonin reuptake inhibitors: A potential combination for adverse interaction. *Journal of Psychoactive Drugs* 30:367–69.

Callaway, J.C., M.M. Airaksinen, D.J. McKenna, G.S. Brito, and C.S. Grob. 1994. Platelet serotonin uptake sites increased in drinkers of *ayahuasca. Psychopharmacology* 116:385–87.

Callaway, J.C., G.S. Brito, and E.S. Neves. 2005. Phytochemical analyses of *Banisteriopsis caapi* and *Psychotria viridis. Journal of Psychoactive Drugs* 37:145–50.

Callaway, J.C., D.J. McKenna, C.S. Grob, G.S. Brito, L.P. Raymon, R.E. Poland, E.N. Andrade, E.O. Andrade, and D.C. Mash. 1999. Pharmacokinetics of hoasca alkaloids in healthy humans. *Journal of Ethnopharmacology* 65:243–56.

Callaway, J.C., L.P. Raymon, W.L. Hearn, D.J. McKenna, C.S. Grob, G.S. Brito, and D.C. Mash. 1996. Quantitation of N,N-dimethyltryptamine and harmala alkaloids in human plasma after oral dosing with Ayahuasca. *Journal of Analytical Toxicology* 20:492–97.

Davis, W. 1996. *One river: Explorations and discoveries in the Amazon rain forest.* New York: Simon & Schuster.

Der Marderosian, A.H., H.V. Pinkley, and M.F. Dobbins. 1968. Native use and occurrence of N,N-dimethyltryptamine in the leaves of *Banisteriopsis rusbyana. American Journal of Pharmacy* 140:137–47.

Dobkin de Rios, M., C.S. Grob, E. Lopez, D.X. da Silviera, L.K. Alonso, and C. Tacla. 2005. *Ayahuasca* in adolescence: Qualitative results. *Journal of Psychoactive Drugs* 37:135–40.

Eliade, M. 1964. *Shamanism: The archaic techniques of ecstasy.* New York: Bollingen Foundation.

Fischman, L.G. 1983. Dreams, hallucinogenic drug states, and schizophrenia: A psychological and biological comparison. *Schizophrenia Bulletin* 9:73–94.

Food and Drug Administration. 2006. Inter-Agency Advisory Regarding Claims That Smoked Marijuana Is a Medicine. FDA Press Office. Http://www.fda.gov.

Grob, C.S., D.J. McKenna, J.C. Callaway, G.S. Brito, E.S. Neves, G. Oberlender, O.L. Saide, E. Labigalini, C. Tacla, C.T. Miranda, R.J. Strassman, and K.B. Boone. 1996. Human pharmacology of hoasca, a plant hallucinogen used in ritual context in Brazil. *Journal of Nervous and Mental Disease* 184:86–94.

Grof, S. 1994. *LSD psychotherapy.* Alameda, CA: Hunter House Publishers.

Hallikainen, T., T. Saito, H.M. Lachman, J. Volavka, T. Pohjalainen, O.P. Ryynanen, J. Kauhanen, E. Syvalahti, J. Hietala, and J. Tiihonen. 1999. Association between low activity serotonin transporter promoter genotype and early onset alcoholism with habitual impulsive violent behavior. *Molecular Psychiatry* 4:385–88.

Harris, G. 2006. FDA dismisses medical benefit from marijuana. *New York Times, Health section,* April 21, 2006.

Harris, O. 2006. *The yage letters redux.* San Francisco: City Lights Books.

Hashimoto, Y., and K. Kawanishi. 1975. New organic bases from the Amazonian *Banisteriopsis caapi. Phytochemistry* 14:1633–35.

Hashimoto, Y., and K. Kawanishi. 1976. New alkaloids from *Banisteriopsis caapi*. *Phytochemistry* 15:1559–60.

Heinrich, C. 2002. *Magic mushrooms in religion and alchemy*. Rochester, VT: Park Street Press.

Hopp, K.H., L.V. Cunningham, M.C. Bromel, L.J. Schermeister, and S.K.W. Kahlil. 1976. In vitro antitrypanosomal activity of certain alkaloids against *Trypanosoma lewisi*. *Lloydia* 39:375–77.

Huether, G. 1999. Acute regulation and long-term modulation of presynaptic serotonin output. *Advances in Experimental Biology and Medicine* 467:1–10.

Huxley, A. 1954. *The doors of perception*. New York: Harper.

Kawanishi, K., Y. Uhara, and Y. Hashimoto. 1982. Shihunine and dehydroshihunine from *Banisteriopsis caapi*. *Journal of Natural Products* 45:637–38.

Langer, S.Z., C.R. Lee, A. Segnozac, T. Tateishi, H. Esnaud, H. Schoemaker, and B. Winblad. 1984. Possible endocrine role of the pineal gland for 6-methoxytetrahydro-β-carboline, a putative endogenous neuromodulator of the [3H]imipramine recognition site. *European Journal of Pharmacology* 102:379–80.

Lee, M.A., and B. Shlain. 1985. *Acid dreams: The CIA, LSD, and the sixties rebellion*. New York: Grove Press.

Leichsenring, F. 2005. Are psychodynamic and psychoanalytic therapies effective?: A review of empirical data. *International Journal of Psychoanalysis* 86 (Pt 3): 841–68.

Lewin, L. 1931. *Phantastica: Narcotic and stimulating drugs, their use and abuse*. London: Paul, Trench, Trubner.

Luna, L.E. 1984. The healing practices of a Peruvian shaman. *Journal of Ethnophramacology* 11: 123–33.

Mabit, J., R. Goive, and J. Vega. 1996. Takiwasi: The use of Amazonian shamanism to rehabilitate drug addicts. In *Sacred plants, consciousness and healing: Cross-cultural and interdisciplinary perspectives. Yearbook of cross-cultural medicine and psychotherapy*, Vol. 6, 257–86. Berlin: Springer-Verlag.

Manske, R.H.F. 1931. A synthesis of the methyltryptamines and some derivatives. *Canadian Journal of Research* 5:592–600.

Mantere, T., E. Tupala, H. Hall, T. Sarkioja, P. Rasanen., K. Bergstrom, J. Callaway, and J. Tiihonen. 2002. Serotonin transporter distribution and density in the cerebral cortex of alcoholic and nonalcoholic comparison subjects: A whole-hemisphere autoradiography study. *American Journal of Psychiatry* 159:599–606.

McKenna, D.J. 2004. Clinical investigations of the therapeutic potential of *ayahuasca:* Rationale and regulatory challenges. *Pharmacology and Therapeutics* 102:111–29.

McKenna, D.J. 2006a. Mescaline: A molecular history. *Fate*, January, 2006.

McKenna, D.J. 2006b. *Ayahuasca:* An ethnopharmacologic history. In *Ayahuasca: Sacred vine of spirits,* ed. R. Metzner, 40–62. Rochester, VT: Park Street Press.

McKenna, D.J., and G.H.N. Towers. 1985. On the comparative ethnopharmacology of the Malpighiaceous and Myristicaceous hallucinogens. *Journal of Psychoactive Drugs* 17:35–9.

McKenna, D.J., L.E. Luna, and G.H.N. Towers. 1995. Biodynamic constituents in *Ayahuasca* admixture plants: An uninvestigated folk pharmacopoeia. In *Ethnobotany: Evolution of a discipline,* ed. S. von Reis and R.E. Schultes. Portland, OR: Dioscorides Press.

McKenna, D., G.H.N. Towers, and F.S. Abbott. 1984. Monoamine oxidase inhibitors in South American hallucinogenic plants: Tryptamine and β-carboline constituents of ayahausca. *Journal of Ethnopharmacology* 10:195–223.

Melchior, C., and M.A. Collins. 1982. The route and significance of endogenous synthesis of alkaloids in animals. *CRC Critical Reviews in Toxicology* 9:313–56.

Metzner, R. 1998. Hallucinogenic drugs and plants in psychotherapy and shamanism. *Journal of Psychoactive Drugs* 30:333–41.

Metzner, R., ed. 2006. *Ayahuasca: Sacred vine of spirits.* Rochester, VT: Park Street Press.

Nichols, D.E., R. Oberlender, and D.J. McKenna. 1991. Stereochemical aspects of hallucinogenesis. In *Biochemistry and physiology of substance abuse,* ed. R. R. Watson, Vol. III, Chapter 1, 1–39. Boca Raton, FL: CRC Press.

Pahkla, R., L. Rago, J.C. Callaway, and M.M. Airaksinen. 1997. Binding of pinoline on the 5-hydroxytryptamine transporter: Competitive interaction with [3H]-citalopram. *Pharmacology and Toxicology* 80:122–26.

Rahwan, R.G. 1974. Speculations on the biochemical pharmacology of ethanol. *Life Sciences* 15:617–33.

Riba, J., and M.J. Barbanoj. 2005. Bringing *ayahuasca* into the clinical research laboratory. *Journal of Psychoactive Drugs* 37:219–30.

Rivier, L., and J. Lindgren. 1972. Ayahausca, the South American hallucinogenic drink: Ethnobotanical and chemical investigations. *Economic Botany* 29:101–29.

Roberts, T.B. 1999. Do entheogen-induced mystical experiences boost the immune system? Psychedelics, peak experiences, and wellness. *Advances in Mind-Body Medicine* 15:139–47.

Rodriguez, E., J.C. Cavin, and J.E. West. 1982. The possible role of Amazonian psychoactive plants in the chemotherapy of parasitic worms: A hypothesis. *Journal of Ethnopharmacology* 6:303–09.

Rommelspacher, H., S. Strauss, and J. Lindemann. 1980. Excretion of tetrahydroharmane and harmane into the urine of man after a load with ethanol. *FEBS Letters* 109: 209–12.

Schultes, R.E. 1957. The identity of the Malpighiaceous narcotics of South America. *Botanical Museum Leaflets, Harvard University* 18:1–56.

Schultes, R.E. 1972. The ethnotoxicological significance of additives to New World hallucinogens. *Plant Sciences Bulletin* 18:34–41.

Shulgin, A.T. 1982. Psychotomimetic drugs: Structure/activity relationships. In *Handbook of Psychopharmacology,* ed. L.L. Iverson, S.D. Iverson, and S.H. Snyder, Vol. 11, 243–333. New York: Plenum Press.

Schultes, R.E., and A. Hofmann. 1980. *The botany and chemistry of hallucinogens.* Springfield, IL: Charles C. Thomas, Publisher.

Schultes, R.E., and R.F. Raffauf. 1960. Prestonia: An Amazon narcotic or not? *Botanical Museum Leaflets, Harvard University* 19:109–22.

Shulgin, A., and A. Shulgin. 1991. *Phenethylamines I Have Known and Loved: A chemical love story.* Berkeley, CA: Transform Press.

Shulgin, A., and A. Shulgin. 1997. *Tryptamines I Have Known and Loved: The continuation.* Berkeley, CA: Transform Press.

Smith, T.A. 1977. Tryptamine and related compounds in plants. *Phytochemistry* 16:171–5.

Stafford, P. 1977. *Psychedelics encyclopedia.* Berkeley, CA: And/Or Press.

Stevens, J. 1987. *Storming heaven: LSD and the American dream.* New York: Atlantic Monthly Press.

Strassman, R. 2001. *DMT: The spirit molecule: A doctor's revolutionary research into the biology of near-death and mystical experiences*. Rochester, VT: Park Street Press.

Strassman, R.J., and C.R. Qualls. 1994. Dose-response study of N,N-dimethyltryptamine in humans I: Neuroendocrine, autonomic, and cardiovascular effects. *Archives of General Psychiatry* 51:85–97.

Stuckey, D.E., R. Lawson, and L.E. Luna. 2005. EEG gamma coherence and other correlates of subjective reports during *ayahuasca* experiences. *Journal of Psychoactive Drugs* 37:163–78.

Supreme Court of the United States. 2006. Certiorari To The United States Court Of Appeals For The Tenth Circuit. No. 04–1084. Alberto R. Gonzales, Attorney General, et al., Petitioners V. O Centro Espirita Beneficente Uniao Do Vegetal et al. (http://www.erowid.org/chemicals/*ayahuasca*/*ayahuasca*_law23.pdf).

Szara, S. 1956. Dimethyltryptamine: Its metabolism in man; the relation of its psychotic effects to the serotonin metabolism. *Experientia* 12:441–42.

Taylor, D.L., P.B. Silverman, and B.T. Ho. 1984. Effects of 6-methoxytetrahydro-β-carboline on 5-hydroxytryptamine binding in rat brain. *Journal of Pharmacy and Pharmacology* 36:125–27.

Tiihonen, J., J.T. Kiukka, K.A. Bergström, J. Karhu, H. Viinamaki, J. Lehtonen, T. Hallikainen, J. Yang, and P. Hakola. 1997. Single-photon emission tomography imaging of monoamine transporters in impulsive violent behavior. *European Journal of Nuclear Medicine* 24:1253–60.

Topping, D. 1998. *Ayahuasca* and cancer: One man's experience. *Bulletin of the Multidisciplinary Association for Psychedelic Studies* 8:22–6.

Udenfriend, S., B. Witkop, B.G. Redfield, and H. Weissbach. 1958. Studies with reversible inhibitors of monoamine oxidase: Harmaline and related compounds. *Biochemical Pharmacology* 1:160–65.

U.S. Controlled Substances Act. 1970. US Code Title 21, Chapter 13. Available at http://www.erowid.org/psychoactives/law/law_fed_csa1.shtml.

Vittetta, L., B. Anton, F. Cortizo, and A. Sali. 2005. Mind-body medicine: Stress and its impact on overall health and longevity. *Annals of the New York Academy of Sciences* 1057:492–505.

Wasson, R.G. 1957. Seeking the divine mushroom. *Life,* May 13, 1957.

Winkelman, M. 2001. Psychointegrators: Multidisciplinary perspectives on the therapeutic effects of hallucinogens. *Complementary Health Practice Review* 6:219–37.

Yasuhara, H. 1974. Studies on monoamine oxidase (report XXIV). Effect of harmine on monoamine oxidase. *Japanese Journal of Pharmacology* 24:523–33.

Yasuhara, H., S. Sho, and K. Kamijo. 1972. Differences in the actions of harmine on the oxidations of serotonin and tyramine by beef brain mitochondrial MAO. *Japanese Journal of Pharmacology* 22:439–41.

3

CONTEMPORARY PSYCHEDELIC THERAPY: AN OVERVIEW

TORSTEN PASSIE

> The future may teach us to exercise a direct influence, by means of particular chemical substances, on the amounts of energy and their distribution in the mental apparatus. It may be that there are other still undreamt-of possibilities of therapy.
>
> —Sigmund Freud, 1939

This chapter focuses on the psychotherapeutic treatment procedures which are referred to as "psycholytic" or "psychedelic" therapy and their foundations. The methods in question use the psychological activating properties of specific substances to reinforce psychotherapeutic treatments. Some typical psychoactive substances are LSD (lysergic acid diethylamide), psilocybin, and MDMA (3,4-methylenedioxymethamphetamine). On the basis of their abilities to restructure and intensify inner experience in a specific manner, these substances are designated as "psycholytic" (soul-loosening) or "psychedelic" (mind-manifesting).

This valuable approach was nearly forgotten as a result of unfortunate historical circumstances. More than 700 scientific publications on the topic clearly demonstrate how actively physicians and psychologists were involved in investigating the therapeutic potential of these substances in the 1950s and 1960s (Abramson 1967; Passie 1997). Because of their increased use by laymen during the end of the 1960s (which developed independently from medical use), a statutory prohibition of these substances was first enacted in 1966 in the United States and Europe. Although the text of the laws basically allowed for exceptional exemptions, the de facto result was a nearly complete cessation of the research efforts which had previously been so multitudinous (Food and Drug Administration 1975; Grinspoon and Bakalar 1979). The number of publications consequently dropped drastically. However, since the late 1980s, changes have begun to take place which make renewed application of such substances in psychotherapy more likely (Grob and Bravo 1995; Mithoefer 2005).

New options for treatment with psychoactive substances are opened up by the entactogens (or empathogens) such as MDMA, MDE (methylenedioxyethylamphetamine), MDA (methylenedioxyamphetamine), and other hallucinogenic substances which have a specified spectrum of action or abilities for better clinical management such as 2-CB, 2-CD, CZ-74, and CEY-19.[1] A complete history of the procedures and their standards is beyond the scope of this chapter, which points to their origins and the scientifically established therapeutic paradigms as well as some recent developments.

A SHORT HISTORY OF THE PSYCHOLYTIC AND PSYCHEDELIC APPROACHES

The first attempts to use pharmacological influences on the state of consciousness in Western psychotherapy go back to before the 20th century, when ether, chloroform, and hashish were used to induce and deepen hypnotic states (Schrenck-Notzing 1891). In the 1920s and 1930s, physicians attempted to intensify the psychotherapeutic treatment options created by hypnosis and psychoanalysis by using subnarcotic doses of barbiturates. These experiments followed the observation that many patients demonstrated an uninhibited flow of speech in the recovery phase of barbiturate narcosis and divulged intimate details. A procedure which became known as "Narcoanalysis" used this barbiturate-induced state of excitation to recall forgotten and repressed memories and conflicts (Horsley 1943).

Although the therapeutic effects of hallucinogenic drugs have been known worldwide for millennia (Furst 1972; Schultes and Hofmann 1979), their scientific investigation first began in the 20th century. Since the 1920s, a variety of human experiments with hallucinogens, especially mescaline, have been conducted. Even though it was possible to provide thorough clinical descriptions of the mescaline intoxication (Beringer 1927), nearly all researchers were of the opinion that the contents of the experiences did not reflect the psychodynamics of the experimental subjects (Passie 1993/1994). But the first clinical experiments with the highly effective hallucinogen LSD, which was discovered in 1943, made evident the psychodynamic components of the hallucinogenic experience (Stoll 1947; Frederking 1955). The further experimental work with LSD led to the first attempts to use hallucinogens as adjuncts in psychotherapy

(Busch and Johnson 1950; Chandler and Hartmann 1960), and evidence of the effectiveness of its personal effects was provided (Leuner 1962; Masters and Houston 1966).

In addition to the influence of its predecessor, "Narcoanalysis," the "psycholytic method" has various other contributory influences:

1. In 1953, the British psychiatrist Ronald Sandison and his coworkers found intensification of affect and abreactive memory actualizations which lead to significant improvements in the condition of neurotic patients after a single LSD application (Sandison and Spencer 1954).

2. Around 1950, Leuner developed a daydream technique in psychotherapy (today established as "Guided Affective Imagery") (Leuner 1984). He determined that by using small doses of hallucinogens, therapeutically useful images could be intensified and deepened. In addition, experiences of regression and catharsis were enhanced (Leuner 1959).

The method designated as "Psycholysis" by Ronald Sandison at the "First European Symposium for Psychotherapy under LSD-25" in 1960 (Barolin 1960) developed under the direction of psychoanalytically oriented therapists. This new method was based on the widely accepted concepts of classical psychoanalysis and supported the activation of unconscious memories, emotional impulses, and conflicts with low doses of hallucinogens. These could produce dreamlike experiences, but mainly a clear altered state of consciousness which was easily remembered and accessible for therapeutic processing.

An approach which must be strictly differentiated from the psycholytic method was developed in the United States and termed the "psychedelic method." This procedure has various origins:

1. Around 1950, proceeding from the observation that many alcoholics remain abstinent after the traumatic experiences of a delirium tremens, Hoffer and Osmond wanted to produce delirium tremens with high doses of LSD to effect abstinence. However, they determined that, in contrast to their hypothesis of the therapeutic effects of the trauma, the lasting therapeutic effects were associated with the positively felt experiences of expanded self-awareness and religious experiences (Hoffer 1967).

2. In 1962, the anesthesiologist Eric Kast conducted a comparative study on the analgesic action of various substances (including LSD) on terminal cancer patients. Surprisingly, he was able to detect a diminution of pain as well as a more relaxed attitude toward death in the LSD subjects. The subjects reported experiencing deepened self and situational insight, as well as an elevated religious awareness (Kast and Collins 1964, 1966).

3. Ethnographic reports suggested that ritual administration of certain hallucinogenic plants (Peyote cult, Brazilian Ayahuasca religion) leads to dramatic positive personality changes in sociopathic and alcohol-dependent individuals (Andritzky 1989; La Barre 1989; MacRae 1992).

Subsequent to their first experiments, Hoffer and Osmond developed the psychedelic treatment technique. This procedure made induction of mystic religious experiences the basis of its therapeutic action. It uses a quasi-religious preparation of the patient, higher dosages, specific surroundings, and music to favor evocation of far-reaching insights and deep religious experiences. The transformative power of certain mystical states of consciousness (mystic union) was particularly emphasized. The psychedelic treatment was further optimized during the 1960s and culminated in the methodically meticulous studies at Spring Grove Hospital, Maryland, and the NIMH Psychiatric Research Center in Catonsville, Maryland (Pahnke et al. 1970; Grof 1975; Yensen and Dryer 1993/1994) (Table 3.1).

Table 3.1   The Two Main Approaches to the Psychotherapeutic Use of Hallucinogens (from Passie 1997)

Psycholytic therapy	Psychedelic therapy
Low doses of LSD (30–200 mcg), psilocybin (3–15 mg), CZ 74 (5–20 mg), MDMA, etc. producing symbolic dream images, regressions, and transference phenomena.	High doses of LSD (400–1500 mcg) leading to so-called cosmic–mystic experiences. Oneness and ecstatic joy are attained.
Activation and deepening of the psychoanalytic process.	Modern transpersonal approaches used to explain structure and effects of experiences.
Numerous sessions required (5–30).	One to three "overwhelming" experiences are aimed at.
Analytic discussion of experienced material in individual and group sessions (focusing on ego-psychology, transference, and defense mechanisms).	Very suggestive quasi-religious preparation and use of specific surroundings and music. Not very detailed discussion of the experience.
Reality comparison, and attempt to adapt experience to everyday life.	Adaption to reality is not the main purpose. Enhancing the meaning of the "psychedelic" experience.
Goal: Cure through restructure of personality in the sense of a maturing process and loosening of infantile parental bonds, requiring several months.	Goal: Symptomatic cure in a change of behavior, but not exactly defined.
Classical indications for psychotherapy: Neuroses, psychosomatic cases, psychopaths, sexual neuroses, and borderline cases. Neither alcoholism nor psychoses.	Alcoholism, neuroses (?), and terminal cancer patients.

A combination of the psycholytic and psychedelic methods was first suggested by Alnaes (1965) and Grof (1967). This "psychedelytic" approach integrates both the intense transformational experiences of individual high-dose psychedelic sessions and the processing of psychodynamic material in low-dose psycholytic serial session (Yensen 1994). It is considered to be the most modern approach and has already been applied in a few pilot studies (Yensen et al. 1976; Benz 1989). As a result of the variety of applications that are described in this chapter, an extremely promising future for hallucinogen-assisted psychotherapy was foreseen by many authors.

In 1985, the SAEPT (Swiss Physicians Society for Psycholytic Therapy) was founded. Between 1988 and 1993, their physicians received a special permit allowing psychotherapy with LSD and MDMA (Benz 1989; Styk 1994). These therapists treated patients in individual and group settings but mainly using recently developed therapeutic group techniques as described below. They used a combination of psycholytic and psychedelic techniques (using high medium doses, impressive music, and sometimes natural settings), expanded by using holotropic breathwork before sessions and combinations of substances (especially MDMA with LSD and MDMA with 2-CB). In the context of their work, some training groups for ongoing psycholytic therapists were created. The SÄPT (Swiss Physician Society for Psycholytic Therapy) group is still working to gain permission for studying MDMA and LSD in psychotherapy in a scientific manner and recently received permission for doing a study of psychotherapy with MDMA in PTSD (post-traumatic stress disorders) patients (Oehen 2005) (Table 3.2).

PRINCIPAL THERAPEUTIC TECHNIQUES: INDIVIDUAL TREATMENTS

The first researchers using LSD in psychotherapy were all psychoanalytically educated and used the LSD-induced state in a conventional individual couch treatment setting. While under the influence of the substance, the patient lies on a couch in a darkened room and is attended to by one attendant (mostly a specially trained nurse) and occasionally visited by the physician. The dosage is

Table 3.2 Substances Typically Used for Psycholytic/ Psychedelic Treatments[2]

Hallucinogens	Entactogens
LSD	MDMA
Psilocybin	MDE
CZ-74	MDA
CEY-19	
2-CB	
2-CD	

individually adjusted in such a manner that the patient remains oriented and in communication with the attendant, and realizes the therapeutic character of the situation. The patient is asked to surrender himself or herself without reservation to the impressions, emotions, and visions which appear. The occasional remarks of the patient are recorded with a tape recorder or in writing and then given to her/him to prepare a retrospective report. In addition to a discussion immediately following the session, the LSD-induced experiences are interpreted and worked through in drug-free sessions between the hallucinogen sessions in accordance with the principles of depth psychology. Therefore, the drug-induced experiences play only a supporting role in primarily conventional psychoanalytical treatments (Grof 1979). As a rule, these extend for months to years, and between 5 and 25 psycholytic sessions are conducted. The individual setting was mainly used with indole hallucinogens like LSD and psilocybin. This may be partly dependent on the fact that these kinds of substances are usually associated with much imagery, cognitive alterations, intense emotions, and regressions. Experiments with conventional psychotherapeutic group settings were abandoned because of the inability to follow-up group interactions because of too much distraction from individual "tripping."

Leuner's (1971) and Sandison and Spencer's (1954) approaches with clinical inpatients used individual settings with attending nurses and a regularly visiting doctor to optimize costs and effects. With this technique, up to four patients can be treated at the same time (Fig. 3.1). After the substances' effects have faded, the individual treatment in separate treatment rooms ends and the patients join together in a group room to discuss their experiences and insights with the doctor, the nurses and the other patients. A further optimization can be seen in the "stationary interval treatment" as developed by Leuner (1983). Here the patients are mainly treated on an outpatient basis, but come to the clinic for two more days for psycholytic sessions.

The individual procedures may be especially useful for treating people with PTSD as shown by the recent study of Mithoefer (2005; also see Chapter 8, this volume). These patients need a special kind of protection by the therapist and freedom from distractions by other people in order to focus on their traumas. Individual treatment techniques were also favored for the psychedelic treatment of alcoholics and the terminally ill (Pahnke et al. 1970).

Some other options may exist for psychotherapeutic treatments of couples with adjunctive use of entactogens (Greer and Tolbert 1990). These treatment options depend on the reduction of anxiety and defensive mechanisms with the entactogens combined with their properties of enhancing interpersonal communication with only marginally altered cognitive functioning. In this specific setting, the patients should be seated facing one with the other. Usually the therapist can be in the background, only softly modulating the unfolding communicative process in moments when it stops or patients may be overcharged (which seems to be rare).

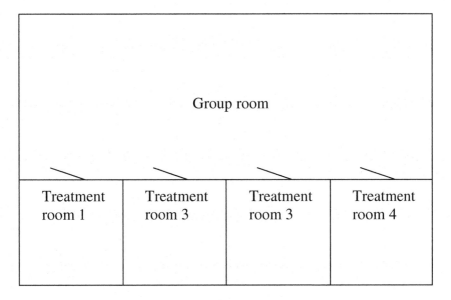

Group room			
Treatment room 1	Treatment room 3	Treatment room 3	Treatment room 4

Figure 3.1   Typical clinical facility for individual sessions as used by Sandison et al. (1954) and Leuner et al. (1983).

PRINCIPAL THERAPEUTIC TECHNIQUES: GROUP TREATMENTS

First applications of the psycholytic/psychedelytic approach in group treatments were conducted during the early 1960s.[3] These approaches used a permissive setting where patients could act out emotions and go through transference processes in the group setting, leading to abreaction of affects and a clarification of defensive patterns and transference tendencies of the individual patients.

Nearly all the therapists at this time also used the individual setting, but the group setting came back with the entactogens (e.g., MDMA and MDE) and the work of the therapists from the SÄPT (Styk 1994). These therapists learned that a group setting can be very productive for facilitating psychotherapeutic processing, especially when entactogens and successive combinations of them with LSD, mescaline, or psilocybin were used. Beside economic advantages, this allows different aspects of the group situation to be used: 1) greater feelings of safety and trust in group setting, 2) making public ones own inconsistencies and traumas, 3) revealing and transparency of transference tendencies and inner defense mechanisms, 4) feeling of belonging to a larger framework than the individuality determined by biographical circumstances, and 5) space for experiencing oneself and others in a new way.

Following some of the early group therapists' experiences[4] and the newer practices from the Swiss group of therapists, a useful setting may be arranged as follows. Patients are treated individually and separately for 10–20 individual (drug-free) sessions. Then they are invited to take part in psycholytic group sessions, which take place in a separate (and nicely furnished) facility on weekends. Patients meet on Friday evening and become accustomed to the rooms and other patients through specific rituals. These may include techniques like centering on one's actual problems by doing a dyadic communication about the actual themes with another group member, who is for these 15 minutes only a witness and does not talk. This is then reversed with the other partner talking about his problems. Following this, a whole group sharing circle allows every participant to speak about the theme of their concerns. The next day starts without breakfast and an optional session for inducing an altered state of consciousness with intensified affectivity by forced breathing (hyperventilation) known as "holotropic breathwork" (Grof 1988) for around 30 minutes and a resting phase of 30 minutes after stopping the hyperventilation. This procedure generates some emergence of individual themes and emotions and may led to abreaction and—most importantly—to a state of very deep psychophysiological relaxation during the resting phase. This very relaxed state enables the patients to "go with the flow" when they go afterwards into the deep process of the psycholytic experience. Then the patients are given the substances by mouth. The dose should be in the medium range like 100–150 mg MDMA or 75–200 mcg of LSD. Patients are then instructed to lie down on individual mattresses and wear headphones and eyeshades. Soft music is played for the whole session. (For people who take LSD/psilocybin instead of MDMA/MDE, the music is available only in the second half of their hallucinogenic experience so as to not disturb the inner flow of experiences to which the hallucinogens make one more vulnerable.) Other therapists use a specific alternation of impressive feeling-enhancing music and stillness. When the effects start, a short introduction is given by the chief therapist to reduce anxiety during the transition to the altered state of consciousness. One or two other therapists may be present depending on the size of the group (usually 8–16 participants). Therapists should be of both sexes to have representatives of both perceptual, psychological, and social aspects of being human.

During the session, people should mainly focus on themselves and not engage in much communication with other group members. Some therapists even instruct the patients to avoid nearly all body movements to facilitate emergence of inner experiences without distraction. Therapists may be recruited to talk with whenever necessary by holding up a hand or directly asking for them. Therapeutic interventions may include talking, facilitating and/or manipulating imagery, body work, or other supportive behaviors.

Ideally, the patients should be offered MDMA for the first three sessions because this substance produces a more easily controllable and benign altered state of consciousness. After these introductory but nonetheless potentially very effective sessions, patients may change to LSD or psilocybin or a combination of MDMA and LSD (in this case, both substances in a lower medium range dosage). Usually the first two hours after the application of the substances will be rather quiet, but then patients may feel greater urge to talk with their therapists. After six to seven hours, the therapists may do a "round" by talking to every patient separately to focus on their problems, give further advice, and check on the state of the patient near the end of the session. At this point, a small meal will be offered. After this "closing ritual," the group will be left alone in the room to give them the opportunity for individual communication with each other. This can be a therapeutically very effective time because people are usually very open and free of anxiety after such a session and may be especially sensitive and talk very openly about their problems, hindrances, resources, and potentials. This may also lead to new valuable experiences in communicating in an open way about problems and may generate a feeling of being very near to one's "inner core," having a very accepting attitude about one's own and also others' difficult habits and behaviors. Another aspect may be the often-seen phenomenon of being very open on a bodily level without any sexual aspirations, which may be a typical psychophysiological effect of the entactogens (Passie et al. 2005a). These tendencies may be especially useful for making gentle body contact with other people. This can be very helpful for reimprinting positive experiences of being near someone without feelings of distrust or being in contact with the bodies of others in general, instead of perpetuating experiences of fear, distance, and distrust in regard to others as is typical with neurotic and PTSD patients.

After a breakfast the next morning, a so-called integration circle is held. In this circle, every participant shares a summary of personal experiences and insights during the psycholytic session with the whole group. Therapists and other participants provide support in interpreting the experiences and/or explaining aspects of their potential helpfulness. These interpretations may point to what to conclude from the experiences and what consequences may be transferred to everyday life to make further progress. As with individual treatment procedures, the participant has to prepare a written report of the experience. Furthermore, the therapist should be available by phone for the week following the session for talking and in case of crises resulting from aftereffects of the experience or what might be evoked by it. Some therapists favored inclusion of shamanic elements (rituals, prayers, and celebration of nature) into the setting, preparation, and treatment procedures (Yensen 1994; Metzner 1998; Styk 2003; also see Chapter 8, Volume 2) (Fig. 3.2).

For the reasons described above, and for economic reasons, group approaches may be the main treatment options for the future. The experiences collected by the SÄPT members during their treatments showed the effectiveness and safety of such group procedures (Gasser 1996). They offer much interpersonal stimulation and facilitate trust and new interpersonal experiences in addition to the individual psycholytic process, which does not appear to be disturbed by the group setting (Table 3.3).

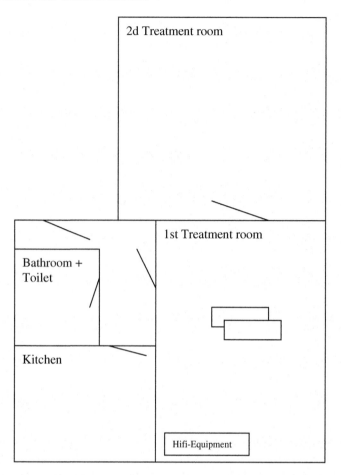

Figure 3.2   Typical treatment facility used for psycholytic group therapy.

INDICATIONS AND CONTRAINDICATIONS

In the first years of the psycholytic approach, nearly all diagnostic groups of neurotic patients were treated, except for the especially infantile and unstable. A summary of diagnostic categories treated with psycholysis compiled by Mascher in 1967 favored some groups in particular (cf. Table 3.4).

Experiences from the following decades confirmed these indications. The new options produced by the specific effects of the entactogens (MDMA, MDE, etc.) seem to broaden the spectrum to nearly all patients with neurotic disorders (some specific addictions, personality disorders, eating disorders, obsessive-compulsive disorders, and PTSD) and perhaps couple therapy (Table 3.5).

Table 3.3 Some Major Recent Developments and Innovations of Psycholytic/ Psychedelic Therapy

1. Group therapy favored

2. Psychedelytic approach

- Medium dose range (e.g., 100–200mcg LSD)
- Use of entactogens
- Stimulating music alternating with stillness
- Inner directedness
- *Optional:* Shamanic ritual elements
- *Optional:* Combination of entactogens and hallucinogens
- *Optional:* Intense chaotic rhythmic music at the end of the session

3. Setting specifications

- Three-day weekend workshops
- Procedure: Introductory phase—individual thematic focusing— psychedelytic process—Group circle for integration
- Instructing patients to move less
- Understanding the psycholytic process as an activation of self-healing capacities
- Nonsexual body contact/body work allowed
- *Optional:* Holotropic breathwork immediately before the psychedelytic session

It seems that a lot of nearly healthy people with some personal problems can greatly benefit from these kind of treatments which may offer to them new opportunities to learn about themselves. As one of the prominent early LSD-researchers Sidney Cohen puts it: LSD "does not construct character, educate the emotions, or improve intelligence. It is not a spiritual labor-saving device, salvation, instant wisdom, or a shortcut to maturity. However, it can be an opportunity to experience oneself and the world in a new way—and to learn from it" (Cohen 1967, p. 1). As far as we can see now from decades of clinical research, it seems that psychotherapeutic treatments assisted by hallucinogens and entactogens are mainly an activation of endogenous self-healing mechanisms by evoking intensification of feelings, visual imagery, activation of repressed memories, broadening of perception combined with new patterns of association, and generation of new attitudes and perspectives. This implies that people with a more healthy inner structure may be able to profit more from it because they can activate more self-healing resources. Psychiatric contraindications for psycholytic treatments include patients with weak ego structures, borderline

Table 3.4   Indications and Effectiveness for Psycholytic Treatment with LSD and Psilocybin as Indicated in a Review of 42 Studies Completed Through 1966 (Mascher 1967)

Diagnosis	Number of studies	Treatment success (%)
Anxiety neuroses	9	70
Depressive neuroses	4	62
Character neuroses	10	61
Sexual perversions	7	50
Obsessive-compulsive neuroses	10	42
Hysteria and conversion neuroses	2	31.5
Substance dependence	6	31

personality disorders, and possibly severe addictions. Contraindications for somatic diseases have to be considered individually and carefully.

During the 1960s, psycholysis was regularly practiced in 18 European treatment centers and more than a hundred outpatients were treated by therapists. Owing to continual processes of development and optimization, one can speak today of a fully developed and therapeutically valuable method. The safety of the procedure was also optimized and led to very few adverse reactions in the later years. Between 1953 and 1968, more than 7,000 patients were treated (Passie 1997).

Possible Risks and Complications

In former years, it was suggested that LSD could damage human chromosomes and that moderate doses of entactogens such as MDMA (even in controlled settings) may destroy serotonergic neurons in the brain. Both assertions were shown in further research to be unfounded when pure substances were applied under medically supervised conditions (for LSD: Grof 1979; for MDMA: Gouzoulis-Mayfrank and Daumann 2006). From decades of experimental research, it can be concluded that the major hallucinogens and entactogens are physiologically well tolerated by healthy humans. No development of physical dependence occurs. The possibility of a minor psychological dependence is

Table 3.5   Potential New Indications and Favorable Substances for Psycholytic Treatment with Entactogens and Hallucinogens

Potential treatable conditions	Favorable substances
Eating disorders	Entactogens + LSD-like hallucinogens
Obsessive-compulsive neuroses	Entactogens
PTSD	Entactogens
Alcohol addiction	Entactogens + LSD-like hallucinogens
Terminal cancer patients	Entactogens + LSD-like hallucinogens
Couples therapy	Entactogens

Table 3.6 Possible Complications During and After Psycholytic/ Psychedelic Treatment Sessions

Complications	Occurrence
During sessions	
Anxiety reactions	Occasionally
Ego-disintegrative crisis	Rare
Agitation or confusion	Rare
Paranoid reactions	Extremely rare
Immediately after the sessions	
Prolongation of the LSD state	Very rare
Depressive reactions	Occasionally
Affective lability	Occasionally

suggested for a very small number of predisposed individuals (Grof 1979; Leuner 1981). More problematic may be complications resulting from their acute psychological effects (Table 3.6).

Some authors also consider the so-called flashback phenomena (reexperiencing fragments of the psycholytic session during the drug-free state) as complications. Exploratory surveys provide the insight that nearly all flashback phenomena, in the rare cases where they emerge, could be controlled by the persons experiencing them and that they were mostly experienced as agreeable (J. Holland 2001). This points to the fact that these phenomena are usually not dangerous and do not make people suffer.

Nearly all of these potential complications can be handled by experienced therapists during the course of the treatment days. Two major surveys in 1960 and 1971 covering psycholytic (and psychedelic) applications with more than 9,000 patients and a more recent retrospective survey from Switzerland show that the risk of major complications is not higher for patients in psycholytic therapy than those in conventional psychotherapy (Table 3.7).

The more recent study from Switzerland indicates that a more advanced handling of indications, patients, and psychotherapeutic processing (plus the application of more benign substances as the entactogens) may lead to even fewer complications (Gasser 1996).

Table 3.7 Suicide Attempts, Suicide, and Prolonged Psychotic Reactions in Psycholytic/ Psychedelic Therapy

Survey	Patients	Suicide attempts	Suicide	Prolonged psychotic reactions
Cohen (1960)	ca. 5,000	1.2:1,000	0.4:1,000	1.6:1,000
Malleson (1971)	ca. 4,300	0.7:1,000	0.3:1,000	0.9:1,000
Gasser (1996)	121	0	0	0

POSSIBLE PSYCHOPHYSIOLOGICAL MECHANISMS OF EFFECTIVENESS

The psychophysiological mechanisms by which these substances generate their potentially helpful effects are indicated by some still valid older concepts and by newer experimental data from studies examining the neurometabolic effects of the hallucinogens and entactogens and their functional implications.

Leuner (1962) first proposed the "psychotoxic basal syndrome" (with LSD-like hallucinogens), which is characterized by a regressive change in normal brain functioning to a more primitive and less-controlled mode of cognitive functioning, combined with an autonomous excitation. This hallucinogen-induced stimulation of affect and instinctual behavior, also called "internal stimulus production," finally captures the sensory apparatus of the central nervous system, and is manifested in optical, acoustical, and other pseudo-hallucinations. Other examples are synesthesia and the broad stream of more rapid and emotionally laden associations that overwhelm the usual thinking process.

The numerous complicated brain-mediated variables of behavior have their biological representations, which can be thought of as specific "functional centers" for activity patterns [as conceptualized by ethological research (Lorenz 1957; Tinbergen 1969)]. These centers or systems are patterned during learning and development (imprinting of motivations) and have a degree of functional autonomy; that is, they basically could operate without outer stimuli and have a "pressure" of their own. These dynamic centers are primarily activated by the inner stimulation caused by hallucinogens. For instance, normal recollections of childhood are "over-stimulated" to appear as the full feeling of being a child ("age regression" as known from psycholytic sessions). Pseudo-hallucinations appear in this model as overstimulated fantasies. The overstimulation also has another effect: highly charged dynamic systems become dominant and control all of psychological activity. As compared with the normal human, whose behavior can be controlled, corrected, and motivated by outer stimuli, this state forces control by the intensified inner stimuli. This has a similar parallel in humans experiencing sensory deprivation, where inner stimuli take the part of the missing outer stimuli and govern the entire psychophysiological system. Another example involves pathological depression in which the deeply experienced melancholy as the "basic affect" selects and regulates all other psychological and even physiological functions. If the energy of one of these "transphenomenal guiding systems" (Leuner) is discharged during a psycholytic session, a rival control system for another category of experience can use it to gain controlling power. The multiplicity of control systems must be thought of as competing for control of inner experience and behavior. In addition, outer stimuli can trigger a new system to discharge its energy. This process lies at the basis of the constantly changing experiences under the hallucinogens and may explain their catalytic and cathartic abilities (Leuner 1967).

The prominent LSD-researcher Stanislav Grof developed a similar concept, proposing systems of condensed experience (COEX-systems) which govern behavior and experience during a LSD-induced state and may be discharged by therapeutic processing. Grof also looked at very deep reaching mystical and so-called transpersonal experiences as major factors for therapeutic change (Grof 1979). Grof's concept of the birth trauma and its relevance for psychedelic treatment and healing cannot be explicated here (cf. Grof 1979 and his chapter in Volume 2).

During recent neurophysiological studies, Franz Vollenweider (2001, 2002) of the Psychiatric University Clinic in Switzerland found some specific alterations of the metabolism in the human brain induced by psilocybin. Simply stated a hypermetabolism in the cortex, especially in the frontal cortex, the putamen, and the thalamus, was found. This metabolic activation pattern corresponds closely to the 5-HT_{2A}-receptor density in the brain (with the exception of the thalamus). Agonistic activity at the 5-HT_{2A}-receptor seems to be the major effect of the indole hallucinogens as indicated by blocking this receptor with pharmacological agents, which results in diminished hallucinogenic activity (Vollenweider et al. 1998). Positron emission tomography was used to verify the hypothesis that the hallucinogens alter the recently characterized and functionally segregated five CSTC (cortico-striato-thalamo-cortical) feedback loops. In this model, the thalamus acts as a "filter" for the extero- and interoceptive information flow to the cerebral cortex. This complex thalamic filtering mechanism is mainly regulated by the five CSTC loops. Altered states of consciousness as induced by the hallucinogens can be considered as complex disturbances that arise from deficits of sensory information processing within the CSTC loops. Studies demonstrated increases of dopaminergic neurotransmission by hallucinogens which result in an opening of the thalamic filter with a subsequent sensory overload of the cortex, which in turn may ultimately cause the sensory flooding, cognitive fragmentation, and ego-dissolution seen in hallucinogen-induced states. From a therapeutic point of view, the subcortical and cortical activation combined with the massive alteration of filtering intero- and exteroceptive input may be responsible for intensification of affectivity, sensory alterations, emergence of repressed memories and ultimately what was called "consciousness-expansion" (Vollenweider and Geyer 2001).

A different model is required to explain the effects of the entactogens such as MDMA or MDE. Neurometabolic studies show a quite different picture than for the hallucinogens. Clinical and experimental studies demonstrated that these substances do alter sensory and cognitive functions much less than those altered by hallucinogens. Neurometabolic studies indicated increased metabolism in the cerebellum, ventromedial prefrontal cortex, ventral anterior cingulate cortex, inferior temporal cortex, and medial occipital cortex. Hypometabolism was indicated in the dorsal and lateral cingulate cortex, insula, and thalamus. Especially significant for the clinical effects of the entactogens seems to be the deactivation of the left amygdala (the brain center for fear responses). This deactivation may be the neurophysiological substrate of the euphoria and loss of anxiety as typically felt during acute effects of entactogens (Gamma et al. 2000). Additionally, the strongly interconnected structures of the ventral and dorsal cingulate cortices, the thalamus, the temporal lobe, and the cerebellum are discussed as a network responsible for the regulation of mood and emotions (George et al. 1995).

Summarizing the working mechanisms of psycholytic therapy (beside the usual mechanisms of psychotherapy which form the basis here too), it can be concluded that stimulation of the reticular activation system, limbic structures, and disturbances of the thalamic filtering for sensory processing may be the major determinants responsible for the psychological alterations induced by hallucinogenic drugs. These functional aberrations change drastically what is being perceived and can activate unconscious memories and feelings which may become available for therapeutic processing. The concepts of Leuner and Grof and newer clinical experiences imply that a lot of therapeutic processing during psycholytic sessions may be seen as activation of self-healing processes. These may work autonomously, driven by the patients' unconscious forces, and lead to discharge of energy from dysfunctional inner tension systems which guide major aspects of the patients' behavior and experience. Slightly different mechanisms may be involved with the healing power of the entactogens. The regression of psychological functioning as hypothesized by Leuner may be not as extreme as with the hallucinogens. During the acute effects of these substances, people may be able to confront and work through painful and repressed memories or aspects of inner and outer reality by decreased activity of the brain's fear networks. The patients may also experience their feelings and memories, as well as actual relationships, circumstances, and problems in new and less fearful ways and find new perspectives, models, and adjustments for their experiential and behavioral dynamics.

ASSESSING EFFECTIVENESS

Psycholytic therapy offers special opportunities to overcome strong and consolidated defense structures in patients who had been previously considered resistant to therapy. Another reported advantage is the ability to use the intensification and deepening of therapeutic processing by psycholysis to improve the effectiveness and shorten the treatment of less severe neurotics to less than half of the usual time, which could save costs.

Psycholytic therapy was developed and researched during the 1950s and 1960s. During that period, scientific research of psychotherapy was still in its initial stages. Therefore, parameters for the scientific evaluation of this procedure were limited. In the first decade of research in psycholytic therapy (1950–1960), observations were primarily collected, the treatment concept was developed, and the treatment practice optimized. Only in the following decade were the first scientific research studies regarding the efficacy of the method performed according to prevailing scientific standards.

With reference to treatment success, most psycholytic therapists reported long-term improvement in approximately two-thirds of their usually difficult and chronic neurotic patients (Mascher 1967). However, these earlier studies only meet the standards of psychotherapy evaluation of that time. Assessed from a current perspective, they are, in most cases, compromised by serious biases (Pletscher and Ladewig 1994). Some of the psychedelic therapists were more rigorous in their methodology. But typically, the psychedelic method was practiced without long-term psychotherapy. Because of that, the initial dramatic improvements of patients were usually not long lasting (Kurland et al. 1971).

Because in Europe psycholytic treatment was primarily used for patients resistant to conventional psychotherapy, several researchers used these patients as their own control group. Thus, in follow-up studies Leuner was able to measure (with standardized evaluation instruments) lasting treatment success with approximately 200 therapy-resistant neurotic patients (Leuner 1994).

Only a few studies exist where psycholytic therapy was performed with at least a minimum of controlled variables (Robinson et al. 1963; Vourlekis et al. 1967; Denson and Sydiaha 1970; Soskin 1973; Soskin et al. 1973). These results suggest that there is little evidence for the superiority of psycholytic therapy compared to conventional psychotherapy. Nevertheless, the double-blind studies performed by Vourlekis et al. (1967) and Soskin et al. (1973) indicate, congruent with many uncontrolled studies, that specific actions of psycholytics can enhance and deepen the psychotherapeutic process.

All aforementioned studies, however, suffered from a number of deficiencies (such as the following) that make the evaluation of their results problematic from today's point of view:

- No standardized diagnostic evaluation.
- No valid use of severity measures to assess patients.
- Only partially blind raters.
- No standardization of psychotherapeutic treatment methods.
- No random assignment of patients to treatment options.
- No control groups.
- Very small patient population numbers.
- Atypically brief treatment periods (6–13 weeks).
- No active placebos.

For these reasons, it seems possible that earlier studies did not conclusively demonstrate efficacy of this treatment method. The aforementioned problems have to be addressed as much as possible. Therefore, for a more specific evaluation of this procedure, it seems justified to conduct an efficacy study constructed with a modern research design (e.g., double-blind design, randomization, control groups, standardized diagnostic and evaluation procedures, blind raters, and follow-ups).

Some other major research obstacles may be characterized as follows. Research in psycholytic/psychedelic therapy is complicated by the unusual combination of pharmacology and psychotherapy. It is not a pure psychotherapy nor a purely psychotherapeutic approach. The unusual psychological effects (including the induction of religious experiences) and the strong sensitivity of the effects to a range of set and setting variables make a scientific evaluation of hallucinogens/entactogens and their therapeutic effects difficult. Other problems are the standardized diagnostic procedures as used today (DSM IV and ICD-10 manuals). These manuals describe psychopathological conditions only by the basic character of the symptom and a very brief assessment of their severity (light, medium, and heavy). This leads to the problem that it is not permissible to select patients who have a psychoneurotic cause of illness instead of a situational (e.g., loss of husband/wife) or endogenous etiology as suitable for a homogenous patient group for study participation. Another problem may be the conventional pharmacotherapeutic treatment as used on nearly all patients suffering from obsessions, depressions, or anxiety (independent from the etiology of their illness). These medications may interact with their improvement during psycholytic/psychedelic therapy in ways difficult to define. The clinical experience shows that patients with good psychological and social resources treated in groups with a mix of different diagnoses profit most from these treatment. The mix of patients may lead to some profitable synergetic effects in the patients group, which may be much less in a group of homogenous (i.e., depressed) patients as usually necessary for scientific studies. A further problem for scientifically rigorous studies may be seen in the fact that most therapist would like to make choice of the substances (or combinations of them) in specific regard to the patient's actual problems.

FUTURE PROSPECTS

New prospects for an adequate examination of the therapeutic potential of these substances first opened up in the late 1980s. The U.S. FDA and equivalent institutions in European countries demonstrated a willingness to permit a renewed examination of psycholytic and psychedelic therapy research. Since that time, more intensive research with hallucinogens has been conducted in the United States, Germany, Switzerland, and Russia (MAPS 2006).

What seems scientifically appropriate and necessary in the near future are controlled studies using the highest standards of modern research design to explore the efficacy of hallucinogen-/entactogen-assisted psychotherapy without prejudices. As the Swiss chairman Ladewig concluded at a recent scientific conference on the subject in 1993: "I consider that only a well-controlled approach can promote research. Restrictive administrative obstacles that block clinical research have to be dismantled....It is hoped that with a better methodology and standardization and, hopefully, with international cooperation, a protocol on psychotherapeutic/psychopharmacological procedures will allow this work to continue" (Pletscher and Ladewig 1994, p. 228).

Three organizations are trying to facilitate this kind of therapy and research: the MAPS (Multidisciplinary Association for Psychedelic studies), the HRI (Heffter Research Institute), and the aforementioned SAEPT. MAPS and SAEPT are on their way to establish some methodologically rigorous studies for proving the effectiveness of these treatments. Both organizations recently established two double-blind and controlled studies regarding treatment-resistant patients with PTSD with the adjunctive use of MDMA (Mithoefer 2005; Oehen 2005). The HRI established a controlled study using psilocybin in the treatment of terminal cancer patients following the approach characterized by Grof and Halifax (1978). It is hoped that the future will give us more opportunities for researching these approaches and developing their full potential to help the suffering patients as much as possible.

Finally, it should be mentioned that besides some reasons founded in our cultural history, one major problem is the fact that the psychedelic substances have no further patent protection, which makes them automatically less interesting for the pharmaceutical industry because of the inability to make profits. This is compounded by the fact that these medications, in contrast to conventional psychopharmacological medications (e.g., neuroleptics and antidepressants), only have to be taken a few times to facilitate a more fundamental healing process, which also is not profitable (Passie and Blackmore 2006).

CONCLUSIONS

In summary, it can be shown that the treatment procedures in question have a very long history. Shamanic practices using hallucinogens obviously have some similar features as described in the practices above (see Schultes and Hofmann 1979). The history of these procedures in modern psychiatry now involves more than 50 years of study and has produced more than 700 scientific publications (Passie 1997). If the historical circumstances surrounding the psychedelics in the late 1960s would have been less unfortunate, these approaches may have been well established by now. But instead we still have a rigid prohibition on these substances, which produces grave hindrances for appropriate research.

Historical and recent developments show that the older separation of the psycholytic and the psychedelic approaches may not stand up in the future. Therapists tried carefully and successfully to combine advantages of both approaches (psychedelytic approach). Furthermore, it seems that the group treatment approach will be the most promising for the near future, if there will be circumstances allowing this. But these group treatments cannot be applied for heavily traumatized patients (such as PTSD), who may be more appropriately treated in safe individual setting (Mithoefer 2005; Oehen 2005). Another relevant development was the introduction of the entactogenic substances which seem to be especially suitable for psychedelytic treatments and may offer new options for treating a broader spectrum of diseases (D. Holland 2001; Passie et al. 2005b).

As has been shown above, some new developments and innovations were made in the procedures using hallucinogens and entactogens in therapy (Table 3.3). These stem in part from illegal psycholytic work carried out by some therapists worldwide (Stolaroff and Zeff 2005) and which were partially integrated into legal (research) contexts.

Older studies of efficacy from the 1960s and 1970s do not meet the research standards of today and may be seen as inadequate evidence for the effectiveness of these treatments. Newer studies were planned and fought for during the 1990s and are now on the way. If their effectiveness could be established within modern research standards, psychotherapy with adjunctive use of hallucinogens and entactogens may become an effective approach to decrease suffering in many patients and save costs by deepening and facilitating the psychotherapeutic process. They may make true during the 21st century, what the founder of Psychoanalysis Sigmund Freud stated in 1939: "The future may teach us to exercise a direct influence, by means of particular chemical substances, on the amounts of energy and their distribution in the mental apparatus. It may be that there are other still undreamt-of possibilities of therapy."

NOTES

1. 2-CB is 4-bromo-2,5-dimethoxyphenethylamine, 2-CD is 2,5-dimethoxy-4-methylphenethylamine, CEY-19 is 4-phosphoryloxy-N,N-diethyltryptamine, and CZ-74 is 4-hydroxy-N,N-diethyltryptamine. These substances are short-acting and nearly side-effect free. They are derived from phenethylamine and psilocybin. CEY-19 and CZ-74 were developed by SANDOZ during the 1960s for applications in psychotherapy and were tested by Leuner and Baer (1965) as well as some other therapists (Alnaes 1965). 2-CD was firstly introduced by a coworker of Leuner and tested during the late 1980s (Schlichting 1989). 2-CB was used especially as a substance to prolong the MDMA-induced state and was found especially useful for its effects in enhancing clear thinking in the after-glow of the MDMA state (Adamson and Metnzer 1988).

2. Ibid.

3. Some early psycholytic researchers experimented with group treatments with (from their perspective) good success. Especially noteworthy are the works of Blewett and Chwelos (1960), Spencer (1963), Alnaes (1965), and Fontana (1965). These authors prepared also for the change to a more open attitude for material emerging from the unconscious like religious or other transpersonal experiences. It should be mentioned that these authors found, because of the fact that more than one therapist was present during the group sessions, a lot fewer transference problems emerge than found by psycholytic therapists in individual dyadic settings.

4. Ibid.

REFERENCES

Abramson, H.A., ed. 1967. *Use of LSD in psychotherapy and alcoholism.* Indianapolis, New York, Kansas City: Bobbs Merrill.

Adamson, S., and R. Metzner. 1988. The nature of the MDMA experience and its role in healing, psychotherapy, and spiritual practice. *ReVision* 10:59–72.

Alnaes, R. 1965. Therapeutic application of the change in consciousness produced by psycholytica (LSD, Psilocybin, etc.). *Acta Psychiatrica Scandinavica* 40 (Suppl. 180):397–409.

Andritzky, W. 1989. Sociotherapeutic functions of ayahuasca healing in Amazonia. *Journal of Psychoactive Drugs* 21:77–89.

Barolin, G.S. 1960. Erstes Europäisches symposion für psychotherapie unter LSD-25, Göttingen, November. *Wiener Medizinische Wochenschrift* 111:266–8.

Benz, E. 1989. *Halluzinogen-unterstützte Psychotherapie.* Medical dissertation, Zürich University.

Beringer, K. 1927. Der Meskalinrausch. Berlin: Julius Springer.

Blewett, D., and N. Chwelos. 1960. The therapeutic use of lysergic acid diethylamide–25: Individual and group procedures. Unpublished manuscript.

Busch, A.K., and W.C. Johnson. 1950. L.S.D. as an aid in psychotherapy. *Diseases of the Nervous System* 11:241–43.

Chandler, A.L., and M.A. Hartmann. 1960. Lysergic Acid Diethylamide (LSD-25) as a facilitating agent in psychotherapy. *Archives of General Psychiatry* 2: 286–99.

Cohen, S. 1960. Lysergic acid diethylamide: Side effects and complications. *Journal of Nervous and Mental Disease* 130:30–40.

Cohen, S. 1967. *The beyond within.* New York: Atheneum.

Denson, R., and D. Sydiaha. 1970. A controlled study of LSD treatment in alcoholism and neurosis. *British Journal of Psychiatry* 116:443–45.

Fontana, A.E. 1965. *Psicoterapia con alucinogenos.* Buenos Aires: Editorial Losada.

Food and Drug Administration. 1975. FDA lists approved LSD research projects. *FDA Consumer* 24–25.

Frederking, W. 1955. Intoxicant drugs (mescaline and Lysergic Acid Diethylamide) in psychotherapy. *Journal of Nervous and Mental Disease* 121:262–66.

Furst, P.T. 1972. *Flesh of the gods: The ritual use of hallucinogens.* New York: Praeger.

Gamma, A., A. Buck, T. Berthold, M.E. Liechti, and F.X. Vollenweider. 2000. 3,4-Methylenedioxymethamphetamine (MDMA) modulates cortical and limbic brain activity as measured by [H(2)(15)O]-PET in healthy humans. *Neuropsychopharmacology* 23:388–95.

Gasser, P. 1996. Die psycholytische Psychotherapie in der Schweiz von 1988-1993. *Schweizer Archiv für Neurologie und Psychiatrie* 147:59–65.

George, M.S., K.A. Ketter, P.I. Parekh, B. Horwitz, P. Herscovitch, and R.M. Post. 1995. Brain activity during transient sadness and happiness in healthy women. *American Journal of Psychiatry* 152:341–51.

Gouzoulis-Mayfrank, E., and J. Daumann. 2006. Neurotoxicity of methylenedioxyamphetamines (MDMA; ecstasy) in humans: How strong is the evidence for persistent brain damage? *Addiction* 101:348–61.

Greer, G.R., and R. Tolbert. 1990. The therapeutic use of MDMA. In *Ecstasy: The clinical, pharmacological and neurotoxicological effects of the Drug MDMA,* ed. S.J. Peroutka, 21–36. Boston, Dordrecht, London: Kluwer.

Grinspoon, L., and J.B. Bakalar. 1979. *Psychedelic drugs reconsidered.* New York: Basic Books.

Grob, C., and G.L. Bravo. 1995. Human research with hallucinogens: Past lessons and current Trends. *Yearbook of Transcultural Medicine and Psychotherapy* 129–142.

Grof, S. 1967. Psycholytic and psychedelic therapy with LSD: Toward an integration of approaches. Unpublished paper presented at the 5th congress of *the European Medical Society of Psycholytic Therapy (EPT)* in Frankfurt (Germany).

Grof, S. 1975. *Realms of the human unconscious: Observations from LSD research.* New York: Viking.

Grof, S. 1979. *LSD psychotherapy.* Pomona, CA: Hunter House.

Grof, S. 1988. *The adventure of self-discovery.* New York: SUNY.

Grof, S., and J. Halifax. 1978. *The human encounter with death.* New York: Dutton.

Hoffer, A. 1967. A program for the treatment of alcoholism: LSD, malvaria and nicotinic acid. In *The use of LSD in psychotherapy and alcoholism,* ed. H.A. Abramson, 343–406. Indianapolis, New York, Kansas City: Bobbs Merrill.

Holland, D. 2001. *Flashback-Phänomene als Nachwirkung von Halluzinogeneinnahme.* M.D. dissertation, Hannover (Germany).

Holland, J., ed. 2001. *Ecstasy: The complete guide.* Rochester, VT: Park Street Press.

Horsley, J.S. 1943. *Narco-analysis.* New York/London: Oxford University Press.

Kast, E.C. 1966. LSD and the dying patient. *Chicago Medical School Quarterly* 26:80–7.

Kast, E.C., and V.J. Collins. 1964. A study of lysergic acid diethylamide as an analgesic agent. *Anesthesia and Analgesia* 43:285–91.

Kurland, A.A., C. Savage, W.N. Pahnke, S. Grof, and J.E. Olsson. 1971. LSD in the treatment of alcoholics. *Pharmakopsychiatry* 2:83–94.

La Barre, W. 1989. *The peyote cult.* 5th ed. Norman/London: University of Oklahoma Press.

Leuner, H. 1959. Psychotherapie in Modellpsychosen. In *Kritische Psychotherapie,* ed. E. Speer, 94–102. Stuttgart: Enke.

Leuner, H. 1962. *Die experimentelle Psychose.* Berlin, Göttingen, Heidelberg: Springer.

Leuner, H. 1967. Basic functions involved in the psychotherapeutic effect of psychotomimetics. In *Neuro-psycho-pharmacology,* ed. H. Brill, 445–8. Amsterdam, New York, London, Milan, Tokyo, Buenos Aires: Excerpta Medica.

Leuner, H. 1971. Halluzinogene in der Psychotherapie. *Pharmakopsychiatrie, Neuropsychopharmakologie* 4:333–51.

Leuner, H. 1981. *Halluzinogene.* Bern, Stuttgart, Wien: Huber.

Leuner, H. 1983. Psycholytic therapy. Hallucinogenics as an aid in psychodynamically oriented psychotherapy. In *Psychedelic reflections,* ed. J. Grinspoon and J.B. Bakalar, 177–92. New York: Human Sciences Press.

Leuner, H. 1984. *Guided affective imagery.* New York: Thieme-Stratton Inc.

Leuner, H. 1994. Hallucinogens as an aid in psychotherapy: Basic principles and results. In *50 Years of LSD. Current status and perspectives of hallucinogens,* ed. A. Pletscher and D. Ladewig, 175–190. New York, London: Parthenon.

Leuner, H., and G. Baer. 1965. Two new short-acting hallucinogens of the psilocybin group. In *Neuro-Psychopharmacology,* ed. D. Bente and P.B. Bradley, Vol. 4, 471–73. Amsterdam, London, New York: Elsevier.

Lorenz, K. 1957. The nature of instinct. In *Instinctive behaviour,* ed. C.H. Schiller, 129–75. New York: International University Press.

MacRae, E. 1992. *Guiado pela luna: xamanismo e uso ritual da Ayahuasca no culto de Santo Daime.* Sao Paulo: Brasiliense.

Malleson, N. 1971. Acute adverse reactions to LSD in clinical and experimental use in the United Kingdom. *British Journal of Psychiatry* 118:229–30.

MAPS (Multidisciplinary Association for Psychedelic Studies). 2006. Available at www.maps.org.

Mascher, E. 1967. Psycholytic therapy: Statistics and indications. In *Neuro-psychopharmacology,* ed. H. Brill, 441–4. Amsterdam, New York, London, Milan, Tokyo, Buenos Aires: Excerpta Medica.

Masters, R.E.L., and J. Houston. 1966. *The varieties of psychedelic experience.* New York, Chicago, San Francisco: Holt, Rhinehart and Winston.

Metzner, R. 1998. Hallucinogenic drugs and plants in psychotherapy and shamanism. *Journal of Psychoactive Drugs* 30:333–43.

Mithoefer, M. 2005. MDMA-assisted psychotherapy in posttraumatic stress disorder. Lecture at the 1st International Conference on MDMA-assisted psychotherapy in Lezion Rishon, Israel, March, 2005.

Pahnke, W.N., A.A. Kurland, S. Unger, C.C. Savage, and S. Grof. 1970. The experimental use of psychedelic (LSD) psychotherapy. *Journal of the American Medical Association* 212:1856–63.

Passie, T. 1993/1994. Ausrichtungen, Methoden und Ergebnisse früher Meskalinforschungen im duetschsprachigen Raum. *Yearbook of the European College for the Study of Consciousness,* 103–12.

Passie, T. 1997. *Psycholytic and psychedelic therapy research 1931–1995: A complete international bibliography.* Hannover, Germany: Laurentius Publishers.

Passie, T., and S. Blackmore. 2006. Psychedelic healing. *New Scientist* 2547:50–1.

Passie, T., U. Hartmann, U. Schneider, H.M. Emrich, and T.H. Kruger. 2005a. Ecstasy (MDMA) mimics the post-orgasmic state: Impairment of sexual drive and function during acute MDMA-effects may be due to increased prolactin secretion. *Medical Hypotheses* 64:899–903.

Passie, T., U. Hartmann, U. Schneider, and H.M. Emrich. 2005b. Was sind Entaktogene? *Suchtmedizin* 7:235–45.

Pletscher, A., and D. Ladewig, eds. 1994. 50 Years of LSD. In *Current status and perspectives of hallucinogens.* New York, London: Parthenon.

Robinson, J.T., L.S. Davis, E.L. Sack, and J.D. Morrissey. 1963. A controlled trial of abreaction with Lysergic Acid Diethylamide. *British Journal of Psychiatry* 109:46–53.

Sandison, R.A., and A.M. Spencer. 1954. The therapeutic value of Lysergic Acid Diethylamide in mental illness. *Journal of Mental Science* 100:491–507.

Schrenck-Notzing, F.v. 1891. *Die Bedeutung narcotischer Mittel für den Hypnotismus.* Leipzig: J.A. Barth.

Schultes, R.E., and A. Hofmann. 1979. *Plants of the gods: Origins of hallucinogenic use.* New York: McGraw Hill.

Schlichting M. 1989. Psychotrope Eigenschaften des Phenathylamins DMM-PEA (2,5-dimethoxy-4-methyl-phenathylamin). Göttingen: Unpublished manuscript.

Soskin, R.A. 1973. The use of LSD in time-limited psychotherapy. *Journal of Nervous and Mental Disease* 157:410–19.

Soskin, R.A., S. Grof, and W.A. Richards. 1973. Low doses of dipropyltryptamine in psychotherapy. *Archives of General Psychiatry* 28:817–21.

Spencer, A.M. 1963. Permissive group therapy with Lysergic Acid Diethylamide. *British Journal of Psychiatry* 109:37–45.

Stolaroff, M.J., and L. Zeff. 2005. *The secret chief revealed.* Sarasota, FL: MAPS.

Stoll, A.W. 1947. Lysergsäure-diäthylamid, ein Phantastikum aus der Mutterkorngruppe. *Schweizer Archiv für Neurologie und Psychiatrie* 60:279–323.

Styk, J. 1994. Rückblick auf die letzten sieben Jahre der Schweizerischen Ärztegesellschaft für Psycholytische Therapie (SAPT). In *Welten des Bewusstseins,* ed. A. Dittrich, A. Hofmann, and H. Leuner, Vol. 4, 149–54. Berlin: VWB.

Styk, J. 2003. Personal communication.

Tinbergen, N. 1969. *The study of instinct.* Oxford: Oxford University Press.

Vollenweider, F. 2002. Brain mechanisms of hallucinogens and entactogens. *Dialogues in Clinical Neuroscience* 3 (5):265–79.

Vollenweider, F.X., and M.A. Geyer. 2001. A systems model of altered consciousness: Integrating natural and drug-induced psychoses. *Brain Research Bulletin* 56:495–507.

Vollenweider, F.X., M.F. Vollenweider-Scherpenhuyzen, A. Babler, H. Vogel, and D. Hell. 1998. Psilocybin induces schizophrenia-like psychosis in humans via a serotonin-2 agonist action. *Neuroreport* 9:897–902.

Vourlekis, A., L.A. Faillace, and S. Szara. 1967. Psychotherapy combined with psychodysleptic tryptamine derivates and an active placebo. In *Neuro-psycho-pharmacology,* ed. H. Brill, 1116–8. Amsterdam, New York, London, Milan, Tokyo, Buenos Aires: Excerpta Medica.

Yensen, R. 1994. Perspectives on LSD and psychotherapy: The search for a new paradigm. In *50 Years of LSD. Current status and perspectives of hallucinogens,* ed. A. Pletscher and D. Ladewig, 191–202. New York, London: Parthenon.

Yensen, R., and D. Dryer. 1993/1994. Thirty years of psychedelic research: The spring grove experiment and its sequels. *Yearbook of the European College for the Study of Consciousness 1993/1994,* 73–102.

Yensen, R., F. DiLeo, J.C. Rhead, W.A. Richards, R.A. Soskin, B. Turek, and A.A. Kurland. 1976. MDA-assisted psychotherapy with neurotic outpatients: A pilot study. *Journal of Nervous and Mental Disease* 163:233–45.

4

THERAPEUTIC GUIDELINES: DANGERS AND CONTRAINDICATIONS IN THERAPEUTIC APPLICATIONS OF HALLUCINOGENS

EDE FRECSKA

INTRODUCTION

There are widespread beliefs about the dangers of hallucinogenic drugs and frequent media reports attributing fatalities to hallucinogens. This media bias was typical in the early 1970s when much attention was focused on supposed chromosome damage and birth defects in children born to mothers who had taken LSD (lysergic acid diethylamide) during pregnancy. Later on, negative results of better-controlled, rigorous investigations (Muneer 1978) refuted the earlier alarmist concerns, but these received very little attention in the media. The controversial nature of the U.S. drug policy and its influence on government-sponsored research of illicit drugs has recently drawn media attention due to investigational flaws of highly publicized research claiming harmful effects (Jennings 2003).

Hallucinogens actually do have a long history of safe administration in legal, controlled research settings (Strassman 1984), contrary to the preconceptions influencing public and professional media. These preconceptions, even when derived from unbiased publications, are related to illicit use (and abuse), rather than responsible clinical use (e.g., see Griffiths et al. 2006). Unfortunately, a hallucinogenic drug's safety has been judged by its abuse and that has been applied to making decisions regarding clinical use. The inconvenient truth is, that the opinion of most of the health care providers and legislation makers on hallucinogenic agents is not well founded scientifically.

The purpose of this chapter is to review safety information available in the literature on hallucinogen *use,* and sort out those data from the reported complications of their *abuse.* The chapter summarizes these analyses in proposing guidelines for clinical application of hallucinogens in anticipation of supportive regulatory changes. Since there is currently no FDA (Food and Drug Administration) approval for therapeutic use of any hallucinogen compound, the therapeutic guidelines presented are tentative and preliminary.

To preview these findings, the various hallucinogenic compounds are physically safe, with the possible exception of the phenethylamine hallucinogens (such as Ecstasy), which have the risk of causing cardiovascular emergencies and liver failure. There are limited records establishing death from overdoses directly attributable to their ingestion alone. The number of annual drug-related deaths in the United States is as follows (based on latest reports from Centers for Disease Control and Prevention)[1]:

- Tobacco kills about 440,000.
- Alcohol kills about 75,000.
- Secondary smoke from tobacco kills about 50,000.
- Cocaine kills about 3,400.
- Heroin kills about 2,000.
- Over-the-counter drugs kill about 2,000.
- Marijuana and LSD kill 0.

All illegal drugs combined kill about 5,500 people per year in the United States, or about 1% of the number killed by alcohol and tobacco. Tobacco kills more people each year than all of the subjects killed by all of the illegal drugs in the last century (NIDA Research Reports).[2] In contrast, the so-called hallucinogens have virtually no fatalities (see below for more details on safety).

Classification, Chemical Structure, and Mechanism of Action

The conventional use of the term "hallucinogen" disproportionately emphasizes perceptual effects, neglecting central actions on emotion and cognition as well. Psychopharmacologists define as hallucinogenic any agent that causes alterations in perception, cognition, and mood in the presence of an otherwise clear sensorium (lucid awareness). Most commonly this classification includes three major groups—indolealkylamines, ergolines, and phenethylamines—and excludes other substances that may induce hallucinations with profoundly altered orientation and vigilance. Excluded are the anticholinergic agents (i.e., plants such as datura), the dissociative anesthetics such as PCP (phencyclidine), and the psychostimulants such as amphetamine and cocaine.

The chemical structures of the classic hallucinogenic drugs are the basis for their classification into three groups: 1) simple indolealkylamine hallucinogens [e.g., DMT (*N,N*-dimethyltryptamine) and psilocybin], which have a common indolealkylamine structure with the neurotransmitter (endogenous signal transferring compound) serotonin; 2) the ergolines, which share an indole group (e.g., LSD); and 3) the ring-substituted phenethylamine hallucinogens (e.g., mescaline and Ecstasy). The indole alkaloid ibogaine is a complex indolealkylamine compound, a beta-carboline derivative akin to harmaline and harmine. The latter is an active, although not the hallucinogenic component of the *ayahuasca* brew (see below).

The indole structure found in serotonin is a common chemical characteristic of these compounds and suggests a specific mechanism of hallucinogenic effect exerted on the serotonergic system. Typical clinico-pharmacological features of classical hallucinogens involve alterations of all cortical functions including perception, mood, and cognition. They share common mechanisms in attaching to serotonin receptors through molecules that bind to the neurotransmitters sites for transferring the signal to the next neuron in the network. It is the activation of the serotonin2A and serotonin2C receptors in the brain that primarily mediates their psychedelic effects.

Epidemiology: Prevalence and Trends of Hallucinogen Use

Hallucinogenic drugs are not commonly used in the Western world, although their use is considered by NIDA to be abuse by definition. Data from the 2004 NSDUH (National Survey on Drug Use and Health) suggests that approximately 34.3 million Americans aged 12 and older reported trying hallucinogens at least once during their lifetimes, representing 14.3% of the population. Approximately 3.9 million reported hallucinogen use during the past year, and 929,000 reported "current" use of hallucinogens (past month). Ecstasy [MDMA (3,4-methylene-dioxy-*N*-methylamphetamine)] and LSD are the most commonly used hallucinogens. Marijuana is the most commonly used illicit drug: according to the 2004 NSDUH, nearly half (about 40%) of Americans over the age of 12 have tried marijuana at least once (Substance Abuse and Mental Health Services Administration 2005).

The incidence of hallucinogen use has exhibited two notable periods of increase. Between 1965 and 1969, there was a tenfold increase in the estimated annual number of initiates. This increase was driven primarily by the use of LSD. The second period of increase in first-time hallucinogen use occurred from around 1992 until 2000, fueled mainly by increases in the use of Ecstasy (MDMA). Lately, there is an overall drop in hallucinogen incidence from 1.6 million to below 1 million, coinciding with decreases in initiation of both LSD and Ecstasy (MDMA) as it was evident in data collected between 2001 and 2004 (Substance Abuse and Mental Health Services Administration 2005).

The yearly national surveys on drug abuse repeatedly indicate that substance use, and in particular hallucinogen use, varies by race and ethnicity. Black youths were less likely to have used any hallucinogen in their lifetime compared with white, Asian, or Hispanic youths. White and Asian youths had similar rates of hallucinogen use, except that whites were much more likely than Asians to have used psilocybin at least once in their lifetime.

HALLUCINOGEN ACUTE TOXICITY

The traditional measure of acute drug toxicity is "therapeutic index": a ratio of the dose that kills 50% of subjects (LD_{50}) to the dose that is effective in 50% of subjects (ED_{50}). According to the Registry of Toxic Effects, the "therapeutic index" for indolealkylamines and ergolines is above 600 (higher numbers indicate a better safety profile). For cannabis, the index is even higher: it is on the order of 10,000s. Therefore, these agents are relatively nonlethal in comparison to other substances. For example, the therapeutic index of aspirin is 199 and for nicotine 21, with the phenethylamine psychostimulants (such as methamphetamine) falling into this range.

There is no known recorded death due to marijuana intoxication at any time in U.S. history. There are no documented toxic fatalities from LSD use either. There was a report (Klock et al. 1974) of accidental overdose of pure LSD that was mistaken for cocaine and snorted by eight individuals in quantities estimated at between 10,000 and 100,000 µg. In this case, the subjects experienced mental status changes characterized by hallucinations and confusion, and suffered from hemorrhage; the latter possibly mediated by LSD antagonism of platelet serotonin function. All subjects have recovered. One *ayahuasca*-related death was reported (Sklerov et al. 2005), an obscure case which needs further clarification (Callaway et al. 2006). All over the world up to the year 2006, at least eight persons have died after having taken ibogaine. One of them was a woman in the United States, who had been previously treated with ibogaine 25 days earlier. In her case, the cause of death was mesenteric arterial thrombosis related to cellulitis, and a role for ibogaine in the fatal outcome was not assumed. Ecstasy (MDMA) leads the group with an estimated annual fatality rate to be about three to four deaths in one million users.[3] Fatal outcome of Ecstasy (MDMA) abuse is due to hyperpyrexia (heatstroke), rhabdomyolysis (muscle breakdown), liver failure, cardiac arrhythmias, strokes, coagulopathy, or drug-related accidents. These fatalities depend on mechanisms that are not specific to Ecstasy (MDMA) but common to all the amphetamines (Kalant 2001), and result from causes which most of the time cannot be separated from alcohol consumption and excessive physical exercise characteristic of rave dancing.

More casualties have been reported, when people abusing hallucinogens used them in combination with other potentially more dangerous drugs and did irresponsible things under their influence. When used in improper settings—mostly outside medical or religious practices—hallucinogen intoxication can be disturbing and on occasions may temporarily increase the risk of suicidal behavior. After large doses of cocaine, amphetamines, LSD, and PCP, certain individuals may experience violent outbursts, probably because of preexisting psychopathology. Crimes or bizarre behavior associated with hallucinogen intoxication are regularly reported by the media. Sensationalization and exaggeration cannot be ruled out in the background, since many more morbidity and mortality cases related to common substances like alcohol are happening every day and those have been less highlighted in the media. Of all psychoactive substances, alcohol is the only one whose consumption has been shown to commonly increase aggression.

Nonetheless, it is recognized that there is significant variability in the response to hallucinogenic agents both interindividually (between individuals) and intraindividually (in the same individual at different times). In part, this is related to the set and setting (Faillace and Szara 1968). In subjects who are unaware of the hallucinogen administration, the incidence of adverse effects is much higher. Generally, uninformed subjects show more anxiety, and cognitive disruption, in contrast to the others who have an excess of euphoric responses. A second set of factors that influence hallucinogenic response are related to the personality of the subject. Acute psychedelic drug intoxication can manifest features of paranoia, confusion, and agitated behavior in a time-limited manner. This was one of the features supporting the proposition that psychedelic drugs were experimentally useful in producing a clinically relevant, discrete episode of psychosis in the "psychotomimetic" (psychosis mimicking) model. Psychosis is the term used for denoting the distortion or disorganization of a person's capacity to recognize reality, think rationally, or communicate with others. The "psychotomimetic" effects of hallucinogenic drugs (e.g., LSD, psilocybin, and mescaline) have been suggested to resemble the symptoms of acute schizophrenia.

Originally, hallucinogens carried the misnomer of "psychotogenic" (psychosis generating) agents, but the hallucinogenic effect is distinct from psychosis on several accounts; essentially, the two experiences are fundamentally different. Reality control is well maintained after minimal experience with hallucinogens, and the psychedelic effect is actively sought by users. Psychosis is neither voluntary nor desired. It is a disordered mental state over which the subject has no control. Hallucinogenic agents, when taken in appropriate settings in a responsible manner, induce a coherent mental state with feeling of increased internal order and personal growth. An experienced hallucinogen user may be regarded as a competent navigator or a "co-dancer" with the drug (Shanon 2002). No such statement applies to a psychotic. Sporadic anecdotal observations noticed a relationship between the onset of schizophrenia and the hallucinogen use in a vulnerable population. However, when schizophrenic symptoms did persist beyond 24 hours, it appeared that the particular syndrome was a hallucinogen-precipitated event in schizophrenia-prone individuals (e.g., those with relatives with psychiatric problems), rather than a specific and genuine hallucinogen-induced persistent psychosis.

Recent reports (Caspi et al. 2005; Henquet et al. 2006) indicate that people with a certain gene variant (Val allele) of the COMT (catecholamine-*O*-methyl-transferase enzyme), an enzyme responsible for the synaptic elimination of dopamine) are more vulnerable to a schizophrenia-like psychosis after cannabis abuse, and regular use of cannabis is a risk factor of schizophrenia. Carriers of the Val allele were most sensitive to cannabis-induced psychotic experiences, but this was conditional on the presence of preexisting psychosis liability. Cannabis abuse had no such adverse influence on individuals with two copies of the Met allele. These findings underline the importance of thorough screening before enrollment into a hallucinogen trial, and explain why such precaution is so helpful for minimizing the risk of adverse outcomes.

Hallucinogens and Pregnancy

It is a well-known fact that drug use in pregnant women can be associated with a number of serious complications for mother and child. There are satisfactory data on harmful effects of alcohol, tobacco, marijuana, and cocaine on pregnancy and neonatal outcome, which usually involves vasoconstriction of the placental vessels resulting in placental abruption, spontaneous abortion, intrauterine growth retardation, preterm delivery, and stillbirth. However, only little evidence is available about the effects of classical hallucinogens like LSD or Ecstasy (MDMA) (von Mandach 2005). The dissociative anesthetic ketamine is an exception: it has been shown to be safe to use in pregnant animals (i.e., no significant adverse effects on the fetus).

Usually, when facing a decision regarding the use of a medication in pregnancy, the therapist has to weigh the risks of using the drug against the risks of not using it (i.e., the effects of the untreated illness itself on pregnancy). The lack of information means that strict precautions have to be maintained, and the therapist must look for alternative treatments. Even in cases of the most positive therapeutic outcome of the ongoing clinical trials with hallucinogens, their use in pregnant women cannot expect any kind of liberalization in the foreseeable future.

Acute Clinical Effects

Common psychedelic experiences include a profound change of perception which can include visual, auditory, olfactory (smell related), gustatory (taste related) and somatic (bodily) illusions or hallucinations, and synesthesias. The latter are unusual blending of sensory modalities, for example, sounds may be perceived as images, or colors may be perceived as smells. At the onset of hallucinogen action, there may be a feeling of energy in the body, and the sense that things are different than usual. As the effects intensify, a wide variety of profound mental changes may occur. The full blown psychedelic experience is usually accompanied by intensified mood, or exaggeration of the emotional state existing at the time of ingestion of the drug. This can include euphoria or elation, depression, anxiety, and panic feelings. Increased visual imagery with closed eyes is the most common perceptual change. Open-eye visual hallucinations are more likely to occur at higher doses, and may affect the behavior of inexperienced or unattended subjects. High-dose effects may also include extreme time-dilation, with seconds or minutes feeling like hours or days. Cognition can be altered to the extent that the experience takes on a mystical quality, and past memories may be reexperienced with picture-like intensity. Advanced users may experience expanded spiritual awareness or a sense of universal understanding through their use of hallucinogens, and report religious revelations, spiritual awakening, dissolution of the ego, near-death experiences, and encounters with seemingly autonomous entities. While these experiences are described by many people as pleasant (good trips), and serve basis for hallucinogen abuse, to some they may be confusing and frightening (bad trips).

ACUTE SIDE EFFECTS

When used in moderate psychedelic doses, hallucinogens may cause common adverse reactions (harmless with minimal care) such as nausea, vomiting, dizziness, headaches, insignificant elevation in pulse and blood pressure, dilated pupils, slightly elevated temperature, raising of skin-hair, impaired coordination, and increased reflexes. These symptoms usually begin within one hour after taking the drug and can last up to several hours (depending on the rate of absorption and metabolism of the drug). Various blood hormones and liver enzymes can also show clinically insignificant, temporary elevation.

Emergency Care of Hallucinogen-Induced Adverse Effects

This chapter is about the risks of hallucinogenic agents used in a clinical, well-controlled, secure setting. After proper and thorough screening of enrolled subjects, fewer complications are expected than from uncontrolled street abuse. Nevertheless, the hospital environment provides less than ideal atmosphere for the psychedelic experience (Strassman 2000). Symptoms of acute hallucinogen drug intoxication may develop, which can manifest in paranoia, confusion, fear of death, and disordered self-control.

The focus of care is to prevent subjects from harming themselves or others and reduce complications related to acute effects until these time-limited phenomena resolve. The toxic psychosis generally resolves in two to six hours. At times aftereffects, such as mild depersonalization–derealization (uneasy feeling of changed personality and reality), may linger for a couple of days. Calm, reassuring, and nonthreatening behavior can be useful in "talking down" patients to allow necessary treatment to be applied and interventions to proceed. Subjects need to be reassured that they are not "crazy," what they sense is "just" the result of a chemical, and will go away soon without a trace, with the eventual return of ordinary reality. The optimal placement of sufferers is under one-to-one supervision (one trained staff person attending the patient), in a quiet room with diminished lighting and other stimuli. Both stimulus deprivation and overstimulation have to be avoided. Bed rest in supine position is not necessary, and is disadvantageous in patients with nausea and vomiting.

Appropriate use of chemical or physical restraints may be required if verbal reassurance is not working. Physical restraints are seldom needed, and must be the last resort. Benzodiazepines are probably the safest sedatives and can be effective for calming most subjects. For fast response, these agents are best administered intravenously. More severe reactions of anxiety or dangerous levels of agitation may require antipsychotic medication. First-generation antipsychotics (such as haloperidol or droperidol) must be avoided because of narrow receptor profile (lack of serotonin blockade) and cardiac side effects. Second-generation antipsychotics with serotonin2A antagonism and parenteral formulation are safer and more effective.

The therapeutic approaches of modern medicine can be combined with some nonintrusive traditional techniques: reciting mantras and gentle, simultaneous massaging of the eyebrow region (6th chakra) and the navel region (3rd chakra).

Tolerance

While hallucinogenic agents are classified as drugs causing dependence, they are physiologically nonaddictive. There is no evidence that these drugs produce physical withdrawal symptoms when their chronic use is stopped (American Psychiatric Association 1994). On the other hand, the tolerance phenomenon is well-known. Psilocybin, LSD, and mescaline users quickly develop a high degree of tolerance for the drug effect: after repeated use, they need increasingly larger doses to produce similar responses. Cross-tolerance is built up for other serotonergic hallucinogenic drugs, such as psilocybin and mescaline, but not for drugs such as marijuana, amphetamines, and PCP, which do not act directly on the serotonin receptors. LSD given daily becomes less effective at the same dose (Isbell et al. 1956). This tolerance is short-lived, lasting only for several days; in humans, tolerance to gross behavioral changes develops in four to seven days of daily administration and lasts approximately three days. Schizophrenic patients may develop tolerance sooner, in two to three days (for review, see Abraham et al. 1996). DMT is unique in this respect: this given frequently does not elicit tolerance neither in animal (Kovacic and Domino 1976) nor in human (Strassman et al. 1996) experiments. Although DMT acts on the same receptors as LSD, its cross-tolerance with LSD and other serotonergic hallucinogens is limited.

LONG-TERM EFFECTS

The widely publicized "flashbacks" associated with the hallucinogenic drugs attest to their long-term effects. A number of chronic clinical syndromes due to hallucinogenic drugs have been recognized, including hallucinogen-induced persistent psychosis and hallucinogen persisting perception disorder (formerly post-hallucinogen perception disorder).

Hallucinogen-Induced Persistent Psychosis

The overwhelming nature of a full-blown psychedelic experience can lead to significant psychological disturbances after the acute drug effects have worn off. Under some hallucinogens, especially LSD, users may experience devastating mental effects that persist longer than one month after the trip has ended. These long-lasting psychosis-like effects of the drug are labeled as a "Hallucinogen-Induced Persistent Psychosis," and distinguished from the "Hallucinogen Persisting Perception Disorder" described subsequently. Hallucinogen-induced persistent psychosis commonly includes a dramatic affective component with mood swings from mania to profound depression, religious thought contents, vivid visual disturbances, and hallucinations not typical in schizophrenia (i.e., not auditory hallucinations of conversing, commenting, or commanding voices). The clinical picture of the hallucinogen-induced persistent psychosis appears to resemble schizoaffective disorders (schizophrenia-like disorder with prominent mood swings) with the not-infrequent addition of visual disturbances. It was noted in an early LSD experiment (Fink et al. 1966, p. 453) with persistent psychotic patients that, "the hazard of LSD administration appears not to be in the precipitation of a schizophrenic-like state but rather in decreasing emotional and affective controls and inducing a persistent state of altered consciousness."

This type of adverse hallucinogen drug effect may also be akin to the pathological sequelae of psychological traumas such as rape, natural disaster, or combat experience. These effects may last for years and can affect people who have no history or other symptoms of psychiatric disorder. Nevertheless, investigators have found early on that it was very uncommon to diagnose hallucinogen-induced persistent psychosis after hallucinogen use in secure, professional settings. The incidence of LSD-related psychosis was estimated to be about 0.8/1,000 in experimental subjects, and one case was reported in 247 LSD users surveyed (Cohen 1960; McGlothlin and Arnold 1971). The low incidence of such unfavorable outcomes was the result of carefully screening volunteers, closely monitoring their sessions, and providing supportive follow-up as indicated (Strassman 1995).

Hallucinogen Persisting Perception Disorder

One of the most common adverse effects of hallucinogens is known colloquially as "flashbacks," and in its severe form called "Hallucinogen Persisting Perception Disorder" by physicians (American Psychiatric Association 1994). "Flashbacks" are spontaneous, repeated, and at times continuous recurrences of one or more of the sensory, cognitive, or emotional symptoms of the hallucinogenic experience after an intervening drug-free period. In earlier decades, "flashbacks" got media attention and were highlighted as a deterrent to recreational use. Most subjects having these experiences find them interesting, enjoyable, and time-limited. Only when such incidences cause distress and interfere with ordinary function do people turn to clinicians. Therefore, it is not well established how often "flashbacks" occur. In addition, because the term "flashback" has been used in many different ways, determining the true incidence of the disorder is even more difficult to determine. Reports from early studies on LSD users (McGlothlin and Arnold 1971) suggested that subjects with less than 10 exposures report "flashbacks" at a rate of 12%, and they were less common in medically controlled settings as compared to street users. This early observation was recently reinforced by Halpern and Pope (2003), who also pointed out that when LSD was used in a therapeutic or research setting, the hallucinogen persisting perception disorder appeared less frequently than when it was used recreationally.

The symptoms of hallucinogen persisting perception disorder are better defined: they most commonly consists of visual disturbances such as simple geometric pseudo-hallucinations (dots, grids, zigzags, spirals, etc.); seeing halos, bright, colorful flashes, or trails attached to moving objects; and perceiving false motion on the edges of the field of vision. There appears to be no strict relationship between the frequency of hallucinogen use and the rate of occurrence: a single dose of LSD can cause the disorder. Stress, fatigue, sleep deprivation, dark environment, marijuana use, depression, and anxiety are the known precipitating or augmenting factors. This condition is typically persistent, and in some cases remains unchanged for years after individuals have stopped using the hallucinogen (Abraham 1983). Given that millions of people have taken hallucinogens, the incidence of hallucinogen persisting perception disorder appears to be very small, and there is presently no fully effective treatment.

The characteristics of the hallucinogen persisting perception disorder suggest that hallucinogens may exert long-lasting physiological changes in the brain with hyperexcitability of the visual system. Psychological studies found abnormalities in visual function, supporting the hypothesis that imagery continued to be processed although the test stimulus had been removed. This dysfunction may arise from a destruction of inhibitory interneurons of the visual pathways that receive serotonergic input and were overstimulated by LSD, with subsequent excitotoxic degeneration. Preclinical research (Gewirtz et al. 2002) showed that the phenethylamine hallucinogen 2,5-dimethoxy-4-iodophenyl-2-aminopropane increased the expression of the brain-derived neurotrophic factor, which can provide another clue to the mechanism by which hallucinogens might exert long-lasting changes in synaptic connections of the nervous system.

Personality Changes

The psychedelic impact a hallucinogen may have on its users need not be confined to the period of the acute drug effects. Having experienced the extraordinary effects induced by the hallucinogen, many partakers feel that they undergo deep personal changes. It is common to hear hallucinogen users testify that they underwent major transformations and their lives were no longer the same. The changes mentioned pertain to new psychological understandings and personal insights; modifications of belief systems, worldviews, and perspectives on life; and religious conversion and adherence to a spiritual lifestyle. Not infrequently, these effects may result in radical decisions and actions, sometimes at variance with family members' conventional expectations (Walsh and Vaughan 1993; Grob 2002a; Shanon 2002).

NEUROTOXIC EFFECTS

There has been an extensive debate in the literature (see Grob 2002b) on the neurotoxic effects of hallucinogenic compounds with more focus on the members of the phenethylamine group, especially on Ecstasy (MDMA). The debate culminated in *Science's* retraction of an erroneous publication (Ricaurte et al. 2002) purporting to show that even onetime use of Ecstasy (MDMA) causes damage to the dopamine system that creates a risk of developing Parkinson's disease later in life. Twenty percent of the studied monkeys died quickly, and another 20% became sick with severe brain damage after their second or third dose of the investigational drug, which later turned out to be methamphetamine. Critics blamed the researchers' and *Science* reviewers' biased mind set for overlooking the extreme fatality rates unusual in recreational Ecstasy (MDMA) users.

MDMA

At variance with the retracted report on dopamine neurotoxicity, extensive studies in animals indicate that high or repeated dose Ecstasy (MDMA) exposure can damage serotonergic nerve fibers as a result of metabolic stress (Green et al. 1995; Baggott and Mendelson 2001). The toxic effect is increased under prolonged physical exertion and high ambient temperature (conditions frequently encountered in rave dancing). Similar changes can be induced by methamphetamine and some other phenethylamine agents (Miller and O'Callaghan 1996; Seiden and Sabol 1996). However, there is controversy over the extent to which analogous changes occur in humans. Ecstasy (MDMA) toxicity has not been documented in controlled research experiments with human subjects, but it has been alleged to occur in settings outside of clinical research. When considering the millions of users taking Ecstasy (MDMA) of unknown origin, purity, and potency (Gore 1999; Henry and Rella 2001), serious toxicity appears to rarely happen (less than four deaths in one million users are estimated).[4] Such users routinely consume estimated Ecstasy (MDMA) doses much higher than those administered in therapeutic protocols. Before the drug was placed into Schedule I, psychiatrists in the United States and Europe reported using Ecstasy (MDMA) in a large number of patients, and these therapists did not report any severe adverse effects occurring during or after MDMA-assisted psychotherapy sessions (Greer and Tolbert 1986, 1998; Gasser 1994). There is now a considerable body of information indicating that the likelihood of significant toxicity is very low from the doses of Ecstasy (MDMA) used in study protocols. To date, Ecstasy (MDMA) has been administered to over 230 people in controlled and uncontrolled trials in clinical settings and has failed to demonstrate toxicity (Grob et al. 1996b; Vollenweider et al. 1999; De La Torre et al. 2000; Gamma et al. 2000; Liechti and Vollenweider 2000). There may nonetheless be legitimate concerns about complications arising as a consequence of polydrug abuse, and the interactions of prescription drugs and food substances with MDMA.

Ibogaine

Several studies have reported cerebellar (Purkinje) cell degeneration in rats after ibogaine administration at doses of 100 mg/kg. However, the neurotoxic effect of ibogaine appears to occur at levels higher than those used for opioid withdrawal or recreational purpose. Moreover, rats appear to be more sensitive to potential ibogaine neurotoxicity compared to other species (including primates). Contrary to expectations from an allegedly abusive drug, since ibogaine has a broad receptor profile with glutamate antagonistic activity at NMDA (N-methyl-D-aspartic acid) specific sites, that feature suggests neuroprotective potential in stroke patients. Ibogaine was reported to protect against methamphetamine neurotoxicity (for review, see Alper 2001).

Indolealkylamines

Very little is known about the neurotoxicity of the indolealkylamine group; in part because they represent the lowest frequency of use, and no controlled studies are available. Conclusions can be drawn from observational reports of sacramental use, that contrary to expectations, the DMT- and beta-carboline–containing *ayahuasca* may have protective effects (Grob et al. 1996a). Some other conjectural evidence supports the notion that this group of hallucinogens may exert neuroprotection. The receptor profile of the indolealkylamines hallucinogens is unique among the classical hallucinogens for their relatively "clean" serotonin1 A agonist (receptor stimulating) property, and neuroprotective action from serotonin1A agonists have been demonstrated in different species (De Vry 1995).

Ergolines

An intermediary position is represented by the ergoline group (e.g., LSD), where the relatively strong flashback-inducing effect may be related to their neurotoxicity within the visual system (Abraham and Mamen 1996). On the other hand, there are circumstances where LSD and other serotonin2A receptor agonists were found to be neuroprotective (Farber et al. 1998).

CHEMICAL INTERACTION COMPLICATIONS

Since the final common pathway of the classical hallucinogenic drugs is the serotonin system, the main concern about drug interactions is primarily in terms of the possibility of an alarming increase in serotonergic effects—a set of symptoms known as the "serotonin syndrome," which is characterized by excessive levels of the neurotransmitter serotonin both in the brain and in the bodily organs. Symptoms are typically initial excitement, nausea, and confusion, followed by tremors, vomiting, convulsions, and loss of consciousness (Isbister and Buckley 2005). The incidence of the "serotonin syndrome" is not known, since most of the cases are mild and resolve undiagnosed. In its severe form if emergency treatment is instituted (which is essentially supportive care for lack of specific antidotes), the syndrome typically resolves within 24 hours. Confusion can last for days, and death has been reported in extreme cases because of circulatory collapse, malignant hyperthermia, or prolonged convulsions (Settle 1998).

Several different drug combinations can lead to this potentially fatal condition. The most common and most dangerous is the mixture of serotonergic agents with MAOIs (monoamine oxidase inhibitors) of the irreversible type. Monoamine oxidase enzymes (MAO-A and MAO-B) are found in the brain, the lung, the liver, and the gastrointestinal system and provide a multiple defense line against invasions of the body from dietary monoamines, particularly tyramine, a food component which can cause extreme high blood pressure. While inhibition of the MAO's action is not intrinsically life threatening—if some dietary constrains are maintained—fatalities from combinations of MAOIs with SSRIs (specific serotonin reuptake inhibitors) have been reported. A mixture of a MAOI with an SSRI results in blockages of the serotonin metabolism by monoamine oxidation and serotonin reuptake into nerve terminals. The production of serotonin continues unaffected while its important pathways of elimination are shut down, causing serotonin accumulation which can increase to toxic levels.[5] Based on an animal study (Santos and Carlini 1983), it was found that sleep-deprived subjects may have slightly increased sensitivity toward serotonin syndrome, calling attention to a risk factor for "*ayahuasca* tourists" owing to long flights and jet lag.

Among hallucinogenic compounds the Amazonian decoctum *ayahuasca* has the greatest potential for a variety of chemical interactions. *Ayahuasca* is a hallucinogenic beverage derived by boiling parts of two or more plants. The brew contains beta-carbolines, which are extremely effective MAOIs, and the potent indolealkylamine hallucinogen DMT. The beta-carbolines, however, are reversible MAOIs, which means they are readily displaced by dietary monoamines or endogenous serotonin, allowing them to be metabolized and thereby avoiding accumulation of these substances to toxic levels. On the contrary, first-generation synthetic MAOIs (such as phenelzine, tranylcypromine, and isocarboxazid) that are used as antidepressants in clinical practice bind tightly (irreversibly) to the enzyme and are not readily displaced. With their use, hypertensive reactions may occur if specific dietary constraints are not maintained. The clinical consequence of the reversible property of beta-carbolines is that strict dietary restrictions may not be required when *ayahuasca* is used in its traditional formulation. There are other features of beta-carbolines which may explain why reports of hypertensive crises following the ingestion of *ayahuasca* have not been documented: beta-carbolines are highly selective inhibitors of MAO-A, a variant of the enzyme (isozyme) which prefers tryptamines (including serotonin) over the pressor agent tyramine as substrates (Yasuhara 1974), and their affinity is lower for liver MAO compared to brain MAO. This complex mechanism would explain the lack of any reports of peripheral autonomic stimulation associated with the ingestion of *ayahuasca* in combination with sympathomimetic drugs or foods containing tyramine (McKenna et al. 1998).

Whilst *ayahuasca* is less likely to induce hypertensive crises with the concomitant administration of sympathomimetic drugs or with tyramine-rich foodstuffs, it still seems wise to advocate care in combining it with potentially interacting medications and to advise a degree of caution with regard to the dietary intake of foodstuffs likely to contain high tyramine content. These typically include fermented or processed food (since bacteria and fungi turn the amino acid tyrosine to tyramine), such as aged cheese, smoked or cured meat, liver products, concentrated yeast or protein extracts, soy foods, fava bean pods, sauerkraut, tap beer, and some brands of red wine. Any protein-containing food or beverage improperly stored or handled should be avoided (Gardner et al. 1996).

Beta-carbolines in *ayahuasca* also retain a potential for adverse interaction with not only sympathomimetic drugs: its concomitant use with serotonin-enhancing drugs (especially SSRIs) and psychostimulants (e.g., amphetamines, MDMA, and methylphenidate) should also be avoided. People interested in using *ayahuasca* are strongly cautioned not to combine this plant medicine with certain classes of psychoactive drugs (Callaway and Grob 1998). Some of the specifically proscribed drugs include Nardil, Parnate, Marplan, Prozac, Paxil, Zoloft, Luvox, Celexa, Lexapro, Effexor, Adipex, Phenphen, Pondimin, and Redux.

As it was previously described, serotonin syndrome is an acute crisis related to a sudden increase of serotonin in the body. There exists a syndrome opposite to it and related to chronic, depleted level of brain serotonin, a condition which can be caused by tryptophan-poor diet (for example, one based on corn). Tryptophan is an essential amino acid and the precursor of serotonin. In studies with humans and nonhuman primates, low serotonin levels were associated with poor impulse control, dysphoric-anxious mood, irritability, recklessness, and social ineptitude (for review, see Bell et al. 2001). When brain serotonin is low, release of testosterone results in a higher rate of self-detrimental and unrestrained aggression (Birger et al. 2003); predispositions which represent a particularly bad mind set for psychedelic experience or community rituals.

The aboriginal tribes of the Amazon basin have developed a bland, salt, spice, and concentrated sugar-free diet (Luna and Amaringo 1999) many generations ago, which prohibits sexual activity and red meat, but permits certain amount of fish and poultry and promotes starchy food like manioc, potatoes, quinoa (a grain), oats, rice, and plantain (a type of banana, which theoretically would be prohibited by the MAOI-safety diet). Some traditions place more emphasis on preceremony diet (even as long as six months), while other traditions stress postceremony diet more. The traditional *ayahuasca* preceremony diet is probably not for prevention of MAOI-related complications: one does not need to follow MAOI diet for days or weeks before a ritual; it would make more sense adhering to a MAOI-safe diet during the hours, and following the ceremony. It is not merely healthy or for spiritual cleansing. The traditional *ayahuasca* diet may serve a very rational purpose: to increase brain serotonin by tryptophan intake.

An Amazonas shaman (*ayahuasquero* among mestizos) definitely does not want his/her people entering the ceremony with "serotonin depletion syndrome" and behaving like "pests." This can be prevented by a tryptophan-rich diet (which can include fish, poultry, papaya, banana, avocado, spinach, cottage cheese, milk, seeds, and nuts), with starch and without competition of amino acids from other sources. Tryptophan needs sugar for facilitated transport into the brain, but from complex carbohydrates (starch) and not from pure sugar. Concentrated, simple sugars induce a sharp increase of insulin release, and insulin helps the transport of rivaling (multiple chain) amino acids (not ring type like tryptophan) into the brain which compete with tryptophan for the transport sites. Promptly activating the brain's serotonin receptors DMT, the psychoactive ingredient of *ayahuasca,* can exert a prosocial effect, somewhat opposite to the serotonin depletion syndrome, and fulfill the role of a "sociointegrator"—one interpretation of the indigenous practice of using *ayahuasca* ceremony for "crisis resolution" in the community.

The use of *ayahuasca* has not been limited to indigenous or mestizo groups, but it is regularly used by members of syncretic religious movements, whose influence is growing in the urban populations of Brazil and recently throughout the Americas and in Europe. Based on the millions of people worldwide who are currently undergoing treatment with SSRIs, the potential for incurring a dangerous serotonin syndrome should not be ignored. The presence of euphoria, confusion, vomiting, and tremor as common as initial symptoms from typical doses of *ayahuasca* makes the diagnosis of "serotonin syndrome" difficult to rule out in people on serotonergic medications.

Beta-carbolines and SSRIs are metabolized in the liver by the same isozyme of the cytochrome P450 enzymatic clearance system denoted as CYP2D6. This common metabolism by CYP2D6 provides another good reason to avoid the combination of SSRIs with *ayahuasca,* since beta-carbolines not only delay elimination of endogenous serotonin but also do the same with the SSRI thus exaggerating the interaction. 5-Methoxy-DMT—a close analogue (chemical kin) of DMT—elicits more intensive undesirable effects, and leads to a less visionary psychedelic experience than its chemical cousin. Essentially, CYP2D6 is a highly specific, high-affinity, high-capacity 5-methoxy-indolealkylamine-*O*-demethylase (Yu et al. 2003) with higher affinity for 5-methoxy-DMT than for DMT, and represents its cardinal metabolic pathway (besides MAO). Therefore, *ayahuasca* (especially pharmahuasca) preparations with high 5-methoxy-DMT contamination can result in a very "rogue" experience in the case where CYP2D6 activity is blocked or deficient. Since the antidepressants paroxetine (Paxil) and fluoxetine (Prozac) are potent CYP2D6 inhibitors, subjects taking these SSRIs are at risk of complex metabolic interactions.

The isozyme CYP2D6 exhibits a wide range of polymorphisms in human populations with interindividual and interethnic variations in its enzymatic activity. This metabolic trait could account for differences in effects between individuals who take *ayahuasca* and makes some ethnic groups more or less vulnerable for *ayahuasca*–drug interactions and 5-methoxy-DMT effects. The frequency of reduced function or nonfunctional gene variants of CYP2D6 is higher in African and Oriental populations (50%) contrasted to Caucasian and Amerindian groups (~30%) (Bradford 2002). The presented picture of polymorphism is not straightforward: Caucasians have higher percentage of poor metabolizers (bimodal distribution with a subgroup of 7% at the slow end) as compared to Orientals (1–2%), but their population metabolizes faster in general (with more rapid metabolizers in the group). In conclusion, one may expect that *ayahuasca* users of African or Oriental descent are somewhat more vulnerable to chemical interactions.

The function of CYP2D6 is not only race-related but also age-dependent as well. CYP2D6 activity increases rapidly after birth to reach a level equivalent to that in the young adult, then gradually decreases and finally declines faster in old age (Tanaka 1998). MAO-B shows a different trend with advanced age: its activity increases (Kumar and Andersen 2004). The combination of these enzyme changes may predispose elderly people for more adverse reactions and decreased DMT effects, since DMT is primarily oxidized by MAO-B in the brain (Suzuki et al. 1981). We have no data regarding age effects on the active reuptake of DMT into the brain, which would probably be more relevant for the distribution (Yanai et al. 1986) and bioavailability of DMT than the physiological, age-related increase of MAO-B activity, since the amounts of beta-carbolines present in a typical dose of *ayahuasca* are usually well above the saturation threshold for MAO inhibition. Based on the observation of difficulties with the experience among elderly ayahuasca users (Luis Luna, pers. comm.), I predict variation in the active DMT transport into the brain with a decline at advanced age.

Summary

The purpose of the above material has been to show that the hallucinogens are much safer than is generally believed by the public and even by the professionals. There nonetheless needs to be strong cautionary statements in the recommendations for use. For instance, one might presume that *ayahuasca* does not need as strict dietary restrictions as many of us might suppose because of its reversible MAOI feature. This seems evident given the many *ayahuasca* tourists who do not care too much about their diet and concomitant medications. These involve thousands of cases with very few, questionable fatalities. The Callaway and Grob (1998) paper is really not a report of a serious serotonin syndrome; it is rather a necessary but overprotective warning. The case is that mild-to-moderate serotonin syndrome is indistinguishable from *ayahuasca* effects (i.e., its vegetative symptoms at the onset essentially represent a mild serotonin syndrome), making the differential diagnosis difficult to ascertain.

GENERAL GUIDELINES FOR THERAPEUTIC USE AND FUTURE RESEARCH

Classic hallucinogens are classified in a combined effort by the Department of Justice and the Department of Health and Human Services as Schedule I drugs, which means a high potential for abuse, with no medical utility, or lack of safety for use of the drug under medical supervision (United States Code 2000).[6] The purpose of this chapter and the whole volume is to point out that none of these statements are defensible. There clearly are instances where a Schedule I hallucinogen can be used safely and does have medical utility (at least in terms of clinical investigation). Under Schedule I, classic hallucinogens are rated worst than the more dangerous and addictive cocaine and amphetamines (Schedule II drugs). Since hallucinogenic agents can have medical use, they should be switched to Schedule II. Alternatively, there ought to be some sort of Ia Schedule, which means that one would need special training or certification to use a Schedule I drug (Strassman pers. comm.). What that training and certification would involve is a complicated issue. Perhaps something akin to psychoanalytic certification is a useful analogy: someone needs to know what the drugs are and do, and must be very well versed in their own psychology and spirituality.

Owing to the diversity of hallucinogenic compounds, only general guidelines can be provided for their clinical use within the constraints of this chapter. Since no hallucinogen has FDA approval for therapeutic indications for the general public, strict guidelines used in experimental protocols are applicable. An exception is ketamine, which is currently Schedule III. However, its use is approved for anesthesia, and off-label use of a controlled substance is very murky; such practices with ketamine may require a certificate of "conscious sedation."

For particular drugs and individual cases, the investigator or the therapist has to use clinical judgment based on a cost-benefit analysis serving the subjects' best interest and in adherence with the directives of local ethics committees. These may include review of the proposed protocol by an ethically and scientifically competent institutional board and acquisition of informed consent from study participants. The informed consent must include, among other considerations: a description of the protocol understandable to a nonspecialist reader; a proper discussion of possible risks and benefits; and a discussion of treatment alternatives; and a statement describing the extent, if any, to which confidentiality of records identifying the subject will be maintained (Code of Federal Regulations 2006).[7] The application of these considerations may justify the experimental or therapeutic use of hallucinogens in the given situation.

Inclusion Criteria for participants, the *Outcome Measures* of treatment, and the *Monitoring Procedures* are dependent on therapeutic goals or the purpose of the particular study, but common elements of a clinical investigational protocol using classical hallucinogenic agents can be generalized as follows.

Exclusion Criteria

Subjects enrolled into hallucinogenic protocols have to undergo a detailed psychiatric diagnostic interview (preferably structured one), and mental disorder comorbidity, substance abuse problems, or a personal or family history of psychosis has to be ruled out. Individuals who carry two copies of the Val allele of the COMT enzyme should be considered for exclusion from cannabis protocols. Participants must be free of any clinically significant comorbid medical illness (other than the targeted one) based on physical examination and routine blood testing. They should not require on a regular basis any prescription or over-the-counter medications interfering with the hallucinogen. Any potentially dangerous medication they may have taken should have been stopped for long enough to allow for their elimination prior to start the administration of the study drug. Women who are pregnant, lactating, or unwilling/unable to practice medically acceptable birth control during the study should also be excluded.

Dietary Restrictions

Subjects are required to refrain from the use of alcohol, drugs of abuse, over-the-counter medications, and medicinal natural products for the duration of the treatment. Dietary recommendations may apply to the use of compounds with MAOI content (such as *ayahuasca* preparations), as it was discussed above. In the latter case, six-hour fasting may be required prior to intake for mitigation of nausea and vomiting.

Specific Considerations

Several special procedures are necessary in order to minimize risk to subjects who participate in clinical studies with hallucinogens. During the early phase of testing, each subject may need constant observation; at the initiation of therapy, they may need to be kept in the hospital overnight and be assessed by the investigator prior to leaving the following day. If subjects are found to be at risk of complications from the procedure at the projected time of discharge, they have to be kept in the hospital until they are felt to be safe. If complications should result during testing, the investigators will be available to treat them as they arise (i.e., psychosis, abnormal mood states, panic attacks, seizures, and others).

FUTURE RESEARCH DIRECTIONS

We are limited in our ability to address all possible complicating factors in the use of hallucinogens as therapies or research medications because of the limited research designs which have thus far been employed. Ascribing adverse effects to a particular hallucinogenic agent (or any kind of drug) is not simple if one is bound to scientific scrutiny. A causal relationship implies a fixed temporal sequence between drug and effect and conclusions based on well-established evidence linking the two. In pharmacological research, different study levels with increasing scientific rigor are instituted for evaluation of a drug.

Uncontrolled Case Reports

This type of design is at the low end of scientific value. Although without statistical power, case reports (e.g., Savage et al. 1966) often become the seed from which more systematic inquiries blossom. In hallucinogenic research, case reports fuel protocols with solid designs for the evaluation of beneficial and adverse drug effects. The exaggerated and at times even fabricated cases in media which capture public attention are even able to influence professional attitudes but do not have scientific value. Nevertheless, those have been dominating the public arena thus far. The controversy is clear: would anyone judge the usefulness of an FDA approved, pharmaceutical company marketed drug based on their abuse, or careless use outside of medical settings? Probably not. Until very recently, hallucinogens could not profit from being tested under neutral academic attention with advanced scientific methods, and mostly have been judged based on reports of their abuse. Not even the "benefit of doubt" has been applied to their case.

Case Series, Case-Controlled Designs

Low levels of validity are represented by case series (e.g., Gill et al. 2002), case-controlled designs, such as comparisons of groups by an unstructured inquiry into their history. In case-control studies, the researcher gathers the data on the dependent variable (e.g., adverse effects) and then looks into the past of the participants to classify them. A good number of these studies are now available, and the majority of literature data on hallucinogen abuse–related psychiatric and medical disorders are based on this kind of approach. Particular concern for any of the above methods is the difficulty in securing a group of hallucinogen users who are free of unrelated psychopathology and/or other psychoactive drug use.

Open-Label Trials

At higher levels of validity are open label trials (e.g., Attal et al. 2004), which provide observational data on the clinical effects of known substances (e.g., without double-blind). Studies with an open label design can be randomized trials, but some do not include a comparison group; therefore, no randomization can be accomplished in these cases. Open label trials lack the strength of a blind design and so are prone to investigator's bias, but the validity of this approach is supported by a controlled dose regimen, prospective design, and statistical analysis of the recorded data. There is no randomization at all in observational studies, where the allocation of treatment is not fully under the control of the investigator. Observational studies are more likely to require difficult statistical adjustments because of the potential for large imbalances. In the research of hallucinogen-related complications, studies with this methodological level are rare.

Double-Blind RPCT (Randomized, Placebo Controlled Trials)

These represent the highest level of validity with the random and blind assignment of subjects to a drug cohort or a placebo control group. This golden standard designed for medication development (double-blind, randomized, rigorous trials) is rarely accomplished in hallucinogenic research. Since the end of the 20-year moratorium on human experimentation with hallucinogens, a series of new studies has emerged utilizing careful attention to experimental design.[8] One remarkable example is the replication of the preeminent Good Friday Experiment (Pahnke 1963) by a group from the Johns Hopkins Hospital (Griffiths et al. 2006; reprinted here in Volume 2) for psilocybin's effect in occasioning mystical experiences. Griffiths' group advanced the methodology of the pioneering study and improved the set and settings as well. Both studies were double-blind, active placebo-controlled trials, but the blind in the Good Friday Experiment was easily broken during the session by the participants' psychedelic experience. Another limitation of the Pahnke study was that it was conducted in a group setting. The Johns Hopkins study used better blinding and comparison control procedures, applied empirically validated measures of mystical experience, and assessed effects in individual participants undisturbed by group interactions. Besides a successful replication of the Good Friday Experiment (its results were even better), an important finding of the Griffiths study was that with careful volunteer screening and preparation, and when sessions are conducted in a comfortable, well-supervised setting, a high dose of psilocybin can be administered safely.

This renaissance is promising but has not yet produced an abundance of well-controlled trials on the putative dangers of hallucinogenic drugs. In order to adequately answer safety concerns related to these compounds, one may need Phase II and III clinical trials.

Clinical trials belonging to the RPCT group and addressing safety and efficacy issues are designated as Phase I, II, or III, based on the type of questions that study is seeking to answer.

In Phase I studies, investigators test a new drug in a small group of healthy volunteers (20–60) for the first time to evaluate its safety, determine a safe dosage range, and identify side effects.

In Phase II trials, the study drug is given to a larger group of ill people (100–400) to further evaluate its safety and to see if it is effective.

In Phase III clinical trials, the size of the treatment group is increased to a larger number of patients (1,000–4,000) to confirm the effectiveness of the drug, monitor its adverse effects, compare it to commonly used treatments, and collect information that will allow its safe use.

Today we are witnessing the entrance of hallucinogens (ibogaine, marijuana, MDMA, and psilocybin) into the Phase II stage of well-controlled trials. As an FDA approved anesthetic, ketamine has already passed these phases, and off-label trials are under way (Zarate et al. 2006). The cost of a Phase III study is so expensive, that usually industry sponsored trials can afford that investment. Appropriate information can also be gained in a cost-effective manner via post-marketing (post-approval) trials (not necessarily RPCT), representing the IVth phase in the development of a therapeutic agent.

CONCLUSIONS

It is apparent that more and better controlled research (at least Phase II) is needed to clarify the adverse effects of hallucinogens. That kind of research would need enrollment of healthy human volunteers. While rigid administrative regulations in the United States are loosening up for the therapeutic use of hallucinogens in severely ill patients, the United States is lagging behind Switzerland and Germany where hallucinogen research is not restricted to sick people. Drug safety can not be reliably evaluated only on individuals with compromised health.

In summary of our current knowledge, when hallucinogens are ingested outside of controlled medical, ceremonial, or research settings, these agents have a relatively low potential to be harmful. Nonetheless, ill-conceived hallucinogen experimentation may induce unstable affect and even precipitate psychotic breaks, especially in individuals with dormant or preexisting psychopathology. What follows is that the recreational use of hallucinogens has not been proven to be "safe."

The situation is less restrictive when under controlled settings, where careful screening of participants, close monitoring of the sessions, and providing follow-up minimize the incidence of serious adverse events to a very low level, below the reasonably accepted threshold. Certainly, one should not judge a drug from its misuse since that way of evaluation is scientifically incorrect, and there is a possibility of well-conducted studies of both therapeutic and socially acceptable use. With the FDA approving several hallucinogen treatment trials and the Supreme Court siding with the *Uniao do Vegetal* in the *ayahuasca* case, that possibility is on a cautious path of realization.

NOTES

1. Centers for Disease Control and Prevention. 2004. Alcohol-attributable deaths and years of potential life lost—United States, 2001. *Morbidity and Mortality Weekly Report* 53:658–61.

Centers for Disease Control and Prevention. 2005. Annual smoking-attributable mortality, years of potential life lost, and productivity losses—United States, 1997–2001. *Morbidity and Mortality Weekly Report* 54:625–48.

2. NIDA Research Report—Heroin Abuse and Addiction: NIH Publication No. 05-4165, Printed October 1997 (Reprinted September 2000; Revised May 2005); NIDA Research Report—Nicotine Addiction: NIH Publication No. 01-4342, Printed 1998 (Reprinted 2001; Revised 2006); NIDA Research Report—Methamphetamine Abuse and Addiction: NIH Publication No. 02-4210, Printed April 1998 (Reprinted January 2002); NIDA Research Report—Cocaine Abuse and Addiction: NIH Publication No. 99-4342, Printed May 1999 (Revised November 2004); NIDA Research Report—Hallucinogens and Dissociative Drugs: NIH Publication No. 01-4209, Printed March 2001; NIDA Research Report—Prescription Drugs: Abuse and Addiction: NIH Publication No. 01-4881, Printed 2001 (Revised August 2005); NIDA Research Report—Marijuana Abuse: NIH Publication No. 05-3859, Printed June 2005; NIDA Research Report—MDMA Abuse (Ecstasy): NIH Publication No. 05-4728, Printed November 2005.

3. Newsletter of the Multidisciplinary Association for Psychedelic Studies. MAPS, Volume 4 Number 1, Spring 1993.

4. Ibid.

5. One may argue that the brain has other adaptive mechanisms remaining unaltered and counteracting the dangerous outcome: self-regulatory autoreceptors can shut down the release of serotonin into the synaptic cleft, and/or another serotonin metabolizing enzyme, the extracellularly located HIOMT (hydroxyindole-O-methyltransferase) enzyme (which is similar to the COMT enzyme mentioned previously in the text) can catalyze deactivation of the excessive neurotransmitter. However, the autoreceptor-mediated feedback regulation becomes less effective after chronic use of SSRIs (Blier et al. 1998), some drugs (such as haloperidol) can block HIOMT, and some people may have genetically deficient HIOMT (Yi et al. 1993). Therefore, in very rare instances though, the number of adaptive processes can eventually get to a dangerously low level.

6. United States Code. 2000. Title 21, Chapter 13, Subchapter I, Part B, § 812. Schedules of controlled substances. Washington, D.C.: House, Office of the Law Revision Counsel.

7. Code of Federal Regulations. 2006. Title 42 – Public Health, Chapter 1 – Public Health Service, Department Of Health And Human Services, Subchapter A – General Provisions. Washington, D.C.: National Archives and Records Administration.

8. The studies of De La Torre et al. (2000), Gamma et al. (2000), Grob et al. (1996b), Liechti et al. (2001), and Vollenweider et al. (1999) represent good examples of the well-controlled RPCT design for studying the supposed neurotoxic effect of Ecstasy (MDMA).

REFERENCES

Abraham, H.D. 1983. Visual phenomenology of the LSD flashback. *Archives of General Psychiatry* 40:884–9.

Abraham, H.D., and A. Mamen. 1996. LSD-like panic from risperidone in post-LSD visual disorder. *Journal of Clinical Psychopharmacology* 16:238–41.

Abraham, H.D., A.M. Aldridge, and P. Gogia. 1996. The psychopharmacology of hallucinogens. *Neuropsychopharmacology* 14:285–98.

Alper, K.R. 2001. Ibogaine: A review. *The Alkaloids: Chemistry and Biology* 56: 1–38.

American Psychiatric Association. 1994. *Diagnostic and statistical manual of mental disorders.* 4th ed. Washington, D.C.: American Psychiatric Press.

Attal, N., L. Brasseur, D. Guirimand, S. Clermond-Gnamien, S. Atlami, and D. Bouhassira. 2004. Are oral cannabinoids safe and effective in refractory neuropathic pain? *European Journal of Pain* 8:173–7.

Baggott, M., and J. Mendelson. 2001. Does MDMA cause brain damage? In *Ecstasy: A complete guide,* ed. J. Holland, 110–45. Rochester, VT: Inner Tradition.

Bell, C., J. Abrams, and D. Nutt. 2001. Tryptophan depletion and its implications for psychiatry. *British Journal of Psychiatry* 178:399–405.

Birger, M., M. Swartz, D. Cohen, Y. Alesh, C. Grishpan, and M. Kotelr. 2003. Aggression: The testosterone-serotonin link. *The Israel Medical Association Journal* 5:653–8.

Blier, P., G. Pineyro, M. El Mansari, R. Bergeron, and C. De Montigny. 1998. Role of somatodendritic 5-HT autoreceptors in modulating 5-HT neurotransmission. *Annals of the New York Academy of Sciences* 861:204–16.

Bradford, L.D. 2002. CYP2D6 allele frequency in European Caucasians, Asians, Africans and their descendants. *Pharmacogenomics* 3:229–43.

Callaway, J.C., and C. Grob. 1998. Ayahuasca preparations and serotonin reuptake inhibitors: A potential combination for severe adverse interactions. *Journal of Psychoactive Drugs* 30:367–9.

Callaway, J.C., C.S. Grob, D.J. McKenna, D.E. Nichols, A. Shulgin, and K.W. Tupper. 2006. A demand for clarity regarding a case report on the ingestion of 5-methoxy-N,N-dimethyltryptamine (5-MeO-DMT) in an Ayahuasca preparation. *Journal of Analytical Toxicology* 30:406–7.

Caspi, A., T.E. Moffitt, M. Cannon, J. McClay, R. Murray, H. Harrington, A. Taylor, L. Arseneault, B. Williams, A. Braithwaite, R. Poulton, and I.W. Craig. 2005. Moderation of the effect of adolescent-onset cannabis use on adult psychosis by a functional polymorphism in the catechol-O-methyltransferase gene: Longitudinal evidence of a gene X environment interaction. *Biological Psychiatry* 57: 1117–27.

Cohen, S. 1960. LSD: Side effects and complications. *The Journal of Nervous and Mental Disease* 130:20–40.

De La Torre, R., M. Farre, P.N. Roset, C. Hernandez Lopez, M. Mas, J. Ortuno, E. Menoyo, N. Pizarro, J. Segura, and J. Cami. 2000. Pharmacology of MDMA in humans. *Annals of the New York Academy of Sciences* 914:225–37.

De Vry, J. 1995. 5-HT1A receptor agonists: Recent developments and controversial issues. *Psychopharmacology* 121:1–26.

Faillace, L.A., and S. Szara. 1968. Hallucinogenic drugs: Influence of mental set and setting. *Diseases of the Nervous System* 29:124–6.

Farber, N.B., J. Hanslick, C. Kirby, L. McWilliams, and J.W. Olney. 1998. Serotonergic agents that activate 5HT2A receptors prevent NMDA antagonist neurotoxicity. *Neuropsychopharmacology* 18:57–62.

Fink, M., J. Simeon, W. Hague, and T. Itil. 1966. Prolonged adverse reactions to LSD in psychotic subjects. *Archives of General Psychiatry* 15:450–4.

Gamma, A., E. Frei, D. Lehmann, R.D. Pascual-Marqui, D. Hell, and F.X. Vollenweider. 2000. Mood state and brain electric activity in ecstasy users. *Neuroreport* 11: 157–62.

Gardner, D.M., K.I. Shulman, S.E. Walker, and S.A. Tailor. 1996. The making of a user-friendly MAOI diet. *Journal of Clinical Psychiatry* 57:99–104.

Gasser, P. 1994. Psycholytic therapy with MDMA and LSD in Switzerland. *MAPS Newsletter* 5:3–7.

Gewirtz, J.C., A.C. Chen, R. Terwilliger, R.C. Duman, and G.J. Marek. 2002. Modulation of DOI-induced increases in cortical BDNF expression by group II mGlu receptors. *Pharmacology Biochemistry and Behavior* 73 (2):317–26.

Gill, J.R., J.A. Hayes, I.S. deSouza, E. Marker, and M. Stajic. 2002. Ecstasy (MDMA) deaths in New York City: A case series and review of the literature. *Journal of Forensic Sciences* 47:121–6.

Gore, S.M. 1999. Fatal uncertainty: Death-rate from use of ecstasy or heroin. *Lancet* 354:1265–6.

Green, A.R., A.J. Cross, and G.M. Goodwin. 1995. Review of the pharmacology and clinical pharmacology of 3,4-methylenedioxymethamphetamine (MDMA or "Ecstasy"). *Psychopharmacology* 119:247–60.

Greer, G.R., and R.A. Tolbert. 1986. Subjective reports of the effects of MDMA in a clinical setting. *Journal of Psychoactive Drugs* 18:319–27.

Greer, G.R., and R.A. Tolbert. 1998. A method of conducting therapeutic sessions with MDMA. *Journal of Psychoactive Drugs* 30:371–9.

Griffiths, R.R., W.A. Richards, U. McCann, and R. Jesse. 2006. Psilocybin can occasion mystical-type experiences having substantial and sustained personal meaning and spiritual significance. *Psychopharmacology* 187:268–83.

Grob, C.S. 2002a. *Hallucinogens: A reader*. New York, NY: Tarcher/Putnam.

Grob, C.S. 2002b. The politics of Ecstasy. *Journal of Psychoactive Drugs* 34:143–4.

Grob, C.S., D.J. McKenna, J.C. Callaway, G.S. Brito, E.S. Neves, G. Oberlaender, O.L. Saide, E. Labigalini, C. Tacla, C.T. Miranda, R.J. Strassman, and K.B. Boone. 1996. Human psychopharmacology of hoasca, a plant hallucinogen used in ritual context in Brazil. *The Journal of Nervous and Mental Disease* 184:86–94.

Grob, C.S., R.E. Poland, L. Chang, and T. Ernst. 1996. Psychobiologic effects of 3,4-methylenedioxymethamphetamine in humans: Methodological considerations and preliminary observations. *Behavior Brain Research* 73:103–7.

Halpern, J.H., and H.G. Pope, Jr. 2003. Hallucinogen persisting perception disorder: What do we know after 50 years? *Drug and Alcohol Dependence* 69:109–19.

Henquet, C., A. Rosa, L. Krabbendam, S. Papiol, L. Fananas, M. Drukker, J.G. Ramaekers, and J. van Os. 2006. An experimental study of catechol-O-methyltransferase Val(158)Met moderation of delta-9-tetrahydrocannabinol-induced effects on psychosis and cognition. *Neuropsychopharmacology* [Epub ahead of print].

Henry, J.A., and J.G. Rella. 2001. Medical risks associated with MDMA use. In *Ecstasy: A complete guide,* ed. J. Holland, 71–86. Rochester, VT: Inner Traditions.

Isbell, H., R.E. Belleville, H.F. Fraser, A. Wikler, and C.R. Logan. 1956. Studies on lysergic acid diethylamide (LSD-25): I. Effects in former morphine addicts and development of tolerance during chronic intoxication. *Archives of Neurology and Psychiatry* 76:468–78.

Isbister, G.K., and N.A. Buckley. 2005. The pathophysiology of serotonin toxicity in animals and humans: Implications for diagnosis and treatment. *Clinical Neuropharmacology* 28:205–14.

Jennings, P. 2003. *World News Tonight,* ABC, September 8.

Kalant, H. 2001. The pharmacology and toxicology of "ecstasy" (MDMA) and related drugs. *Canadian Medical Association Journal* 165:917–28.

Klock, J.C., U. Boerner, and C.E. Becker. 1974. Coma, hyperthermia and bleeding associated with massive LSD overdose. A report of eight cases. *The Western Journal of Medicine* 120:183–8.

Kovacic, B., and E.F. Domino. 1976. Tolerance and limited cross-tolerance to the effects of N,N-dimethyltryptamine (DMT) and lysergic acid diethylamide-25 (LSD) on food-rewarded bar pressing in the rat. *Journal of Pharmacology and Experimental Therapeutics* 197:495–502.

Kumar, M.J., and J.K. Andersen. 2004. Perspectives on MAO-B in aging and neurological disease: Where do we go from here? *Molecular Neurobiology* 30: 77–89.

Liechti, M.E., and F.X. Vollenweider. 2000. Acute psychological and physiological effects of MDMA ("Ecstasy") after haloperidol pretreatment in healthy humans. *European Neuropsychopharmacology: The Journal of the European College of Neuropsychopharmacology* 10:289–95.

Liechti, M.E., A. Gamma, and F.X. Vollenweider. 2001. Gender differences in the subjective effects of MDMA. *Psychopharmacology* 154:161–8.

Luna, L.E., and P. Amaringo. 1999. *Ayahuasca visions: The iconography of a Peruvian Shaman.* Berkeley, CA: North Atlantic Books.

McGlothlin, W.H., and D.O. Arnold. 1971. LSD revisited. A ten-year follow-up of medical LSD use. *Archives of General Psychiatry* 24:35–49.

McKenna, D.J., J.C. Callaway, and C.S. Grob. 1998. The scientific investigation of ayahuasca: A review of past and current research. *The Heffter Review of Psychedelic Research* 1:65–76.

Miller, D.B., and J.P. O'Callaghan. 1996. Neurotoxicity of d-amphetamine in the C57BL/6J and CD-1 mouse. Interactions with stress and the adrenal system. *Annals of the New York Academy of Sciences* 801:148–67.

Muneer, R.S. 1978. Effects of LSD on human chromosomes. *Mutation Research* 51: 403–10.

Pahnke, W. 1963. Drugs and mysticism: An analysis of the relationship between psychedelic drugs and the mystical consciousness. PhD thesis, Harvard University.

Ricaurte, G.A., J. Yuan, G. Hatzidimitriou, B.J. Cord, and U.D. McCann. 2002. Severe dopaminergic neurotoxicity in primates after a common recreational dose regimen of MDMA ("Ecstasy"). *Science* 297:2260–3. (Retracted article.)

Santos, R., and E.A. Carlini. 1983. Serotonin receptor activation in rats previously deprived of REM sleep. *Pharmacology, Biochemistry, and Behavior* 18:501–7.

Savage, C., J. Fadiman, R. Mogar, and M.H. Allen. 1966. The effects of psychedelic (LSD) therapy on values, personality, and behavior. *International Journal of Neuropsychiatry* 2:241–54.

Seiden, L.S., and K.E. Sabol. 1996. Methamphetamine and methylenedioxymethamphetamine neurotoxicity: Possible mechanisms of cell destruction. *NIDA Research Monograph* 163:251–76.

Settle, E.C., Jr. 1998. Antidepressant drugs: Disturbing and potentially dangerous adverse effects. *Journal of Clinical Psychiatry* 59 (Suppl. 16):25–30; discussion 40–42.

Shanon, B. 2002. *Antipodes of the mind: Charting the phenomenology of the ayahuasca experience.* New York, NY: Oxford University Press.

Sklerov, J., B. Levine, K.A. Moore, T. King, and D. Fowler. 2005. A fatal intoxication following the ingestion of 5-methoxy-N,N-dimethyltryptamine in an ayahuasca preparation. *Journal of Analytical Toxicology* 29:838–41.

Strassman, R.J. 1995. Hallucinogenic drugs in psychiatric research and treatment. Perspectives and prospects. *The Journal of Nervous and Mental Disease* 183: 127–38.

Strassman, R.J. 2000. *DMT: The spirit molecule. A doctor's revolutionary research into the biology of near-death and mystical experiences.* Rochester, VT: Park Street Press.

Substance Abuse and Mental Health Services Administration. 2005. *Results from the 2004 National Survey on Drug Use and Health: National Findings* (Office of Applied Studies, NSDUH Series H-28, DHHS Publication No. SMA 05-4062). Rockville, MD: SAMHSA.

Suzuki, O., Y. Katsumata, and M. Oya. 1981. Characterization of eight biogenic indoleamines as substrates for type A and type B monoamine oxidase. *Biochemical Pharmacology* 30:1353–8.

Tanaka, E. 1998. In vivo age-related changes in hepatic drug-oxidizing capacity in humans. *Journal of Clinical Pharmacy and Therapeutics* 23:247–55.

Vollenweider, F.X., A. Gamma, M. Liechti, and T. Huber. 1999. Is a single dose of MDMA harmless? *Neuropsychopharmacology* 21:598–600.

von Mandach, U. 2005. Drug use in pregnancy. *Therapeutische Umschau: Revue Thérapeutique* 62:29–35.

Walsh, R., and F. Vaughan. 1993. *Paths beyond ego.* New York, NY: Tarcher/Putnam.

Yanai, K., T. Ido, K. Ishiwata, J. Hatazawa, T. Takahashi, R. Iwata, and T. Matsuzawa. 1986. In vivo kinetics and displacement study of a carbon-11-labeled hallucinogen, N,N-[11C]dimethyltryptamine. *European Journal of Nuclear Medicine* 12:141–6.

Yasuhara, H. 1974. Studies on monoamine oxidase (report XXIV). Effect of harmine on monoamine oxidase. *Japanese Journal of Pharmacology* 24:523–33.

Yi, H., S.J. Donohue, D.C. Klein, and O.W. McBride. 1993. Localization of the hydroxyindole-O-methyltransferase gene to the pseudoautosomal region: Implications for mapping of psychiatric disorders. *Human Molecular Genetics* 2: 127–31.

Yu, A.M., J.R. Idle, T. Herraiz, A. Kupfer, and F.J. Gonzalez. 2003. Screening for endogenous substrates reveals that CYP2D6 is a 5-methoxyindolethylamine O-demethylase. *Pharmacogenetics* 13:307–19.

Zarate, C.A., Jr, J.B. Singh, P.J. Carlson, N.E. Brutsche, R. Ameli, D.A. Luckenbaugh, D.S. Charney, and H.K. Manji. 2006. A randomized trial of an N-methyl-D-aspartate antagonist in treatment-resistant major depression. *Archives of General Psychiatry* 63:856–64.

PART II

MEDICAL APPLICATIONS

5

RESPONSE OF CLUSTER HEADACHE TO PSILOCYBIN AND LSD

R. ANDREW SEWELL AND JOHN H. HALPERN

Disorders of pain are arguably the most interesting of the CNS (central nervous system) diseases, spanning the divide between neurology and psychiatry, and of the pain disorders, the trigeminal autonomic cephalgia known as "cluster headache" is the most fascinating. By understanding cluster headache, one understands the circadian rhythm; by understanding *both,* one understands dreams, mania, and depression—half of psychiatry—as well as the sympathetic and parasympathetic nervous system—half of neurology! Although the use of psychedelics to treat psychiatric disorders has been well described (Grinspoon and Bakalar 1981; Halpern 1996), accumulating evidence suggests that cluster headache may be the first purely neurological disorder to respond to psilocybin and LSD (lysergic acid diethylamide).

WHAT IS A CLUSTER HEADACHE?

Although fragmentary descriptions of cluster headache were written prior to 1745, the earliest and most complete description comes from Gerhard van Sweiten, one of the most prominent medical men of his day, who wrote in that year:

A healthy, robust man of middle age [was suffering from] troublesome pain which came on every day at the same hour at the same spot above the orbit of the left eye, where the nerve emerges from the opening of the frontal bone; after a short time, the left eye began to redden and to overflow with tears; then he felt as if his eye was slowly forced out of its orbit with so much pain that he nearly went mad. After a few hours, all these evils ceased, and nothing in the eye appeared at all changed. (Isler 1993)

The headache pain is one-sided, almost always on the same side, but it can switch sides from cluster period to period. Unlike migraine pain, which is described as dull and throbbing, the cluster headache pain is sharp, steady, and intense. It has been compared with having a lighted cigarette held to the side of one's face and as "giving birth through the eye socket." Men who have experienced both kidney stones and cluster headache rate the cluster attacks more painful. Women with cluster headache who have given birth without anaesthesia rate the pain of a cluster attack as being worse (Leone 2004). While migraineurs generally feel better lying down in a dark room, cluster headache patients are restless and agitated, and compelled to pace around, press their temples, and sometimes even bang their heads on walls and doors (Blau 1993). The best way to appreciate the pain of a cluster attack is to see someone suffering from one. One such attack is available for viewing over the Internet (Ott 2005).

But the most striking feature of cluster headaches—and the one missed by van Sweiten—is their periodicity, which is their cardinal feature. At peak, there can be between one and eight attacks a day, usually at the same times each day and—most predictably—about 90 minutes after going to sleep, as attacks have been shown to be associated with the onset of REM (rapid eye movement) sleep. These nocturnal attacks frequently lead to sleep deprivation, or "sleep fear" (Dodick et al. 2000). The first cluster period usually lasts four to eight weeks and recurs thereafter once or twice a year. This pattern does vary but is strikingly consistent for any given patient. Figure 5.1 shows the headache diary of a patient who has cluster periods every two years that each last almost exactly 50 days, and illustrates several features of a typical cluster period. The attacks occur at almost exactly the same time every day—around noon; they start as mild, build slowly to a point at which sufferers often consider suicide, and then die away. This is characteristic of *episodic* cluster headache, but 10% of cluster headache patients have the *chronic* form, which has no remission period. The attacks are ever present. If these patients are treatment nonresponders, they frequently kill themselves; this has led to the informal term "suicide headache" for this disorder (Horton 1961).

Causes of Cluster Headaches

What causes cluster headache? Opinion was evenly divided as to whether it was a central disorder or a peripheral disorder of the trigeminal nerve until functional imaging performed during an actual cluster attack demonstrated

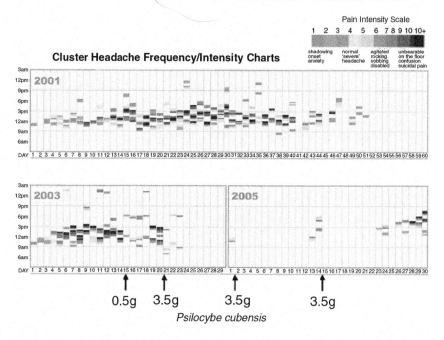

Figure 5.1   Cluster attack diary, case no. 47. The 2001 cluster period is medication-free. Effects of psilocybin administration are evident in 2003 and 2005.

conclusively that such attacks were correlated with an abnormal activation of the posterior hypothalamus (May et al. 1998). Migraine, by contrast, is associated with abnormal activation in the brainstem (Weiller et al. 1995). Other clues to hypothalamic etiology are the abnormal levels and timing of a variety of neuroendocrine hormones such as cortisol, prolactin, adrenocorticotropic hormone, and growth hormone seen in these patients (Leone and Bussone 1993), and that—unlike migraine, which is often keyed to the menstrual cycle—cluster headache follows a clear circadian rhythm (the suprachiasmatic nucleus, which regulates the circadian rhythm, is in the hypothalamus). Abnormal hypothalamic activation then does two things. First, it activates the trigeminal nerve, causing pain in a trigeminal distribution, although why the pain is so intense is not clear. Second, it causes sympathetic dysfunction in the form of a drooping eyelid and constricted pupil (Horner's syndrome), and parasympathetic overactivity that is responsible for the runny eye and stuffy nose that accompany most attacks.

The exact cause of the pain in cluster headache remains obscure. Although the central hypothalamic dysfunction that underlies the disorder has been conclusively demonstrated through positron emission tomography (May et al. 1998), the sharp "boring," penetrating nature of cluster pain is at odds with the dull burning usually described with central pain and points more to a peripheral origin. Nevertheless, hypothalamic dysfunction is behind the circadian abnormalities described in cluster headache patients (Leone et al. 1995; Strittmatter et al. 1997) and the striking periodicity shown in the waxing and waning of symptoms. Cluster headaches can be triggered by the administration of mCPP (meta-chlorophenylpiperazine), which affects the serotonin 1_A and 2 receptors, suggesting sensitivity at those receptors (Leone et al. 1997). A down-regulation of serotonin 2_C receptors in the paraventricular hypothalamic nuclei also leads to a blunted cortisol response to mCPP administration that is characteristic of cluster headache sufferers (Bagdy and Makara 1995).

Cluster headache predominantly affects young men in their twenties, but it can start at any age. The male-to-female ratio is 6:1, although a small spike in incidence around menopause decreases that ratio in older cohorts. Unlike migraine, it does not seem to be strongly genetic, although rarely it can run in families. A prior head injury doubles the odds of developing cluster headache, but there do not seem to be any other predisposing factors (Granella and Cooperative Study Group on the Epidemiology of Cluster Headache 1999), and the disorder otherwise develops apparently randomly in 0.1% of the population.

TREATMENT OF CLUSTER HEADACHE

Of the many available treatments, all have drawbacks. Treatments fall into two classes: *acute,* to treat an individual attack, and *prophylactic,* to prevent attacks during a cluster period. Oxygen will reliably stop an attack in 70% of patients, but the impracticality of carrying around a heavy oxygen tank often incapacitates such patients and keeps them at home for months. Triptans such as sumatriptan are extremely effective—close to 90% effective in some studies. Unfortunately, insurance generally covers only a handful of injections a month, not the required several a day, and the too frequent use of triptans can have cardiac complications (Welch et al. 2000). Prednisone works well, but chronic use can result in immunosuppression, osteoporosis, cataracts, and psychosis, and cluster attacks frequently recur when prednisone is discontinued.

Of prophylactic medications, verapamil is somewhat effective in decreasing the frequency and intensity of attacks, but it rarely leads to complete relief (Leone et al. 2000). Lithium has a narrow therapeutic window and can cause kidney and thyroid damage. Methysergide has an unpredictable propensity to cause retroperitoneal fibrosis, a massive overgrowth of scar tissue that chokes internal organs (Graham et al. 1966). Ergotamine is contraindicated in the presence of many heart conditions, and almost everyone will develop a heart condition if they live long enough. About 10% of patients are treatment resistant and do not respond to any medications. For these, there are surgical solutions. Pioneered in Italy, hypothalamic deep brain stimulation, which involves implanting an electrode deep within the hypothalamus, can reliably stop cluster headaches (Leone et al. 2006). Other surgical solutions, which destroy the trigeminal nerve peripherally, usually stop the pain temporarily, but because the disorder has a central rather than a peripheral etiology, the cluster attacks sometimes return on the other side of the head.

The Discovery of Psychedelic Treatment for Cluster Headache

The response of cluster headache to psilocybin and LSD was discovered serendipitously in 1995 by one patient, Craig Adams.[1]

PATIENT ZERO

A 34-year-old Scottish man with no other medical conditions, except for infectious mononucleosis at age 24, had his first onset of episodic cluster headache at the age of 16. Attacks occurred regularly every seven months; they consisted of one month of four to six left orbital attacks a day that lasted from 30 minutes to three hours and were precipitated by alcohol and stress. At worst, he rated the pain of the attacks as being 10 out of 10 in intensity, and they occurred almost continually for five days in the third week of each cluster period. He was prescribed the histamine receptor blocker pizotifen, which was ineffective. In January 1993, at the age of 22, he took LSD recreationally and was surprised when his anticipated February attack did not occur. Over the next two years, he took LSD three or four times and missed the next four consecutive clusters. In April 1995, at age 24, following a 12-month abstinence from LSD, he experienced another attack and was prescribed propanolol and amitriptyline, both of which were ineffective. Suspecting that his use of a psychedelic had prevented his cluster periods from recurring, the following October, he ingested *Psilocybe* mushrooms and did not experience his anticipated November cluster. After that, until December 1996, he consumed 10 to 12 fresh "Liberty Cap" mushrooms every three months—about a quarter of the usual recreational dose required for psychedelic effects. He did not suffer any attacks until he discontinued his use of the mushrooms to test whether there was a correlation between their use and the absence of cluster periods. In January 1998, his next cluster period began, and he was again prescribed propanolol, which mitigated some of his attacks but which he was unable to tolerate because of slowed heart rate. His first post to the Internet on this subject was on July 28, 1998, and from then on, he ingested psilocybin every six months and has since been almost pain-free on this regimen, with two exceptions. The first was in 2001 when he took a smaller than usual dose after he had destroyed his supply because he feared being discovered by the police. This resulted in a seven-day cluster period. He was prescribed oxygen, but the episode ended before his insurance approved this treatment. Another episode occurred in April 2003 when he deliberately took a smaller dose as an experiment and again suffered a week of attacks that he then aborted with a second dose of psilocybin.

The 38th person to try the psilocybin treatment on the basis of Mr. Adam's recommendations was Bob Wold, a Midwesterner with treatment-resistant cluster headache. Although reluctant to ingest psilocybin, his only alternatives at that point were either gamma knife or microvascular decompression, so Mr. Wold took several doses of psilocybin and was amazed to find that his cluster attacks stopped, thus obviating the need for further medication or brain surgery. Furious that his doctors had not told him about psilocybin as a possible treatment for cluster headache, in 2001, he formed a group called the "Clusterbusters," which is dedicated to publicizing the psilocybin treatment of cluster headache and bringing it to the attention of mainstream medicine. After having gathered a hundred or so cases, he approached our research group at McLean Hospital, which is part of Harvard Medical School. We were skeptical but interested, as we would be in any potential cure for an uncommon disease.

SCIENTIFIC STUDY OF THE ANECDOTAL EVIDENCE

Starting with the 120 cases provided to us by the Clusterbusters, we added a statement "Do you consent to have Andrew Sewell, M.D. or John Halpern, M.D. of McLean Hospital contact you to ask you questions about your cluster headache?" to an already existing online questionnaire on cluster headache (Clusterbusters 2006). This drew another 242 people whom we could guarantee were not psilocybin enthusiasts associated with the Clusterbusters. A further 21 subjects heard of our interest in cluster headache on Internet forums and independently contacted us to ask to participate. Of this total, 197 consented to take part in the study; of these, 78 had taken psychedelics. Our final step was to obtain medical records to verify that subjects were who they said they were, and that they had done what they said they had done. *How many cluster headache patients would be willing to send documented evidence of illegal activity to a faceless authority figure over the Internet merely to help develop a potential cure for their disease?* To our surprise, we had only two refusals. We terminated the study at 50 subjects on the grounds that more cases than that would not necessarily be more convincing; three more medical records arrived subsequent to that, so our final analysis contained 53 subjects.

Quantitative Results

The demographic indices and cluster headache features of the 53 qualifying participants are summarized in Table 5.1. They are typical for cluster headache patients, with the exception of the number of attacks per day, which is high,[2] and the proportion of women, which likely reflects the greater presence of women on Internet support forums. We did not find any statistically significant differences between men and women with regard to any of the demographic indices or headache features.

Table 5.1   Cluster Headache Characteristics by Gender and Subtype

Cluster headache subtype	n	Age, mean (SD)	Attack length, minutes (SD)	Attacks/day at peak, n (SD)	Cluster period length, weeks (SD)	Remission period length, weeks (SD)
Episodic						
Men	26	45 (8)	97 (66)	5.5 (3.7)	13 (10)	11 (10)
Women	6	45 (11)	66 (34)	6.2 (3.0)	15 (10)	9 (5)
Total	32	45 (8)	91 (60)	5.6 (3.5)	13 (10)	11 (9)
1° chronic						
Men	6	48 (8)	79 (57)	9.8 (7.4)	N/A	N/A
Women	1	38 (N/A)	90 (N/A)	8.0 (N/A)		
Total	7	47 (8)	81 (53)	9.6 (6.8)		
2° chronic						
Men	10	45 (6)	105 (70)	6.9 (3.0)	N/A	N/A
Women	4	46 (10)	139 (64)	7.5 (1.0)		
Total	14	45 (7)	115 (68)	7.1 (2.5)		

SD refers to standard deviation. *1° chronic* refers to cluster headache subjects who have had the chronic subtype since the disorder started; *2° chronic* refers to subjects who initially had episodic cluster headache but transformed into the chronic form; *N/A* means not applicable as standard deviation cannot be calculated from an "*n*" of 1, and chronic cluster headache has neither cluster periods nor remission periods.

We were interested in effects in three categories. First, as an abortive: how did LSD or psilocybin, taken sublingually in what is called the "SPUT" method—*s*mall *p*iece *u*nder the *t*ongue—measure up to oxygen or triptans? Second, how effective were they as preventive medications? We defined "effective" as being a total cessation of all cluster attacks. Most trials of prophylactic medication define "effective" as a greater than 50% reduction in the number of cluster attacks, but in our study, even one subsequent attack was enough for us to reclassify the medication as "partially effective," thus artificially depressing the efficacy rates recorded for conventional medications. Third, remission extension: what happened when subjects took LSD or psilocybin a month before their cluster period was about to begin?

DOSING SCHEDULE

The dosing schedule varied considerably from subject to subject, but most adhered to the following guidelines that were determined empirically by Cluster-busters members to increase the likelihood of headache remission. Subjects discontinued all of their prophylactic and abortive medications for at least five

Table 5.2   Effects on Therapeutic Effect Noted when Combining Psilocybin and Other Medications

Blocks psilocybin effect	May block effect	Does not block effect
Triptans	Benzodiazepines	Albuterol
Ergotamine	Bupropion	Antibiotics
Dihydroergotamine	Gabapentin	Aspirin
Methysergide	5-Hydroxytryptophan	Dimenhydrinate
Prednisone	Ketanserin	Insulin
	Kudzu	Meclizine
	Levothyroxine	NSAIDs
	Lithium	Omeprazole (PPIs)
	Melatonin	Ranitidine (H2-blockers)
	Mianserin	
	Ondansetron	
	Opioids	
	Polygala tenuifolia	
	Prochlorperazine	
	Selective serotonin reuptake inhibitors	
	Topiramate	
	Verapamil	

days prior to treatment. Several found this impossible and devised a way to replace their abortive medications by ingesting small amounts of psilocybin in the form of brewed mushroom tea or as a small piece of mushroom. After the five days, subjects consumed either mushroom tea or dried or fresh mushrooms according to one of two basic dosing schedules: 1) three 0.5 g subpsychedelic doses of dried mushrooms, spread over one day, and the same split-dose regimen repeated five days later; a higher dose used only if this was ineffective; or 2) one to three equal doses of 1.0 to 1.5 g dried mushrooms taken in single sessions separated by five-day intervals; patients determined their total number of doses by the effects on their headaches. If the subject was apprehensive about using a compound with psychedelic properties, the initial dose was sometimes smaller than that recommended by Clusterbusters, but if the subject was not, it was larger. Subsequent doses were sometimes increased if the subject felt the initial dose was too low, or decreased if the first dose was effective but the headaches did not completely remit. Occasionally, an interval of increased frequency and intensity of attacks appeared two days following psilocybin administration, and against Clusterbusters' recommendations, some subjects took a second smaller dose. Those who did not wait five days between doses often required more doses to end the cluster period. Medications that have been empirically determined to interact with the psilocybin treatment are listed in Table 5.2, but no pharmacological assays or clinical trials have been conducted to verify these reported interactions.

Table 5.3   Reported Efficacy of Several Treatments for Cluster Attacks, Cluster Periods, and Remission Extension

Medication	Effective, n (%)	Partially effective, n (%)	Ineffective/ intolerable, n (%)	Total, N
Abortive				
Oxygen	24 (51%)	19 (40%)	4 (9%)	47
Triptans	33 (73%)	8 (18%)	4 (9%)	45
Psilocybin	22 (85%)	0 (0%)	4 (15%)	26
LSD	1 (50%)	0 (0%)	1 (50%)	2
Prophylactic				
Propanolol	0 (0%)	2 (9%)	20 (91%)	22
Lithium	1 (5%)	8 (40%)	11 (55%)	20
Amitriptyline	0 (0%)	4 (16%)	21 (84%)	25
Verapamil	2 (5%)	22 (58%)	14 (37%)	38
Prednisone	15 (43%)	5 (14%)	15 (43%)	35
Psilocybin	25 (54%)	18 (39%)	3 (7%)	46
LSD	7 (88%)	0 (0%)	1 (12%)	8
Remission extension				
Psilocybin	20 (91%)	0 (0%)	2 (9%)	22 (31)
LSD	4 (80%)	0 (0%)	1 (20%)	5 (7)

Nine additional subjects had taken psilocybin and two additional had taken LSD purposefully for remission extension but were not yet due for another cluster period at the time of our evaluation; hence, for them, efficacy could not be scored (Sewell et al. 2006)

REPORTED RESPONSE RATES

The participants reported high rates of response to psilocybin and LSD, both for the acute treatment of headaches and for the prophylaxis of clusters; response rates that equaled or were better than their reported response rates to conventional medications (Table 5.3). Note also that prophylaxis with conventional medications involves taking the medication daily at the onset of a cluster period, whereas prophylaxis with psilocybin or LSD typically requires taking only a single dose of LSD or several doses of psilocybin at the onset of a cluster period, rather than daily dosing.

Twenty-four (45%) of the 53 participants had taken one or more doses of psilocybin or LSD during a symptom-free interval between clusters in an attempt to prevent the onset of an anticipated cluster. Of these 24 individuals, 22 (92%) reported that psilocybin or LSD had apparently prevented an anticipated cluster. We classified this novel property as "remission extension."

Chronic cluster patients who used psilocybin experienced varied remission periods ranging from 24 hours to eight months, and some no longer met the criteria for *chronic* cluster headache. Of two chronic participants who tried LSD, one experienced 10 pain-free days, which he described as "miraculous," and the other was free of pain for two months.

Of the 52 participants who used psilocybin for acute, prophylactic, or remission extension treatment, 22 (42%) reported that they achieved therapeutic responses with subpsychedelic doses that produced at most a mild sense of altered state of consciousness and brighter colors. Of the nine who used LSD, two (22%) reported benefit from a subpsychedelic dose. It is not possible to estimate the milligrams of psilocybin ingested, since participants used primarily dried *Psilocybe cubensis* mushrooms of varied sizes, and mushrooms vary widely in potency (Bigwood and Beug 1982), as does LSD.

As a result of taking either psilocybin or LSD, 34 (64%) of the participants currently report that they no longer take prophylactic or abortive medications of any kind. Seven (13%) still take conventional medications in addition to psilocybin or LSD; of these, five (10%) still require occasional standard abortive medication but no longer take prophylactic medication (two are in the process of re-dosing with psilocybin), and two (4%) remain on verapamil. Twelve (23%) no longer take psilocybin or LSD; of these, four (8%) cite an incomplete response to psilocybin, one (2%) reports it ineffective, four (8%) report that they are unable to obtain further supplies of psilocybin or LSD, two (4%)—both with chronic cluster headache—are unwilling to take psilocybin as often as is necessary for complete relief, and one (2%) has discontinued use, citing concerns about being arrested. Eleven of these 12 have resumed conventional medications, and one reports partial efficacy with kudzu plus LSA (lysergic acid amide) obtained from Hawaiian baby woodrose seeds (*Argyreia nervosa*). None discontinued use of psilocybin or LSD because of intolerable side effects. Most found psilocybin or LSD to be more effective than conventional medications.

Representative Case Reports

The typical characteristics of these cases of self-treatment are illustrated in the following case studies, which show the lack of response to conventional medications and the powerful personal relief afforded by these treatments.

CASE 5

Bob Wold, the founder of Clusterbusters, is a 51-year-old man without other medical conditions who has, since age 25, suffered from episodic cluster headaches that occur for six or seven months out of the year, usually from late fall to early summer, with four or five months of respite between each cluster. At worst, attacks occur 12 times a day and last 45 minutes each. Attacks are usually left-sided, consisting of a sudden-onset sharp, searing pain that quickly builds to a maximum and is associated with unilateral nasal congestion and rhinorrhea. In the early 1990s, his cluster headache became chronic for five years, but eventually reverted to being episodic, which it now remains. Trials of propanolol and amitriptyline were ineffective, and the combination of lithium and verapamil proved only partially effective for prophylaxis. Triptans aborted individual attacks, but Mr. Wold was limited with respect to how often he could use them. Oxygen, which he used first during his chronic stage, aborted every attack within 15 minutes but ceased to work after nine months. Over the years, he completed 65 other medication trials without success.[3] With equally disappointing results, he also tried various alternative medical procedures (acupuncture, biofeedback, chiropractic, cold showers, hot showers, feverfew, and massage therapy). In 2001, he ingested two 2 g doses of psilocybin-containing mushrooms and was amazed to find that he was pain-free for 12 hours (an interval during which he usually experienced six attacks). The following day, he took another 2 g dose and again experienced 12 pain-free hours. Then, over several weeks, he gradually discontinued all of his medications (about 15, at that time) and then took a third dose—this time, 1.5 g of dried *Psilocybe*. This immediately ended his cluster period four months early. He attributes this increase in effectiveness of the *Psilocybe* to his discontinuation of his other medications. In subsequent cluster periods, one dose of psilocybin would not only abort an attack but would also offer complete relief for 24 hours, and two or three repeated doses taken five days apart would end the cluster period. He also discovered that taking a dose of psilocybin every three to six months during a remission period prevented a new cluster period from occurring, although cluster periods occasionally began again if he waited for too long. When he aborts a cluster period with psilocybin, after the second dose, he experiences a number of "phantom attacks"—autonomic signs of a cluster attack without the pain—that herald the end of the cluster. In July 2004, a new cluster period began, and he used one perforated square of LSD-coated blotter for the first time, getting slight sensory distortions but nothing more. He found that the single dose terminated the cluster period completely and he has not needed medications since then. He uses cigarettes and alcohol every couple of months and no other recreational drugs.

CASE 25

A 37-year-old man with carpal tunnel syndrome, migraines, hypertension, shoulder tenosynovitis, and C4-5 hemiplegia caused by a swimming pool accident at age 14 has also suffered from episodic cluster headaches since he was 12. They occurred every February and lasted for about one month. The attacks were blinding, frequently nauseating, and at worst, occurred four times a day for 90 minutes each. At age 14, he smoked cannabis for the first time and noticed that it dulled his pain and dispelled his nausea. Subsequently, every February, he began a campaign of aggressive self-medication. At 16, he took approximately 75 mg of LSD for the first time, experiencing only minimal visual distortions—much to his disappointment at the time. For the following three years, as he continued his recreational use of psychedelics, the patient had no cluster headaches. His drug use included cannabis, psilocybin, 3-methylenedioxyamphetamine, 4-bromo-2,5-dimethoxyphenethylamine (2C-B), LSD, and cocaine, on which he became dependent until 1990 when, at age 22, he stopped all substance use. Within two years, his cluster attacks returned, following their usual pattern. He found prednisone and propanolol ineffective, but oxygen, cold air, and triptans were partially effective as abortives. In November 2001, the patient ingested 3 g of *Psilocybe* mushrooms with his wife on their honeymoon—the first psychedelic he had used in 11 years. By March 2002, he realized that he had missed his yearly cluster period. He concluded that the reason for this could only be that he had taken psilocybin, and he realized, in hindsight, that he must have inadvertently been treating his cluster headaches with psilocybin during the attack-free period he had had in his youth. Since then, he has maintained himself with two 2 g psilocybin sessions a year. He finds that, taken during an attack, the psilocybin terminates it, and although he is still prone to occasional attacks during the time of his regular cluster period, the intensity, frequency, and duration are dramatically diminished and controllable with ergotamine and cannabis. He continues to use cannabis daily as well as infrequent LSD and MDMA (3,4-methylenedioxy-methamphetamine).

CASE 27

A 42-year-old man from the Netherlands, with no other medical conditions, was diagnosed with primary chronic cluster headaches at age 34. These occurred as often as six times daily and typically lasted an hour each. He found propanolol ineffective and verapamil effective in treating his attacks, but after six months, the verapamil ceased to work. His attacks could be aborted with oxygen if administered immediately, although he noted that oxygen use increased his attack frequency. He first tried a quarter of a square of LSD-coated blotter paper that was offered to him at age 39, and he was surprised when, for the next 10 days, he experienced only "phantom attacks" without pain. At that point, he switched to psilocybin, because the mushrooms are legal in his country, and he dosed himself with 1.5 g of dried *Psilocybe cubensis* every two weeks for the next six months. He continued to experience one "phantom attack" a day and ultimately stopped taking psilocybin in January 2002 after a "bad trip." He has now been pain-free and off medications for three years, with the exception of two cluster attacks triggered by his emergence from general anaesthesia in September 2004 and March 2005; both were quickly aborted with oxygen. He currently smokes tobacco and, rarely, cannabis, and he drinks coffee. He has not used alcohol since the onset of his cluster headache.

CASE 31

Following a seizure, a 40-year-old South African with a benign pineal cyst was diagnosed with a slow-growing right-hemisphere glioma in 1993. In August 2000, the tumor had reached a size sufficient to prompt a craniotomy and biopsy; this revealed a grade II astrocytoma, and he had 34 sessions of radiation therapy. For 20 months after the end of this therapy, the patient had no problems other than two small areas of post-radiation vasculitis and occasional seizures. On September 9, 2002, he suffered his first cluster attack and was rushed to the emergency room. At first, attacks were bimonthly, but they increased in frequency to weekly and sometimes daily, occurring every day at 10 p.m., so he was diagnosed with chronic cluster headache. With little success, he attempted to control the headaches with pethadrine and omnipon (semisynthetic opiates), pentazocine, prednisone, melatonin, zolmitriptan, and clonazepam, and used oxygen as an abortive. In September 2004, he took a small dose of LSD (likely ~25 mg), but he had his regular evening attack on schedule and unaltered. Seven days later, he took a larger dose and experienced a mild reaction, perceiving more-intense colors and some illusory motion. His cluster attacks ceased abruptly. His headache diary is detailed in Figure 5.2. After three symptom-free months, on December 9, he had another attack, at which point he re-dosed with LSD. This second dose was of comparable strength to the first, but it was not as efficacious, and he continues to suffer attacks approximately once a week; he treats these with oxygen.

CASE 37

This 46-year-old man with restless legs syndrome began to suffer cluster headaches at age eight. He was taken to many doctors and suffered severe disruptions of his schooling owing to his need for frequent hospitalization. His headaches came without warning, were described as being "like a red hot poker being poked through my eye," and were associated with runny nose, drooping eyelid and teary eye on one side, and whole-body perspiration. The pain was overwhelming and rendered him incapable of speaking or doing anything. He often screamed, flailed around, pounded his head with his fists, and banged against anything he could find without regard for his personal safety. He described these episodes as "degrading" and "exhausting"—he was woken two or three times a night by an attack—and distressing for his companions. Until his mid-twenties, his cluster periods were regular—twice a year—and lasted six to eight weeks, but as he grew older, the cluster periods gradually lengthened, and 10 years ago, they became secondary chronic, at which point he had to stop working and was classified as disabled, not leaving his home for months on end. In 1998, he participated in a functional imaging study that demonstrated, for the first time, hypothalamic perfusion changes during a cluster attack (May et al. 1998). He found amitriptyline, propanolol, and lithium ineffective in controlling his headaches. Verapamil was partially effective, and oxygen

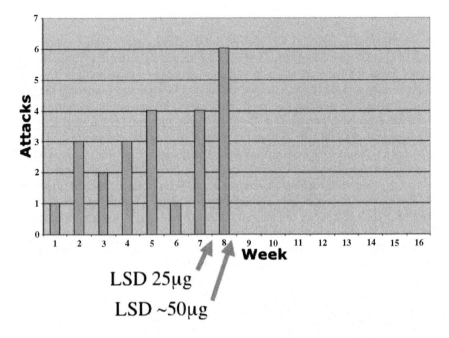

Figure 5.2   Response of chronic cluster headache to LSD (case no. 31). The pain-free period persisted for 12 weeks beyond the second LSD administration, at which point cluster attacks resumed their former pattern.

and sumatriptan worked well as abortives; prednisone was also effective. In November 2004, he took a 2 g dose of psilocybin mushrooms but did not note any change in his headaches. After a second dose a week later, however, his headaches remitted completely and have not returned as of July 2006. He is now able to sleep through the night and is resuming a "normal life" completely without medications. He currently uses tea, coffee, cigarettes, and cannabis daily, but no other drugs except for a subpsychedelic maintenance dose of psilocybin every two or three months.

Discussion

Several limitations of this study should be considered.

1. How do we know that the subjects were, in fact, ingesting LSD and psilocybin?
   The purity of street drugs is notoriously low. One recent analysis of seized Ecstasy
   tablets found that nearly half contained no MDMA at all (Sherlock et al. 1999).
   Two facts argue against such misidentification in this case. First, LSD is the only drug
   that comes in the form of blotter.[4] This is because it is the most potent psychoactive
   recreational drug (other than carfentanyl—a synthetic opioid about 10,000 times more
   potent than morphine). Since a square of blotter paper holds at most a milligram of

substrate, any psychoactive blotter can contain little else but LSD. Second, psilocybin is the drug of choice for most cluster headache patients, who generally are not recreational drug users and do not know where to obtain LSD. Psilocybin spore syringes are readily available over the Internet, however, and since the spores themselves do not contain psilocybin, they are legal to ship and own in 47 of the 50 states. Since subjects grew their own mushrooms from legally available *Psilocybe* spore prints, it is likely that this was what they were ingesting.

2. A second consideration is the possibility of selection bias, in that individuals with a good outcome may have been more likely to participate. When we expanded our analysis to include the 147 additional respondents who failed to provide medical records or declined to be contacted, however, their outcomes were no different from those of the 53 participants who were included in the final analysis (Table 5.4). Although this observation does not exclude the possibility of serious selection bias, it suggests that the 53 participants who met the criteria for inclusion were not substantially different from the respondents who did not. Selection bias could also be present in the 28 cases that were derived from the Clusterbusters group—individuals who might arguably have an interest in exaggerating the efficacy of psilocybin. The other 25 cases were derived from unrelated contacts, however, and from the results of a survey that asked only incidentally about psychedelic use, yet these 25 individuals reported rates of efficacy comparable to the rates reported by the Clusterbusters members. That being said, selection bias can ultimately only be avoided with a carefully controlled trial.

3. Participants were nonblind to their treatment, and that raises the possibility of a placebo response. But cluster headache is known to respond poorly to placebo; controlled trials have shown a placebo response of 0% to prophylactic medications such as verapamil (Leone et al. 2000), capsaicin (Marks et al. 1993), and melatonin (Leone et al. 1996), and less than 20% to abortive medications such as sumatriptan (van Vliet et al. 2003). Thus, it seems unlikely that we would have found more than 50 cases of an apparent response to psilocybin or LSD through placebo effects alone.

4. The findings are subject to recall bias, since the study relies primarily on participants' retrospective reports. Six participants, however, provided detailed headache diaries that corroborated their recall. Two examples of such a diary can be seen in Figures 5.1 and 5.2. In addition, three (6%) of the 53 participants and two additional participants not included in the primary analysis tried psilocybin for the first time after their inclusion in our initial pool of participants; three of these five showed a complete response and two a partial response—a prospective response rate that matches our retrospective findings.

Our observations must be regarded as preliminary in that they are unblinded, uncontrolled, and subject to the additional limitations described. Therefore, our findings likely overestimate the response rate of cluster headache to psilocybin and LSD. On the other hand, it is difficult to dismiss this entire series of cases as an artifact of these limitations; it appears that these drugs, possibly in subpsychedelic doses, may have beneficial effects on cluster headache in some individuals.

To our knowledge, the use of psilocybin or LSD to treat cluster headache specifically has not, up to now, been described in the scientific literature.[5]

Table 5.4   Efficacy of Psilocybin in Ending a Cluster Period in Selected Groups

Efficacy	A (*n*=53)	B (*n*=146)	C (*n*=184)	Total (*n*=383)
Ineffective, *n* (%)	3 (6)	3 (13)	7 (5)	13 (6)
<75%, *n* (%)	6 (11)	2 (8)	16 (12)	24 (11)
>75%, *n* (%)	15 (29)	7 (29)	36 (27)	58 (27)
100%, *n* (%)	25 (48)	10 (42)	66 (49)	101 (48)
Unclear, *n* (%)	4 (8)	2 (8)	10 (7)	16 (8)
Nonuser, *n*	0	122	49	171

Group A, the case study subjects; Group B, those who consented to participate but did not provide medical records; Group C, those who did not consent to participate but either completed the online survey or posted freely about their experiences on public Internet forums.

Frequent references to LSD's effects on headache appear in the psychiatric literature, however. One investigator describes the case of "Mrs. M., age 51. A happily married drama teacher who had complained of severe migraine since age 9.... She had six weekly sessions of LSD in doses of 40 to 90 mcg. Eight months since her last treatment, she has had no more attacks of migraine" (Ling and Buckman 1960). Other writers describe a similar phenomenon (Stevens 1987):

> A number of therapists talked about the serendipitous side effects that they sometimes saw in their patients. They would be in the middle of a post-session interview, perhaps two or three weeks after the original LSD session, and the patient would suddenly say, "Oh, and the headache is gone too." "What headache?" they'd ask. "Why, the headache I've had for ten to fifteen years," would be the answer.

In every case, however, resolution of the headache was attributed to resolution of underlying psychodynamic conflicts. No author before now has suggested that it might be a direct pharmacologic effect of the drug itself.

Clinical observations with LSD in the treatment of other types of pain also suggest that it has effects that may sometimes persist long after acute administration. For example, some patients with phantom limb pain, another central pain syndrome, noted striking improvement when given sub-psychedelic doses of LSD (25–50 mg) daily for three weeks (Fanciullacci 1977). These analgesic effects persisted for weeks and then slowly declined after the LSD was discontinued, suggesting that its benefits extended well beyond the period of acute pharmacologic effect. This effect of LSD on phantom limb pain has been replicated elsewhere (Kuromaru 1962). Early studies with LSD in terminal cancer patients have also described analgesic effects that, in a substantial proportion of patients, last for weeks after acute administration, although investigators did not know to control for the concurrent use of opioids, which may have led to the less consistent results reported (Kast and Collins 1964; Kast 1967;

Pahnke et al. 1969). There are no reports on the use of psilocybin for headaches or for pain in general.

PROPOSED MECHANISMS

If psilocybin and LSD are indeed effective for cluster headache, as our observations suggest, the mechanism of this action remains unclear. Methysergide is almost structurally identical to LSD, and ergotamine is little more than two LSD molecules combined, which is why it is a commonly used precursor in LSD manufacture (Fig. 3). Thus, the idea that these substances have efficacy for headache has a certain "face validity" on structural grounds alone.

Clues to mechanism of action may be found in an examination of the receptor affinities of the two drugs. LSD is a weak partial agonist[6] at the serotonin 2_A receptor, but it has greater affinity for the serotonin 1_A receptor and also binds the serotonin 1_B, 1_D, 2_C, 5_A, 6, and 7 receptors, the dopamine 1 and 2 receptors, and the α_1 and α_2 adrenergic receptors (Nichols 2004). Psilocin—the active metabolite of psilocybin—has an affinity for serotonin 1_A, 2_A, and 2_C comparable to that of LSD (Nichols 2004) and also binds the serotonin 1_D receptor. Methysergide, mianserin, pizotifen, and cyproheptadine—medications all shown effective in the treatment of vascular headache—are serotonin 2_B antagonists (Kalkman 1994) and might also share a mechanism of action with psilocybin and LSD. Antidepressants that are clinically effective in prophylaxis of migraines either

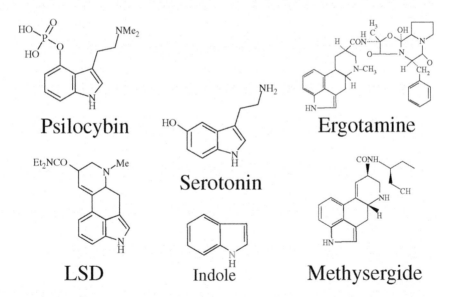

Figure 5.3   Structural homologies between indole, serotonin, and selected anti-cluster headache drugs.

inhibit norepinephrine and serotonin reuptake or, like LSD, can antagonize serotonin 2 receptors (Richelson 1990). In rats with lesions of the hypothalamus, the sympathomimetic effects of LSD-25 are not as pronounced (Sankar 1972), suggesting a possible site of action for the drug there. Triptan medications that abort acute attacks do so by stimulating serotonin 1_B and 1_D receptors in the periaqueductal grey matter of the brainstem (Hargreaves et al. 1999), and since psilocybin and LSD affect the same receptors, that may explain their putative acute abortive effects.

Triptans, like LSD and psilocybin, have a structure based on an indole group. Many nonpsychedelic indole alkaloids that are structurally related to psilocybin and LSD, for example, methysergide, ergotamine, dihydroergotamine, and methylergonovine, can be used as treatments for cluster headache, although they lack the properties of being able to abort a cluster period and extend remission noted with psilocybin and LSD. Thus, it is quite possible that the efficacy of psilocybin and LSD is entirely unrelated to the psychedelic properties of these drugs; in fact, a dissociation between the autonomic and the psychedelic properties of psilocybin has already been described (Fischer and Warshay 1968).

One of the most striking findings in our study was that 22 participants reported taking psilocybin or LSD during a remission period and thereby seemingly averted an anticipated future cluster. We are not aware of any other medication that shows this property. Ergotamine is frequently given as a nocturnal prophylactic, but it does not have therapeutic effects that outlast its presence in the body, and it does not change the timing or frequency of other attacks in the cluster. Yet there is no doubt that LSD is known to have other persisting effects. LSD use can cause long-lasting occipital EEG hypersynchrony (Abraham and Duffy 2001) and hallucinogen persisting perceptual disorder (Halpern and Pope 2003). Binocular rivalry was strikingly affected in one subject 10 hours after dosing with LSD (Carter and Pettigrew 2003) but the effects had disappeared when the subject was retested two months later. Rabbits administered with LSD show an enhancement of conditioned response acquisition (Harvey 1988), which could be a sign of increased synaptic plasticity leading to permanent brain changes. Similarly, psilocybin has been noted to have a potent serotoninergically mediated activity on smooth muscle that appears to be irreversible (Woolley and Campbell 1962).

This prolonged efficacy in terminating cluster periods and extending remission periods is more difficult to explain as a consequence of receptor stimulation or antagonism, which should persist only for the duration of acute pharmacologic effect, or receptor up- or down-regulation, which generally resolves over two weeks to two months. A number of other possibilities present themselves:

1. Disruption of the circadian rhythm through serotonin 1_A, 2_C, or 7 modulation (I. Jerome, pers. comm.).

    Serotonin 2_C receptors may be involved in regulating the circadian response to light (Kennaway et al. 2003), possibly by affecting the melatonin system

(Raghavendra and Kulkarni 2003). Psilocybin, LSD, and all related psychedelics bind to serotonin 2_C receptors sometimes with even greater affinity than they bind to the 2_A receptors that cause hallucinations (Nichols 2004). Animal studies also indicate that drugs that activate serotonin 1_A and 7 receptors can produce significant phase shifts in hamster and rat circadian rhythms (Antle et al. 2003; Sprouse et al. 2004; Duncan et al. 2005; Gannon and Millan 2006), so psilocybin and LSD may interrupt cluster periods through their actions on serotonin 1_A or 7 receptors, or the cascade of chemical changes that follow as well as the genes subsequently expressed. Even if a phase shift in the circadian rhythm is an acute drug effect, it is possible that such an abrupt phase shift can lead to the attenuation of cluster attacks in the same way that crossing time zones while flying in a plane can.

2. Disruption of the circadian rhythm through serotonin 2_A gene induction.

Drugs that activate serotonin 2_A receptors cause the production of several gene products. Even very low doses of LSD induce the expression of seven genes, two of which mediate synaptic plasticity and thus have the potential to mediate permanent long-term changes in the brain (Nichols 2004). Indeed, LSD has been noted to cause an increase in the area of synaptic contacts when given to frogs (Kemali and Kemali 1980). Two genes are expressed early—*c-fos,* which increases twofold in the rat prefrontal cortex and anterior cingulate (Gresch et al. 2002), and *arc,* which increases fivefold. *Arc* protein is specifically localized to dendrites, and is predicted to be involved in cytoskeletal rearrangements during the process of synaptic plasticity (Lyford et al. 1995). Ninety minutes post LSD administration, five other genes are expressed—*sgk* (serum glucocorticoid kinase), $I\kappa\beta\alpha$, *Nor1* (neuron-derived orphan receptor 1), which is still elevated five hours later, *ania3,* and *krox-20,* which is also known as *egr-2* (Nichols and Sanders-Bush 2002) with maximal expression after 90 minutes.These genes have diverse effects. *Ania3* is involved in glutamate signaling. *Krox-20* is a zinc-finger transcription factor gene that is coregulated with *c-fos* and has been shown to be necessary for normal brain development (Seitanidou et al. 1997) and may be involved in the maintenance of long-term potentiation, in other words, permanent brain changes (Inokuchi et al. 1996). *Nor1* is a nuclear receptor of the steroid/thyroid family that was recently discovered to be involved in the brain's response to opiate and cocaine administration (Maruyama et al. 1995).

LSD also induces *egr-1* and *period-1. Egr-1* (early growth response protein 1) encodes another zinc-finger transcription factor that links cellular signaling cascades with changes in gene expression patterns, and numerous biological functions have been attributed to it (Liu et al. 1996). *Egr-1* is up-regulated in the hippocampus by repeated high-frequency neuronal stimulation (Wisden et al. 1990) and learning and memory retrieval (Nicolaev 1992), and it is also activated under painful conditions (Lanteri-Minet et al. 1993). Pain causes synaptic transmission in the CNS to undergo long-lasting changes that alter the brain's perception of future sensory stimuli (Woolf and Salter 2000). Stimuli that cause the activation of *egr-1* also induce long-term strengthening of synapses in the anterior cingulate (Wei et al. 2000), suggesting that *egr-1* has a role in pain-related synaptic potentiation. *Egr-1* knockout mice[7] show reduced pain response behaviors to persistent inflammatory pain (Ko et al. 2005), so LSD could well have a modulatory effect on subjective pain experience through this gene.

Period-1 is a circadian rhythm gene (Cermakian et al. 2001), and it is one of three to five genes that are crucial in maintaining basic cellular rhythms. Unlike the other genes induced by LSD, which show induction in cortical cultures, *period-1* is induced only in intact animals, suggesting that its regulation is mediated by neuronal circuitry. Possibly it is through the modulation of this gene combined with other effects on long-term synaptic plasticity that LSD is able to disrupt a cluster cycle.

Future Directions for Research

These observations suggest several possible directions for further study. The first is a clinical trial of LSD vs. psilocybin for the treatment of cluster headache to avoid the methodological flaws inherent in a case series and thus demonstrate the efficacy of these substances in a more scientifically rigorous manner. The second is an extension of the observational study to include mescaline. The third is a prospective study of LSA made possible by our accumulation of a database of cluster headache patients.

LSD VS. PSILOCYBIN VS. PLACEBO

We plan to submit a protocol for a pilot escalating-dose study of psilocybin vs. LSD vs. "treatment as usual" that, if it demonstrates safety and efficacy, could be used as a springboard to a larger dose–response study. This protocol will require the approval of the Institutional Review Board and the Food and Drug Administration, and the granting of Schedule I research registration for both psilocybin and LSD by the Drug Enforcement Administration.

MESCALINE

There are no anecdotal reports to indicate whether mescaline has any effects on cluster headache. Mescaline shows cross-tolerance with LSD, but not with psilocybin (Isbell et al. 1961; Wolbach et al. 1962), implying that similarities in psychoactive effects are not necessarily caused by identical receptor activity. We propose to work with the Indian Health Service to identify whether or not the 250,000 peyote-using members of the Native American Church have a significantly different incidence of cluster headache from that of nonpeyote-using Native Americans. Although the logistical challenges are formidable, the answer should provide important clues about the mechanism of action of psilocybin and LSD in controlling cluster headache.

LSA

LSA, also known as ergine, is an ergoline alkaloid that, unlike LSD, is found in nature in four plants—three found in the United States (Hawaiian baby woodrose, morning glory, and sleepygrass) and one (*ololiuhqui*) found in

South America. Hawaiian baby woodrose is a perennial climbing vine that was native to the Indian subcontinent but is now present worldwide. Its psychedelic properties were discovered only in the 1960s when socioeconomically disadvantaged people in Hawaii, Haiti, and Puerto Rico consumed the seeds for a cheap "buzz" as an alternative to alcohol. Seven or eight seeds will cause a 4- to 12-hour trip similar to LSD but with diminished visual effects and with severe nausea, flatulence, and vomiting. Morning glory is a dicot climbing vine whose seeds contain LSA; it was originally used by Aztec priests in Mexico to commune with their gods. Other native healers in shamanic healing ceremonies likewise used *ololiuhqui,* and it was the most commonly used psychedelic drug in most of South America. It is still used by the Zapotecs, Chinantecs, Mixtecs, and Mazatecs, who live in the southern mountains of Mexico. In Spanish, it is called *semilla de la virgen,* or "little seeds of the virgin Mary." It was identified as *Rivea corymbosa* in 1941 by Harvard professor Richard Evans Schultes, and the active constituent LSA identified in 1960 by Albert Hofmann (Halpern and Sewell 2005). Sleepygrass (*Achnatherum robustum* or *Stipia robusta*), which grows in the American Southwest, sometimes contains LSA, but there have been no reports of it being used either ritually or recreationally. LSA is categorized in Schedule III, the same class as buprenorphine and anabolic steroids, and not in Schedule I as psilocybin and LSD are.

Only one of the original 383 cluster headache subjects in the study had tried LSA. We successfully contacted 214 of these subjects a year later and found that 18 more had subsequently tried LSA to control their cluster headache. This will enable us to evaluate the effects of LSA prospectively and to address the methodological flaw of retrospective bias that hampered the psilocybin/LSD case series. Better yet, the discrete nature of LSA-containing seeds means that by recording the number of seeds ingested by a particular patient and analyzing seeds from the same batch, it is possible to calculate exactly how much LSA was ingested by the patient, to correlate it with a clinical response, and to construct a dose–response relationship. Data collection for this study is under way.

CONCLUSIONS

Keen observation by individual patients and persistence by a patient group that is otherwise uninterested in psychedelic drugs have brought the previously unsuspected properties of psilocybin and LSA to the attention of medical science. These substances may have efficacy in aborting the acute attacks of cluster headache, terminating cluster periods, and extending remission periods, frequently with sub-psychedelic doses. The latter two properties are not found in any conventional medication. An appropriate evaluation in the form of a randomized, placebo-controlled trial will be necessary to verify these observations. Investigations are in progress.

NOTES

1. Both Craig Adams and Bob Wold have granted permission for us to use their real names.

2. However, only three of the fifty-three subjects endorsed the criterion "More than five attacks more than half the time," suggesting that by asking about attacks "at peak," we generated an artificially inflated value for peak number of attacks. Of the three, one subject had increased frequency only following ingestion of LSD but met criteria for cluster headache prior to that; the other two had average attack frequencies only slightly higher than the "5 per day" cutoff, and typical attack lengths of 75 and 90 minutes, respectively, unresponsive to indomethacin. This is inconsistent with paroxysmal hemicrania, which is characterized by pain similar to that of cluster headache but attacks of shorter length and higher frequency and which would be the most likely alternate diagnosis that would explain the symptoms.

3. These are clonidine, anticonvulsants (phenobarbital, carbamazepine, divalproex, tiagabine, and topiramate), antidepressants (bupropion, doxepin, and fluoxetine), antihistamines (chlorpheniramine, cyproheptadine, hydroxyzine, and IV histamine—which was effective in terminating his cluster period two out of four times), calcium-channel blockers (nicardipine and verapamil), antipsychotics (chlorpromazine and olanzapine), ergot derivatives (dihydroergotamine, ergotamine, methylergonovine, methysergide, and Bellergal, which combines ergotamine, phenobarbital, and belladonna alkaloids), intranasal preparations (capsaicin, prescription cocaine, and lidocaine), muscle relaxants (baclofen, clonazepam, cyclobenzaprine, chlorzoxazone, and tizanidine), nonopioid painkillers (indomethacin, ketorolac, rofecoxib, Excedrin, which combines aspirin, acetamenophen, and caffeine, and Midrin, which combines acetaminophen, isometheptene, and dichloralphenazone), nutritional supplements (calcium, cobalamin, magnesium, melatonin, and riboflavin), opiates (butorphanol, fentanyl patches, hydrocodone, meperidine, methadone, Darvocet, which combines propoxyphene and acetamenophen, and Norgesic, which combines orphenadrine, aspirin, and caffeine), corticosteroids (adrenocorticotrophic hormone injections, beclomethasone, and dexamethasone injections and tablets), and surgery (transcutaneous nerve stimulation unit and tooth extractions); all produced only marginal relief.

4. Since the completion of this study, DOB (2,5-dimethoxy-4-bromoamphetamine) and bromo-dragonfly [1-(8-bromobenzo[1,2-b;4,5-b']difuran-4-yl)-2-aminopropane] have appeared in blotter form, but these are rare and can be readily distinguished from LSD by their effects.

5. In 1963, Sicuteri treated 390 headache patients, including 25 cluster headache patients, with a variety of lysergic acid derivatives, and reported that LSD in subhallucinogenic doses prevented migraine successfully but not as effectively as methysergide (Sicuteri 1963). He did not specifically describe the effects of LSD on the cluster headache subgroup, however, or assess cluster period termination or prophylaxis. More recently, Russo (1997) is investigating hallucinogenic botanicals at sub-psychedelic doses as a treatment for migraine.

6. A "partial agonist" refers to a drug that partially activates a receptor, but not as much as a neurotransmitter, and will actually block the receptor in the presence of enough neurotransmitter.

7. Mice that are genetically engineered to lack the *egr-1* gene.

REFERENCES

Abraham, H.D., and F.H. Duffy. 2001. EEG coherence in post-LSD visual hallucinations. *Psychiatry Research* 107 (3):151–63.

Antle, M.C., M.D. Ogilvie, G.E. Pickard, and R.E. Mistlberger. 2003. Response of the mouse circadian system to serotonin 1A/2/7 agonists in vivo: Surprisingly little. *Journal of Biological Rhythms* 18 (2):145–58.

Bagdy, G., and G.B. Makara. 1995. Paraventricular nucleus controls 5-HT2C receptor-mediated corticosterone and prolactin but not oxytocin and penile erection responses. *European Journal of Pharmacology* 275 (3):301–5.

Bigwood, J., and M.W. Beug. 1982. Variation of psilocybin and psilocin levels with repeated flushes (harvests) of mature sporocarps of Psilocybe cubensis (Earle) Singer. *Journal of Ethnopharmacology* 5 (3):287–91.

Blau, J.N. 1993. Behaviour during a cluster headache. *Lancet* 342 (8873):723–25.

Carter, O.L., and J.D. Pettigrew. 2003. A common oscillator for perceptual rivalries? *Perception* 32 (3):295–305.

Cermakian, N., L. Monaco, M.P. Pando, A. Dierich, and P. Sassone-Corsi. 2001. Altered behavioral rhythms and clock gene expression in mice with a targeted mutation in the Period1 gene. *EMBO Journal* 20 (15):3967–74.

Clusterbusters. 2006. Quality of Life Survey #2 of 2. Retrieved July 18, 2006, from http://www.clusterbusters.com/phpsurveyor/index.php?sid=3.

Dodick, D.W., T.D. Rozen, P.J. Goadsby, and S.D. Silberstein. 2000. Cluster headache. *Cephalalgia* 20 (9):787–803.

Duncan, M.J., K.M. Franklin, V.A. Davis, G.H. Grossman, M.E. Knoch, and J.D. Glass. 2005. Short-term constant light potentiation of large-magnitude circadian phase shifts induced by 8-OH-DPAT: Effects on serotonin receptors and gene expression in the hamster suprachiasmatic nucleus. *European Journal of Neuroscience* 22 (9):2306–14.

Fanciullacci, M., E. Del Bene, G. Franchi, and F. Sicuteri. 1977. Phantom limb pain: Sub-hallucinogenic treatment with lysergic acid diethylamide (LSD-25). *Headache* 17 (3):118–9.

Fischer, R., and D. Warshay. 1968. Psilocybin-induced autonomic, perceptual and behavioral change. *Neuro-psycho-pharmkologie* 1:291–302.

Gannon, R.L., and M.J. Millan. 2006. Serotonin1A autoreceptor activation by S 15535 enhances circadian activity rhythms in hamsters: Evaluation of potential interactions with serotonin2A and serotonin2C receptors. *Neuroscience* 137 (1):287–99.

Graham, J.R., H.I. Suby, P.R. LeCompte, and N.L. Sadowsky. 1966. Fibrotic disorders associated with methysergide therapy for headache. *New England Journal of Medicine* 274 (7):359–68.

Granella, F., and Cooperative Study Group on the Epidemiology of Cluster Headache. 1999. Case-control study on the epidemiology of cluster headache. In *Cluster Headache & Related Conditions,* ed. J. Oleson and P.J. Goadsby, 37–47. Oxford: Oxford University Press.

Gresch, P.J., L.V. Strickland, and E. Sanders-Bush. 2002. Lysergic acid diethylamide-induced Fos expression in rat brain: Role of serotonin-2A receptors. *Neuroscience* 114 (3):707–13.

Grinspoon, L., and J. Bakalar. 1981. The psychedelic drug therapies. *Current Psychiatric Therapies* 20:275–8.

Halpern, J. 1996. The use of hallucinogens in the treatment of addiction. *Addiction Research* 4 (2):177–189.

Halpern, J., and H. Pope. 2003. Hallucinogen persisting perception disorder: What do we know after 50 years? *Drug and Alcohol Dependence* 69 (2):109–19.

Halpern, J., and R. Sewell. 2005. Hallucinogenic botanicals of America: A growing need for focused drug education and research. *Life Science* 78 (5):519–26.

Hargreaves, R., R. Hargreaves, and S. Shepheard. 1999. Pathophysiology of migraine— new insights. *The Canadian Journal of Neurological Sciences* 26 (3):12–9.

Harvey, J.A., I. Gormezano, V.A. Cool-Hauser, and C.W. Schindler. 1988. Effects of LSD on classical conditioning as a function of CS-UCS interval: Relationship to reflex facilitation. *Pharmacology Biochemistry and Behaviour* 30 (2):433–41.

Horton, B.T. 1961. Histaminic cephalgia (Horton's headache or syndrome). *Maryland State Medical Journal* 10:178–203.

Inokuchi, K., A. Murayama, and F. Ozawa. 1996. mRNA differential display reveals Krox-20 as a neural plasticity-regulated gene in the rat hippocampus. *Biochemical and Biophysical Research Communications* 221 (2):430–6.

Isbell, H., A.B. Wolbach, A. Wikler, and E.J. Miner. 1961. Cross tolerance between LSD and psilocybin. *Psychopharmacologia* 2:147–59.

Isler, H. 1993. Episodic cluster headache from a textbook of 1745: van Swieten's classic description. *Cephalalgia* 13 (3):172–4; discussion 149.

Kalkman, H. 1994. Is migraine prophylactic activity caused by 5-HT2B or 5-HT2C receptor blockade? *Life Science* 54 (10):641–4.

Kast, E. 1967. Attenuation of anticipation: A therapeutic use of lysergic acid diethylamide. *Psychiatric Quarterly* 41 (4):646–57.

Kast, E., and V. Collins. 1964. Study of lysergic acid diethylamide as an analgesic agent. *Anesthesia and Analgesia* 43:285–91.

Kemali, M., and D. Kemali. 1980. Lysergic acid diethylamide: Morphological study of its effect on synapses. *Psychopharmacology* 69:315–7.

Kennaway, D.J., A. Voultsios, T.J. Varcoe, and R.W. Moyer. 2003. Melatonin and activity rhythm responses to light pulses in mice with the Clock mutation. *American Journal Physiology Regulatory Integrative Comparative Physiology* 284 (5): R1231–40.

Ko, S.W., I.V. Kunjumon, A. Hushan, A. Gallitano-Mendel, F. Wei, J. Milbrandt, and M. Zhuo. 2005. Selective contribution of egr1 (Zif/268) to persistent inflammatory pain. *The Journal of Pain* 6 (1):12–20.

Kuromaru, S., S. Okada, M. Hanada, Y. Kasahara, and K. Sakamoto. 1962. [Effect of LSD25 on the phantom limb; the problem of body scheme and the therapeutic use of LSD25 on phantom pain.] *Folia Psychiatr Neurol Japan* 64:604–13.

Lanteri-Minet, M., J. de Pommery, T. Herdegen, J. Weil-Fugazza, R. Bravo, and D. Menetrey. 1993. Differential time course and spatial expression of Fos, Jun, and Krox-24 proteins in spinal cord of rats undergoing subacute or chronic somatic inflammation. *Journal of Comparative Neurology* 333 (2):223–35.

Leone, M. 2004. Chronic cluster headache: New and emerging treatment options. *Current Pain and Headache Reports* 8 (5):347–52.

Leone, M., and G. Bussone. 1993. A review of hormonal findings in cluster headache. Evidence for hypothalamic involvement. *Cephalalgia* 13 (5):309–17.

Leone, M., A. Attanasio, D. Croci, G. Libro, L. Grazzi, D. D'Amico, A. Nespolo, and G. Bussone. 1997. The m-chlorophenylpiperazine test in cluster headache: A study on central serotoninergic activity. *Cephalalgia* 17 (6):666–72.

Leone, M., D. D'Amico, F. Frediani, F. Moschiano, L. Grazzi, A. Attanasio, and G. Bussone. 2000. Verapamil in the prophylaxis of episodic cluster headache: A double-blind study versus placebo. *Neurology* 54 (6):1382–5.

Leone, M., D. D'Amico, F. Moschiano, F. Fraschini, and G. Bussone. 1996. Melatonin versus placebo in the prophylaxis of cluster headache: A double-blind pilot study with parallel groups. *Cephalalgia* 16 (7):494–6.

Leone, M., A. Franzini, G. Broggi, and G. Bussone. 2006. Hypothalamic stimulation for intractable cluster headache: Long-term experience. *Neurology* 67 (1):150–2.

Leone, M., V. Lucini, D. D'Amico, F. Moschiano, C. Maltempo, F. Fraschini, and G. Bussone. 1995. Twenty-four-hour melatonin and cortisol plasma levels in relation to timing of cluster headache. *Cephalalgia* 15 (3):224–9.

Ling, T. M., and J. Buckman. 1960. The use of lysergic acid in individual psychotherapy. *Proceedings of the Royal Society of Medicine* 53:927–9.

Liu, C., A. Calogero, G. Ragona, E. Adamson, and D. Mercola. 1996. EGR-1, the reluctant suppression factor: EGR-1 is known to function in the regulation of growth, differentiation, and also has significant tumor suppressor activity and a mechanism involving the induction of TGF-beta1 is postulated to account for this suppressor activity. *Critical Reviews in Oncology* 7 (1–2):101–25.

Lyford, G. L., K. Yamagata, W. E. Kaufmann, C. A. Barnes, L. K. Sanders, N. G. Copeland, and D. J. Gilbert, N. A. Jenkins, A. A. Lanahan, and P. F. Worley. 1995. Arc, a growth factor and activity-regulated gene, encodes a novel cytoskeleton-associated protein that is enriched in neuronal dendrites. *Neuron* 14 (2):433–45.

Marks, D. R., A. Rapoport, D. Padla, R. Weeks, R. Rosum, F. Sheftell, and F. Arrowsmith. 1993. A double-blind placebo-controlled trial of intranasal capsaicin for cluster headache. *Cephalalgia* 13 (2):114–6.

Maruyama, K., T. Tsukada, S. Bandoh, K. Sasaki, N. Ohkura, and K. Yamaguchi. 1995. Expression of NOR-1 and its closely related members of the steroid/thyroid hormone receptor superfamily in human neuroblastoma cell lines. *Cancer Letters* 96 (1):117–22.

May, A., A. Bahra, C. Buchel, R. Frackowiak, and P. Goadsby. 1998. Hypothalamic activation in cluster headache attacks. *Lancet* 352 (9124):275–8.

Nichols, D. E. 2004. Hallucinogens. *Pharmacology and Therapeutics* 101 (2):131–81.

Nichols, C., and E. Sanders-Bush. 2002. A single dose of lysergic acid diethylamide influences gene expression patterns within the mammalian brain. *Neuropsychopharmacology* 26 (5):634–9.

Nicolaev, E., B. Kaminska, W. Tischmeyer, H. Matthies, and L. Kaczmarek. 1992. Induction of expression of genes encoding transcription factors in the rat brain elicited by behavioral training. *Brain Research Bulletin* 28:479–84.

Ott, J. 2005. Clusterheads: A documentary film about the daily life of cluster headache sufferers. Retrieved May 1, 2006, from http://homepage.mac.com/justinott/clusterheads.htm.

Pahnke, W. N., A. A. Kurland, L. E. Goodman, and W. A. Richards. 1969. LSD-assisted psychotherapy with terminal cancer patients. *Current Psychiatric Therapy* 9: 144–52.

Raghavendra, V., and S.K. Kulkarni. 2000. Melatonin reversal of DOI-induced hypophagia in rats; possible mechanism by suppressing 5-HT$_{2A}$ receptor-mediated activation of HPA axis. *Brain Research* 860 (1–2):112–8.

Richelson, E. 1990. Antidepressants and brain neurochemistry. *Mayo Clinic Proceedings* 65 (9):1227–36.

Russo, E. 1997. Schedule 1 research protocol: An investigation of psychedelic plants and compounds for activity in serotonin receptor assays for headache treatment and prophylaxis. *Newsletter of the Multidisciplinary Association of Psychedelic Studies* 7 (1):4–9.

Sankar, D.V.S. 1972. Interrelations of endocrine function and LSD-25: Effect of psychoactive drugs and of removal of endocrine glands on oxygen uptake in the rat. *Research Communications in Chemical Pathology and Pharmacology* 3 (2):321–38.

Seitanidou, T., S. Schneider-Maunoury, C. Desmarquet, D.G. Wilkinson, and P. Charnay. 1997. Krox-20 is a key regulator of rhombomere-specific gene expression in the developing hindbrain. *Mech Dev* 65 (1–2):31–42.

Sewell, R., J. Halpern, and H. Pope, Jr. 2006. Response of cluster headache to psilocybin and LSD. *Neurology* 66 (12):1920–2.

Sherlock, K., K. Wolff, A.W. Hay, and M. Conner. 1999. Analysis of illicit ecstasy tablets: Implications for clinical management in the accident and emergency department. *Journal of Accident and Emergency Medicine* 16 (3):194–7.

Sicuteri, F. 1963. Prophylactic treatment of migraine by means of lysergic acid derivatives. *Triangle* 67:116–25.

Sprouse, J., L. Reynolds, X. Li, J. Braselton, and A. Schmidt. 2004. 8-OH-DPAT as a 5-HT7 agonist: Phase shifts of the circadian biological clock through increases in cAMP production. *Neuropharmacology* 46 (1):52–62.

Stevens, J. 1987. *Storming heaven: LSD and the American dream.* New York: Harper and Row.

Strittmatter, M., G. Hamann, F. Blaes, C. Fischer, M. Grauer, K.H. Hoffmann, and K. Schimrigk. 1997. [Faulty regulation of the hypothalamo-hypophyseal-adrenal axis and chronobiological manifestations in cluster headache]. *Fortschr Neurol Psychiatry* 65 (1):1–7.

van Vliet, J.A., A. Bahra, V. Martin, N. Ramadan, S.K. Aurora, N.T. Mathew, M.D. Ferrari, and P.J. Goadsby. 2003. Intranasal sumatriptan in cluster headache: Randomized placebo-controlled double-blind study. *Neurology* 60 (4):630–33.

Wei, F., Z.C. Xu, Z. Qu, J. Milbrandt, and M. Zhuo. 2000. Role of EGR1 in hippocampal synaptic enhancement induced by tetanic stimulation and amputation. *Journal of Cell Biology* 149 (7):1325–34.

Weiller, C., A. May, V. Limmroth, M. Juptner, H. Kaube, R.V. Schayck, et al. 1995. Brain stem activation in spontaneous human migraine attacks. *Nature Medicine* 1 (7):658–60.

Welch, K.M., N.T. Mathew, P. Stone, W. Rosamond, J. Saiers, and D. Gutterman. 2000. Tolerability of sumatriptan: Clinical trials and post-marketing experience. *Cephalalgia* 20 (8):687–95.

Wisden, W., M.L. Errington, S. Williams, S.B. Dunnett, C. Waters, D. Hitchcock, G. Evan, T.V. Bliss, and S.P. Hunt. 1990. Differential expression of immediate early genes in the hippocampus and spinal cord. *Neuron* 4 (4):603–14.

Wolbach, A.B., Jr., H. Isbell, and E.J. Miner. 1962. Cross tolerance between mescaline and LSD-25, with a comparison of the mescaline and LSD reactions. *Psychopharmacologia* 3:1–14.

Woolf, C.J., and M.W. Salter. 2000. Neuronal plasticity: Increasing the gain in pain. *Science* 288 (5472):1765–9.

Woolley, D., and N. Campbell. 1962. Serotonin-like and antiserotonin properties of psilocybin and psilocin. *Science* 136:777–8.

6

PSILOCYBIN TREATMENT OF
OBSESSIVE-COMPULSIVE DISORDER

FRANCISCO A. MORENO AND PEDRO L. DELGADO

I am such an awful person. I feel repulsion for my husband and I know this hurts his feelings; now I can't stand my own child's kisses...

I love them, but I have this urge to bite them and pinch them, I can't help it, it drives me crazy...

I can't visit my parent's house because they use that chemical, I had to get rid of my car, and can't even go in the grocery store because it's there...

THE NATURE OF OBSESSIVE-COMPULSIVE DISORDER

Millions of people throughout the world suffer in silence for too long because of shame and lack of understanding regarding OCD (obsessive-compulsive disorder), an often-devastating medical condition. The American Psychiatric Association's Diagnostic and Statistical Manual of Mental Disorders (Fourth Edition) is a broadly accepted standardized compendium of modern psychiatric diagnoses (American Psychiatric Association 1994). It describes OCD as a condition characterized by the presence of either obsessions and/or compulsions that are usually recognized as excessive, unreasonable, and a product of the individuals own mind. These symptoms are time consuming (lasting at least one hour per day), and cause marked distress or significant interference in the person's ability to function. Obsessions are defined as recurrent thoughts, impulses to do something, or intrusive mental images said to resemble a photograph or a short video. Obsessions are not simply excessive worries about real-life problems. Their content is usually related to fears of being harmed or harming others, and concerns with contamination, or preoccupations with perfectionist arranging and symmetry, among others. They generally cause marked anxiety or distress especially since the content may involve unacceptable thoughts or urges that go against the individual's moral, religious, or sexual beliefs or practices. Compulsions are excessive repetitive behaviors or mental acts that are aimed at preventing or reducing distress, or preventing some dreaded event. Consistent with the most common obsessions, compulsions often involve behaviors such as excessive checking, cleaning, arranging, or performing a series of rituals mentally or physically in response to an urge or the belief that if not performed an irrational but highly undesirable consequence may ensue.

OCD is typically a chronic or highly recurring condition with a lifetime prevalence of 2–3% (Karno et al. 1988), which makes it the fourth most frequent psychiatric diagnosis after phobias, depression, and alcohol dependence or abuse. This statistics may surprise lay people and professional alike, as they often consider OCD to be a rarely encountered disorder. This is true in part because patients with OCD are generally very secretive about it and will often delay or altogether avoid pursuing professional care. Of those who seek treatment, many remain improperly diagnosed and treated due in part to attention given to associated conditions such as other anxiety disorders or co-occurring depression, panic, delusions, suicidality, substance abuse, physical health issues, and/or interpersonal difficulties (Kessler et al. 1994). OCD often starts in the second or third decade of life, so it impacts academic achievement, career aspirations, relationships, and self-esteem. It is estimated that OCD is one of the most financially burdensome diseases worldwide, leading to more economic impact than disorders such as illegal and prescription drug abuse (excluding alcohol) (Murray and Lopez 1996).

Although OCD may in some ways resembles psychosis because of the sense of near paranoia, overvalued ideas, or near delusional beliefs, it is actually classified as a primary anxiety disorder. Despite the fact that anxiety is commonly experienced by most people, and can sometimes have an adaptive or positive purpose, it becomes obviously dysfunctional when danger is perceived as larger than it in fact is, or when the individual underestimates his or her ability to deal with such perceived threats.

Disease Mechanisms

Although much is known about treatment and natural course of OCD, the underlying psychological and biological dysfunctions that cause the disorder remain unclear.

PSYCHODYNAMIC THEORIES

The well-known early psychiatrist Sigmund Freud developed a psychoanalytic conceptualization of anxiety. According to this theory, anxiety is not defined as pathological or functional but rather as material to be understood and mastered. Of course, excessive and maladaptive anxiety represented the core of neurotic conditions, one of which, "Obsessional Neurosis," was described nearly a century ago by Freud. He proposed that in this condition, anxiety caused a regression to more primitive stages of psychosexual development, specifically the "Anal Phase." Evidence supporting this formulation comes from the observation that the very same defense mechanisms believed to be prevalent during the Anal Phase often coincided with those found in obsessional neurosis. These include "reaction formation" (transforming an unacceptable wish or impulse into its opposite), "undoing" (attempting to negate unacceptable implications from a comment or an internal process by clarifying or doing the opposite), and "isolation of affect" (isolating an idea from its associated emotional state to avoid turmoil) (Gabbard 2001, 2005). However, despite this formulation, OCD is notoriously refractory to improvement with psychoanalytic therapy.

BIOLOGICAL THEORIES

It is known that OCD is heritable; identical twins that share 100% of their genetic information have a five to nine times greater rate of concordant diagnosis than fraternal twins who only share half of their genes. OCD also runs in families, and it is observed four times more frequently in relatives of people with OCD than in the general population (Hettema et al. 2001). Molecular genetic studies suggest a higher representation of certain genes related to serotonin function in patients with OCD (McDougle et al. 1998). Several neurotransmitters, neurohormones, and immunological alterations have been proposed as explanation for symptom generation, and treatment response. The serotonergic system, however, is among the most broadly supported given the seemingly selective pharmacological response to serotonin acting agents, the reports of serotonin-related changes in the central nervous system, and other alterations in peripheral markers of serotonin function in OCD patients. An interesting finding is that laboratory-induced reductions in brain serotonin availability in patients recovered from OCD do not lead to a worsening of obsessive-compulsive symptoms. In contrast, specific blockade of serotonin subtype-2 receptors in patients recently improved and receiving treatment with serotonin-enhancing medications causes an acute return of OCD symptoms (Benkelfat et al. 1989; Delgado and Moreno 1998). Although more research is clearly warranted, these findings suggest that it is not the global availability of serotonin but the activity of certain serotonin receptors subtypes in selected brain regions which mediates OCD symptoms. Other neurotransmitters also associated with OCD include the dopamine system, but this issue needs to be further studied.

Brain imaging studies point to the involvement of a specific circuit that includes interconnections between the orbitofrontal cortex, the caudate nucleus, the thalamus, and the anterior cingulate gyrus in the genesis of OCD (Baxter et al. 1996). Serotonin neurons are richly distributed in this loop, moderating its activity (Swerdlow 1995). For this reason, serotonin-activating drugs are well positioned both pharmacologically and anatomically to help regulate this circuitry dysfunction.

OCD Treatment

Not only is OCD frequent, debilitating, and underdiagnosed, it often also represents a significant treatment challenge. The U.S. FDA (Food and Drug Administration) has approved a small number of agents to treat this disorder. They are all potent serotonin reuptake inhibitors that lead to an increase in serotonin function and include clomipramine (Anafranil® and others), fluoxetine (Prozac® and others), fluvoxamine, sertraline (Zoloft®), and paroxetine (Paxil® and others). In spite of their established selective efficacy (Goodman et al. 1990), a number of shortcomings limit their ability to improve a patient's function. For example, the length of time required for improvement in patients undergoing these treatments appears to be quite long. Most patients that will ultimately improve do not show significant effects until at least one to three months of continuous treatment; only about half of the patients will reach a satisfactory response, while most patients that do improve only have a one-third to one-half decreases in severity. Their residual symptoms continue to cause dysfunction and increase vulnerability to complications and exacerbations (Goodman 1999).

Drugs such as desipramine and bupropion, which may act primarily by enhancing the function of norepinephrine and/or dopamine, have been found to be ineffective at treating OCD (Vulink et al. 2005). Although agents that block dopamine are also effective in treating some aspects of OCD, the apparent selectivity of treatment response to medication that act on the serotonin system and the finding that serotonin blockers cause a relapse of OCD symptoms further justify pursuing options related to serotonin actions in this population.

Cognitive behavioral psychotherapy is another approach often used to treat OCD. Specific techniques commonly used include Exposure and Response Prevention (Foa and Goldstein 1978). This technique essentially consists of gradually providing exposure first by imagining specific events or situations, and then in reality to a recognizable trigger of anxiety while attempting to prevent the usual obsessive and/or compulsive response. It has been the mainstay of nonanalytic therapy and a first choice treatment for OCD.

Although both pharmacotherapy and psychotherapy can be useful alone, the most effective outcomes typically occur through a combination of these treatment forms (pharmacology and cognitive behavioural therapy) (March et al. 1997). When these treatments fail, a series of atypical drug combination strategies may be tried with the hope of diminishing symptom severity. Electroshock treatment, a form of therapy reserved for highly treatment resistant mental disorders, has limited efficacy for OCD as well. At times prolonged hospitalizations are required, and in cases where all these interventions fail, extreme measures such as psychosurgery may be indicated. During psychosurgery, brain lesions are surgically produced in order to alter pathway function in areas of the central nervous system believed to be involved in OCD symptom production. This dramatic and irreversible procedure is associated with risks of complications and mortality, and has a limited clinical success rate. For these reasons, identifying new options for treatments of patients with severe and treatment-resistant OCD has become a high priority.

HALLUCINOGENS AND OCD TREATMENT

Shamans and traditional healers in cultures worldwide have utilized psychedelic agents for millennia. One may speculate that the constructs prompting their use may have included afflictions of the spirit, mind, or body, fitting with their concepts of wellness. Modern psychiatry incorporated the use of psychedelic agents to its therapeutic armamentarium half a century ago. Ingestion of psychedelics such as LSD (lysergic acid diethylamide) or psilocybin was believed to enhance therapy progress by facilitating the development of psychological insights, especially when strong psychological resistance compromised the progress of therapy (Grof 2001).

Anecdotal reports regarding the effects of hallucinogens and OCD have been published in the scientific literature. In 1962, a young male with depression and violent sexual thoughts (obsessions) was reported to have improved dramatically and permanently with psychotherapy facilitated by two doses of LSD (Delgado and Moreno 1998). In 1977, Brandrup and Vanggaard (1977) described another young patient with chronic and severe obsessions and compulsions; he received many doses of LSD and reported improvement that was partially evident early on, and continued over several months until he went into remission which lasted for years. There are additional reported cases of the beneficial effects of serotonin-related hallucinogenic drugs (psilocybin, mescaline, and LSD) unrelated to psychotherapy or medical treatment in patients with OCD. In 1987, Leonard and Rapoport reported the case of a teenage boy with chronic and severe OCD who noticed that repeated LSD use after an initial exacerbation of symptoms led to complete symptom resolution for several hours. Use of psilocybe mushrooms and mescaline also resulted in similar improvement. In our practice, we encountered a young man who had suffered from OCD symptoms (e.g., checking and counting compulsions, performing actions a specific number of times, and a variety of cleaning rituals) since age six. He started using marijuana and alcohol at age 12, which led to decrease in anxiety but no changes in OCD core symptoms. He also used cocaine, which exacerbated obsessions and compulsions; eventually during his college years, he begun using freeze-dried psilocybe mushrooms recreationally. He observed consistently that during the psilocybe mushroom intoxication, he was free of obsessions or compulsions. Repeated use induced tolerance to the psychedelic effects, but he continued to experience relief of his OCD symptoms despite the lack of a "high." Chronic use of this hallucinogenic plant led to a symptomatic remission, which lasted for about two years after discontinuing use (Moreno and Delgado 1997).

Psilocybin's Pharmacology

Psilocybin (4-phosporyloxy-N,N-dimethyltryptamine), an indolealkylamine, is the main active compound of many species of the genus "Psilocybe" commonly known as "magic mushrooms." It binds potently and selectively activates the serotonin receptors 1A, 2A, and 2C, while other serotonin receptors are less affected (McKenna et al. 1990). Behavioral pharmacology and electrophysiological research show that activation of serotonin-2 receptors strongly predicts hallucinogenic effects in humans and stimulus effects (a proxy for hallucinogenic effects) in laboratory animals (Glennon et al. 1995; Vollenweider et al. 1998; Aghajanian and Marek 1999). Activity at serotonin 1A is also supported (Carter et al. 2005). Functional imaging studies suggest that psilocybin has primary activity in the areas hypothesized to be involved in OCD neurocircuitry, namely the frontal cortex, anterior cingulate, and to a lesser extent the caudate nucleus, putamen, and thalamus (Vollenweideret al. 1997). After oral ingestion and absorption in the intestinal track, psilocybin is extensively transformed by the liver before reaching the systemic circulation. Psilocybin is converted primarily to psilocin, which is believed to be responsible for the psychotropic effects observed after psilocybin administration (Hasler et al. 2004; Passie et al. 2002).

Clinical Research with Psilocybin

Based on the serotonergic selectivity of OCD pharmacotherapies, the reversal of antiobsessional effects after selectively blocking serotonin-2, and the anecdotal reports of acute reduction in OCD symptoms with psilocybin and similar agents, the following prospective study was proposed. We sought to evaluate the safety, tolerability, and potential therapeutic effect of psilocybin use in people affected with OCD who had failed to respond to at least one adequate standard treatment. Because at least one subject described improvement in his symptoms after ingesting psilocybin, in the absence of psychedelic effects, we sought to explore the relationship of intensity of the psychedelic experience and the potential decrease in obsessions and compulsions during psilocybin use.

All research involving human subjects requires that a number of procedures be put in place to safeguard the safety of the participants, and the ethics of the proposed protocol. As part of these safeguards, an independent review board for human subjects' protection must evaluate the appropriateness of any clinical research involving people. In this case, the University of Arizona IRB

(Institutional Review Board) assessed, helped revise, and approved our project. Given that this study involved the use of a pharmacologically active substance, the U.S. FDA was also involved in oversight of the study. The FDA provided us an IND (Investigational New Drug) number and approved the project as a Phase I study, meaning that the study goal was to demonstrate safety of psilocybin for human consumption. Additionally, since psilocybin is a Schedule I–controlled substance, the U.S. DEA (Drug Enforcement Agency) was also involved. The DEA provided approval of the site and the investigators for shipment, possession, prescription, and dispensation of psilocybin, but only under the auspices of the approved research protocol.

All participants signed written informed consent, which included a detailed discussion of potential physical and mental effects of psilocybin and risks of participation. Psilocybin was obtained from a domestic manufacturer who provided us with synthetic psilocybin, which met the FDA specifications for human consumption after testing.

Determining the study inclusion and exclusion criteria for participants was the result of extensive discussions between the investigators, a large group of supportive collaborators, the University of Arizona IRB, and the FDA. Nine adult subjects (seven male; two female) with OCD diagnosis based on a standardized and validated diagnostic questionnaire were recruited through word of mouth, Internet postings, and local advertisement. They had failed to improve after an average of 3.4 treatments with known antiobsessional medications. The participants had an average baseline Y-BOCS (Yale-Brown Obsessive-Compulsive Scale) (Goodman et al. 1989) score of 24.1 (which is considered severe), and ranged from 18 (moderate) to 36 (extreme) on the first test day. Potential participants were excluded if they had any concurrent major psychiatric illnesses, active substance use disorders, unstable medical conditions, or pregnancy. Owing to safety concerns over potential adverse reaction to psychedelic drugs, subjects were required to have tolerated well at least one prior exposure to psychedelics and had no personal or family history of psychosis. They were also required to abstain from use of antidepressants for at least two weeks (six weeks for fluoxetine), or any other pharmaceutical or nutritional supplement, for at least a week before testing. The reason to exclude antidepressants was twofold: first, the concern with a potentially hazardous interaction between psychedelic drugs and serotonin-enhancing antidepressants called serotonin syndrome (Coore 1996); and second, the reported decrease in ability to experience a full hallucinogenic experience in patients using antidepressants (Bonson et al. 1996). Additionally, subjects were free of any other prescription or over-the-counter medication, nutritional supplements, or drugs of abuse, as it is customary in all Phase I studies.

Psilocybin sessions were conducted in a specially adapted room in the outpatient offices of the Psychiatry Research Program. The room was altered to give the appearance of a casual living room rather than a hospital ward or a professional office. An initial preparatory session allowed us to: further establish rapport; make sure the subjects had the right mindset; re-explain the testing procedure; and make sure that subjects were comfortable with the physical environment. On the day of testing, patients arrived at the testing room where they received their assigned dose. Four doses were selected to allow a range from nonhallucinogenic to definitely hallucinogenic. The low (100 mcg/kg), medium (200 mcg/kg), and high (300 mcg/kg) doses were assigned in that order to assure escalating tolerability, and a very low dose (25 mcg/kg) thought to be nearly inactive was inserted randomly and in double-blind fashion at any time after the first dose. The testing days were separated by at least one week; in several cases, it varied by an additional week or so. During testing, subjects were asked to wear comfortable loose clothing and they were provided with eyeshades and headphones and were encouraged to keep them on throughout most of the session, most importantly during the first six hours or so. They listened to a standardized set of music for several hours; music of the patient's choice was generally introduced at the end of the session to facilitate reintegration. We also attempted to minimize interactions and interruptions during the sessions in order to favor an internalized experience with minimal external environment interactions. Trained sitters were present at all times. Whenever possible a male and a female sitter were present simultaneously, and included at least one of the investigators. As the psychedelic experience wore off, generally between the fifth- and the eighth-hour of testing (higher doses generally lasted longer), subjects were gradually allowed to modify the above described routine, and started debriefing with the principal investigator (FM) regarding aspects of their experience. At the end of eight hours, the participants went into our inpatient psychiatric unit for an overnight stay or the medical–surgical unit in the rare instance that a psychiatric bed was not available. During testing, we measured vital signs, OCD symptom severity, and at the end of each testing day, we also measured the quality and intensity of the hallucinogenic experience with a scale that quantified sensory perception, emotion, thinking, and intensity (Riba et al. 2001).

Study Outcome

The synthetic psilocybin was clearly able to induce a psychedelic experience, and the patient group had a clear correlation between the dose of psilocybin used and the intensity of psychedelic response. Subjects underwent psychedelic experiences of different qualities and intensities. The theme of OCD was not necessarily a central content to many participants' psilocybin experience, but it was closely related in others. Some patients experienced death, birth, and space travel, similar to the classic descriptions of LSD-facilitated altered states of consciousness (Grof 1976).

Subjects generally tolerated the procedure well, none of the participants experienced psychotic or mood complications nor any kind of dangerous behaviors. One individual experienced a transient asymptomatic elevation of blood pressure, which was not associated with nervousness, or the content of his psychedelic experience. Some of the subjects were uncomfortable with the overnight stay in the psychiatric unit, and two decided not to continue primarily for this reason.

Clinically, the most remarkable finding was the acute decrease in OCD symptoms of variable degree observed in every study participant during one or more of their test sessions. Improvement ranged from a modest reduction (23%) to a complete (100%) but temporary resolution of symptoms. For the group as a whole, psilocybin led to a comparable reduction in obsessions and compulsions (Moreno et al. 2006).

For example, one of the participants described being plagued by obsessions and compulsions involving the theme of contamination and would not allow any part of his body or his clothing to be in direct or indirect contact with the floor except for the soles of his shoes. During his first psilocybin session, he noticed a brief and modest reduction in symptom severity. The same evening when the patient was admitted to the inpatient unit, he experienced a significant increase in anxiety as he observed the nurses handling his shoes and placing them in a bag that allowed the sole of one shoe to "contaminate" aspects of the other one. Staff offered him a pair of "booties," which he considered an ineffective protection from contamination, further increasing his anxiety. This patient had larger and longer lasting effects in remaining sessions. Ultimately during his "high dose" session, the patient sat up about six hours into the session and said "Doc, I am ready to play ball. . ." As he elaborated further, he explained that it had been years since he touched a basketball because of his concern with contamination, and as he sat with his feet and hands in direct contact with the ground he said again, "I am ready to play some ball. . ." This very acute improvement in OCD symptoms lasted several hours before his symptoms gradually returned. Very similarly, two-thirds of the subjects maintained an equal or greater than 50% reduction in OCD symptoms for at least 24 hours in at least one of the testing doses. Two of the subjects reported that their symptomatic improvement lasted most of the following week after repeated testing, and one of them remained in remission for at least six months.

Another participant, also during his fourth session, which happened to involve the high dose, reportedly had an opportunity to explore himself from a "higher place in consciousness, in a more transcendental way," describing in detail the following interesting aspects.

> I could view it through my third eye chakra (pointing at his forehead). I was in this beautiful garden where there was no more need to know, the sense that always drives me to read and look for answers so much, was gone. It was so perfect and so pretty, without real need for anything, like I already had it all.

Although this person was not involved in psychotherapy with us, it was very evident that a number of relevant anxiety-generating issues were symbolically visited during his psilocybin experience. For example, he had told us about his struggle with the Christian faith, as he resented his involvement as a youth with what he described as an extremist, cult like church that was in conflict with his own beliefs and life style. During his psilocybin experience he described:

> I told Jesus I am sorry but you have to go...Then there was then this child Buddha and we started playing, I looked him in the eye and felt a truly strong connection... After a while Jesus came back, I told him that I was sorry that things were whatever they were, and gave him a hug and I felt that we made our peace.

During debriefing, the patient commented on the sense of acceptance and lack of fear with which he confronted several other anxiety generating themes. He mentioned that although he had taken psilocybin, he had reached those "places" through his own mind and stated: "True answers come from within...I feel a lot of healing!"

Another patient who had a minimal improvement in OCD symptoms, mentioned how enriching and beneficial the whole study experience had been for him. It is interesting that in some cases, people's perception of wellness does not accurately reflect health as it relates to established psychiatric constructs, or recognized medical conditions.

Interestingly as well, one of the subjects had a clear increase in symptom severity during the high dose in the last session. When asked what he made of the experience, he mentioned that he really tried to take advantage of the last session and really wanted to heal himself, so he purposely confronted psychological aspects that he intuitively anticipated would yield the best outcome. This is interesting, as we noticed that in a study geared at documenting safety and tolerability, we had asked our patients to follow their thoughts wherever their experience would take them. It is not clear what might be the outcome should more subjects pursue the strategy of confronting known anxiety provoking themes during psilocybin use. This was a very small study and the increase in the severity score in one outlier patient during the high dose session may have resulted in the loss of a more significant study dose–response relationship in the study.

Study Conclusions

When administered in a supportive clinical environment, psilocybin appeared to be safe, well tolerated, and was associated with transient symptomatic reduction of OCD symptoms in subjects with treatment-resistant OCD.

The study size was small, as was the number of sessions per participant, which limits what we can say about long-term safety and, of course, the efficacy in this population. The use of "Very Low Dose," anticipated to be almost inactive, led to higher responses than anticipated, so our study does not rule out the possibility of a placebo effect. It may be possible for subjects to experience a decrease in symptoms by the mere artifact of mindset and setting (known to affect the psychedelic experience), the contextual expectation of improvement, the distracting effects of a "pleasurable experience," or an intriguing psychedelic trip with supportive company and the "allure of research." It should be noted that for some of the patients, study participation was perceived as a stressful event for a number of reasons. In some cases, testing represented a time without access to the usual distractions that ordinarily help the patients minimize their obsessions. Furthermore, for most, the overnight stay in the hospital represented an important source of stress. Although this setting was not ideal, adhering to this protocol was important to insure safety and facilitate monitoring. This issue may have introduced selection bias since we restricted participations to subjects who tolerated travel, prolonged hotel stays, and repeated psychiatric hospitalization. Other methodological concerns include the fact that we used a modified blinded protocol that may have influenced expectations in both subjects and clinical raters, and utilized a hallucinogenic rating scale that still requires improvements in validity.

WHAT HAVE WE LEARNED?

In spite of the above limitations, the findings described are highly deserving of replication and further exploration. When administered in a supportive clinical environment, psilocybin appears to be safe, well tolerated, and causes at least a transient decrease of OCD symptoms in patients with treatment resistance. Most subjects reporting symptom reduction experienced a period of relief that extended beyond the pharmacologically expected life of the drug and beyond the 24-hour assessment. This lingering effect, which extends clearly beyond the "high" or psychedelic state, raises a number of intriguing mechanistic questions. One may speculate that these prolonged pharmacological effects may be related to a rapid adaptive cascade of events such as postsynaptic serotonin receptor accommodation, or early gene expression that affect the function of certain circuits.

A large body of evidence indicates that hallucinogen administration in animal models and human subjects leads to a decrease in postsynaptic serotonin-1A and -2A receptor activity similar to what is observed with long-term antidepressant use (El Mansari and Blier 2005; Gresch et al. 2005). LSD has been reported to induce changes in intracellular signaling that are different to the effects of naturally occurring serotonin in the same receptor site (Backstrom et al. 1999), and also decreases gene expression in rat brain after a single dose administration (Nichols and Sanders-Bush 2002). These changes in receptor activity, intracellular signaling, and gene expression may result in physiological alterations that explain the extended effect described above.

RECOMMENDATIONS

Ingestion of psilocybin and similar substances will facilitate in many subjects the experience of altered states of consciousness that may lead to the development of powerful insights and profound existential and spiritual realizations.

The ability to induce these extraordinary effects in people may represent both potential benefits and liabilities. Although it is possible that marked acute decreases in OCD severity represent a mere pharmacological effect on symptom expression, and/or the disease process, the potential gains—psychological, existential, spiritual, or otherwise—may influence the individual's overall perception of wellness. Similarly, the purely pharmacological effects of psilocybin may lead to complications such as flashbacks, anxiety, mood, or psychotic episodes. The described powerful realizations may influence behavior, emotions, and thinking, facilitating potential complications that may alter function or safety when not dealt with properly. The use of psilocybin therefore should be approached with caution to minimize exposure to individuals who are vulnerable to psychosis, overvalued ideas, or violence toward self or others. Facilitators should carefully consider the subject's mindset prior to exposure, address concerns developed during the psychedelic experience through careful debriefing, and secure competent and supportive continuity during follow up.

In spite of these concerns, given that OCD is associated with a great deal of human suffering and financial burden, and that treatment resistance is very prevalent and requires interventions such as prolonged hospitalization, electroconvulsive therapy, and brain surgery, the potential benefit derived from psilocybin may represent a less burdensome alternative, one worth investigating further. The authors, however, strongly discourage the use of psychedelics for the treatment of people with severe mental illness either autonomously or delivered by unskilled individuals, or in unfit environments. On the other hand, we enthusiastically encourage patients, physicians, and scientists to pursue this line of research and are wholeheartedly thankful to our study participants for the generosity of their time and efforts to support this effort.

NOTE

The study described in this chapter was supported by grants from the Heffter Research Institute, the Multidisciplinary Association for Psychedelic Studies, and the Nathan Cummings Foundation, with the support and encouragement of Richard A. and Roberta Friedman Cummings. We thank Eric Schindler, Ph.D., for his editorial assistance with the manuscript and the Arizona Hispanic Center of Excellence for logistical support.

REFERENCES

Aghajanian, G.K., and G.J. Marek. 1999. Serotonin and hallucinogens. *Neuropsychopharmacology* 21 (Suppl. 2):16S–23S.

American Psychiatric Association. 1994. *Diagnostic and statistical manual of mental disorders.* 4th ed. Washington, D.C.: American Psychiatric Association.

Backstrom, J.R., M.S. Chang, H. Chu, C.M. Niswender, and E. Sanders-Bush. 1999. Agonist-directed signaling of serotonin 5HT2C receptors: Differences between serotonin and lysergic acid diethylamide (LSD). *Neuropsychopharmacology* 21:77S–81S.

Baxter, L.R., S. Saxena, A.L. Body, R.F. Ackermann, M. Colgan, J.M. Schwartz, Z. Allen-Martinez, J.M. Fuster, and M.E. Phelps. 1996. Brain mediation of obsessive-compulsive disorder symptoms: Evidence from functional brain imaging studies in the human and non-human primate. *Seminars in Clinical Neuropsychiatry* 1:32–47.

Brandrup, E., and T. Vanggaard. 1977. LSD treatment in a severe case of compulsive neurosis. *Acta Psychiatrica Scandinavica* 55 (2):127–41.

Benkelfat, C., D.L. Murphy, and J. Zohar. 1989. Clomipramine in obsessive-compulsive disorder: Further evidence for a serotonergic mechanism of action. *Archives of General Psychiatry* 46 (1):23–8.

Bonson, K.R., J.W. Buckholtz, and D.L. Murphy. 1996. Chronic administration of seroto-nergic antidepressants attenuates the subjective effects of LSD in humans. *Neuropsy-chopharmacology* 14 (6):425–36.

Carter, O.L., D.C. Burr, J.D. Pettigrew, G.M. Wallis, F. Hasler, and F.X. Vollenweider. 2005. Using psilocybin to investigate the relationship between attention, working memory, and the serotonin 1A and 2A receptors. *Journal of Cognitive Neuroscience* 17 (10):1497–508.

Coore, J.R. 1996. A fatal trip with ecstasy: A case of 3,4-methylene-dioxy-methamphetamine toxicity. *Journal of the Royal Society of Medicine* 89:51–2.

Delgado, P.L., and F.A. Moreno. 1998a. Different roles for serotonin in anti-obsessional drug action and the pathophysiology of obsessive-compulsive disorder. *British Journal of Psychiatry* 173 (Suppl. 35):21–5.

Delgado, P.L., and F.A. Moreno. 1998b. Hallucinogens, serotonin, and obsessive-compulsive disorder. *Journal of Psychoactive Drugs* 30 (4):359–66.

El Mansari, M., and P. Blier. 2005. Responsiveness of 5-HT1A and 5-HT2 receptors in the rat orbitofrontal cortex after long-term serotonin reuptake inhibition. *Journal of Psychiatry and Neuroscience* 30 (4):268–74.

Foa, E.B., and A. Goldstein. 1978. Continuous exposure and complete response preven-tion in the treatment of obsessive-compulsive neurosis. *Behavioral Research and Therapy* 9:821–9.

Gabbard, G.O. 2001. Psychoanalytically informed approaches to the treatment of obsessive-compulsive disorders. *Psychoanalytic Inquiry* 21 (2):208–21.

Gabbard, G.O. 2005. Anxiety disorders. In *Psychodynamic psychiatry in clinical practice,* ed. G.O. Gabbard, 249–82. Arlington, VA: American Psychiatric Publish-ing, Inc.

Glennon, R.A., M. Titeler, and J.D. McKenney. 1995. Evidence for 5-HT2 involve-ment in the mechanism of action of hallucinogenic agents. *Life Science* 35: 2505–11.

Goodman, W.K. 1999. Obsessive-compulsive disorder: Diagnosis and treatment. *Journal of Clinical Psychiatry* 60 (Suppl. 18):27–32.

Goodman, W.K., L.H. Price, P.L. Delgado, J. Palumbo, J.H. Krystal, L.M. Nagy, S.A. Rasmussen, G.R. Heninger, and D.S. Charney. 1990. Specificity of serotonin reuptake inhibitors in the treatment of obsessive-compulsive disorder. *Archives of General Psychiatry* 47:577–85.

Goodman, W.K., L.H. Price, S.A. Rasmussen, C. Mazure, R.L. Fleischmann, C.L. Hill, GR. Heninger, and D.S. Charney. 1989. The Yale-Brown Obsessive Compulsive Scale. I. Development, use, and reliability. *Archives of General Psychiatry* 46 (11):1006–11.

Gresch, P.J., R.L. Smith, R.J. Barrett, and E. Sanders-Bush. 2005. Behavioral tolerance to lysergic acid diethylamide is associated with reduced serotonin-2A receptor signaling in rat cortex. *Neuropsychopharmacology* 30:1692–1702.

Grof, S. 1976. *Realms of the human unconscious: Observations from LSD Research.* New York: EP Dutton.

Grof, S. 2001. *LSD psychotherapy.* 3rd ed. Sarasota, FL: The Multidisciplinary Association of Psychedelic Studies.

Hasler, F., U. Grimberg, and M.A. Benz. 2004. Acute psychological and physiological effects of psilocybin in healthy humans: A double-blind, placebo-controlled dose-effect study. *Psychopharmacology* 172 (2):145–56.

Hettema, J.M., M.C. Neale, and K.S. Kendler. 2001. A review and meta-analysis of genetic epidemiology of anxiety disorders. *American Journal of Psychiatry* 158:1568–78.

Karno, M., J.M. Golding, S.B. Sorenson, and R.A. Burnbaum. 1988. The epidemiology of obsessive compulsive disorder in 5 US communities. *Archives of General Psychiatry* 45:1094–99.

Kessler, R.C., K.A. McGonagle, S. Zhao, C.B. Nelson, M. Hughes, S. Eshleman, H.V. Wittchen, and K.S. Kendler. 1994. Lifetime and 12-month prevalence of DSM-II-R psychiatric disorders in the United States. *Archives of General Psychiatry* 51:8–19.

Leonard, H.L., and J.L. Rapoport. 1987. Relief of obsessive-compulsive symptoms by LSD and psilocin. *American Journal of Psychiatry* 144 (9):1239–40.

March, J.S., M. Liebowitz, D. Carpenter, D.A. Kahn, and A. Francis. 1997. The Expert Consensus Guideline Series. Treatment of obsessive compulsive disorder. Journal of *Clinical Psychiatry* 58 (Suppl. 4):5–72.

McDougle, C.J., C.N. Epperson, L.H. Price, and J. Gelernter. 1998. Evidence for linkage disequilibrium between the serotonin transporter protein and obsessive-compulsive disorder. *Molecular Psychiatry* 3:270–4.

McKenna, D.J., D.B. Repke, L. Lo, and S.J. Peroutka. 1990. Differential interactions of indolealkylamines with 5-hydroxytryptamine receptors subtypes. *Neuropharmacology* 29:193–8.

Moreno, F.A., and P.L. Delgado. 1997. Hallucinogen-induced relief of obsessions and compulsions. *American Journal of Psychiatry* 154 (7):1037–8.

Moreno, F.A., C.B. Wiegand, K. Taitano, and P.L. Delgado. Safety, tolerability, and efficacy of psilocybin in obsessive-compulsive disorder. *Journal of Clinical Psychiatry* 67:735–40.

Murray, C.J., and A.D. Lopez, eds. 1996. A comprehensive assessment of mortality and disability from diseases, injuries, and risk factors in 1990 and projected to 2020. *The Global Burden of Disease.* Boston, MA: The Harvard School of Public Health on Behalf of the World Health Organization and The World Bank.

Nichols, C.D., and E. Sanders-Bush. 2002. A single dose of lysergic acid diethylamide influences gene expression patterns within the mammalian brain. *Neuropsychopharmacology* 26:634–42.

Passie, T., J. Seifert, U. Schneider, and H.M. Emrich. 2002. The pharmacology of psilocybin. *Addiction Biology* 7:357–64.

Riba, J., A. Rodriguez-Fornells, R.J. Strassman, M.J. Barbanoj. 2001. Psychometric assessment of the Hallucinogen Rating Scale. *Drug and Alcohol Dependence* 62 (3):215–23.

Swerdlow, N.R. 1995. Serotonin, obsessive compulsive disorder and basal ganglia. *International Review of Psychiatry* 7 (1):115–29.

Vollenweider, F.X., K.L. Leenders, C. Scharfetter, P. Maguire, O. Stadelmann, and J. Angst. 1997. Positron emission tomography and fluorodeoxyglucose studies of metabolic hyperfrontality and psychopathology in the psilocybin model of psychosis. *Neuropsychopharmacology* 16 (5):357–72.

Vollenweider, F.X., M.F. Vollenweider-Scherpenhuyzen, A. Babler, H. Vogel, and D. Hell. 1998. Psilocybin induces schizophrenia-like psychosis in humans via a serotonin-2 agonist action. *Neuroreport* 9 (17):3897–902.

Vulink, N.C.C., D. Denys, and H.G.M. Westenberg. 2005. Bupropion for patients with obsessive-compulsive disorder: An open label, fixed dose study. *Journal of Clinical Psychiatry* 66 (2):228–30.

7

THERAPEUTIC USES OF MDMA

GEORGE GREER AND REQUA TOLBERT

There have been several scientifically controlled studies of the psychological and physiological effects of MDMA (methylenedioxymethamphetamine) in humans, and books and media reports have told many stories about the use of MDMA in healing. However, no scientifically controlled studies of MDMA in treatment have ever been published or completed. The first such study is underway at present and is described by Michael Mithoefer, MD, in these volumes. At the time of this writing in mid-2006, other therapeutic projects in the United States, Israel, Spain, and Switzerland are beginning. Other than small studies using ketamine for depression (Berman et al. 2000) and studies by Evgeny Krupitsky, MD (chapter in this publication) for addiction as described in these volumes, as of this writing in mid-2006, no controlled studies on the therapeutic use of any psychedelic drug have been published since the early 1970s (Mangini 1998).

MDMA has been used therapeutically since the late 1970s, and there have been two systematic follow-up studies. However, these studies employed only customized questionnaires administered before and after the MDMA sessions. All of this work was done in the context of purely clinical psychiatric practice, and there were no control groups or sessions, or standardized or quantitative assessments. The first study (Greer and Tolbert 1986) reported on the first 29 people administered with MDMA from 1980 to 1983, before it became a controlled substance in the United States in 1985. The second report by Swiss psychiatrist Peter Gasser (Gasser 1995) describes the results of courses of treatment involving both MDMA and LSD (lysergic acid diethylamide) in the same patients conducted by a small, organized group of Swiss psychiatrists from 1988 until 1993, when all psychedelic therapy was halted by the Swiss government. This chapter will summarize and comment on the findings of these two studies.

GREER AND TOLBERT RESEARCH

For our study, Greer synthesized MDMA in the laboratory of Alexander Shulgin, a biochemist who with David Nichols first reported on the subjective effects of MDMA (Shulgin and Nichols 1978), comparing it to low doses of MDA (methylenedioxyamphetamine), which had been used therapeutically (Yensen et al. 1976). The ethical context for this work included informed consent and peer review, utilizing all scientific information available at the time. Because the primary purpose of the project was to assist the subjects in achieving their particular and varied goals for having the sessions, only vital signs during sessions and phenomenological descriptions of the therapists' observations and of the subjects' experiences before, during and after the sessions were recorded.

All subjects were referred by psychotherapists or friends specifically for the purpose of having an MDMA session for various reasons, and none were referred from the author's (Greer) private psychiatric practice. A questionnaire[1] designed for screening and preparing the subjects for MDMA sessions was filled out, and lengthy informed consent information about the possible side effects that could occur was explained both verbally and in writing. Subjects with any known medical conditions that might be worsened by MDMA—such as hypertension, heart disease, hyperthyroidism, diabetes mellitus, hypoglycemia, seizure disorder, glaucoma, liver disease, and pregnancy—were excluded, as were subjects who had ever had functional problems resulting from a psychiatric disorder, other than substance intoxication. Of the 29 subjects, 14 reported relatively mild psychological problems before the sessions.

The treatment model utilized was derived from the method established by psychiatrist Stanislav Grof for LSD psychotherapy (Grof 2001) and psychologist Leo Zeff for MDMA psychotherapy (Stolaroff 2004). To optimize the therapeutic alliance and mindset of everyone involved in the sessions, the life histories of the subjects were discussed as well as their intentions and goals for the session. This is the same general model being employed in the current therapeutic trials with MDMA and psychedelic drugs, including the Mithoefer MDMA study.

An extensive preparatory session was held to establish a close relationship with the subjects. At that time, subjects were told that they should not take

MDMA unless they were certain that they were willing to deal with any disturbing experience they might have, including but not limited to previous psychological difficulties. Following Zeff's method, the following agreements were made with the therapists before the session to ensure an atmosphere of psychological security and physical safety during the session:

1. Everyone agreed to remain on the premises until the session was over, and the therapists determined that it was safe to leave;
2. The subjects agreed to refrain from any destructive activity to self, others, or property;
3. All agreed that there would be no sexual activity between the therapists and the subjects; and
4. The subjects agreed to follow any instructions given by a therapist when explicitly stated as part of the structure of the session.

Sessions were conducted with individuals, couples, and small groups, usually at the homes of the subjects or sometimes the facilitators. A six-hour fast was instituted to ensure rapid absorption of the MDMA and to prevent nausea. Before the dose was administered, there was time to reestablish contact with the therapists and to answer questions. A dose of 75–150mg of MDMA was then given by mouth. Lower doses were used in interpersonal sessions, and higher doses were given to heavier people. During individual sessions, the subjects listened to instrumental music—with or without headphones and/or eyeshades—to facilitate an internal experience. During interpersonal sessions, music was usually played in the background. The therapists were attentive and available to respond to requests or needs, to receive and record communications, and to interact with subjects as was deemed appropriate.

When subjects noticed that the effect of MDMA was beginning to subside, usually before two hours, they were offered a second dose of 50mg or rarely, 75mg. The purpose of the second dose was to prolong the session and to provide a more gradual return to their usual state of consciousness. Some subjects were offered diazepam/Valium, 5mg, at the beginning of the session, or propranolol/Inderal, 20–40mg, every 3½–4 hours, to reduce unwanted sympathomimetic side effects such as muscle tension. Others received l-tryptophan, 500mg, to help reduce various emotional discomforts occurring late in the sessions.

When the sessions were over, the subjects' ability to drive was assessed before they were allowed to drive a car. The usual duration of sessions was five to eight hours, depending on the dosage and setting. Follow-up was conducted verbally soon after the session, and much later by written questionnaire. DSM-III (Diagnostic and Statistical Manual of Mental Disorders, Third Edition) psychiatric diagnoses were made retrospectively. Subjects completed the follow-up between two months and two years after the last session with most around nine months, though one subject wrote a letter two years later instead of the questionnaire.

Side Effects and Complications

These subjects (19 of 29) reported undesirable emotional symptoms:

- anxiety or nervousness during the session (5);
- mild depression the day after (2);
- mildly distracting thoughts for a few days (4);
- panic attacks a few weeks later; that subject had had panic attacks before (1);
- guilt around men for a while, related to an insight about the childhood death of her brother (1);
- miscellaneous emotional symptoms (6).

All 29 of the subjects reported some undesirable physical symptoms:

- jaw tension or shaking, or teeth clenching (22);
- fatigue (23);
- some insomnia the night after the session (11).

Benefits

Twenty-eight of the subjects had a specific purpose for the session. Of these, 16 had their purposes completely realized and 11 had them partially realized, as indicated in the following:

- A more cognitive understanding of themselves (of the nine, three were fully realized and two partially realized);
- A peak experience or a sense of wholeness, connectedness, or enlightenment (of the eight, six were realized);
- A personal or spiritual growth or self-exploration (all five were realized);
- Increased communication with spouse or someone else taking MDMA with them (of these, five were fully satisfied and one partially realized);
- To facilitate creative writing (all five, who took 50 mg, were satisfied);
- Fun, enjoyment, or increased awareness (all six were achieved);
- A change in their personality or behavior patterns in some lasting way (of the three, two were satisfied and one partially satisfied);
- To experience a different state of consciousness (both of the two were satisfied);
- More awareness of their feelings (both of the two were satisfied).

The nine subjects with formal DSM diagnoses reported significant relief from their problems. They include

- Two with full and lasting remissions (one, dysthymic disorder; one, simple phobia);

- Four with improvement of depressive disorders;
- Three with improvement of personality disorders.

All 29 reported benefits during sessions, including positive changes in their attitudes or feelings:

- felt closer and more intimate with anyone present (27),
- all 21 who had sessions in couples or groups experienced more closeness and/or enhanced communication,
- various cognitive benefits (22).

All 29 reported improvements in relationships:

- (spouses present but not using MDMA)—more closeness and/or improved communication with spouses, two briefly and the other still at follow-up after 10½ months (3),
- closeness and enhanced communication with people other than their mates (14),
- resolved conflicts with others after the session, five with partners not at the session (10),
- increase in the interpersonal expression of feelings afterwards (7),
- increase in acceptance and/or tolerance of others afterwards (6).

Of the five couples who had sessions with their partners:

- closeness and enhanced communication present during sessions continued for a few days to two years at follow-up (three couples),
- resolved prior conflicts after the session (two couples),
- enhanced sexual enjoyment afterwards—partly due to delayed orgasm (one couple),
- more awareness of their prior sexual problems (one couple).

Fifteen subjects changed some of their life goals after sessions; all implying that they were positive:

- sought more positive kinds of experiences in life (9),
- avoided negative experiences in life more (9),
- improved self-actualization, with insight into psychological problems, and less guilt and limiting beliefs (13).

Of the 28 subjects who answered follow-up questionnaires, 14 reported a decrease in the use of mind- or mood-altering substances, and 3 reported increase:

- Alcohol (six decreased and one increased);
- Marijuana (six decreased and one increased);
- Caffeine (five decreased and one increased much later);
- Tobacco (two decreased and one increased urge to smoke);
- Cocaine (only two users in the study; one stopped and one had less desire);
- LSD (one decreased);
- Psychedelics (one desired less and one desired more).

There were also a variety of miscellaneous changes reported by the 29 subjects, such as

- positive attitude lasting from a week to a follow-up time of two years (23),
- positive mood or emotional state, lasting from several hours to several weeks and averaging about one week (18),
- positive beliefs about themselves and/or their relations to others or the world, including self-confidence and ability to pursue spiritual growth (16),
- positive at work since their sessions (16),
- more spiritual or physical practice (14),
- see dying as less fearful or not an end (4),
- eventual termination of relationships that were failing before the sessions; partners were not at the sessions (4).

MDMA was administered to approximately 50 more individuals with similar results before being placed in Schedule I by the Drug Enforcement Administration in 1985. To provide a window into what MDMA therapy is like for someone, a case report follows of the person who, among the total of 80 people administered MDMA, experienced the most dramatic improvement in emotional and physical health and quality of life.

Case Study

A married man in his early seventies, father to an adult son and daughter, had successful careers as a geophysicist and farmer. At the time of his sessions, he had been told that he was among the longest-lived survivors with multiple myeloma to date. This metastatic, cancerous condition of the bone marrow had been diagnosed about 10 years earlier. For two years before his cancer diagnosis, he had had group therapy to help with depression over family problems. On being diagnosed with cancer, he began a different type of therapy in a group format in which he learned deep relaxation, meditation, and visualization to combat his cancer and assist in pain control. He was able to achieve states where his pain was as reduced as well as it was with narcotics, but he still endured much pain.

At the time of our first meeting, his main complaint was "movement pain" from four collapsing vertebrae due to the cancer. Over the prior months, the pain had increased, decreasing his physical and sexual activity and his ability to go fishing and to fly his plane. He was also troubled by depression that usually followed the numerous fractures of his spine, which necessitated confinement to bed. The goal for his session with MDMA, which he wished to take with his wife, was to cope with his pain in a better way and to receive help in adjusting to his current life changes.

During his first session, he and his wife remained in separate rooms listening to music with eyeshades and headphones on for five hours. He hummed along with the classical music being played. Shortly after an extra dose of 50 mg of MDMA, he announced ecstatically that he was free of pain and began singing aloud with the music, repeatedly proclaiming his love for his wife and family. He spent several hours in this elated state. Afterwards he said it was the first time he had been completely pain free in the four years of the current relapse of his myeloma. He described his beautiful experience of being inside his vertebrae, straightening out the nerves, and "gluing" fractured splinters back together. In a letter two weeks after his session, he stated that his pain had returned, but that his ability to hypnotically "re-anchor" his pain-free experience greatly assisted him in reducing the pain by himself.

He had four MDMA sessions spaced over the course of nine months, and each time he achieved relief from his physical pain and had greater success in controlling painful episodes in the interims by returning himself to an approximation of the MDMA state. He noted in particular that the feelings of "cosmic love," and especially forgiveness of himself and others, would usually precede the relief of physical pain. He describes an episode from his second session:

> As I was finishing the meditation, time ceased to exist, my ego fell away, and I became one with the cosmos. I then started my visualization of my body's immune system fighting my cancer, of the chemo[therapy] joining with my immune system to kill the cancer cells in my vertebrae and of positive forces coming from the cosmos to fight my cancer. Gradually I went deeper in to where the feeling of love, peace and joy were overwhelming. Although I had heard the new age music before, many details of the music became clear and more beautiful.

His sessions stopped when MDMA was placed in Schedule I by the Drug Enforcement Administration in 1985, and the Food and Drug Administration denied permission to continue the treatment pending further animal studies. He remained quite functional and mostly pain free for a few months after the last session, but eventually his pain began to return. He died very peacefully in his wife's presence soon afterwards.

SWISS RESEARCH

Between 1988 and 1993, the Swiss Federal Office for Public Health gave permission to five psychiatrist members of the Swiss Medical Society for Psycholytic Therapy to conduct psychotherapy with MDMA and LSD in private practice.

Among the five, Jurai Styk, MD, and Samuel Widmer, MD, administered both MDMA and LSD to their patients, and Dr. Marianne Bloch, MD, administered only MDMA, and Gasser reported the combined results for all three, without reporting the results of sessions or patients with MDMA and LSD separately.

There were 171 patients who completed treatment with one of the three psychiatrists by the end of the period. All were sent a standardized questionnaire about the patients' reasons for treatment, social situation, other treatments, self-evaluation of improvement during and after treatment, summary of the sessions, and life situation after treatment. Diagnosis, duration of therapy, number of non-drug and drug sessions, and duration of the follow-up were obtained from the medical records. There were 121 follow-up questionnaires completed.

The MDMA and LSD sessions were conducted in small groups, combining elements of the psycholytic therapy of Dr. Hanscarl Leuner, MD—low to medium dosage, group setting, and continuous verbal therapy—with those of the psychedelic therapy of Grof—high dosage, individual session and use of music and silence as a therapeutic method. A dose of 125 mg of MDMA or 100–400 mcg of LSD was used in the sessions. Average duration of therapy was three years and average follow-up was two years. Nondrug sessions occurred in an average of every two weeks, with an average of seven drug sessions per patient, or a session about every five months after 10 nondrug sessions.

Two-thirds of the patients sought treatment for interpersonal problems and two-thirds for psychological symptoms. About 30% wanted help for somatic symptoms, and 57% wanted the treatment for self-exploration. About 20% sought help for nondrug addictive behaviors such as "need to be used (co-dependency) and excessive sexual or workaholic behavior." Patients were diagnosed only by their presenting problem: 38% had a personality disorder, 26% an adjustment disorder, 25% an affective disorder, and 7% eating disorders. "Addiction, Psychosis and Sexual Deviation" affected just under 2% each.

Results

Eighty-five percent of the patients reported good to slight improvement during treatment and 91% at follow-up. The treatment was helpful emotionally to 65% of the patients and interpersonally to 56%. Forty-nine percent said they had important biographical insights. Thirty-six percent said the sessions helped them make important life decisions, such as about their careers and relationships. Five percent had spiritual and religious experiences, 7% reported improved self-esteem and self-confidence, and 3% reported more creativity and awareness.

As for important experiences during the sessions, 71% reported important experiences of unity and/or love, 45% reported religious or spiritual experiences, and 40% reported visions, though there is no determination as to whether MDMA or LSD was involved.

Most (84%) said their quality of life was improved, but 3% said it worsened. Most (82%) reported more self-acceptance and 3% less. Sixty-eight percent reported more autonomy and only 3% less. Eighty-one percent had better relationships with family members and 3% had worse. Work involvement was better for most (57%) and worse for 3%. Seventy-four percent reported "a better approach to the Divine" and 1% worse. Fifty-eight percent had less fear of death and 2% more fear. These changes were attributed to the drug sessions with LSD or MDMA.

Gasser (1995, pp. 6–7) concludes:

> Nine out of ten patients declared themselves to have experienced good improvement or slight improvement concerning the problems that brought them to therapy.

The feedback of the ex-patients permits us to say that psycholytic psychotherapy is a safe treatment. In the personal notes, only one patient complained of persistent depression that appeared three months after his last psycholytic session. During psycholytic therapy (which lasted an average of three years), none of the patients committed suicide, were hospitalized in a psychiatric hospital, or had a psychotic episode for more than 48 hours.

This result is consistent with other studies. In a 1960 paper by Cohen, the complication rate from 44 therapists with about 5,000 patients and 25,000 applications of LSD or mescaline was 0.04% for suicide and 0.18% for the risk of a psychosis longer lasting than 48 hours. In a 1971 study by Malleson, the complication rate for 4,300 patients and 49,500 applications of LSD was 0.07% for suicide and 0.9% for a longer psychotic crisis.

PSYCHOLOGICAL MECHANISMS OF ACTION

It appears that in the right circumstances, MDMA reduces or somehow eliminates the neurophysiological fear response to a perceived threat to one's emotional integrity. The main neurotransmitter effects of MDMA are the release of serotonin, norepinephrine, and dopamine (Vollenweider et al. 2002). Therefore, this release is likely the reason why MDMA reduces the primary somatic symptoms of fear: the tightness and nervous feelings in the throat, chest, abdomen, and skeletal musculature. There is also a moderate anesthesia to pain (but not to touch) in the skin during the acute effect, which may parallel the anesthesia to emotional pain or fear without reducing emotional sensitivity.

With this experience of fear eliminated, a loving and forgiving awareness seems to occur quite naturally and spontaneously. Subjects found it comfortable to be aware of, to communicate, and to remember thoughts and feelings that are usually accompanied by fear and anxiety. Alcohol, antianxiety drugs, and beta sympathetic nervous system blockers also can reduce fear. However, they have no effect after the pharmacological effects have ended, and they do not facilitate intimate and emotional communication, access to repressed memories or feelings, or the learning of new attitudes and beliefs or social behaviors.

Unresolved emotional conflicts from the past perpetuate conditioned fear responses, which drive people to avoid having certain feelings or thoughts symbolically associated with those conflicts. Without the conditioned fear, access to the information contained in these thoughts, feelings, or memories is enhanced, allowing value judgments about the past, relationships, and self-worth to be based on more accurate interpretations of experiential data. A corrective emotional experience then can occur once psychological defenses are no longer needed. One can then reassess their life and relationships from a broader perspective of security and love rather from one of vulnerability and fear. It then becomes easier to trust the validity of one's own feelings without fear, as well as those of a significant other who is experiencing the same state with them. As the subjects reported, they can then remember and integrate these healthier psychological processes into their everyday lives.

Couples who had a session together frequently reported basing their relationships much more on love and trust than on fear and suspicion after their MDMA sessions. These results were achieved by the patients making decisions based on what they learned during their MDMA experience and by their cognitively and emotionally remembering and applying those decisions after the session was over.

Because MDMA did not significantly distort perception, thinking, or memory (except in doses well over 100–150mg), new insights and behaviors can be carried over into everyday life. Therapeutic learning occurs with the normal structure of the ego and personality intact, unlike an experience with a psychedelic drug such as LSD, psilocybin, or mescaline.

POTENTIAL APPLICATIONS OF MDMA FOR HEALING

MDMA's use as an adjunct to insight-oriented psychotherapy for a variety of problems was specifically recommended by six subjects in the Greer and Tolbert study. Many felt that MDMA enhanced self-understanding and was useful in their personal and spiritual growth. Given the consistently positive experience that people have and the lack of complications, many psychiatric conditions could be helped by MDMA-assisted treatment.

Anxiety Disorders

Given the improvements in mood, attitude, and self-confidence, treatment for anxiety disorders, such as in terminal illness and post-traumatic stress, is already being pursued through controlled studies internationally.

Relationship disorders

The enhancement of emotional intimacy and communication that occurs with MDMA therapy could dramatically improve treatment for dysfunctional relationships. Regardless of the mechanism, most subjects expressed a greater ease in relating to their partners, friends, and coworkers for days to months after their sessions. Once a therapeutically motivated person has experienced the lack of true risk involved in direct and open communication, it can be practiced without the assistance of MDMA. This ability can help resolve existing conflicts and prevent future ones from occurring due to unexpressed fears or misunderstandings.

Substance Use Disorders

A value in treating at least mild alcohol and other drug abuse disorders was indicated by the decreased use of substances that have psychological dependence potential. Some subjects mentioned that these substances seemed less appealing after experiencing MDMA. The ability not only to feel free of conflict—which can be provided by many drugs of abuse—but also to learn how to prevent conflicts in everyday life seems unique to MDMA as a therapeutic adjunct. Inadequate parenting, with its traumas and deprivations, is a major factor in the development of both addictive behaviors and the codependency of family members that helps sustain the addiction. If those at risk can acquire the skills of becoming aware of and communicating their deepest feelings to family members who can learn to receive and accept them, it could prevent the transmission of dysfunctional family relationships from one generation to the next. Such potential benefits of the careful therapeutic use of MDMA should be considered when evaluating the potential medical risks.

In addition, MDMA's diminished pleasurable effects and markedly increased side effects when taken in either larger doses or with greater frequency distinguish it from most drugs of abuse, though cases of frequent and abusive use of MDMA at high doses do occur. Two subjects took four 50 mg supplements after their initial dose and found the fourth to cause only more agitation and confusion without any pleasant effects at all. Some subjects reported using MDMA on their own, but only one used it twice in the same week. The second experience was therapeutically useful but left her depressed and exhausted for about two days. Therefore, both the positive experience of MDMA and the relative impracticality of using it frequently can motivate people to find other ways to achieve a desirable state of mind in everyday life. Sixteen subjects began or increased their meditation practices or exercise programs, supporting this conclusion.

CONCLUDING THOUGHTS

Double-blind controlled experiments of treatment with MDMA are necessary to prove the efficacy of MDMA under current scientific standards, and the Mithoefer study is the first of this type to occur. However, it is important to keep in mind that double-blind, placebo-controlled conditions necessarily change the mindset of the subject and facilitator because it requires that neither the client nor the therapist know that MDMA is being ingested. The knowledge that there is only a chance that a subject is actually receiving MDMA could result in less motivation to prepare for the session and less hopefulness about its outcome, on the part of both therapist and subject.

Therefore, changing the purpose of the session from treatment to treatment research can have an important influence on the outcome of a session. Also, motivation could be affected if therapists and clients believe that the primary goal of the session was to study the therapeutic effects of the drug to help others, rather than for the patients to receive benefit mainly for themselves. Just the difference of a patient paying the therapist for the drug and their service during a session or not can change the mindset of both.

Because the therapeutic method is not fully separable from the ingestion of MDMA, a carefully considered compromise is necessary in research design. This is exemplified in the Mithoefer study, involving a combination of sessions for which some sessions it is known that MDMA will be administered, and others for which it is not known. Hopefully this will generate valuable data about how the variable of blindness to drug vs. nondrug session affects therapeutic outcome.

NOTES

Portions of this chapter have been excerpted from the following articles in the *Journal of Psychoactive Drugs* and reprinted with permission from Haight Ashbury Publications, 856 Stanyan Street, San Francisco, CA. Greer, G., & Tolbert, R. (1986). "Subjective reports of the effects of MDMA in a clinical setting." *Journal of Psychoactive Drugs* 18 (4): 319–27 and Greer, G., & Tolbert, R. (1998). "A method of conducting therapeutic sessions with MDMA." *Journal of Psychoactive Drugs* 30 (4): 371–79.

1. The data from the questionnaires before and after the session are reflected in the Results section.

REFERENCES

Berman, R.M., A. Cappiello, A. Anand, D.A. Oren, G.R. Heninger, D.S. Charney, and J.H. Krystal. 2000. Antidepressant effects of ketamine in depressed patients. *Biological Psychiatry* 47 (4):351–4.

Gasser, P. 1995. Psycholytic therapy with MDMA and LSD in Switzerland. *Bulletin of the Multidisciplinary Association for Psychedelic Studies* 5 (3):3–7. (Full text at http://www.maps.org/news-letters/v05n3/05303psy.html.)

Greer, G., and R. Tolbert. 1986. Subjective reports of the effects of MDMA in a clinical setting. *Journal of Psychoactive Drugs* 18 (4):319–27. (Full text at http://www.heffter.org/pages/subjrep.html.)

Greer, G., and R. Tolbert. 1998. A method of conducting therapeutic sessions with MDMA. *Journal of Psychoactive Drugs* 30 (4):371–9. (Full text at http://www.heffter.org/pages/sessions.html.)

Grof, S. 2001. *LSD psychotherapy.* Sarasota, FL: Multidisciplinary Association for Psychedelic Studies.

Mangini, M. 1998. Treatment of alcoholism using psychedelic drugs: A review of the program of research. *Journal of Psychoactive Drugs* 30 (4):381–418.

Shulgin, A.T., and D.E. Nichols. 1978. Characterization of three new psychotomimetics. In *The psychopharmacology of hallucinogens,* ed. R.C. Stillman and R.E. Willette, 76–77. New York: Pergamon Press.

Stolaroff, M.J. 2004. *The secret chief revealed.* Sarasota, FL: Multidisciplinary Association for Psychedelic Studies.

Vollenweider, F.X., M.E. Leichti, A. Gamma, G. Greer, and M. Geyer. 2002. Acute psychological and neurophysiological effects of MDMA in humans. *Journal of Psychoactive Drugs* 34 (2):171–84.

Yensen, R., F. DiLeo, J.C. Rhead, W.A. Richards, R.A. Soskin, B. Turek, and A.A. Kurland. 1976. MDA-assisted psychotherapy with neurotic outpatients: A pilot study. *Journal of Nervous and Mental Disease* 163:233–45.

8

MDMA-ASSISTED PSYCHOTHERAPY FOR THE TREATMENT OF POST-TRAUMATIC STRESS DISORDER

MICHAEL MITHOEFER

INTRODUCTION

In the history of psychotherapy, therapeutic methods have often been developed and used in clinical practice before their efficacy has been evaluated by controlled research trials. This is true in the case of MDMA (methylenedioxymethamphetamine)-assisted psychotherapy (Holland 2001), albeit primarily because all legal use was abruptly halted by government prohibition before formal research could be undertaken. With the end of sanctioned use, the process of open exploration and communication about the therapeutic potential of MDMA and other psychedelics virtually disappeared from the scientific literature. Only recently, more than twenty years later, has legal research been allowed to resume. Consequently, this research is still in the early stages of development. Much of the discussion in this chapter is based on the ongoing study I have been conducting since early 2004 in collaboration with my wife, Ann Mithoefer, Mark Wagner, and others (Mithoefer 2003). As of this writing several other controlled MDMA treatment trials are now beginning elsewhere in the world, but none have yet been completed.

Against this background, I will first discuss general principles of MDMA-assisted psychotherapy for PTSD (post-traumatic stress disorder) as well as some specific observations from our research. Our sample size is small (14), our data are preliminary, and our results have not yet undergone peer review for publication.

In deference to these limitations, I am giving a descriptive account of what we have gleaned rather than presenting the data itself. Our research design is based on the modern standard of double-blind, placebo-controlled trials. This approach has important advantages and inherent limitations. While we expect our statistical results to add to the understanding of MDMA-assisted psychotherapy, we also know that statistical data alone cannot tell the whole story of this rich and complex subject that has been discussed in a more descriptive way by previous authors.

Despite the limitations in our current level of knowledge, the therapeutic tool we are studying is not new, and our controlled data do not comprise the only information at hand. Mankind has a rich history of using psychedelic substances to catalyze healing, spiritual experience, and community ritual, dating back millennia (Grob 2002, p. 5). Western psychology has its own tradition with psychedelics involving clinical use, as well as formal clinical research with some substances. In the case of MDMA, it is estimated that in the early 1980s, approximately 4,000 therapists in the United States were using it as an adjunct to psychotherapy (Holland 2001, p. 12). Though formal outcome research was not done prior to our study, much has been learned from clinical experience about the use of MDMA in therapy and the appropriate role of the therapist in this setting. We are indebted to those whose published accounts, formal instruction, and personal conversations have taught us much about how to approach this work.

WHY MDMA-ASSISTED THERAPY FOR PTSD

Approximately 10% to 20% of people who experience a major trauma go on to develop PTSD, resulting in an estimated 8% prevalence in the general U.S. population (Kessler et al. 1995). In the National Comorbidity Study, the median time to remission was 36 months with treatment and 64 months without treatment. In either subgroup, more than one-third still had symptoms several times per week 10 years later (Kessler et al. 1995). More recent studies confirm that a significant percentage of patients do not respond adequately to current established treatments (Spinazzola et al. 2005). Consequently PTSD is a public health problem that causes a great deal of suffering and accounts for a significant portion of health care costs. Research into a wider array of more effective treatments is called for.

Revisiting traumatic experiences in psychotherapy is widely recognized as an important element of PTSD treatment. However, the symptoms of PTSD, which fall into three groups (reexperiencing, avoidance, and hyperarousal), can themselves constitute serious barriers to this treatment. People with PTSD, vigilant for possible betrayal and danger, may have difficulty developing enough trust in a therapist to establish an effective working alliance, especially if they have been abused by someone in a helping role and/or an authority figure. Likewise, patients may have levels of anxiety (hyperarousal) and intense reexperiencing phenomena that make them unwilling to revisit their trauma in therapy, or their efforts to do so may produce such high levels of anxiety that the experience is re-traumatizing rather than therapeutic. Conversely, they may have pronounced emotional numbing (avoidance) that renders them unable to make the emotional connection to traumatic memories necessary for therapeutic change. They may also lack self-compassion in the face of guilt and shame that so often follow trauma. This difficulty, which can lead to harsh and relentless self-judgment and a distorted perspective about the trauma and about present reality, may perpetuate a cycle of ongoing traumatic inner experience.

In anecdotal reports of early therapeutic use of MDMA,[1] results suggest that MDMA has the potential to be particularly effective in treating PTSD by removing or lowering these barriers to treatment. The reported results include decreased fear and anxiety, increased openness, trust and interpersonal closeness, improved therapeutic alliance, enhanced recall of past events with an accompanying ability to examine them with new insight, calm objectivity, and compassionate self-acceptance. These effects are consistent with the hypothesis that MDMA can increase the effectiveness of PTSD treatment. Thus far, the preliminary results of our study reported below support this hypothesis.

While my focus is on the possible benefits of MDMA as a catalyst for the psychotherapeutic process in PTSD, the accompanying effects on neurochemistry and possibly even brain structure should be noted. Chronic PTSD causes changes in the hypothalamic pituitary axis and other aspects of the stress response that may lead to changes in volume and cellular make up of the hypothalamus and possibly other areas of the brain (Van der Kolk 2003). Treatment goals for PTSD should include both alleviating symptoms and interrupting the stress-induced neurochemical abnormalities produced by the condition. MDMA-assisted therapy may accomplish the latter by decreasing or eliminating chronic hyperarousal and acute stress reactions to internal and external triggers.

Comparison to Other Therapies

The most recent American Psychiatric Association Practice Guidelines recommend three psychotherapeutic interventions for treating PTSD: cognitive and behavioral therapies, eye movement desensitization and reprocessing, and psychodynamic psychotherapy (Ursano et al. 2004). MDMA-assisted psychotherapy includes all the elements that, to varying degrees, are important in these other approaches—prolonged exposure, cognitive restructuring, anxiety management training/stress inoculation training, addressing transference, and addressing somatic manifestations of PTSD.

The unique properties of MDMA-assisted therapy compared to the other approaches, aside from the obvious differences in format, are that:

- MDMA-assisted psychotherapy stimulates subjects to arrive at the necessary therapeutic process spontaneously with little or no specific direction from therapists.

- The therapeutic outcome can be reached over a much shorter period of time and in a more intense manner than in most other approaches.
- People are often able to connect deeply with positive, affirming aspects of their present lives, in addition to processing difficult emotions and past experiences.

ELEMENTS OF THE MDMA-ASSISTED THERAPEUTIC PROCESS

A major influence on the method of therapy in our study is the work of Stanislav Grof, MD, PhD.[2] My comments about MDMA-assisted therapy for PTSD are informed not only by the research we are currently doing but also by extrapolation from what we learned in the Grof training program for Holotropic Breathwork facilitators and from our subsequent experience using Holotropic Breathwork and other experiential therapies with PTSD patients.

Some important common principles apply to any therapeutic method using nonordinary states of consciousness, whether induced by a substance or a nondrug technique. Scrupulous attention to these four elements is especially required:

- participant safety,
- subject and therapist preparation and resulting mindset,[3]
- physical setting,
- integration of the experience in the days and months that follow.

The following discussion of these elements focuses on issues particular to MDMA-assisted therapy and assumes a basic foundation of therapist training, healthy boundaries, and therapeutic alliance.

Participant Safety

Potential participants in MDMA-assisted psychotherapy for PTSD should be screened for underlying medical and psychiatric problems. Because MDMA raises blood pressure and pulse, it can pose a risk for individuals with hypertension and/or preexisting cardiovascular or cerebrovascular disease. Even if such medical conditions are not detected during screening, occult disease could become symptomatic as a result of the emotional and cardiovascular effects of MDMA. During 22 MDMA research sessions, in which we have closely monitored blood pressure, pulse, and temperature, all subjects have experienced transient elevations. None of these has resulted in symptoms or the need for medical intervention. Blood pressure and pulse usually peak at two to two and a half hours after MDMA administration and gradually subside thereafter, although there may also be periodic elevations in these parameters associated with intense emotions and apparently independent of the direct cardiovascular effects of MDMA. If MDMA-assisted therapy is eventually approved as a clinical tool, standard procedures will likely include some monitoring of vital signs and arrangements for medical backup in the unlikely event of a complication.

Psychiatric screening of potential subjects is also important but perhaps less clear-cut. Most people with PTSD also meet DSM-IV (Diagnostic and Statistical Manual) criteria for other psychiatric disorders, especially mood and anxiety disorders. Usually this comorbidity is not a contraindication to MDMA-assisted therapy. In our study, we have excluded people with psychotic disorders, bipolar disorder type 1, eating disorder with active purging, active substance abuse, borderline personality disorder, or dissociative identity disorder (though lower levels of dissociation are common). We also exclude anyone who is at significant risk for suicide or re-traumatization, or who requires ongoing psychotropic medication other than as-needed benzodiazepines or medication for insomnia. As clinical experience accumulates, more will be learned about the degree to which these criteria may be appropriately adjusted. Some may continue to be absolute contraindications. Others will likely prove to be relative contraindications, dependent upon the degree of ongoing support available, the setting in which the therapy takes place, and the specific characteristics of the individual subject.

Therapist Preparation

A team of male and female co-therapists offers many important advantages. This configuration provides a sense of safety for participants that is particularly important during the vulnerability of nonordinary states of consciousness and in situations involving physical touch (Taylor 1995). It also presents opportunities for working with transference toward both sexes.

The therapists must have developed the ability to work together in a trusting and cooperative way. They should be attentive to maintaining good communication with each other and addressing any disagreements or conflicts that may arise between them. Subjects in a nonordinary state of consciousness may be exquisitely sensitive to dynamics between therapists, and to therapists' responses to any challenges that arise. It is especially important in this situation that therapists cultivate their own abilities to respond with openness and without defensiveness or blame.

Therapists should have personal experience themselves with nonordinary states of consciousness as participants in a therapeutic set and setting. This will better prepare them to understand and be comfortable with a subject's experiences, which may at times take a painful and seemingly circuitous course toward healing. Ideally, therapists have undergone MDMA-assisted therapy; however, if that is not possible, a nondrug method such as Holotropic Breathwork may suffice.

Subject Preparation: Orientation to the
Therapeutic Approach

The development of a therapeutic mindset is especially important in MDMA-assisted psychotherapy. This requires a significant effort in advance, during which the therapists educate the subject about the approach to therapy that will be taken during MDMA-assisted sessions. The basic concept to be conveyed is the empirically derived perspective that it is most useful to allow an individual's therapeutic process to unfold spontaneously rather than to try to predict or direct it according to preconceived assumptions. Healing may involve a temporary intensification of painful memories and emotions, as well as periods of relief and joy. The subject's willingness and ability to consciously direct awareness toward whatever arises can facilitate the natural course of their inherent healing process.

Other key points to be stressed during preparatory nondrug therapy sessions are as follows.

USING THE BREATH AND DIRECTING ATTENTION

We talk to subjects about using the breath and directing attention in three similar but distinct ways:

1. As an anxiety management technique in situations where it is necessary or advisable to set anxiety aside and relax the body as much as possible. This may be the case if intense, painful emotions arise in the course of daily life, or in the first hour of an MDMA session when autonomic arousal itself may trigger anxiety. If subjects do not already have an effective technique for this, we usually teach them focused diaphragmatic breathing.

2. As an aid to maintaining attention on an experience that they might otherwise distract themselves from. We encourage people to practice "breathing into" whatever they are experiencing (including painful memories, emotions, or body sensations) and notice any tendency for the mind to redirect attention toward familiar thought patterns or outer distractions. In this way, subjects learn to use their breath to bring attention back into their bodies and emotions.

3. As an ongoing daily practice to support both anxiety management and integration of lessons and emotional shifts resulting from therapy. This may involve simply focused diaphragmatic breathing or more specific techniques a subject may choose such as vipassana meditation, yoga, tonglen, contemplative prayer, or guided imagery.

SETTING ASIDE PRECONCEPTIONS AND JUDGMENTS ABOUT HEALING
PROCESSES

Subjects with PTSD should be prepared for the likelihood that they will revisit traumatic events during the sessions. They should be encouraged to be as open as possible to fully experiencing any accompanying painful emotions as well as any positive, even blissful, experiences that may occur. In a therapeutic setting, the effects of MDMA may enable them to revisit trauma without either being overwhelmed by fear or needing to emotionally distance themselves. They may also have a new depth of emotional connection with affirming, nurturing experiences and positive aspects of their lives. It is best not to make assumptions about what particular mix of these experiences is needed for a given person. A useful mindset with which to approach an MDMA-assisted therapy session is that the innate healing intelligence of the psyche, catalyzed by MDMA and the therapeutic setting, will determine the nature and content of the experience. The result may be quite different from anything the intellect could have anticipated or devised. For this to occur, both the subject and the therapists should refrain from attempting to direct or prematurely judge or analyze the experience.

One particular form of judgment that should be discussed beforehand is the possible tendency to judge the nature of the MDMA experience itself. Subjects may have periods of feeling "stuck" and thinking that they should be having a different kind of experience. It helps to regard such self-judgment and stuck feelings as important patterns themselves, rather than merely as obstacles to something else. This approach presents the opportunity to bring greater awareness and healing to these difficult patterns that undoubtedly arise in relation to PTSD symptoms as well as other areas of life. This is somewhat similar to the psychodynamic principle of working with resistance directly when it comes up, rather than pushing to overcome it.

COMMUNICATING WITH THE THERAPISTS

Subjects are encouraged to begin the session in a reclining position, with eyeshades on, listening to music through headphones. They may speak to the therapists at any time. If they have not spoken within one hour of ingesting MDMA, the therapists check in with them. The suggested approach is to alternate periods of talking with periods of inner focus. While conversation with the therapists can be valuable, it is important that subjects also spend time with eyes closed and attention directed toward their inner experience. The timing of these alternating periods should be flexible and largely determined by the spontaneous flow of the subject's process though some guidance from the therapists may be required to maintain a balance.

ESTABLISHING PARAMETERS FOR PHYSICAL CONTACT

It should be made explicit that (1) subjects will determine whether or not there is physical touch during therapy and (2) there will be no sexual contact. In this method of therapy, withholding touch can be as problematic as touching inappropriately. Subjects are told that the therapists are comfortable with providing nurturing touch by either or both of them (such as placing a hand on the shoulder, hand-holding, or hugging) and that it is equally acceptable if the subject prefers not to be touched.

Physical Setting

The physical setting should be comfortable and as aesthetically pleasing as possible. It should provide freedom from interruptions and outside noises and should convey to the subject a sense of privacy and safety. Stanislav Grof's recommendations about the physical setting for LSD (D-lysergic acid diethylamide) psychotherapy apply to MDMA-assisted therapy as well, "The treatment room should be quiet, comfortable, tastefully decorated, and furnished in a homelike fashion. Much attention should be paid to the choice of fabrics, pictures and flower arrangements" (Grof 2001). Ralph Metzner has described the ideal setting as a "serene, simple, comfortable room in which the person can recline...and the therapist or guide can sit nearby" (Metzner and Adamson 2001). Both these authors emphasize the beneficial influence of any elements of nature that can be included, such as flowers and other plants, water, fire, and ideally the possibility of being outside in natural beauty.

Follow-up and Integration of the Experience

Insights and emotional shifts that occur in a contained therapeutic setting under the influence of MDMA must be integrated into daily life and ordinary consciousness if they are to be of therapeutic value. Follow-up psychotherapy sessions play an important role in facilitating this process. In our study, three MDMA-assisted sessions that occur over a three- to four-month period are accompanied by 15 scheduled 90-minute follow-up sessions with both co-therapists, and additional sessions are added if needed. In all subjects thus far, follow-up therapy and attention to ongoing personal inner practice have appeared to play an important role in allowing them to integrate and make full use of their experiences from experimental sessions, and in facilitating a continuing process of growth and healing. For some, this integration has been relatively easy, requiring only a modest amount of input from therapists. For others, the MDMA experience has catalyzed a longer and more challenging road to healing, calling for considerable personal commitment by the subjects and support from therapists. *If there are temporary periods of heightened anxiety, grief or other PTSD symptoms following MDMA sessions, proper support is vital.*

PROGRESSION OF SESSIONS

Sessions build on each other. While this is true of any therapy, this phenomenon may be more pronounced in the relatively short course of MDMA-assisted therapy.

In the first session I saw the Pollyanna, optimistic veneer I put on to avoid pain. Tomorrow I'll be ready to get down to the rumbling constant turmoil underneath that's always bubbling. Now I see a thread rather than chaos, and I want to weave it together.[4]

THE TRAJECTORY OF DIFFICULT EMOTIONS FOLLOWING MDMA SESSIONS

Anxiety, anger, grief, and other difficult feelings often increase temporarily during some periods of the days or weeks following an MDMA session. This is usually best understood as a challenging but important part of the healing process, rather than a worsening of PTSD or any other disorder.

One subject, four days after her first MDMA session (which she had finished feeling calm and happy), called from work to say that her anxiety was very high and she was "afraid of losing it." I prescribed one dose of lorazepam to help her get through the rest of the day at work. We met with her that evening and encouraged her to fully feel and express the anxiety. As a result, it dissipated within an hour, and she regarded the experience as part of her healing process. Several other transient peaks of anxiety occurred over the next month; we approached them in the same manner, and they also resolved quite quickly. Each episode seemed to lead to further self-awareness and deeper resolution of the pain related to her trauma.

CHALLENGES OF INTEGRATING RAPID CHANGE

Rapid changes in symptoms or outlook may lead to various challenges in integration. In the days that follow an MDMA-assisted session, subjects are sometimes fearful of losing new-found benefits or they may be skeptical about the validity of what occurred. People with PTSD in particular are typically accustomed to long-standing avoidance or hypervigilance, and may have difficulty adjusting to these defenses. Conversely, subjects who expected dramatic results may be disappointed if symptoms are not resolved. Considerable time and attention are generally required to address these challenges and to incorporate rapid psychological changes into emotional, social and working life, and the dynamics of intimate relationships. The need for careful attention to integration appears to be heightened by the fact that in MDMA sessions, psychological shifts not only occur rapidly rather than gradually, but they also occur in a nonordinary state of consciousness and must then be integrated into ordinary consciousness.

After all these years of not talking about it, was it really safe to reveal that I felt physical pleasure along with horror when I was abused?

Now that the medicine has worn off I sometimes feel guilty for saying the things I did about my parents not being emotionally available. I know it wasn't about blame, but there's still that judging voice that says we don't talk about any of this.

During MDMA sessions, subjects with PTSD may become more aware of habitual patterns such as emotionally distancing themselves from others or not speaking the truth about their own experience. They may have a profound sense of the value of letting go of these old patterns and opening to deeper emotional connection and honest self-expression. But sometimes when subjects attempt to bring this new attitude into everyday life, they find that those around them are unresponsive to or even threatened by their efforts to communicate. This can be a painful experience, especially during the state of openness and vulnerability that may follow an MDMA session.

One subject said, "Since I've realized how shut down I had been I don't ever want to go back to being that way, so I'm having a hard time in business situations or with my father knowing when not to say everything I'm feeling."

Follow-up integration sessions can help subjects find a new, appropriate balance in this respect.

Toward the end of an MDMA session one subject said,

> I feel a peacefulness and also some anxiety about coming back into the world, about how to just be, don't know what that is.
>
> I feel as if a layer has been scraped off, and there are raw nerve endings, a sense of newness, almost like being a newborn, not knowing what will happen.
>
> There's some sense of bewilderment, not knowing what to do now after so many years of being secretive and angry.

BOUNDARIES IN INTEGRATION

After MDMA sessions, subjects may encounter a period of some dysregulation regarding openness vs. appropriate boundaries for self-protection. This may involve increased projection of feelings related to their trauma.

> My husband tries to be supportive, but it feels intrusive.
>
> The most noteworthy thing since last visit is that I'm now experiencing anger at women; I realize it has a lot to do with my mother. I see the way it can get projected onto other women.

After this male subject who was experiencing anger toward women worked with it in the integration sessions and established an agreement with Annie about expressing anger safely in the presence of a woman, he concluded that, "My mother and my abuser now have top billing for my anger, it's a big relief not to have it directed toward myself."

CURRENT STUDY: PHASE II CLINICAL TRIAL TESTING THE SAFETY AND EFFICACY OF MDMA-ASSISTED PSYCHOTHERAPY IN SUBJECTS WITH CHRONIC PTSD

The full protocol of this study is available at the sponsor's website, www.maps.org/mdma/protocol. All subjects have treatment-resistant PTSD with significant symptoms that have failed to resolve with prior psychotherapy and medication treatment. Most subjects have had years of both. Fourteen subjects have thus far completed our three-month, double-blind protocol consisting of two eight-hour MDMA-assisted or placebo-assisted psychotherapy sessions, eleven 90-minute nondrug psychotherapy sessions, and four testing sessions to measure PTSD symptom levels. Four subjects who received placebo have gone on to an open-label protocol in which they have had two MDMA-assisted sessions and nine additional nondrug therapy sessions. Two subjects have had a third MDMA-assisted session and accompanying nondrug sessions as now allowed in our revised protocol.

Preliminary observations reveal four patterns of response:

1. Dramatic and lasting reduction in PTSD symptoms in response to MDMA-assisted therapy.
2. Partial reduction in PTSD symptoms in response to MDMA-assisted therapy.
3. Dramatic, though temporary, response to placebo.
4. No response to placebo, followed by dramatic or partial response to MDMA.

All subjects have told us they found MDMA helpful, which was also our clinical impression, supported by preliminary outcome data. Some have felt that the effect of two MDMA-assisted sessions was dramatic and even life saving; however, others have reported disappointment that MDMA was not a "magic bullet" to remove all their symptoms, or have said it would have been helpful to have one or a few additional sessions.

Observations from the Current Study

The formal outcome measures used in our study are well-established, validated psychological symptom scales. Our primary outcome measure is the CAPS (Clinician Administered PTSD Scale). The CAPS was also used in the clinical trials of sertraline and paroxitine that led to their becoming the only drugs currently approved by the U.S. FDA (Food and Drug Administration) for treating PTSD. Our preliminary results based on these tests are very promising; however, we are not in a position to draw statistical conclusions until the study is complete. The observations provided below are descriptive. With the exception of the first one, the categories discussed below are not variables that we had set out in advance to measure formally. They are empirically derived from our experiences with the 16 subjects who have thus far enrolled in the study. The nature of subjects' experience has varied over quite a broad range, and an effort is made here to communicate a sense of their experiences, emphasizing common elements without drawing conclusions about the likelihood that a given subject will have a particular trajectory of experience. A great deal remains to be learned about the mechanisms of change in MDMA-assisted psychotherapy, and we are currently collaborating with other researchers who are formally studying recordings of our study sessions to learn more in this area. What appears to be true from our observations thus far is that much of the growth and healing that may occur in MDMA-assisted therapy is the result of greater access to and more accurate perspective about affirming experiences, as well as the ability to experience and process difficult emotions and accompanying somatic experience without being overwhelmed by fear or shut down by emotional numbing. Most of the difficulties that subjects encounter have to do with the challenge of carrying these abilities into everyday life. This usually involves resolving conflicts between these new experiences and perspectives, and old patterns of emotional and somatic reactivity, thought, and behavior in order to integrate change into their lives and relationships.

DISTRESS LEVEL

High levels of anxiety or other distress may be part of the therapeutic trajectory of an MDMA session. Our research protocol stipulates that the SUD (Subjective Units of Distress) scale be tracked approximately every 90 minutes during experimental sessions. A typical pattern is for subjects to have a high SUD rating just before starting the first session, then a dramatically lower rating as they realize that the experience will not only be manageable but also can help them connect with feelings of safety and joy, perhaps for the first time in many years. They may then start the second MDMA session a month later with a very low SUD rating only to have it climb steeply as they begin to process their trauma in more depth. Distress levels may stay high for several hours. A succession of difficult emotions may emerge, such as fear, anger, self-blame, and grief. These are often interspersed with periods of insight and a sense of healing and resolution, or by a temporary return to emotional numbness or dissociation. Of course, the specific distress levels usually vary considerably from one subject to another, but a given individual's unique trajectory of experience usually concludes with low levels of distress by the end of a session.

The anxiety that comes up may be directly related to the trauma:

> I was just feeling another wave of fear and wanting to shut down, but now I see it more clearly and I'm willing to feel it to the very core.
> I'm being shown many layers of the fear.
> I'm torn between going away and feeling fear in the abdomen. I hated my body. The shame! It betrayed me because it responded. I can see him (the abuser from childhood), but I also know that I'm here with two people who aren't hurting me. Now I can wake up instead of the old pattern of going away.

Frequently, subjects encounter painful realizations and emotions about difficult circumstances from the past, such as lack of nurturing or protection during childhood, distinct from any discrete trauma to which their PTSD is attributed, or realizations about current unhealthy situations or relationships, all of which may be contributing to their ongoing symptoms. This phenomenon is consistent with the psychoanalytic observation that symptoms are "overdetermined" or with Stanislav Grof's broader concept of "systems of condensed experiences" (COEXs) linking experiences with similar characteristics (Grof 2001). Examples of this are provided below under the section "Insights."

AFFIRMING EXPERIENCES

Pleasurable, joyful, or otherwise affirming experiences may be essential components of the therapeutic process. They may serve both as elements of healing in their own right and as a foundation upon which the strength and perspective necessary for subsequent deeper processing of painful experience may be built.

After a period of intense anxiety about being raped 15 years before, one subject went on to connect deeply with the fact that not only had she survived the rape but also now had a loving and supportive husband and family. "I've known that intellectually but I have never really been able to feel it before. I've always been waiting for the other shoe to drop. . . . I finally feel loved and protected." She reported that this new level of emotional realization was profoundly healing and was accompanied by a great sense of relief.

> There's so much beauty you could live a million lifetimes and not capture it all.
>
> I was happy going off into the forest with that man (when I was seven years old) having fun, not a care in the world, sense of sheer pleasure, sun shining, enjoying the world. He took that from me. I haven't felt it since, until today—I felt some of it again.
>
> There are possibilities in life now. . .the difference between walking around in darkness and pain and not knowing why and not even knowing there's anything different. Sometimes I didn't even try because I didn't really believe there was anything different. You really have to know an alternative to strive for something different; you have to have felt another possibility at least for a moment.
>
> I had never before felt what I felt today in terms of loving connection. I'm not sure I can reach it again without MDMA but I'm not without hope that it's possible. Maybe it's like having an aerial map so now I know there's a trail.
>
> I got a glimpse of more of what I'm capable of growing into. . .I'm motivated to keep practicing openness until it gets more developed and comes from the heart place, but I need safe relationships to do that in.

RESOLUTION OF SYMPTOMS

Some specific symptoms may resolve abruptly. The weight of emotional pain may lift dramatically during an MDMA-assisted session. Some subjects report striking and lasting decreases in or even resolution of certain symptoms during a single session.

The low level of background anxiety is gone, fear of disapproval is gone.
The fear's not there, that's kind of unusual not to feel the fear
Whatever I do, at least I'll have the remaining years of my life free of shame.
I feel the truth of that in my belly, not just in my head.

Other subjects have reported resolution or marked improvement dating from a particular MDMA session with respect to depersonalization, chronic insomnia, decreased concentration, panic, startle response, and chronic pain.

LEARNING TO PROCESS DIFFICULT EMOTIONS

A major benefit of MDMA sessions is the direct experience of being able to withstand difficult emotions without either being overwhelmed or resorting to emotional numbing or dissociating. This provides a template for handling emotional pain that may carry over into the future.

For some subjects, this is a more prominent result than dramatic symptom resolution. In the weeks following MDMA sessions, some subjects have described periods of greater well-being than they had ever experienced previously, but also difficult periods of low mood and emotional reactivity that have challenged them to use what they learned in the MDMA sessions about relating to painful emotions.

What's most comforting is knowing now I can handle difficult feelings without being overwhelmed.
A positive aspect is that I can feel the vulnerability even though I don't like it. I couldn't feel it before. At some level I know that is a good thing and on other levels it doesn't feel good.
One of the main things I took from the MDMA experience was that I'd never before felt so free to tap into my feelings.
I know I can revisit the attack in my mind to a greater extent and know it's not going to overwhelm me. I know there are levels I still haven't dealt with, but it's certainly better.
If I move past the anger and relax, I feel sadness. If I stay with that I feel myself getting dizzy. When I stayed with that I felt gladness. It doesn't have to be all suffering.
That has been a stunning revelation. I didn't understand how much a role I've played in holding onto the anger and how I can breathe into it and experience what's under it. I have a chance now to let it go.
It feels good to experience all the emotions; and knowing they come and move through, I don't get stuck.
I have respect for my emotions now.

INSIGHTS

Important insights and associated emotions often occur spontaneously. These may include revelations about early family dynamics or other life experience relevant to their developing PTSD, as well as insights about current patterns of behavior, thought, and emotion. Many of our subjects have experienced spontaneous painful realizations and accompanying grief and anger about a lack of nurturing, acceptance, and protection during childhood in general, as well as the absence of an effective response to their trauma by those around them. They have often realized that these early omissions contributed to their vulnerability to being traumatized and to their likelihood of developing PTSD. Most had discussed this material in past therapy, but most said it had not resonated as deeply for them before.

Now I feel sadness and loneliness I didn't feel as a child; it was just the way life was. I thought I had to just suck it up and move on when I was raped.

My mother was so emotionally needy I couldn't express my feelings. The rape was the straw that broke the camel's back. I was probably more willing to get in the car with a stranger because I was lonely.

Other valuable insights may also occur:

Blaming myself was a way of distracting myself from the fear.

I realize I've had the belief that I don't deserve anything good.

I realize that I got up early and drove myself so hard in school to get away from my father.

I wasn't able to separate the present moment from the rape and all the associated feelings before, now I'm able to. I feel like I'm coming back into my own.

I used to feel I had to hold onto all that garbage to keep on guard and safe. Now I realize that didn't serve me.

He said I liked it too. He was telling a lie, but I pretended. Since then (43 years) I have thought if I stopped pretending I would die. I don't have to pretend anymore. It's hard to fathom that.

I'm still awestruck by the deep realization last time that that I'm not 7 years old.

Maybe this will also help me let go of my need to control other people. Before control equaled survival.

I realize the way I used to release the anger with bitter, cynical humor; but that only goes so far, it doesn't get to the heart of it.

I feel safer. I realize the way I was in fighting stance all the time, protecting myself, and that actually made me feel less safe and not as safe for other people.

Compassion for themselves as well as others may allow subjects to let go of self- blame about the trauma.

Despite what I thought intellectually there was an impenetrable wall. I knew emotionally I was bad. Now that's changed. The most horrible secret is out and I'm OK. I wasn't responsible for my body responding.

BODY AWARENESS

Subjects often become more aware of connections between emotional and somatic symptoms and may experience spontaneous body movements, sounds, pain or tension, sensations of energy movement, or a feeling of great comfort in the body. At times it may be helpful for therapists to work directly with these physical manifestations. For example, one of our subjects, who experienced an increase in anger several days after an MDMA-assisted session in which she revisited a past sexual assault, reported a dream about having enough energy to kill two male assailants. After the dream, she was distressed by the anger and described it as feeling, "like a raging river inside." In a follow-up session, she agreed to work with this body sensation by lying on a mat with male and female therapists sitting on either side. We offered resistance with our hands as she followed her body's urge to push against us and to express her rage with movement and sounds. Afterwards she reported, "My body feels good. The river is now strong and flowing and full of life, but not raging. My body feels relaxed."

During MDMA sessions, subjects often move with the music, and sometimes make sounds that they experience as arising spontaneously. One subject chanted tones for 40 minutes. Later he commented, "Ahh, I can feel it in my chest, the heaviness lifting. The sound took some of it away and I can breathe better." He associated the chest heaviness with the weight of a sexual assailant.

Other subjects also reported helpful shifts in body awareness and in the quality of their somatic perceptions following MDMA sessions.

You mean I can relax! Forty three years of fear and not being able to feel my body. Now I can feel my body without pain.

I can feel my body without having to make reference to the attack. My body is more than a victim. My body is my own; it's not there for somebody else.

There's an energy that flows inside when you feel that you matter. I like the way that feels.

I tried to eat this morning without the usual distraction to keep from feeling body sensations. I could taste it so much more. Before I didn't want to taste anything. Until yesterday I didn't really understand how separated I was from my body.

I gained trust in my body in the session. That was really important and gives me more confidence when I feel in a stuck place lately.

I've had all these insights on a deeper level than just intellectual, in my body.

TRANSFERENCE

Transference may be heightened during MDMA-assisted sessions and may involve shifts in focus between the male and the female therapists. This possibility is discussed with subjects beforehand to frame it as an anticipated and useful aspect of the therapeutic process. Often subjects direct their attention and conversation toward one of the therapists for as long as 45 minutes at a time. It can be helpful to offer interpretations of the transference; however, this is often unnecessary because subjects frequently talk specifically and insightfully about it without prompting. Contrary to a strictly psychodynamic approach, we find that responding to requests for nurturing touch or other corrective experience within the framework of the transference is helpful and does not interfere with efforts to understand and explore the transference as well.

> It's hard to hear a man's voice. I want to talk just to Annie.
>
> I feel really safe now; you must be a really good mom. I'm sad my mother is not different.
>
> Michael, will you give me a hug. . . .. This was the first time I've ever been touched by a father figure in a non-sexual way. It felt really healing.
>
> I notice the way I cut off Michael when he talks, I have to jump in and be a know-it-all so he'll not think I'm stupid and abandon me. That's what I did with my mother's boyfriends, hoping they would stay and take care of me and my mother. . .now I'm having the experience of really being able to listen to you, Michael, and stay present.
>
> Annie, would you brush my hair? My mother never did when I was little, and it was so hard not to be clean and neatly dressed like other kids.

IMAGERY

Vivid imagery may arise spontaneously and serve as a vehicle for subjects to revisit traumatic experience without feeling overwhelmed.

> In the second session revisiting the trauma was not chaotic like in the first. I had the image of going down a ladder gradually; I had more control.
>
> I felt deeply connected to painful feelings of the traumas as I saw them go by contained in transparent spheres, but it didn't cause anxiety. I felt deep sadness in my heart (tears) but also deep happiness that I was healing and letting it go.
>
> A tiger came and we're running together, yes, this is life, we're free! I remember riding on your back when I was little; you never left me I just forgot you were there.
>
> The tree isn't afraid, and it reflects light; that helps me.
>
> I had the image of floating in the universe in a uterus; then being born, head out with a smile.
>
> I have the image of water buffalo carrying me and my burdens. He's dropping my burdens off slowly so it won't be too much of a shock. I don't have to be afraid anymore.
>
> I see huge white doors with beautiful white glass—so huge and heavy—but a master has engineered them so you can open them with one hand. It's only without the fear that the doors are so light. How interesting; if I go up to them with all the fears it makes me weak. I'm taking those fears out of different parts of my body, looking at them and saying 'it's OK but I'm leaving you here.' The fear served me well at one time, but not now for going through these doors.
>
> I'm a huge pile of fertilizer composting and turning into beautiful rich soil. It's a perfect time to have rain. I'm a converter, I'm the earth, I am. Leaves, rain, even acid rain hit me, and I have a powerful ecosystem, all can be absorbed. What we're doing here is turning compost.

DISSOCIATION

Some degree of dissociation is invariably present in people with PTSD. In our study, potential subjects who met criteria for DID (Dissociative Identity Disorder) were excluded, but most who were included had some features of DDNOS (Dissociative Disorder Not Otherwise Specified). Subjects commonly had periods of feeling and appearing quite regressed. Some described the tendency to "space out" or "feel floaty" in response to addressing painful experience. Others become more aware of distinct ego states.

> I'm more aware of the self critical voice in my mind. I realize that's the voice that saved me when I had to escape from the room.

This subject was able to arrive at feelings of relief and trust after revisiting and processing her traumatic experiences; however, self-deprecation later transiently intensified as a result. Harsh self-criticism was a reaction that followed comfort and trust. This well-established defense became more intense, presumably as an unconscious attempt to regain the illusion of self-protection and control associated with hypervigilance and disdain for her own vulnerability. During this period, close follow-up and support were necessary to prevent relapse into a prior pattern of self-harm. With proper support, this subject and others with similar dynamics were able to move through such periods of heightened difficulty and to develop greater awareness of the role that dissociation had played in their response to trauma. This resulted in less use of dissociation as a defense.

Other subjects had transient periods of increased anxiety, anger, grief, and other difficult feelings following MDMA-assisted sessions. It was helpful in all cases that both the subjects and their significant others had been prepared for the likelihood of these waves of memories and emotions and had been introduced to the perspective that such phenomena are often part of the progression of a deep healing process, rather than a sign of relapse or deterioration.

GROWTH

Subjects may experience growth that goes well beyond the resolution of PTSD symptoms. The following comments from follow-up sessions reflect this phenomenon.

> I'm not so rigid and compulsive; a lot calmer and more rational. I feel wiser. Life has a deeper level.
> There's a loosening of the reins, more sharing responsibility with my husband. The stress level at home is way down.
> I'm like the old me, but a new old me.
> I'm experiencing a whole deeper level of consciousness, calmer, peacefulness. I don't remember ever having this. My mind has never been at peace like this.
> I feel more efficient, grounded, at ease, whole.

It's a challenge to no longer being willing to settle for work that is not consistent with my abilities.

Letting go of shame and responsibility for the abuse feels like it's also opened new possibilities. I don't have to work off the old fear paradigm; I can open to the world in a way that wasn't there before.

Growth may involve what subjects consider to be important spiritual experiences and/or an enhancement of their sense of spirituality.

It wasn't an easy experience but it was so worth it. It was a very spiritual experience, very expansive. I feel a sense of calm and stability now.

I'm taking in healing from a sense of cosmic spirituality filling in the nooks and crannies with healing where I've released things today.

I feel the thread of connectedness of things, a sense of spiritual awakening. I'm reconnecting with feelings I used to have doing meditation years ago just before the rape.

I have a sense of much greater connection with a wise inner voice, inner knowing. It used to happen occasionally over the years, but now since the MDMA sessions it's very common. Some think it's my inner wisdom, I think it's God.

SUMMARY OF EXPERIENCES IN THE CURRENT STUDY

Many subjects have summarized the essential effect of MDMA-assisted therapy for PTSD with striking clarity:

That's where the MDMA is very powerful—helping you let go of old patterns, helping you discover what's real and helping you be less fearful about facing it.

I feel solidness where there wasn't before, a foundation where there used to be a hole.

Last night I had a clear sense that I got where I needed to get. What was missing has been found. What I needed I've gotten. I don't feel like I need to do it again. I think there are still other issues in my life that I can work on with less intense methods.

I don't think I would have survived another year. It's like night and day for me compared to other methods of therapy. Without MDMA I didn't even know where I needed to go. Maybe one of the things the drug does is let your mind relax and get out of the way because the mind is so protective about the injury. It wasn't cognitive about the session. I said things I'd never thought before. It's not like I'd remember something cognitively and then say it; I'd just say it and then say 'Wow, where'd that come from?' Like part of me talking that I wasn't aware of before.

There's still grief but I have my faculties back to deal with it.

It feels like I've started the journey of integration, a whole new reformatting.

The self awareness is enough. I don't want to cling to good feelings just for the sake of it, don't want to interfere with the progression of growth. If I just get real with myself then the time will come for sorting it out.

What I experienced in the sessions is still so present and comforting, such a delight.

There are things about this experience I can't refute. Things will have to shift a bit.

THE FUTURE OF MDMA AS A THERAPEUTIC TOOL

We do not know what the final outcome of our study will be. We can say that the preliminary results are encouraging, particularly given that they have occurred in treatment-resistant subjects and in the context of a controlled clinical trial that places significant limitations on the number of sessions and the time course of treatment. It is clear that MDMA-assisted therapy can be used safely in people with PTSD and that it shows the potential of proving effective. Continued research with this approach will certainly be warranted. In the next several years, outcome data will be available from our study and from similar MDMA/ PTSD studies in Israel and Switzerland. By then investigators and regulatory agencies will be in a position to decide whether to move forward with large-scale clinical trials. The future of MDMA as a therapeutic tool will depend not only on the results of scientific research but also on the degree of objectivity with which these results are interpreted by regulators, mental health professionals, and the culture at large.

NOTES

1. Greer and Tolbert (1998), Downing (1986), Shulgin and Shulgin (2005), Metzner and Adamson (2001), Greer (1985–1986), Downing (1985–1986), and Grinspoon (1985–1986), and in phase I studies (Vollenweider et al. 1998; Cami et al. 2000; Liechti et al. 2001; Tancer et al. 2001; Harris et al. 2002).

2. As expressed in his writings (Grof 2000, 2001) and in personal communication primarily in the context of his training program in Holotropic Breathwork, a nondrug method of working with nonordinary states of consciousness that is based on his extensive experience with psychedelic research.

3. In this chapter, I refer to people undergoing MDMA-assisted psychotherapy as "subjects" or "participants" rather than "patients," "clients," or "inner explorers" because we are doing this work in the context of research. My intent is to convey respect for these individuals and their willingness and intentions to heal.

4. Our observations about the nature of MDMA-assisted therapy for PTSD are illustrated with brief clinical vignettes or quotes from subjects in our study. (Portions of some quotes have been paraphrased for brevity or clarity.)

REFERENCES

Cami, J., M. Farre, M. Mas, P.N. Roset, S. Poudevida, A. Mas, L. San, and R. de la Torre. 2000. Human pharmacology of 3,4-methylenedioxymethamphetamine ("ecstasy"):

Psychomotor performance and subjective effects. *Journal of Clinical Psychopharmacology* 20:455–66.

Downing, J. 1986. The psychological and physiological effects of MDMA on normal volunteers. *Journal of Psychoactive Drugs* 18 (4):335–40.

Downing, J. 1985–1986. Testimony DEA Administrative Law Judge hearings on the scheduling of MDMA. Transcripts and documents from of these hearings can be found on the MAPS website at http://www.maps.org/dea-mdma/ (in Section 6).

Greer, G.R., and R. Tolbert. 1998. A method of conducting therapeutic sessions with MDMA. *Journal of Psychoactive Drugs* 30:371–9.

Greer, G.R. 1985–1986. Testimony DEA Administrative Law Judge hearings on the scheduling of MDMA. Transcripts and documents from of these hearings can be found on the MAPS website at http://www.maps.org/dea-mdma/ (in Section 6).

Grinspoon, L. 1985–1986. Testimony DEA Administrative Law Judge hearings on the scheduling of MDMA. Transcripts and documents from of these hearings can be found on the MAPS website at http://www.maps.org/dea-mdma/ (in Section 6).

Grob, C.S. 2002. Hallucinogens revisited. In *Hallucinogens, a reader,* ed. C.S. Grob, 1–13. New York, NY: Jeremy P. Tarcher/Putnam.

Grof, S. 2000. *Psychology of the future.* Albany, NY: State University of New York Press.

Grof, S. 2001. *LSD psychotherapy.* Sarasota, FL: Multidisciplinary Association for Psychedelic Studies.

Harris, D.S., M. Baggott, J. Mendelson, J.E. Mendelson, and R.T. Jones. 2002. Subjective and hormonal effects of 3,4-methylenedioxymethamphetamine (MDMA) in humans. *Psychopharmacology* (Berl.) 162:396–405.

Holland, J. 2001. The history of MDMA. In *Ecstasy: The complete guide,* ed. J. Holland, 12–20. Rochester, VT: Inner Traditions.

Kessler, R.C., A. Sonnega, E.J. Bromet, M. Hughes, and C.B. Nelson. 1995. Posttraumatic stress disorder in the National Comorbidity Survey. *Archives of General Psychiatry* 52:1048–60.

Liechti, M.E., A. Gamma, and F.X. Vollenweider. 2001. Gender differences in the subjective effects of MDMA. *Psychopharmacology* 154:161–8.

Metzner, R., and S. Adamson. 2001. Using MDMA in healing, psychotherapy and spiritual practice. In *Ecstasy: The complete guide,* ed. J. Holland, 182–207. Rochester, VT: Inner Traditions. Originally published in ReVision 10(4) (1988). The nature of the MDMA experience and its role in healing, psychotherapy, and spiritual practice.

Mithoefer, M.C. 2003, Revised 2005. Study Protocol Phase II clinical trial testing the safety and efficacy of 3,4-methylenedioxymethamphetamine (MDMA)-assisted psychotherapy in subjects with chronic posttraumatic stress disorder. Study # 63-384 Original Protocol: September 24, 2003, Protocol Amendment #1: November 17, 2004, Protocol Amendment #2: June 23, 2005, http://www.maps.org/research/mdma/ptsd_study/protocol/protocol030605.html.

Shulgin, A.T., and A. Shulgin. 2005. Frontiers of pharmacology: Chemistry and consciousness. In *Higher wisdom,* ed. R. Walsh and C. Grob, 69–90. Albany, NY: SUNY Press.

Spinazzola, L., M. Blaustein, and B.A. van der Kolk. 2005. Posttraumatic stress disorder treatment outcome research: The study of unrepresented samples? *Journal of Traumatic Stress* 18:425–36.

Tancer, M.E., and C.E. Johnson. 2001. The subjective effects of MDMA and mCPP in moderate MDMA users. *Drug and Alcohol Dependence* 65:97–101.

Taylor, K. 1995. *The ethics of caring*. Santa Cruz, CA: Hanford Mead.

Ursano, R.J., C. Bell, S. Eth, M. Friedman, A. Norwood, B. Pfefferbaum, R. Pynoos, D. Zitzick, and D. Benedek 2004. *The American Journal of Psychiatry* V161 (11) Supplement.

Van der Kolk, B.A. 2003. The neurobiology of childhood trauma and abuse. *Child and Adolescent Psychiatric Clinics* 12:293–317.

Vollenweider, F.X., A. Gamma, M. Liechti, and T. Huber. 1998. Psychological and cardiovascular effects and short-term sequelae of MDMA ("ecstasy") in MDMA-naive healthy volunteers. *Neuropsychopharmacology* 19:241–51.

9

PSYCHEDELIC THERAPY FOR THE TREATMENT OF DEPRESSION

MICHAEL MONTAGNE

The effectiveness of psychedelic drugs for the treatment of depression was recognized during the golden age of research and clinical use of these substances in the 1950s and 1960s. Before these drugs became prohibited from medical research and use, a great deal of interest and work had occurred to identify how they might be applied therapeutically. Over the past decade or so, a new generation of scientists and therapists, who have learned and still are learning from those who worked in the golden age, have renewed efforts to determine the role of psychedelic drugs in the treatment of a variety of mental illnesses including depression.

Depression is a complex condition that affects an individual's health and well-being. Many different types of therapy have been developed and studied to treat this condition and its associated symptoms. The dominant therapeutic approach is based in pharmacology and thus the use of pharmaceuticals. The effectiveness of this approach varies considerably, and some critics believe it is flawed and more destructive than productive (Ford 2006). What can psychedelic drugs show or tell us about depression and the best way to treat it? (Riedlinger and Riedlinger 1994).

The psychedelics that have been considered and studied in this regard include LSD (lysergic acid diethylamide), psilocybin/psilocin (found in "magic" mushrooms), MDMA (methylenedioxymethamphetamine or "Ecstasy") and MDE (methylenedioxyethylamphetamine or "Eve"), DMT (dimethytryptamine), mescaline (found in peyote), ketamine, ibogaine (found in Iboga), and ayahuasca. These substances are active on specific receptors and neurotransmitters that influence mood, anxiety, sensory processing, memory, and many other functions carried out by the central nervous system. They also carry significant social–cultural meanings and experiences that can enhance a depressed patient's ability to heal.

The nature and extent of depression, its symptoms, and therapies to treat it are reviewed. This provides background for understanding the biochemical basis of depression as the dominant model for describing this disease. This biological model, however, is not necessarily the best or only approach for appreciating the causes and context of how and why an individual might suffer from depression. Psychedelic drugs were studied and used therapeutically during a golden age of medical research on these substances after the Second World War. Researchers and therapists discovered that psychedelic drugs were useful in treating psychiatric conditions, such as depression, especially in conjunction with psychotherapy. Prohibitions on the use and medical study of psychedelics have curtailed any activity since the late 1960s. Psychedelic drug research has returned however, and studies are being planned and conducted to reassess the safety and effectiveness of these drugs for the treatment of depression.

WHAT IS DEPRESSION AND HOW IS IT TREATED?

Studies on the extent of depression have shown that the lifetime risk for major depression in adults ranges from 10% to 25% for women and from 5% to 12% for men. Major depression tends to occur most in the 25- to 44-year-old age group and is more common among first-degree biological relatives of persons with the disorder than in the general population (APA 2000).

The experience, perception, and description of the symptoms of depression can be influenced by cultural background. In some cultures, depression may be experienced largely in physical terms rather than emotional states such as sadness or guilt. In Latino and Mediterranean cultures, individuals may complain of "nerves" and headaches. In some Asian cultures, individuals may complain of weakness, fatigue, or imbalance. In Middle Eastern cultures, depression is viewed as a problem of the heart, and in some Native American cultures, it is expressed as being "heart-broken." Cultures also differ in their perception of the seriousness of depression.

Symptoms of a major depressive episode usually develop over a period of time. According to the diagnostic criteria for a major depressive episode, primary requirements for a diagnosis are either a depressed mood or the loss of interest or pleasure in nearly all activities for at least two weeks. These symptoms must exist for most of the day and for nearly every day. Five or more of the following symptoms must also be present during that same two-week period of time, and they must represent a change from previous functioning: 1) significant weight gain or weight loss, or a decrease or increase in appetite nearly every day; 2) insomnia or excessive sleeping nearly every day; 3) psychomotor retardation or agitation; 4) fatigue or loss of energy; 5) feelings of worthlessness, or excessive or inappropriate guilt; 6) diminished ability to think or concentrate, or indecisiveness; and 7) recurrent thoughts of death, suicidal ideas, or a suicide attempt (APA 2000). The mood in a major depressive episode is often described as feeling sad, hopeless, discouraged, or "down in the dumps." It thus is reasonable to consider major depression as a potentially life-threatening illness.

Because there are no clinical laboratory findings that are definitively diagnostic for major depression, distinguishing between many different medical and psychiatric syndromes can be difficult. Anxiety disorders, drug-induced mood disorders, manic episodes, attention-deficit hyperactivity disorder, adjustment disorders, and bereavement are examples of other psychiatric conditions with similar symptoms. Anxiety can coexist with depression in many patients. Major depression may be associated with chronic medical conditions as well. Up to 25% of individuals with certain medical conditions (e.g., diabetes, myocardial infarction, cancer, stroke, and AIDS) will develop major depression during the course of their illness. Periods of sadness are inherent aspects of the human experience, but they should not be diagnosed as a major depressive episode (APA 2000).

Depression then is both a biologically based disease and a state of mind and being in a social–cultural context. The word depression has many meanings, and the state of depression can refer to a great variety of symptoms. What brings about a state of depression and what are the different ways of treating it? There is a difference between the transitory state of feeling sad or "blue" and depression. As an individual experiences various physical and mental changes, and how they respond to them, a set of symptoms becomes defined, often as depression (as opposed to feeling blue, being down).

Current Treatments

Current treatment for depression ranges from the most popular pharmacological therapy to psychotherapy and electroconvulsive or shock therapy. These therapies are sometimes, but not often enough, used in combination and tailored to the individual patient's needs and symptoms. Different types and severity of symptoms and presumed causes of the depressive state often dictate the type of therapy to be used. Most types of therapy tend to be effective for most patients, but not necessarily for long periods of time. The key is that most cases of depression are not truly cured as we normally think of a "cure" in the context of an infectious disease. The goal usually is to treat the symptoms to the point where the patient feels he or she can function again in everyday life. For cases of severe depression, however, the goal may be to access, confront, or accept the cause of the depressive state, especially traumatic episodes, through psychotherapy.

Current pharmaceuticals are based on molecular relationships with the neurotransmitters, or brain chemicals, which relay messages along nerve cells and their receptors throughout the brain and central nervous system to maintain or change physical and mental states of being (Julien 2001). These drugs require daily dosing. Tolerance to a drug's activity may develop over time, and there then may be the need to increase doses or switch to other drugs. The receptors and neurotransmitter systems thought to be involved in depression include dopamine, norepinephrine, serotonin, GABA (gamma-amino butyric acid), and more recently glutamate. The biochemical basis of depression is poorly understood, and thus the use of pharmacologically active substances becomes problematic. Antidepressant medications have proven effective, at least in terms of treating symptoms, for many depressed patients (ranging from 30% to 60%), but not for all of them.

Treatment of depression before the development of the tricyclic antidepressants was crudely based on elevating mood with stimulants such as amphetamines and methylphenidate (Ritalin®). The tricyclics, such as amitriptyline (Elavil®) and imipramine (Tofranil®), ushered in the era of the biogenic amine theory of depression in the 1960s. Depression became a biological, more specifically a biochemical, disorder. These drugs are active on dopamine and norepinephrine and to a lesser extent on serotonin neurotransmitter systems (see Table 9.1). At the same time, another class of drugs was developed and found to be somewhat effective in treating depression, the monoamine oxidase inhibitors. Monoamine oxidase is an enzyme that breaks down neurotransmitters, so this category of drugs works by preventing the breakdown process thus increasing the concentration of the "mood" neurotransmitters in nerve cells. The most popular current type of antidepressant medication prescribed for treatment of depression has activity on serotonin and are called selective serotonin reuptake inhibitors or SSRIs (Prozac®, Zoloft®, and Paxil®), in reference to how they work. Benzodiazepine tranquilizers act on the GABA system and are used to treat anxiety. They also can be effective in treating depressed patients who are experiencing anxiety as a component of their condition. Antidepressants conversely can be effective in treating anxiety. Current research has focused on SNRIs (selective norepinephrine reuptake inhibitors) to treat depression (Julien 2001).

The pharmacological treatment of depression has ranged over almost all of the body's neurotransmitter systems. Each category of antidepressant medication acts primarily on one of the major receptor–neurotransmitter systems, but they often have some activity on other systems. While the specific mechanism of action of these drugs in terms of nerve cell receptors and chemicals is known, it still is not clear how this equates to the medical condition called depression. In essence, instead of first identifying the biochemical cause of depression, medical research has defined the "cause" in terms of those chemicals (neurotransmitters) which act specifically to perform certain functions in the nervous system and seem to be related to the various symptoms of depression.

Table 9.1 Relationships Between Receptors/Neurotransmitters, Pharmaceuticals, and Psychedelics in the Treatment of Depression

Receptor/ neurotransmitter	Functions	Pharmaceuticals	Psychedelics
Dopamine	Mood Stimulation Concentration	Cocaine Amphetamines Tricyclic antidepressants Bupropion	MDMA/MDE Mescaline
Norepinephrine	Mood Memory Learning Sleep Anxiety Sensory processing	Tricyclic antidepressants SNRI antidepressants	MDMA/MDE Mescaline
Serotonin	Mood Sleep Hallucinations Emotional and pain processing	SSRI antidepressants	LSD Psilocybin DMT Ibogaine Ayahuasca
GABA	Anxiety Sedation Anesthesia	Benzodiazepine tranquilizers	
Acetylcholine	Memory Sensory transmission	Tricyclic antidepressants	Scopolamine
Glutamate	Memory Excitatory functions		Ketamine Ibogaine
Opioid receptors (Endorphins)	Pain Emotional states	Tricyclic antidepressants	Ibogaine

THE "GOLDEN AGE" OF MEDICAL RESEARCH THROUGH USE OF PSYCHEDELICS

The possibility that psychedelic drugs could help facilitate the modern psychotherapeutic process was realized in the late 1940s after the synthesis and discovery of LSD-25 by the Sandoz chemist Albert Hofmann. Hofmann later extracted and identified psilocybin and psilocin from the "magic" mushroom. Mescaline had been known since the turn of the 20th century, and some investigators suspected it could have a role in treating mental conditions.

From the late 1940s to the mid-1960s, a couple of thousand publications describing tens of thousands of patients who had taken part in psychedelic drug therapy or other clinical research trials were published, as well as several dozen books. A number of international conferences on psychedelic drug therapy were held. Two different types of psychedelic drug–assisted psychotherapy emerged. One emphasized a mystical or conversion experience and its after effects (psychedelic therapy). This type of therapy was thought to be especially effective in treating alcoholics and "reforming" criminals using high doses of LSD (greater than 200 mcg). The other type of therapy (psycholytic) explored the unconscious through psychoanalysis. It focused on the treatment of neuroses and psychosomatic disorders using low doses of LSD (100 to 150 mcg), as well as other psychedelic drugs (Aaronson and Osmond 1970; Grinspoon and Bakalar 1979, 1983).

By the mid-1950s, it was recognized that psychedelics function as nonspecific amplifiers, drugs that project into consciousness (amplify) memories, fears, and other subjectively variable (nonspecific) psychological material that was previously repressed or unconscious. Among the first announcements of this highly significant finding was a report titled *Ataractic and Psychedelic Drugs in Psychiatry,* written by a team of international experts convened by the World Health Organization in 1958. This report challenged the prevailing idea that psychedelic drugs were psychotomimetic, capable of inducing a model of temporary psychosis. It was made clear that the issues of set (the user's expectations) and setting (the environment of the drug experience) must be taken into account when using psychedelics.

Another important issue that was realized in drug-assisted psychotherapy was that, unlike mood elevating or stabilizing drugs that patients must use on a daily basis, psychedelic drugs would be used only a few times, under the supervision of a therapist, in the initial sessions that begin the psychotherapeutic process toward healing. Grinspoon and Bakalar (1986) have emphasized: "It is a misunderstanding to consider psychedelic drug therapy as a form of chemotherapy, which must be regarded in the same way as prescribing lithium or phenothiazines." Instead, it is more like "a hybrid between pharmacotherapy and psychotherapy" that incorporates features of both.

Despite early reports of success with drug-assisted psychotherapy, both psychedelic and psycholytic therapies have certain limitations. In most cases, those studies were either anecdotal or lacked a control group in their experimental design. Anecdotal reports can be questioned for several reasons including placebo effects and the patient's and therapist's biases in judging improvement. The lack of a control group is also a problem. It is generally agreed upon that a good study design must include the presence of a group of subjects, for comparison, who underwent the entire procedure (psychotherapy) without taking the drug in question for comparison. The effects of psychedelics are so unmistakable that most researchers argue using them effectively would rule out a blinded study design. With these few limitations acknowledged, however, it is clear that human research using psychedelic drugs produced some promising results with implications for the treatment of depression, as well as other psychiatric disorders (Riedlinger and Montagne 2001).

Another problem was that the classic psychedelics are time-consuming to use, despite claims that they accelerate psychotherapy. Even low doses have pronounced psychoactive and behavioral effects lasting five or more hours. Patients needed to be supervised throughout this period and for several hours afterward to minimize adverse effects. The incidence of adverse reactions to psychedelic drugs was low when individuals (both normal volunteers and patients) were carefully screened, supervised, and followed up, especially when given judicious doses of pharmaceutical quality drug.

One program was conducted for several years in the early 1960s by Stolaroff (1994) and his colleagues at the International Foundation for Advanced Study in Menlo Park, California. Therapy required several preliminary meetings for psychological screening and other preparatory work, a full day for the LSD session, and supervision for all of the following day by someone who had previously finished the same program. Bishop's *The Discovery of Love* (1963) is a subjective account of this program by one of the clients. Grof (1980) also was an early pioneer in the use of drug-assisted psychotherapy at the Maryland Psychiatric Research Center in Baltimore. Some of his work focused on the use of LSD in terminal cancer patients to decrease their anxiety and depression and to increase their serenity, calmness, inner peace, and intensity of interpersonal closeness.

These previous experiences with the use of psychedelics in psychotherapy involved therapists, researchers, and patients interested in finding an alternate route to treating or resolving depression. Outside the traditional pharmaceutical treatments for depression, what have patients on their own or with their therapists discovered can help them? Many patients have searched for alternatives to traditional antidepressant medications, and they have claimed to receive effects and benefits from other drugs including stimulants (amphetamines and cocaine), cannabis, and psychedelics. Some psychedelic drug users were not interested initially in symptom treatment, but more in hallucinatory experience. They discovered, however, that these drugs had an impact on the symptoms of their depression, or more significantly, allowed them to recognize and explore the traumatic basis of their symptoms and condition (Riedlinger and Montagne 2001).

CONTEMPORARY RESEARCH ON PSYCHEDELICS AND DEPRESSION

A new golden age of medical research on the therapeutic benefits of psychedelic drugs has begun. After nearly 30 years of repression, researchers are returning to these drugs and exploring their effectiveness, safety, and utility in treating depression. Much of this effort was initiated and championed by the MAPS (Multidisciplinary Association for Psychedelic Studies, see www.maps.org/research) and later by the Heffter Research Institute (see www.heffter.org). See these websites for all current research activity.

This new generation of researchers and clinical investigators are using many of the classic psychedelic drugs in a variety of studies and experiments to open new avenues in the treatment of depression. These drugs have pharmacological activity related to the body's receptor–neurotransmitter systems and to the types of antidepressant medications that are prescribed for depressed patients (Table 9.1).

Substances That Act on Dopamine and Norepinephrine

The first category of psychedelic drug research focuses on those substances that act on dopamine and norepinephrine: MDMA, MDE and related molecules, and to a lesser extent, mescaline (Eisner 1989; Julien 2001).

The use of MDMA in psychotherapy does have something in common with the classic psychedelic and psycholytic therapies. The patient must be given MDMA under supervision of an experienced practitioner. The effects, however, are not as intense as for a classic psychedelic like LSD, but the potential does exist for individual variance, and set and setting continue to be a factor. In any case, the use of MDMA in psychotherapy to stimulate positive feelings such as openness and empathy would seem to recommend a possible clinical role in treating depression. Because it is a potent releaser of serotonin, and because of its short duration of activity, MDMA would seem to be both effective and efficient as a drug for the medical treatment of depression. It works in minutes, instead of weeks (as is the case for most prescription antidepressants), and is effective when administered infrequently, perhaps on weekly or monthly dosing intervals (Greer 1985; Greer and Tolbert 1990).

The notion that MDMA might be useful in treating suicidal depression is based on a comparison of psychological patterns in suicidal patients and MDMA's psychoactive effects. Many suicidal cases seem to be manifestations of alienation. Such people often find it hard to deal with the conflicts and demands of interpersonal relationships. They withdraw into a private, lonely world, and the isolation typically starts to feel irreversible. They feel there is no possibility of ever establishing meaningful contact with other human beings or any aspect of life (Riedlinger and Montagne 2001).

When MDMA was reintroduced in the 1970s by Shulgin and Shulgin (1991), they and a few psychiatrists and therapists realized this potential in MDMA and began using it in therapy with depressed patients. It was used as an aid to psychotherapy for over 10 years until it became a Schedule I–controlled substance (no medical use) in 1986. It appeared to enhance the therapeutic alliance by inviting self-disclosure and enhancing trust. Some patients also reported changes that lasted several days, weeks, or longer and changes in symptoms such as improved mood, greater relaxation, heightened self-esteem, and enhanced relations with others. It heightened the user's capacity for introspection and intimacy without the significant perceptual changes, emotional unpredictability, and other adverse reactions that are associated with LSD (Baylen and Rosenberg 2006).

Anecdotal reports by the hundreds of people who have taken MDMA in therapeutic settings are important. Their testimonies indicate that certain psychological effects occur consistently across a broad spectrum of use. This is evident in Adamson's (1985) collection of about 50 such testimonies. The foreword, by Ralph Metzner, observes that these firsthand accounts include words such as "empathy, openness, acceptance, forgiveness, and emotional bonding" in reference to MDMA's effects. These are the opposite terms often used to describe the psychological distress of suicidal people: anguish, alienation, recalcitrance, rejection, blame and guilt, and emotional withdrawal. The therapeutic process becomes accelerated. According to Metzner, "one therapist has estimated that in five hours of one Adam (MDMA) session clients could activate and process psychic material that would normally require five months of weekly sessions." Eisner (1989) also describes several cases of MDMA-assisted psychotherapy in which depression is mentioned specifically as one of the conditions successfully treated.

From 1988 to 1993, therapists with the Swiss Medical Society for Psycholytic Therapy used MDMA and LSD to assist in psychotherapy. A questionnaire-based evaluation of 171 of these patients was conducted (Gasser 1994–1995). Nine out of ten patients declared themselves to have experienced good or slight improvement concerning the problems that brought them to therapy, and they felt that psycholytic psychotherapy was a safe treatment. Clinical trials of MDMA-assisted psychotherapy for treatment of PTSD (post-traumatic stress disorder) have been proposed recently in Spain, Israel, Switzerland, and the United States and have begun in some cases (see the MAPS website for the current status of these studies). Volunteers in the United States study undergo two experimental sessions in which they receive 125 mg MDMA or placebo, as well as up to 10 nondrug-assisted therapy sessions. As traumatic events are considered the source or "cause" of major depressive episodes for many patients, the results of these trials will be very important in identifying new approaches to treating some forms of major depression. Early results of these trials have confirmed the safety of MDMA-assisted psychotherapy and also have suggested that this therapeutic approach is effective.

As depression can occur in patients with serious medical conditions, particularly in advanced stages, and can coexist with anxiety, studies have begun to examine the effectiveness of psychedelics in assisting psychotherapy in these patients. A study at Harvard Medical School is focusing on the use of MDMA in reducing anxiety in advanced stage cancer patients.

There also has been interest in the use of mescaline in treating depression. Nonmedical users of peyote and mescaline have reported anxiety and depressive symptoms, though in many cases, these conditions were present, and even diagnosed, prior to the use of that drug. There are anecdotal accounts, however, by some individuals that their mescaline experiences helped them to remember or confront the potential source (again usually a traumatic event) of their depression. These reports, in conjunction with the known pharmacological activity of mescaline on dopamine and norepinephrine, suggest that mescaline might be effective in drug-assisted psychotherapy. No studies are currently planned or being conducted to examine this hypothesis, and the potential benefit of mescaline in treating depression is more ambiguous than the obvious role of MDMA.

Substances That Act on Serotonin

The second category of psychedelics that are being explored in the treatment of depression include LSD and other substances active on serotonin, such as psilocybin, DMT, and ibogaine. The evaluation study of LSD-assisted psycholytic therapy in Switzerland has already been discussed. Another Swiss study and an American study are focusing on the use of LSD in reducing anxiety in advanced stage cancer patients, and another American study is using psilocybin for the same therapeutic purpose.

These studies are extensions, or perhaps continuations, of the medical research performed with these compounds during the golden age of psychedelic research. The obvious connection is that LSD, psilocybin, DMT (Strassman 2000), ibogaine (De Rienzo and Beal 1997), and the components of ayahuasca (Metzner 2005) are active on the serotonin neurotransmitter system, which has been the center of attention in the development of the most popular pharmaceutical medications to treat depression, the SSRIs. These psychedelics should show beneficial effects for the treatment of depression. Based on the research performed in the 1950s and 1960s, contemporary anecdotal user accounts of the benefits of these drugs in alleviating symptoms of depression or providing insight into the reasons why they are depressed, and the pharmacological relationships to neurotransmitters that affect mood, research on these psychedelics in the treatment of depression should show beneficial effects (Shulgin and Shulgin 1997; Riedlinger and Riedlinger 1994).

A Substance That Acts on Glutamate

Ketamine is a psychedelic which is active on the glutamate receptor–neurotransmitter system, and it has shown promise in treating depression. Ketamine-assisted psychotherapy has been shown to reduce levels of anxiety and depression in patients. In one study by Berman et al. (2000), the intravenous administration of ketamine, without psychotherapy, produced significant improvement in depressive symptoms within 72 hours. A recent study by Zarate et al. (2006) has generated a great deal of media attention. Intravenous administration of ketamine again produced a rapid and profound antidepressant effect in 12 of 17 patients. The most spectacular aspects of this study are that these patients had been severely depressed for a long time and had been resistant to the effects of a variety of pharmaceutical antidepressants and that five of them met the criteria for remission of their condition the day after treatment. In addition to identifying the potential value of ketamine as an antidepressant, these studies suggest that the glutamate neurotransmitter system might have a much more significant role in depression than previously thought. The major limitation is that the lasting effects and long-term benefits of ketamine therapy are not known.

Ketamine-assisted psychedelic therapy also has been used to treat heroin addiction (Krupitsky et al. 2000). Research in Russia has shown its effectiveness in reducing the craving for heroin and reducing relapse to drug use. Relevant to ketamine's role as an antidepressant is that many heroin addicts also reported a reduction in the symptoms of depression.

THE MYSTICAL–SPIRITUAL ASPECTS OF PSYCHEDELICS

A final aspect that may be very important in terms of the effectiveness of psychedelics in treating depression is the mystical–spiritual component to the experiences these drugs can produce for many users. Depression can be examined clinically, but there is an element of this disorder that affects the psyche in ways that are difficult to explain in traditional Western scientific terms. The element of the soul or spirit is very important in healing and religious practices in many cultures, but the Western scientific community is still reluctant to accept the idea of spirituality having an influence on illness. Depression in the spiritual sense can be considered a sickness of the soul. It represents a soul that is disconnected from society, family, and friends. There is a loss of faith that the universe will support and nourish the individual ultimately resulting in the conviction that life is just not worth living. In this state, one feels unloved and unable to love, and personal conflicts cannot be resolved only perpetuated (Grinspoon and Bakalar 1983; Riedlinger and Montagne 2001).

Accounts from users and therapists who have employed MDMA therapeutically describe a reconnection of the patient with a deep appreciation of their place in the universe and a feeling of being loved by it (Adamson 1985). A recent study at Johns Hopkins University examined the role of psychedelics in producing mystical experiences. Griffiths et al. (2006) are performing a series of studies to investigate the effects of psilocybin in healthy volunteers. The first was a double-blind experimental study evaluating the psychological effects of psilocybin relative to methylphenidate administered under comfortable, supportive conditions to 36 psychedelic-naive adults reporting regular participation in religious or spiritual activities. On psilocybin, 22 of the subjects had a full mystical experience. Two months after the study, almost three-quarters of the subjects rated their psilocybin experience as among the five most "spiritually significant" experiences of their lifetimes. They also reported that it had increased their current sense of personal well-being or life satisfaction. Some of the subjects, however, reported significant fear and strong anxiety during their psilocybin session.

THE FUTURE OF PSYCHEDELICS AS HEALING AGENTS FOR DEPRESSION

Psychedelic drugs appear to have value in the treatment of depression, but the benefits are limited. Their greatest utility is in the treatment of major depressive disorders produced by traumatic events, such as PTSD, and by the advanced or terminal stages of certain illnesses (cancer and AIDS). In these situations, the use of specific psychedelics would consist of limited dosing and duration of use regimens, though the actual dose used in a therapeutic session could vary considerably. These drugs would not and could not be used on a daily basis over any extended period of time.

The future role of psychedelic drugs in treating depression will be through pharmaceutical discovery and development that was not permitted to occur from the late 1960s to the 1990s. These molecules need to be placed in the hands of medicinal chemists, pharmacologists, and clinical researchers for molecular modification, pharmacological testing, and therapeutic assessment. This traditional process of pharmaceutical development allows for the enhancement of specific antidepressant activity while reducing the occurrence or severity of side effects and adverse reactions, especially those related to hallucinatory activity.

Encouraging results from a few ongoing studies recommend strongly for increased research on all types of psychedelics, with special emphasis perhaps on those (MDMA) which cause substantially less distortion of normal consciousness than classic psychedelics such as LSD or mescaline. Those drugs could be more easily assimilated into existing psychotherapy approaches, in which they would function to accelerate and enhance the normal psychotherapeutic process rather than serving as a maintenance medication. Their usefulness in such an application is mainly at the start of psychotherapy to reduce the client's "fear response" that often inhibits their ability to deal with repressed traumatic material; facilitate the client's interpersonal communications with the therapist, spouse, or significant others; and accelerate formation of a therapeutic alliance between client and therapist.

A new golden age of psychedelic medicine has dawned (Sessa 2005). These drugs and their effects must be explored for the benefit of depressed patients, particularly those for whom traditional therapies have been ineffective. Molecular variations of these drugs can lead to the discovery of new types of antidepressant medications. Psychedelic drugs also can help us see beyond a purely biological approach to treating depression. Psychedelic drug effects provide for mystical experiences, spiritual insights, and an unlocking of the closed self and repressed mind and soul. Psychedelic-assisted psychotherapy is a patient-centered approach to the healing process that can provide a long-term resolution to major depression.

REFERENCES

Aaronson, B., and H. Osmond, eds. 1970. *Psychedelics: The uses and implications of hallucinogenic drugs.* New York: Anchor Books.

Adamson, S. 1985. *Through the gateway of the heart: Accounts of experiences with MDMA and other empathogenic substances.* San Francisco: Four Trees Publications.

APA (American Psychiatric Association). 2000. *Diagnostic and statistical manual of mental disorders DSM-IV-TR.* 4th ed. (Text Revision). Washington, D.C.: American Psychiatric Publishing.

Baylen, C.A., and H. Rosenberg. 2006. A review of the acute subjective effects of MDMA/ecstasy. *Addiction* 101:933–47.

Berman, R.M., A. Cappiello, A. Anand, D.A. Oren, G.R. Heninger, D.S. Charney, and J.H. Krystal. 2000. Antidepressant effects of ketamine in depressed patients. *Biological Psychiatry* 47:351–4.

Bishop, M.G. 1963. *The discovery of love: A psychedelic experience with LSD-25.* New York: Dodd, Mead & Co.

De Rienzo, P., and D. Beal. 1997. *The Ibogaine story: Report on the Staten Island project.* New York: Autonomedia.

Eisner, B. 1989. *Ecstasy: The MDMA story.* Berkeley, CA: Ronin.

Ford, J. 2006. *Antidepressants and the critics: Cure-alls or unnatural poisons?* Broomall, PA: Mason Crest Publishers.

Gasser, P. 1994–1995. http://www.maps.org/news-letters/v05n3/05303psy.html.

Greer, G. 1985. Using MDMA in psychotherapy. *Advances: Journal of the Institute for the Advancement of Health* 2:57–9.

Greer, G., and R. Tolbert. 1990. The therapeutic use of MDMA. In *Ecstasy: The clinical, pharmacological and neurotoxicological effects of the drug MDMA,* ed. S.J. Peroutka, 21–36. Boston: Kluwer Academic Publishers.

Griffiths, R.R., W.A. Richards, U. McCann, and R. Jesse. 2006. Psilocybin can occasion mystical-type experiences having substantial and sustained personal meaning and spiritual significance. *Psychopharmacology* 187:268–83.

Grinspoon, L., and J.B. Bakalar. 1979. *Psychedelic drugs reconsidered.* New York: Basic.

Grinspoon, L., and J.B. Bakalar. 1983. *Psychedelic reflections.* New York: Human Sciences Press.

Grinspoon, L., and J.B. Bakalar. 1986. Can drugs be used to enhance the psychotherapeutic process? *American Journal of Psychotherapy* 40:393–404.

Grof, S. 1980. *LSD psychotherapy.* Pomona, CA: Hunter House.

Julien, R.M. 2001. *A primer of drug action.* 9th ed. New York: Worth Publishers.

Krupitsky, E., A. Burakov, T. Romanova, I. Dunaevsky, R. Strassman, and A. Grinenko. 2000. Ketamine psychotherapy for heroin addiction: Immediate effects and two-year follow-up. *Journal of Substance Abuse Treatment* 23:273–83.

Metzner, R. 2005. *Sacred vine of spirits: Ayahuasca.* Rochester, VT: Park Street Press.

Riedlinger, J., and M. Montagne. 2001. Using MDMA in the treatment of depression. In *Ecstasy: The complete guide,* ed. J. Holland, 261–72. Rochester, VT: Park Street Press.

Riedlinger, T., and J. Riedlinger. 1994. Psychedelic and entactogenic drugs in the treatment of depression. *Journal of Psychoactive Drugs* 26:41–55.

Sessa, B. 2005. Can psychedelics have a role in psychiatry once again? *British Journal of Psychiatry* 186:457–8.

Shulgin, A., and A. Shulgin. 1991. *PiHKAL: A chemical love story.* Berkeley, CA: Transform Press.

Shulgin, A., and A. Shulgin. 1997. *TiHKAL: The continuation.* Berkeley, CA: Transform Press.

Stolaroff, M.J. 1994. *Thanatos to eros: 35 years of psychedelic exploration.* Lone Pine, CA: Thaneros Press.

Strassman, R. 2000. *DMT: The spirit molecule.* Rochester, VT: Park Street Press.

World Health Organization. 1958. *Ataractic and hallucinogenic drugs in psychiatry: Report of a study group.* Technical Report Series No. 152. Geneva, Switzerland: WHO.

Zarate, C.A., J.B. Singh, P.J. Carlson, N.E. Brutsche, R. Ameli, D.A. Luckenbaugh, D.S. Charney, and H.K. Manji. 2006. A randomized trial of an N-methyl-D-aspartate antagonist in treatment-resistant major depression. *Archives General Psychiatry* 63:856–64.

10

MARIJUANA AND AIDS

DONALD I. ABRAMS

CANNABIS AS MEDICINE: A BRIEF HISTORY

Use of cannabis as medicine dates back at least 2,000 years (Abel 1980; Chan et al. 1995; Joy et al. 1999; Mack and Joy 2001; Booth 2003). Widely employed on the Indian subcontinent, cannabis was introduced into Western medicine in the 1840s by W.B. O'Shaughnessy, a surgeon who learned of its medicinal benefits firsthand while working in the British East Indies Company. Promoted for reported analgesic, sedative, anti-inflammatory, antispasmodic, and anticonvulsant properties, cannabis was said to be the treatment of choice for Queen Victoria's menstrual cramps. In the early 1900s, medicines that were indicated for each of cannabis' purported activities were introduced into the Western armamentarium, making its use less widespread.

Physicians in the United States were the main opponents to the introduction of the Marihuana Tax Act by the Treasury Department in 1937. The legislation was masterminded by Harry Anslinger, Director of the Federal Bureau of Narcotics from its inception in 1931 until 1962, who testified in Congress that "Marijuana is the most violence-causing drug in the history of mankind." The Act imposed a levy of one dollar an ounce for medicinal use and one hundred dollars an ounce for recreational use, which in 1937 dollars was a prohibitive cost. By using the Mexican name for the plant and associating it with nefarious

South-of-the-Border goings-on, the proponents fooled many physicians. The Act was opposed by the American Medical Association who felt that objective evidence that cannabis was harmful was lacking and that its passage would impede further research into its medical utility. In 1942, cannabis was removed from the U.S. Pharmacopoeia.

Mayor Fiorello LaGuardia of New York commissioned an investigation into the reality of the potential risks and benefits of cannabis. That report in 1944 indicated that the substance was not associated with increased risk of criminal activity, addiction, and insanity as had been claimed (New York Academy of Medicine 1944). The LaGuardia Committee Report, as well as the subsequent similar investigations that have been commissioned every 10 to 20 years since, has been largely ignored.

In 1970, with the initiation of the Controlled Substances Act, marijuana was classified as a Schedule I drug. Where both Schedule I and Schedule II substances have a high potential for abuse, Schedule I drugs are distinguished by having no accepted medical use. Other Schedule I substances include heroin, LSD, mescaline, methylqualone, and most recently, gamma hydroxybutyrate. In 1973, President Nixon's investigation into the risks and benefits of marijuana, the Shafer Commission, concluded that it was a safe substance with no addictive potential that had medicinal benefits (National Commission on Marihuana and Drug Abuse 1973). Again, this report was largely ignored as was the subsequent National Academy of Sciences investigation published in 1982 (National Research Council of the National Academy of Sciences 1982).

Cannabinoids and the Wasting Syndrome

Despite the fact that it was perceived to have no medical use, marijuana was distributed to patients by the U.S. government on a case-by-case basis by way of a Compassionate Use IND (Investigational New Drug) program established in 1978. In the late 1980s and early 1990s, many people living with human immunodeficiency virus developed the wasting syndrome as a preterminal event. In one collaborative network database, wasting was second only to *Pneumocystis carinii* pneumonia as the most frequent diagnosis in the six months prior to death (Chan et al. 1995). The wasting syndrome, characterized by anorexia, weight loss of greater than 10% body weight, and frequently fever and diarrhea, created hordes of emaciated individuals in search of any potential therapeutic intervention. Many turned to smoking marijuana (Abrams et al. 1995; Abrams 2000; Werner 2001). Fearful that there might be a run on the Compassionate Use program, the Bush administration shut it down in 1992, the same year that dronabinol [delta-9-THC (tetrahydrocannabinol), Marinol] was approved for treatment of anorexia associated with the AIDS wasting syndrome.

Delta-9-THC is one of the 60 cannabinoids found in the cannabis plant and is felt to be the main psychoactive component. Overall, the plant contains 400 compounds, many of which may contribute to its medicinal effect. Synthetic delta-9-THC in sesame oil was licensed and approved in 1986 for the treatment of chemotherapy-associated nausea and vomiting. Clinical trials done at the time determined that dronabinol was as effective, if not more so, than the available antiemetic agents (Sallen et al. 1975). The potent class of serotonin receptor antagonists which have subsequently revolutionized the ability to administer emetogenic chemotherapy had not yet come to market.

Dronabinol was investigated for its ability to stimulate weight gain in patients with the AIDS wasting syndrome in the late 1980s. Results from a number of trials suggested that although patients reported an improvement in appetite, no statistically significant weight gain was appreciated (Gorter et al. 1992; Beal et al. 1995). In one trial evaluating megestrol acetate and dronabinol alone and together, the cannabinoid seemed to negate some of the weight increase seen in those receiving the hormone alone (Timpone et al. 1997).

CANNABINOID CHEMISTRY AND BIOLOGIC EFFECTS

Cannabinoids are a group of 21 carbon terpenophenolic compounds produced uniquely by *Cannabis sativa* and *C. indica* (Grothenhermen and Russo 2002). These plant compounds may also be referred to as phytocannabinoids to distinguish them from pharmaceutical compounds and endogenous cannabinoids. Although delta-9-THC is the primary active ingredient in cannabis, there are number of non-THC cannabinoids and noncannabinoid compounds that also have biologic activity. It is postulated that these secondary compounds may enhance the beneficial effects of delta-9-THC, for example, by modulating the THC-induced anxiety, anticholinergic effect, or immunosuppressive effect. Cannabinol, cannabidiol, cannabichromene, cannabigerol, tetrahydrocannabivirin, and delta-8-THC are just some of the additional cannabinoids that have been identified and thought to have biologic activity. In addition, cannabis contains terpenoids and flavonoids that may increase cerebral blood flow, enhance cortical activity, kill respiratory pathogens, and provide anti-inflammatory activity (McPartland and Mediavilla 2002).

The neurobiology of the cannabinoids has only been identified within the past 20 years during which time an explosion of knowledge has occurred (Devane et al. 1988, 1992; Pertwee 1997; Felder and Glass 1998). In the mid-1980s, researchers developed a potent cannabinoid agonist to be used in research investigations. In 1986, it was discovered that cannabinoids inhibited the accumulation of cAMP (cyclic adenosine monophosphate), suggesting the presence of a receptor-mediated mechanism. By attaching a radiolabel to the synthetic cannabinoid, the first cannabinoid receptor, CB1, was identified in the brain in 1988. The CB1 receptor is coupled to G-proteins and inhibits adenylate cyclase. Activation of the receptor inhibits N-type voltage-gated calcium channels, increases potassium conductance in hippocampal neurons, and increases prostaglandin production—all of these events leading to a decrease in the release of neurotransmitters. Each of these changes influence cellular communication. Cannabinoids generally inhibit neurotransmission, although findings are somewhat variable and depend on the specific neurotransmitter. Among the neurotransmitters and neuromodulators impacted by the cannabinoids are acetylcholine, dopamine, gamma-aminobutyric acid, histamine, serotonin, glutamine, norepinephrine, prostaglandins, and opioid peptides (Grothenhermen and Russo 2002). By 1990, investigators had cloned the CB1 receptor, identified its DNA sequence, and mapped its location in the brain, with the largest concentration being in the cerebellum, hippocampus, and cerebral cortex. In 1993, a second cannabinoid receptor, CB2, was identified outside the brain. They were originally detected in macrophages, tissue immune system cells, and the marginal zone of the spleen; however, the highest concentration of CB2 receptors is located on the B lymphocytes and natural killer cells, suggesting a possible role of the cannabinoids in the functioning of the immune system.

The existence of cannabinoid receptors has subsequently been demonstrated in animal species all the way down to invertebrates. Are these receptors present in the body solely to bind with ingested phytocannabinoids? The answer came in 1992 with the identification of a brain constituent that binds to the cannabinoid receptor. This first endocannabinoid was named anandamide from the Sanskrit word for bliss. Subsequently, 2-arachidonyl-glycerol has also been confirmed as part of the body's endogenous cannabinoid system. These endocanabinoids function as neurotransmitters. As the ligands for the seven-transmembrane domain cannabinoid receptors, endocannabinoid binding leads to G-protein activation. The cascade of events that transpires results in the opening of potassium channels, which decreases cell firing, and the closure of calcium channels, which decreases neurotransmitter release, as described above.

The function of the endogenous cannabinoid system in the body is becoming more appreciated through advances in cannabinoid pharmacology. The identification of the cannabinoid receptors has lead to a host of agonists and antagonists being synthesized. Utilizing these tools, investigators are discovering that the system is likely to be important in the modulation of pain and appetite, suckling in the newborn, and the complexities of memory. [Pollen (2001) in *The Botany of Desire* gives a particularly entertaining description of the natural function of endocannabinoids in memory.] In addition to being utilized to learn more about the natural function of the endocannabinoid system, a number of these cannabinoid receptor agonists and antagonists are being developed as potential pharmaceutical therapies. In the meantime, dronabinol and cannabis are the currently available cannabinoid therapies in the United States.

Through the receptors described above, cannabis delivered by way of inhalation or orally can produce a host of biologic effects. These effects impact on psyche and perception, cognition and psychomotor performance, the nervous system, body temperature, the cardiovascular system, the respiratory system, the gastrointestinal tract, the eye, and the immune system (Grothenhermen and Russo 2002). Well-known effects of cannabis include euphoria, alteration of time perception, enhanced creativity, disturbed memory, unsteady gait, muscle relaxation, appetite stimulation, antinausea effects, rapid heart rate, postural hypotension, injected conjunctivae, decreased intraocular pressure, dry mouth, reduced bowel movements, and possibly reduced sperm counts and menstrual irregularity.

The Institute of Medicine report makes the following general conclusions about the biology of cannabis and cannabinoids (Joy et al. 1999).

- Cannabinoids likely have a natural role in pain modulation, control of movement, and memory.
- The natural role of cannabinoids in immune systems is likely multifaceted and remains unclear.
- The brain develops tolerance to cannabinoids.
- Animal research has demonstrated the potential for dependence, but this potential is observed under a narrower range of conditions than with benzodiazepines, opiates, cocaine, or nicotine.
- Withdrawal symptoms can be observed in animals but appear mild compared with those of withdrawal from opiates or benzodiazepines.

PHARMACOLOGY OF CANNABIS

As physicians began to prescribe dronabinol to patients with the AIDS wasting syndrome when it became available for that indication in 1992, a number of patients previously experienced in smoking marijuana complained about the effects of the synthetic alternative. Many reported that the onset of the appetite stimulating effect was delayed and the central nervous system effects could not be titrated and in fact, seemed to exceed the effect from smoking marijuana. When assessing the pharmacokinetics of smoked versus oral cannabis, it becomes clear that the patients were correct. When taken by mouth, there is a low (6–20%) and variable oral bioavailability (Agurell et al. 1986). Peak plasma concentrations occur after one to six hours (2.5 hours in our trial) and remain elevated with a terminal half-life of 20 to 30 hours. When consumed orally, delta-9-THC is initially metabolized in the liver to 11-OH-THC, a potent psychoactive metabolite. On the other hand, when smoked, the cannabinoids are rapidly absorbed into the bloodstream with a peak concentration in 2 to 10 minutes which rapidly declines over the next 30 minutes. Smoking thus achieves a higher peak concentration with a shorter duration of effect. Less of the psychoactive 11-OH-THC metabolite is formed.

Cannabinoids can interact with the liver's cytochrome P450 enzyme system (Watanabe et al. 1995; Yamamoto et al. 1995). This is the system responsible for the metabolism of many other drugs as well. For example, the antiretroviral drugs—particularly the potent protease inhibitors—are broken down by this pathway. An early report of a patient dying of an overdose of Ecstasy while taking protease inhibitors highlighted the serious consequences of casually mixing protease inhibitors with recreational substances. The potential for a cannabinoid interaction with cytochrome P450 and hence, possibly protease inhibitor metabolism opened the door for an initial clinical investigation of smoked marijuana in patients with HIV infection (Acosta et al. 2000; Piscitelli and Gallicano 2001).

SHORT-TERM SAFETY OF CANNABINOIDS IN HIV

In the early 1990s, thousands of San Francisco Bay Area patients with the HIV wasting syndrome were obtaining cannabis for treatment from the increasing number of buyers' clubs that were being established for distribution in an area of the country that has always been tolerant to marijuana smoking (Child et al. 1998; Werner 2001). In an effort to ascertain whether smoking marijuana was of benefit to patients with AIDS wasting syndrome, the Community Consortium of Bay Area HIV Care Providers submitted two applications requesting marijuana and/or funding from the NIDA (National Institute on Drug Abuse) in 1994 and 1996 (Abrams 1998). Both were denied. This reflected NIDA's Congressional mandate to study these agents as substances of abuse and not as potential therapeutic interventions.

In November 1996, the people of California voted to pass the Compassionate Use Act, allowing for physicians to recommend use of marijuana to their patients for a number of medical conditions. Shortly thereafter, the United States Drug Czar, flanked by the Attorney General and the Secretary of Health and Human Services, warned California physicians that they best not enter into such discussions with their patients. This led to the filing of a lawsuit to protect First Amendment rights of physicians and increasing demand from the medical community for more research in the medical marijuana arena (Annas 1997; Kassirer 1997; Kane 2001). By this time, with the increasing availability of protease inhibitor therapies, the AIDS wasting syndrome had all but disappeared as a clinical problem. However, the potential for a cytochrome P450–mediated interaction between cannabinoids and protease inhibitors allowed us to be first in line with a reformatted application in response to public demands for more research into the medical marijuana question. In May 1998, the first patient was randomized into our study of the short-term effects of cannabinoids in patients with HIV-1 infection (Abrams et al. 2003). The objective of the trial was to determine the short-term effects of smoked marijuana on the viral load in HIV-infected patients. Cannabinoid use could potentially alter HIV RNA levels by two postulated mechanisms: immune modulation directly or by way of a cannabinoid; protease inhibitor interaction leading to a change in plasma levels of the antiviral agent. If either condition existed, the study was also designed to assess whether the interaction was different if the cannabinoids were smoked versus swallowed. In this prospective, placebo-controlled trial, participants were randomized to receive either a 3.95% THC marijuana cigarette, a 2.5 mg dronabinol capsule, or a placebo capsule three times daily before meals for 21 days. The study was conducted in the inpatient General Clinical Research Center at San Francisco General Hospital.

Sixty-seven participants enrolled in the study; 62 were eligible for the primary endpoint (marijuana 20; dronabinol 22; placebo 20). Overall, no change in HIV RNA levels was detected over the 21-day study period in any of the treatment conditions; this likely reflected the fact that the majority of the participants had HIV RNA levels that were undetectable at baseline. There were no clinically significant pharmacokinetic interactions noted between the cannabinoids and the protease inhibitors (Kosel et al. 2002). It was felt that the magnitude of changes observed was not likely to have any short-term clinical consequences and that the use of marijuana or dronabinol was not likely to impact on antiretroviral efficacy.

No adverse effect of smoking marijuana was seen in an exhaustive battery of immune testing (Bredt et al. 2002). We examined the number and function of various T lymphocyte subsets. CD4+ T lymphocytes are the building blocks of the cellular immune system that is attacked by the HIV virus. As HIV infection progresses, continued depletion of the CD4+ helper lymphocyte population leads to immune deficiency and the development of opportunistic infections and malignancies. The CD8+ T lymphocyte is the suppressor cytotoxic cell that is involved in the suppression of virally infected cells. With regard to CD4+ T lymphocytes, both cannabinoid groups actually demonstrated increased counts over the 21-day experimental exposure period when compared to the placebo recipients. The marijuana group alone also demonstrated a statistically significant increase in CD8+ T lymphocytes compared to the placebo recipients. More extensive assays of immune phenotype (including flow cytometric quantification of T cell subpopulations, B cells, and natural killer cells) and immune function (including assays for cytokine production, natural killer cell function, and lymphoproliferation) were performed weekly. Patients randomized to the cannabinoid treatment conditions showed no clear discernable negative changes when compared with placebo recipients over the 21-day study period. The few statistically significant changes that were noted did not constitute any meaningful pattern of changes in immune phenotype or function. These results, coupled with the lack of any cannabinoid-associated effect on viral load or the metabolism of protease inhibitors, indicated that the short-term use of cannabinoids was well tolerated in this patient population.

Although energy intake and weight changes were not the primary endpoint of our initial safety study, we did note significant weight gain in the dronabinol (3.2 kg) and marijuana (3.0 kg) treatment conditions compared to the placebo group (1.1 kg) over the 21-day study period. Only the marijuana smoking group reported an increased appetite associated with study drug intake over the experimental period. Of note, these patients were not malnourished at baseline, so these results do not fully support either cannabinoid intervention as a treatment for HIV-associated wasting syndrome. On analysis of body composition, the increased weight in all patient groups was found to be in the fat compartment and not the more desirable lean body mass (Mulligan et al. 2001). No detrimental effect on serum testosterone levels was noted, nor were any consistent changes in levels of insulin, insulin-like growth factor, or leptin seen over the course of the study (Mulligan, pers. comm.).

Cannabis in HIV-Related Peripheral Neuropathy

Having completed a trial which suggested short-term safety of smoked marijuana in HIV patients on protease inhibitor–containing antiviral regimens, we were interested in investigating the potential efficacy of smoked marijuana for a difficult to treat HIV-related condition—painful peripheral neuropathy. The establishment of the Center for Medicinal Cannabis Research at the University of California in August 2000 provided a mechanism to fund studies investigating the potential therapeutic utility of cannabis products (University of California Center for Medicinal Cannabis Research). The NIDA established a mechanism to provide marijuana to peer-reviewed trials that would be funded by an outside sponsor. This opened the door for the Center for Medicinal Cannabis Research to fund three studies of smoked marijuana in patients with painful peripheral neuropathy including our inpatient General Clinical Research Center based placebo-controlled trial.

Elevated levels of the CB1 receptor are found in areas of the brain that modulate nociceptive processing (Facci et al. 1995; Calignano et al. 1998; Fields and Meng 1998; Walker et al. 1999). CB1 and CB2 agonists have peripheral analgesic effects and may also exert anti-inflammatory effects. Although apparently linked to the opioid system, the analgesic effects of cannabinoids are not blocked by opioid antagonists. Cannabinoids have also been shown to be of potential benefit in an animal model of neuropathic pain. With this background and further fueled by patients' anecdotal reports of benefit, we completed a 16 patient open-label pilot study of smoked marijuana in patients with painful HIV-related peripheral neuropathy. To anchor our evaluation, we subjected participants to a heat–capsaicin experimental pain model. Participants had a patch of skin on their forearm heated to 40°C for 10 minutes followed by application of a capsaicin cream. The surrounding area of abnormal sensations—allodynia and hypesthesia—was carefully measured before and after smoking the cannabis cigarettes. Thus we were able to simultaneously assess the effect of marijuana on the patient's chronic neuropathic pain and the acute experimental pain condition—a much less subjective outcome measure (Petersen and Rowbotham 1999). The objective of the pilot study was to ascertain whether there was a significant clinical effect, and if so, to estimate the effect size to be able to calculate the sample size for a subsequent randomized placebo-controlled trial.

Sixteen patients (14 men) with neuropathy felt to be related to HIV (3), antiretroviral therapy (8), or both (5) were enrolled in the open-label pilot study (meaning all participants received active marijuana and there were no placebo controls). The participants smoked one 3.56% THC-containing marijuana cigarette three times daily for seven days (Jay et al. 2004). Pain was assessed using a visual analog scale where patients rated their pain by pointing to where on a line from 0 (none) to 100 (most ever) their pain scored. Patients reported a mean duration of neuropathy of six years. In the open-label pilot study, overall 10 of the 16 participants experienced at least a 30% reduction in their average daily pain score upon smoking marijuana. During the experimental pain procedures implemented after smoking the first cigarette on day 1 and the last one on day 7, 13 of the 16 participants reported an acute 30% reduction in their neuropathic pain on day 1. Fourteen experienced a comparable reduction in their experimental pain mapped during the heat–capsaicin model done concurrently. The correlation between those patients reporting relief in their neuropathic pain and those demonstrating a response in the much less subjective heat–capsaicin experiment was excellent suggesting that cannabis was able to impact both pains effectively.

From the results of the pilot study, we calculated that the randomized placebo-controlled trial would require 50 participants to demonstrate convincing effectiveness. The results of this subsequent trial confirmed the findings of the initial pilot study showing a benefit of smoking THC compared to placebo for relief of both the chronic neuropathic and the acute experimental pain (Abrams et al. 2005, 2007). Hopefully, the three trials funded by the Center for Medicinal Cannabis Research in patients with HIV-related peripheral neuropathy will be comparable enough that their results can be ultimately pooled in a meta-analysis to provide a conclusive and compelling answer to the question.

ALTERNATIVE DELIVERY SYSTEMS

What if clinical trials were to demonstrate that smoked marijuana may be of benefit to patients with a condition like, for example, painful peripheral neuropathy? It is not likely that even a meta-analysis of a number of similar studies in any condition would convince the necessary regulatory bodies that cannabis should be reinstated to the U.S. Pharmacoepia and made widely available to patients who may benefit from its use. The Institute of Medicine Report in 1999 already stated that the accumulated data indicate a potential therapeutic value for cannabinoid drugs particularly in the areas of pain relief, control of nausea and vomiting, and appetite stimulation. They went on to suggest that the "goal of clinical trials of smoked marijuana would not be to develop it as a licensed drug, but as a first step towards the development of non-smoked, rapid-onset cannabinoid delivery systems" (Joy et al. 1999, p. 7). To this end, we completed a trial comparing the blood levels of cannabinoids achieved upon inhaling marijuana that has been vaporized in the Volcano® device with those obtained upon smoking a comparable dosed cigarette (Gieringer et al. 2004; Hazekamp et al. 2006). The results of this trial suggest that vaporization is a safe and effective way of delivering cannabinoids than smoking (Abrams et al. 2006).

Guidelines for Providers

The Institute of Medicine is aware that the development and acceptance of smokeless marijuana delivery systems "may take years; in the meantime there are patients with debilitating symptoms for whom smoked marijuana may provide relief" (Joy et al. 1999, p. 7). Ironically, the U.S. Food and Drug Administration felt compelled in April 2006 to issue a statement to the effect that there is no evidence that marijuana has any medicinal benefit.

So what is a provider to do? Patients with HIV infection have a number of possible conditions that may be responsive to cannabinoid therapies. On screening for our initial safety study where abstinence from marijuana for 30 days prior to entry was an eligibility criterion, our study coordinator was struck by the number of potential participants who opted out of the trial after hearing this requirement, claiming that they would be unable to take their antiretroviral regimen if they had to forego the antinausea benefits of their smoked cannabis. This observation was confirmed in a larger study of 252 people living with HIV that found recent use of marijuana to be positively associated with moderate to severe nausea (Prentiss et al. 2004). The authors concluded that medicinal use of marijuana may facilitate, rather than impede, adherence to antiretroviral regimens (De Jong et al. 2005). Many patients rely on cannabis to stimulate their appetite and maintain their weight. A recent study concluded that for experienced marijuana smokers with clinically significant muscle mass depletion, both high-dose dronabinol and marijuana produce significant increases in food intake without adverse effects (Haney et al. 2005). As well as for control of pain, some patients also utilize medical marijuana as a sedative or hypnotic or even an antidepressant. Many providers would frown upon the use of a relatively benign smoked psychotropic agent while freely writing prescriptions for pharmaceutical agents with significantly greater cost, potential for addiction or abuse, and more negative societal impact overall.

The Medical Board of California in their July 2004 Action Report provides a model for how those states with medical marijuana legislation should advise physicians (Medical Board of California 2004).

> The intent of the board at this time is to reassure physicians that if they use the same proper care in recommending medical marijuana to their patients as they would any other medication or treatment, their activity will be viewed by the Medical Board just as any other appropriate medical intervention.... If physicians use the same care in recommending medical marijuana to patients as they would recommending or approving any other medication or prescription drug treatment, they have nothing to fear from the Medical Board. (Medical Board of California 2004, p. 2)

The Board recommends following the accepted standards that would be used in recommending any medication. A history and physical examination should be documented. The provider should ascertain that medical marijuana use is not masking an acute or treatable progressive condition. A treatment plan should be formulated. A patient need not have failed all standard interventions before marijuana can be recommended. Discussion of potential side effects and obtaining verbal informed consent are desirable. Periodic review of the treatment efficacy should be documented. Consultation should be obtained when necessary. Proper record keeping that supports the decision to recommend the use of medical marijuana is advised. Despite all these guidelines, the California Medical Board still reminds physicians that making a written recommendation "could trigger a federal action."

THE FUTURE

Our prospective studies to date suggest that patients with HIV infection appear to have little risk of significant clinical detriment from the short-term use of smoked marijuana. Many such patients may benefit from potential therapeutic effects. The dose that may be effective is highly variable depending on a number of host- and herb-related issues (Carter et al. 2004). Hopefully, more results from well-designed, carefully controlled clinical trials will be forthcoming in the future to assist practitioners of evidence-based medicine that this long-utilized botanical therapy may have a role to play in certain patient populations. As well, the field of cannabinoid therapies based on receptor agonists and an tagonists also stands poised to provide us with exciting novel therapies in the not too distant future.

NOTE

Acknowledgments: With gratitude to the entire research team and especially to research coordinators Roz Leiser, R.N. and Hector Vizoso, R.N. for their tireless efforts in making our studies possible. Thanks to the research nursing staff of the San Francisco General Hospital General Clinical Research Center for their meticulous attention to detail and compassionate care. This work was funded in part by NIH Grants 1RO1 DA/MH11607, 5-MO1-RR00083, and the University of California Center for Medicinal Cannabis Research. Finally, thanks to all of our study participants who contributed valuable inpatient time to make our trials possible.

REFERENCES

Abel, E.L. 1980. *Marijuana: The first twelve thousand years.* New York: Plenum Press.
Abrams, D.I. 1998. Medical marijuana: Tribulations and trials. *Journal of Psychoactive Drugs* 30:163–9.
Abrams, D.I. 2000. Potential interventions for HIV/AIDS wasting: An overview. *Journal of AIDS* 25:S74–80.
Abrams, D.I., C.C. Child, and T. Mitchell. 1995. Marijuana, the AIDS wasting syndrome and the US government. *New England Journal of Medicine* 333:670–1.

Abrams, D.I., J.F. Hilton, R.J. Leiser, S.B. Shade, T.A. Elbeik, F.T. Aweeka, N.L. Benowitz, B.M. Bredt, B. Kosel, J.A. Aberg, S.G. Deeks, T.F. Mitchell, K. Mulligan, J.M. McCune, and M. Schambelan. 2003. Short-term safety of cannabinoids in HIV infection: Results of a randomized, controlled clinical trial. *Annals of Internal Medicine* 139:258–66.

Abrams, D.I., C. Jay, S. Shade, H. Vizoso, K. Petersen, and M. Rowbotham. 2005. The effects of smoked cannabis in HIV-related painful peripheral neuropathy: Results of a randomized, double-blind, placebo-controlled trial. 2005 Symposium on the Cannabinoids, International Cannabinoid Research Society, Burlington, VT, p. 51.

Abrams, D.I., H.P. Vizoso, S.B. Shade, C. Jay, M.E. Kelly, and N. Benowitz. 2006. Symposium on the cannabinoids. International Cannabinoid Research Society, Burlington, VT, p. 65.

Abrams, D.I., C.A. Jay, S.B. Shade, H. Vizoso, H. Rede, S. Press, M.E. Kelly, M.C. Rowbotham, and K.L. Petersen. 2007. Cannabis in painful HIV-associated sensory neuropathy. AAN Enterprises, Inc.

Acosta, E.P., T.N. Kakuda, R.C. Brundage, P.L. Anderson, and C.V. Fletcher. 2000. Pharmacodynamics of human immunodeficiency virus type-1 protease inhibitors. *Clinical Infectious Diseases* 30 (Suppl. 2):S151–9.

Agurell, S., M. Halldin, and J. Lindgren. 1986. Pharmacokinetics and metabolism of delta1-tetrahydrocannabinol and other cannabinoids with emphasis on man. *Pharmacology Review* 38 (1):21–43.

Annas, G.J. 1997. Reefer madness- the Federal response to California's medical-marijuana law. *New England Journal of Medicine* 337:435–9.

Beal, J.E., R. Olson, L. Laubenstein, J.O. Morales, P. Bellman, B. Yangco, L. Lefkowitz, T.F. Plasse, and K.V. Shepard. 1995. Dronabinol as a treatment for anorexia associated with weight loss in patients with AIDS. *Journal of Pain and Symptom Management* 10 (2):89–97.

Booth, M. 2003. *Cannabis: A history.* New York: St. Martin's Press.

Bredt, B.M., D. Higuera-Alhino, S.B. Shade, S. Herbert, J.M. McCune, and D.I. Abrams. 2002. Short-term effects of cannabinoids on immune phenotype and function in HIV-1-infected patients. *Journal of Clinical Pharmacology* 42:82S–9S.

California physicians and medical marijuana. 2004. Action Report. Medical Board of California, 90, 1–4, available at www.caldocinfo.ca.gov.

Calignano, A., G. LaRana, A. Giuffrida, and D. Piomelli. 1998. Control of pain initiation by endogenous cannabinoids. *Nature* 394:277–81.

Carter, G.T., P. Weydt, M. Kyashna-Tocha, and D.I. Abrams. 2004. Medicinal cannabis: Rational guidelines for dosing. *IDrugs* 7:464–70.

Chan, I.S.F., J.D. Naton, L.D. Saravolatz, L.R. Crane, and J. Osterberger. 1995. Frequencies of opportunistic diseases prior to death among HIV-infected persons. *AIDS* 9:1145–51.

Child, C.C., T.F. Mitchell, and D.I. Abrams. 1998. Patterns of therapeutic marijuana use in two community-based cannabis buyers' cooperatives. 12th World AIDS Conference, Geneva, abstract 60569, 1105.

De Jong, B.C., D. Prentiss, W. McFarland, R. Machekano, and D.M. Israelski. 2005. Marijuana use and its association with adherence to antiretroviral therapy among HIV-infected persons with moderate to severe nausea. *Journal of Acquired Immune Deficiency Syndrome* 35:43–6.

Devane, W.A., F.A. Dysarc, M.R. Johnson, L.S. Melvin, and A.C. Howlett. 1992. Determination and characterization of a cannabinoid receptor in rat brain. *Molecular Pharmacology* 34:605–13.

Devane, W.A., L. Hanus, A. Breuer, R.G. Pertwee, L.A. Stevenson, G. Griffin,D. Gibson, A. Mandelbaum, A. Etinger, and R. Mechoulam. 1988. Isolation and structure of a brain constituent that binds to the cannabinoid receptor. *Science* 258:1946–9.

Facci, L., R. Dal Toso, S. Romanello, A. Buriani, S.D. Skaper, and A. Leon. 1995. Mast cells express a peripheral cannabinoid receptor with differential sensitivity to anandamide and palmitoylethanolamide. *Proceedings of the National Academy of Science United States of America* 92:3376–80.

Felder, C.C., and M. Glass. 1998. Cannabinoid receptors and their endogenous agonists. *Annual Review of Pharmacology and Toxicology* 38:179–200.

Fields, H.L., and I.D. Meng. 1998 Watching the pot boil. *Nature Medicine* 4:1008–9.

Gieringer, D., J. St. Laurent, and S. Goodrich. 2004. Cannabis vaporizer combines efficient delivery of THC with effective suppression of pyrolytic compounds. *Journal of Cannabis Therapy* 4:7–27.

Gorter, R., M. Seefried, and P. Volberding. 1992. Dronabinol effects on weight in patients with HIV infection. *AIDS* 6:127.

Grothenhermen, F., and E. Russo, eds. 2002. *Cannabis and cannabinoids: Pharmacology, toxicology, and therapeutic potential.* Binghamton, NY: The Haworth Press.

Haney, M., J. Rabkin, E. Gunderson, and R.W. Foltin. 2005. Dronabinol and marijuana in HIV+ marijuana smokers: Acute effects on caloric intake and mood. *Psychopharmacology,* March 19 [Epub ahead of print].

Hazekamp, A., R. Ruhaak, L. Zuurman, J. van Gerven, and R. Verpoorte. 2006. Evaluation of a vaporizing device (Volcano®) for the pulmonary administration of tetrahydrocannabinol. *Journal of Pharmaceutical Science* 95:1308–17.

Jay, C., S. Shade, H. Vizoso, H. Reda, K. Petersen, M. Rowbotham, and D. Abrams. 2004. The effect of smoked marijuana on chronic neuropathic and experimentally induced pain in HIV neuropathy: Results of an open-label pilot study. Proceedings 11th Conference on Retroviruses and Opportunistic Infections, abstract 496, p. 243.

Joy, J.E., S.J. Watson, and J.A. Benson, eds. 1999. *Marijuana and medicine: Assessing the science base.* Washington, D.C.: National Academy Press.

Kane, B. 2001. Medical marijuana: The continuing story. *Annals of Internal Medicine* 134:1159–62.

Kassirer, J.P. 1997. Federal foolishness and marijuana. *New England Journal of Medicine* 336:366–7.

Kosel, B.W., F.T. Aweeka, N.L. Benowitz, S.B. Shade, J.F. Hilton, P.S. Lizak, and D.I. Abrams. 2002. The effects of cannabinoids on the pharmacokinetics of indinavir and nelfinavir. *AIDS* 16 (4):543–50.

Mack, A., and J.E. Joy. 2001 *Marijuana as medicine?—The science beyond the controversy.* Washington, D.C.: National Academy Press.

McPartland, J.M., and V. Mediavilla. 2002. Noncannabinoid components. In *Cannabis and cannabinoids: Pharmacology, toxicology and therapeutic potential,* ed. F. Grothenhermen and E. Russo, 401–9. Binghamton, NY: The Haworth Press.

Mulligan, K., D.I. Abrams, R.J. Leiser, and M. Schambelan. 2001. Body composition changes in HIV-infected men consuming self-selected diets during a placebo-controlled inpatient study of cannabinoids. Proceedings 8th Conference on Retroviruses and Opportunistic Infections, Chicago, abstract 647, p. 238.

National Commission on Marihuana and Drug Abuse. 1973. Marihuana, a signal of misunderstanding. Accessed at http://www.druglibrary.org/schaffer/Library/studies/nc/ncmenu.htm (9/24/2006).

National Research Council of the National Academy of Science. 1982. An analysis of marijuana policy. Accessed at http://www.druglibrary.org/schaffer/library/studies/nas/AMPMenu.htm (9/24/2006).

New York Academy of Medicine. 1944. The LaGuardia Committee Report: The Marihuana Problem in the City of New York. Accessed at http://www.druglibrary.org/schaffer/Library/studies/lag/lagmenu.htm (9/24/2006).

Pertwee, R.G. 1997. Pharmacology of cannabinoid CB1 and CB2 receptors. *Pharmacology Therapy* 74:129–80.

Petersen, K.L., and M.C. Rowbotham. 1999. A new human experimental pain model: The heat/capsaicin sensitization model. *NeuroReport* 10:1511–6.

Piscitelli, S.C., and K.D. Gallicano. 2001. Drug therapy: Interactions among drugs for HIV and opportunistic infections. *New England Journal of Medicine* 344:984–96.

Pollan, M. 2001. *The botany of desire: A plant's eye view of the world.* New York: Random House.

Prentiss, D., R. Power, G. Balmas, G. Tzuang, and D.I. Israleski. 2004. Patterns of marijuana use among patients with HIV/AIDS followed in a public health care setting. *Journal of Acquired Immune Deficiency Syndrome* 35:38–45.

Sallen, S.E., N.E. Zinberg, and E. Frei. 1975. Antiemetic effect of delta-9-THC in patients receiving cancer chemotherapy. *New England Journal of Medicine* 293:795–7.

Timpone, J.G., D.J. Wright, N. Li, M.J. Egorin, M.E. Enama, J. Mayers, and G. Galleto. 1997. The safety and pharmacokinetics of single-agent and combination therapy with megestrol acetate and dronabinol for the treatment of the HIV wasting syndrome. The DATRI 004 Study Group. *AIDS Research and Human Retroviruses* 13:305–15.

University of California Center for Medicinal Cannabis Research. Accessed at http://www.cmcr.ucsd.edu (9/24/2006).

Walker, J.M., S.M. Huang, N.M. Strangeman, K. Tsou, and M.C. Sanudo-Pena. 1999. Pain modulation by release of the endogenous cannabinoid anandamide. *Proceedings of the National Academy of Sciences United States of America* 96 (21):12198–203.

Watanabe, K., T. Matsunaga, I. Yamamoto, Y. Funae, and H. Yoshimura. 1995. Involvement of CYP2C in the metabolism of cannabinoids by human hepatic microsomes from an old woman. *Biological Pharmacology Bulletin* 18:1138–41.

Werner, C.A. 2001. Medical marijuana and the AIDS crisis. *Journal of Cannabis Therapeutics* 1:17–33.

Yamamoto, I., K. Watanabe, S. Narimatsu, and H. Yoshimura. 1995. Recent advances in the metabolism of cannabinoids. *International Journal Biochemistry and Cell Biology* 27:741–6.

11

THE USE OF PSILOCYBIN IN PATIENTS WITH ADVANCED CANCER AND EXISTENTIAL ANXIETY

CHARLES S. GROB

INTRODUCTION

Major advances in the medical and surgical treatments of many types of cancers have occurred over the past several decades. Our knowledge of pathophysiological mechanisms of tumor genesis and growth has evolved significantly, along with new and innovative treatment regimens, some of which have had success in prolonging survival time. Unfortunately, addressing the psychological and spiritual needs of patients with end-stage cancers has often received far less attention. Even with the lengthening life span of some patients, the final months for individuals dying of cancer are often burdened with extreme levels of suffering, both physical and mental. Along with the physical pain often associated with the spread of cancer, the patient approaching death frequently encounters variable degrees of anxiety, depression, and psychological isolation. The inevitable and impending death often provokes feelings of defeat, helplessness, and despair not only in the patient but also in family members and even among attending medical personnel. Our modern system of medical care is often successful in increasing the amount of time a terminal cancer patient has to live, but very little is customarily done to enhance the quality of intra- and interpersonal life during the patient's final months (Derogatis et al. 1983; Cochinov 2000).

There has been in recent years a growing appreciation that efforts directed at addressing the psychological, spiritual, and existential crises often encountered by patients and families need to be addressed more vigorously (Rousseau 2000; Breitbart et al. 2004). Beyond conventional psychotherapies and psychotropic medication regimens, however, a model also exists for intensively addressing the core psychological processes of individuals inflicted with drastic, end of life medical illnesses. From the late 1950s to the early 1970s, investigators trained and authorized to administer hallucinogens to carefully selected patients with end-stage cancers described a number of individual cases and clinical research studies with impressive treatment outcomes. Along with efforts designed to explore the application of an hallucinogen treatment paradigm in such conditions as refractory alcoholism and drug addiction, infantile autism, antisocial personality, and psychosomatic and neurotic disorders, published accounts from that era revealed promising results from the highly structured and controlled administration of hallucinogens to dying patients suffering from profound psychospiritual demoralization (Grinspoon and Bakalar 1979; Grof 1980; Grob 1998, 2002; Walsh and Grob 2005).

Past Hallucinogen Research with Cancer Patients

Eric Kast, a Chicago internist specializing in pain treatment in the seriously medically ill, pioneered the utilization of low-dose LSD (lysergic acid diethylamide) in patients with terminal cancer. Exploring the effects in several hundred end-stage cancer patients, Kast and his colleagues found that 100 micrograms of LSD induced superior analgesia compared to hydromorphone (Dilaudid) and meperidine (Demerol), on the order of several days as opposed to several hours. Significant reductions in pain perception were observed for several weeks following treatment, with a diminished need for narcotic medication. Additional findings included relief of depression, improved sleep, and lessened fear of death. Kast suggested that his patients' pain was controlled through a process he described as the "attenuation of anticipation," a liberation from anxiety about loss of control through dying and death (Kast 1962, 1966a,b, 1970; Kast and Collins 1964). Another prominent internist, Sidney Cohen of UCLA (University of California, Los Angeles) administered LSD to several dying persons and confirmed Kast's findings, quoting a patient: "Ah yes, I see what you have done. You have stripped away ME. This is a touch of death—a preparation for the big one when the No Me will be permanent" (Cohen 1965, p. 72).

A comprehensive program designed to explore the effects of the psychedelic experience on terminal cancer patients was conducted at the Spring Grove State Hospital and Maryland Psychiatric Research Institute, University of Maryland School of Medicine, from 1965 to the early 1970s. A director of the program for many of those years was Walter Pahnke, a Harvard-trained doctor of divinity and psychiatrist who reported that the most dramatic effects came in the wake of a mystical experience. Pahnke reported that two-thirds of his treated cancer patients reported improvement, with decreased "tension," depression, pain, and fear of death. In the *Harvard Theological Review,* Pahnke described that he observed

> an increase in serenity, peace and calmness. Most striking was a decrease in the fear of death. It seems as if the mystical experience, by opening the patient to usually untapped ranges of human consciousness, can provide a sense of security that transcends even death. Once the patient is able to release all the psychic energy which has tied him to the fear of death and worry about the future, he seems able to live more meaningfully in the present. He can turn his attention to the things which have the most significance in the here and now. This change of attitude has an effect on all the people around him. The depth and intensity of interpersonal closeness can be increased so that honesty and courage emerge in a joint confrontation and acceptance of the total situation. (Pahnke 1969, p. 12)

One of the final studies exploring the therapeutic potential of hallucinogens before clinical research was shut down for a thirty-year hiatus was led by Stanislav Grof, one of the most accomplished psychiatric investigators in Europe and the United States from the 1950s to early 1970s. Before his program was terminated by political pressure, Grof studied 60 terminal patients with either LSD or dipropyltryptamine, of whom 29% improved dramatically and 41.9% moderately. Grof described that "probably the most surprising of the findings were the changes in the attitude toward death and in the concept of death itself. Increased acceptance of death usually followed sessions in which the patients reported deep religious and mystical experiences, whereas improvement of the emotional condition of the patients and relief of pain was frequently observed even after sessions with predominantly psychodynamic content" (Grof et al. 1973, p. 143).

PSILOCYBIN

Psilocybin is 4-phosphoryloxy-N,N-dimethyltryptamine and occurs in nature in many species of mushrooms, including the genera Psilocybe, Conocybe, Gymnopilus, Panaeolus, and Stropharia. Psilocybin mushrooms grow in many parts of the world, including the United States and Europe, but until recently they have been consumed primarily in Mexico and Central America, where they were called by the ancient Aztec name of teonanacatl (flesh of the gods). Employed for religious purposes by the Native peoples, the use of mushrooms was condemned under the laws of the Holy Inquisition in the early 17th century following European conquest and domination of the New World. Driven underground by repression and forced conversion to Christianity, the ceremonial use of psilocybin-containing mushrooms was believed to be extinct until their "rediscovery" in 1955 by New York banker and amateur mycologist R. Gordon Wasson. Permitted to attend a healing ritual conducted in the hills of Oaxaca,

Mexico, by a native curandera, Maria Sabina, Wasson was allowed to ingest samples of a mushroom later identified as *Psilocybe mexicana.* Wasson would later write an account of his profound experience with the legendary magic mushrooms of Mexico for Life magazine, in 1957, and in so doing stimulated interest among other Westerners in this previously unknown phenomenon (Riedlinger 1990; Metzner 2004).

Several years after Wasson's discovery, specimens sent to the Basel, Switzerland, laboratory of Sandoz medicinal chemist, Albert Hofmann, yielded the isolation of the two active indole alkaloids, identified as psilocybin and psilocin. As is the case with LSD and mescaline, psilocybin is an extremely potent agonist at 5-HT(2A) and 5-HT(2C) receptors, and their binding potency to these receptors is directly correlated with their human potency as hallucinogens (Presti and Nichols 2004). Although not provided the extensive degree of investigation received by the prototype hallucinogen, LSD, psilocybin was subjected to a variety of research studies during the 1960s employed to establish its psychopharmacological profile of action. Psilocybin was determined to be active in the 10 to 20mg range and was found to be about thirty times stronger than mescaline and approximately 1/200 as potent as LSD. The experience lasts from four to six hours. Physiologically, psilocybin was observed to be similar to LSD but gentler. Psychological effects were also observed to be very similar to LSD, with psilocybin evaluated as more strongly visual, less intense, more euphoric and with fewer panic reactions and less chance of paranoia than LSD.

Contemporary Psilocybin Research

After almost three decades of inactivity, the hallucinogen treatment model is again being examined in formal psychiatric settings. Essential physiological and psychological examinations of the effects of psilocybin have been conducted in healthy normal volunteer subjects at the Heffter Research Center and the University of Zurich in Switzerland. Effects on cardiovascular function, blood chemistries, and neuroendocrine secretion were all determined to be modest and within normal limits. Overall, the investigators concluded that psilocybin was not hazardous to somatic health (Hasler et al. 2004). A recent study conducted at Johns Hopkins administered high dose (30mg/70kg) psilocybin to 36 healthy volunteer subjects, with no sustained deleterious physiological or psychological effects. The investigators also corroborated findings from previous decades that psilocybin could reliably catalyze mystical experiences in prepared subjects (Griffiths et al. 2006).

Groundbreaking work has also been done, exploring the effects of psilocybin on the central nervous system. Franz Vollenweider and his colleagues at the University of Zurich have administered psilocybin to research subjects undergoing PET (positron emission tomography) scans of their brain. These PET studies found that psilocybin produced a global increase in cerebral metabolic rate of glucose with significant and most marked increase in the frontomedial and frontolateral cortexes, anterior cingulate, and temporomedial cortex. This metabolic hyperfrontality in particular may be related to states of ego disintegration and derealization phenomena. Such work not only elucidates the range of neurophysiologic effects of hallucinogens but also provides valuable knowledge of neurotransmitter function needed to advance our knowledge of the neurobiological substrate of major mental illnesses and their psychopharmacological treatment (Vollendweider et al. 1997).

The first approved psilocybin treatment study in several decades in the United States was recently conducted at the University of Arizona under the direction of Francisco Moreno. Examining the effects of psilocybin on patients with severe, refractory OCD (obsessive-compulsive disorder), a disorder notorious for its difficulty responding to conventional treatments, Moreno's study has established an important precedent demonstrating that it is possible once again to conduct sanctioned clinical treatment research with hallucinogens (see also Chapter 6, this volume). Interestingly, what motivated these mainstream investigators to explore psilocybin's potential efficacy treating OCD was both the recognition that the drug's specific effects on the serotonergic neurotransmitter system should theoretically ameliorate the disorder and the examination of published and unpublished anecdotal accounts over the past half-century describing the apparently successful self-medication use of hallucinogens (psilocybin and LSD) to treat OCD. The conclusions of the recent University of Arizona pilot study were that psilocybin is safe and well tolerated in subjects with OCD and may be associated with "robust acute reductions" in core OCD symptoms (Moreno et al. 2006; also see Chapter 6, this volume).

The Harbor–UCLA Psilocybin Treatment of Cancer Anxiety Project

Since 2004, work has been under way at Harbor–UCLA Medical Center and the Los Angeles Biomedical Research Institute studying the potential therapeutic efficacy of psilocybin in advanced-stage cancer patients with anxiety. Given that this is the first approved study using a hallucinogen as treatment for this patient population in more than thirty years, it was considered prudent to include a double-blind, placebo-controlled research design. Although investigators from the 1960s had not found the need for placebo controls, adhering to contemporary methodological standards at this point in time is necessary to pass scientific scrutiny. Each subject in this approved study functions as his or her own control, participating in two research sessions, on one occasion receiving the active medicine, psilocybin (0.2mg/kg), and the other occasion receiving a placebo. Actual treatment sessions are spaced several weeks apart, and neither the subject nor the research staff is aware of what order the sessions will occur. For ethical reasons, it was decided that all subjects would have an opportunity to receive the experimental medicine and that none of the subjects, all with grave life-threatening disease, would be denied the active treatment.

Prospective subjects are rigorously screened to exclude those with central nervous system involvement, either primary or metastatic disease to the brain, severe cardiovascular illness, and lifetime history of severe mental illness. Several preparatory meetings are arranged for the subject to establish rapport with the investigators and to examine the intention and purpose of their participation in the treatment study. Sessions take place on the GCRC (General Clinical Research Center) at Harbor–UCLA Medical Center, where a single room has been allocated and prepared for the study. Sessions are six hours in length, during which time the investigators remain continuously with the subject. The treatment model is similar to that developed by the Spring Grove research team in the 1960s and early 1970s, with the subject instructed to lie down on a bed with eyeshades on and listening with headphones to preselected music. Subjects are encouraged to relax and go deeply into their experience. At every hour point, the subject's blood pressure is taken and the investigators check in and inquire about their experience. Short reports are encouraged, and then the subject is instructed to put on the eyeshades and head phones again, lie down, and go deeply back into their experience. Toward the end of the session, usually around the five-hour point, more extensive discussions of the subject's experience and associations to it are elicited.

In the days, weeks, and months following the sessions, investigators stay closely in touch with the research subjects, providing assistance with integrating the experience and evaluating the effects of treatment. Prior to the actual treatment sessions, subjects are asked to complete questionnaires examining their level of anxiety, depression, general psychological status and level of physical pain perception, as well as additional measures exploring questions of religion and spirituality and quality of life specific for patients with cancer. Questionnaires are again administered at various intervals following treatment, up to the six month follow-up point.

The study was developed and supported with funding from the Heffter Research Institute. Contact information as well as details on inclusion/exclusion criteria can be found at www.canceranxietystudy.org.

CASE VIGNETTE

P. is a 58-year-old Japanese-American woman, who presented with stage IV colon cancer. P. had been in good health until two years previously, when routine colonoscopy identified and resected a polyp. Histopathological inspection of the polyp revealed adenocarcinoma. Further examination of the polyp revealed that the resection had not yielded cancer-free margins. Inexplicably, P.'s health maintenance organization refused to authorize further intervention. Several months later, the cancer had spread to her lungs, peritoneum, and diffuse lymph nodes.

In the previous year, P. had had to undergo surgical excision of the primary tumor in the colon, as well as extensive cancer chemotherapy. P. and her husband had also filed a malpractice law suit against the health maintenance organization and the physicians who had elected to forego further excision of the cancerous polyp. In several meetings with research staff prior to her treatment with psilocybin, P. expressed considerable distress over the ordeal she had experienced, and in particular the anger she had directed towards the poor judgment employed by her physicians and the health system which had allowed the cancer to metastasize from its primary site. Although she expressed some gratification at having won a fairly sizable court settlement from her HMO (Health Maintenance Organization), she remained distraught that their ineptitude had resulted in her health being severely damaged.

P. was the only child of second-generation immigrants who during the period of intense xenophobia following Pearl Harbor had been arrested and then taken from their homes and forced to live in internment camps where they remained until the end of World War II. P. had had long-term employment in a computer business and had never sought mental health treatment. Until her colon cancer, she had had good physical health. She reported no substance use history, except for physician-recommended use of "medical cannabis" to help her with her physical pain and discomfort and cancer chemotherapy-induced nausea.

During what is presumed to have been her experimental psilocybin session, P. reported experiencing a pleasant and sustained reverie with noticeable improvement of affect and relaxation of tension. However, at approximately the four and a half–hour point, she appeared distressed and spontaneously began to cry, which she continued for approximately twenty minutes. Later, when processing the session, P. stated that her tearfulness was in response to internally experiencing a psychological state of very powerful empathic rapport with her husband, with whom she had had a very close long-term relationship. She further explained that in this experience, she had "become" her husband, and in particular could feel the tremendous pain of loss he would inevitably have to undergo upon her death.

In the months following her single active session treatment, P. has reported sustained positive mood, less anxiety, and greater acceptance of her situation. In particular, she has described a further strengthening of her bond with her husband as well as greater interest and motivation in spending "quality time" with important friends in her life. The only criticism she has had regarding her participation in the research study was that the protocol only allowed for one psilocybin treatment study. P. strongly expressed her viewpoint that an additional "booster" session (or two) might further amplify the positive effects she attributes to her experience with the psilocybin treatment model.

IMPLICATIONS FOR PSYCHO-ONCOLOGY

Since earlier efforts investigating the safety and effectiveness of hallucinogens in ameliorating the psychospiritual distress seen in individuals with advanced cancer were forced to halt over three decades ago, significant advances have been achieved within mainstream culture, sensitizing the medical system to the needs of dying patients. Development of the hospice movement and the field of palliative care have provided greater and more humane attention to the treatment of physical pain, as well as to providing a supportive structure, often within the home, for the dying process itself. Nevertheless, it is an unavoidable fact that innumerable individuals approaching the final phase of their life experience terrible psychological anguish that precludes a peaceful, tranquil, and dignified death (Rousseau 2000). This profound spiritual suffering shares many features of depression, including hopelessness, worthlessness, and meaninglessness. Indeed, depression and hopelessness are associated with poorer survival rates in cancer patients and with dramatically higher rates of suicide, suicidal ideation, desire for hastened death, and interest in physician-assisted suicide (Breitbart et al. 2000; Cochinov 2000).

The psychotherapeutic approach to working with end of life issues often emphasizes the significance of spirituality and meaning as important resources for coping with the emotional and existential suffering encountered as one nears death. The crisis of dying may include overwhelming fear, panic, anxiety, anger, and dependency which must be addressed. Acquiring meaning and purpose become pivotal existential resources for helping patients reconcile with their past, come to terms with their present, and accept an uncertain future (Breitbart et al. 2004). Indeed, there is no greater existential crisis than of facing one's own death. One of the founders of the existential psychiatry movement, Victor Frankl, himself a survivor of Auschwitz Concentration Camp, has emphasized that "meaning can be found in life up to the last moment, up to the last breath, in the face of death" (Frankl 1988, p. 76). The goal and outcome of finding meaning at the end of life is to transform anxiety, despair, and hopelessness into new ways of exploring relationship to self and others, and to promote emotional and spiritual well-being.

The hallucinogen treatment model for the existential anxiety crisis often encountered at the end of life was first suggested by the expatriate British writer Aldous Huxley, who during the final decade of his life, ending in 1963, devoted considerable attention to closely examining the implications of psychedelics to society. Huxley, according to his close colleagues, often said that "the last rites should make one more conscious rather than less conscious, more human rather than less human" (Huxley 1977, pp. 257–258), and true to his personal vision received from his personal physician an injection of 100 micrograms of LSD several hours prior to his demise from cancer. Subsequently, medical and psychiatric investigators explored the capacity of hallucinogens to reduce the intensity and tenacity of physical pain without the mental dulling and awareness constricting effects often observed with narcotic analgesia. The transcendent state of expanded consciousness frequently reported in patients undergoing psychedelic experiences was also found to enhance their capacity to maintain interest in their lives, and helped create, in the words of early researcher Eric Kast, "a new will to live and a zest for experience which against a background of dismal darkness and preoccupying fear produces an exciting and promising outlook. In human terms the short but profound impact upon the dying patient is impressive" (Kast 1966b, p. 85).

A remarkable opportunity to address the universal existential dilemma faced by the dying is offered by careful examination of the hallucinogen treatment model. Recent research contributions by Griffiths et al. (2006) demonstrate that psilocybin administered under optimal conditions may reliably induce legitimate mystical experience in normal volunteers, strengthening the case for the judicious use of hallucinogens with patients in profound psychospiritual crisis. Indeed, such treatment may be considered as *existential medicine* designed to directly intervene and ameliorate the emotional and spiritual suffering of dying patients. Under the influence of hallucinogens, individuals transcend their primary identification with their bodies and experience ego-free states before the time of their actual physical demise, and return with a new perspective and profound acceptance of the life constant, change. Experiencing oneself in a transitional state and with a new equilibrium and consciousness, identification with the dying body ceases. This implicit acceptance of the inevitable cycles of life leads to a drastically altered approach to what time is remaining without the panic, fear, pain, and dependency that were previously so overwhelming (Fisher 1969, 1970).

The facility which hallucinogens, when taken under optimal conditions, have in catalyzing genuine mystical experiences provides a rich area for further study. Reports of patients with advanced-stage cancer suggest a strong positive correlation between heightened spiritual consciousness induced by these compounds and subsequent improved psychological status during their remaining time. Finally, there are serious transpersonal and ontological implications of administering hallucinogens to individuals approaching the end of life. On this matter, Walter Pahnke, in his Ingersoll Lecture to the Harvard Divinity School, elegantly suggested that "although the questions of human immortality may always remain a tantalizing enigma, the psychedelic mystical experience at least teaches that there is more to the range of human consciousness than we might ordinarily assume. Because the answer cannot be definitely proved either way, there is certainly no cause for pessimistic despair. Perhaps it is not so unfortunate that each person must ultimately find out for himself. The psychedelic mystical experience can prepare one to face that moment with a sense of open adventure" (Pahnke 1969, pp. 20–21).

CONCLUSIONS

During the 1960s and early 1970s, investigators initiated research studies exploring the use of hallucinogens to treat the existential anxiety, despair, and isolation often associated with terminal cancer. Reports from that time were highly encouraging, describing critically ill individuals undergoing psychospiritual epiphanies, often with powerful and sustained improvement in mood and anxiety regulation, as well as diminished pain perception and need for narcotic pain medication. Unfortunately, the political and cultural turmoil of that historical period led to the inevitable shut down of all clinical research with hallucinogens. In spite of the promising preliminary studies of Eric Kast (1962, 1966a,b, 1970; Kast and Collins 1964), Walter Pahnke (1969), Stanislav Grof (1980; Grof et al. 1973), William Richards (Grof et al. 1973), Gary Fisher (1969, 1970), and Sidney Cohen (1965), several decades would have to pass before the work of these pioneer investigators would be reexamined.

Beginning in the early 1990s, a few Phase 1 research investigations of hallucinogens were permitted in the United States, followed a decade later by several pilot clinical treatment trials. Psilocybin in particular has recently been explored in an adjunctive therapeutic model, with promising preliminary reports. Questions have been raised; however, concerning the choice of psilocybin in these studies over other classical or novel hallucinogens. One important advantage psilocybin has over the better known LSD is that it carries less political baggage and consequently has a far less sensationalized reputation. The more recently prominent drug MDMA (methylenedioxymethamphetamine), popularly known as Ecstasy, has also been suggested as a possible treatment for cancer anxiety, however, the clear advantage of psilocybin over MDMA is its far safer range of cardiovascular effects. While MDMA has demonstrated therapeutic potential with people suffering from post-traumatic stress disorder, these are usually individuals in good physical health. On the other hand, patients with advanced cancer often have multiple organ system failures, and are consequently more sensitive to the sympathomimetic effects of MDMA. Furthermore, psilocybin's greater capacity than MDMA to catalyze transcendent and psychospiritual states of consciousness would, according to the early investigators, lead to a more therapeutic outcome.

As clinical research with hallucinogens experiences renewed activity, great sensitivity will have to be utilized in selecting the psychotherapists who will do the actual work. It is imperative that, in addition to the requisite psychological acumen, therapists will also need to possess sufficient emotional maturity, psychological stability, and ethical integrity to be able to conduct their work effectively and safely. Patients under the influence of hallucinogens are exquisitely sensitive to environmental stimuli, including the individual and collective input of the therapy team. Consequently, as both past and recent history attest, attentiveness to set and setting remains paramount when conducting clinical investigations with hallucinogens.

After a hiatus of several decades, there are encouraging signs that hallucinogen research is beginning to receive the sanctions necessary to move forward again. The promising findings of a previous generation of researchers now need to be replicated using contemporary state-of-the-art research methodologies. Early work with advanced-stage cancer patients in particular demonstrated the promise of effective intervention for psychospiritual crises often observed at the end of life. A critical element that is necessary to support such a program of research, which was not available to our predecessors but is to an increasing degree today, is a stable political and professional environment. Given the universality of the essential existential dilemma, and the potential for the optimally conducted hallucinogen treatment model to significantly enhance the quality of the end of life period, there is clearly a need to develop further research that will demonstrate the utility of this field of hallucinogen medicine.

REFERENCES

Breitbart, W., C. Gibson, S.R. Poppito, and A. Berg. 2004. Psychotherapeutic interventions at the end of life: A focus on meaning and spirituality. *Canadian Journal of Psychiatry* 49:366–72.

Breitbart, W., B. Rosenfield, H. Pessin, M. Kaim, E.J. Funesti, and M. Galietta. 2000. Depression, hopelessness and desire for death in terminally ill patients with cancer. *JAMA* 284:2907–11.

Cochinov, H.M. 2000. Psychiatry and terminal illness. *Canadian Journal of Psychiatry* 45:143–50.

Cohen, S. 1965. LSD and the anguish of dying. *Harper's,* September, pp. 69–78.

Derogatis, L.R., G.R. Morrow, J. Fetting, D. Penman, S. Piasetsky, A.M. Schmale, M. Henrichs, and C.L.M. Carnicke. 1983. The prevalence of psychiatric disorders among cancer patients. *JAMA* 249:751–7.

Fisher, G. 1969. Death, identity and creativity. *Voices: Art and Science of Psychotherapy* 5:36–9.

Fisher, G. 1970. Psychotherapy for the dying: Principles and illustrative cases with special reference to the use of LSD. *OMEGA* 1:3–15.

Frankl, V. 1988. *The will to meaning.* New York: Meridian.

Griffiths, R., W. Richards, U. McCann, and R. Jesse. 2006. Psilocybin can occasion mystical-type experiences having substantial and sustained personal meaning and spiritual significance. *Psychopharmacology* 187:268–83.

Grinspoon, L., and J.B. Bakalar. 1979. *Psychedelic Drugs Reconsidered.* New York: Basic Books.

Grob, C.S. 1998. Psychiatric research with hallucinogens: What have we learned? *Heffter Review of Psychedelic Research* 1:8–20.

Grob, C.S., ed. 2002. *Hallucinogens: A reader.* New York: Tarcher/Putnam.

Grof, S. 1980. *LSD psychotherapy.* Pomona, CA: Hunter House Publishers.

Grof, S., L.E. Goodman, W.A. Richards, and A.A. Kurland. 1973. LSD-assisted psychotherapy in patients with terminal cancer. *International Pharmacopsychiatry* 8:129–44.

Hasler, F., U. Grimberg, M.A. Benz, T. Huber, and F.X. Vollenweider. 2004. Acute psychological and physiological effects of psilocybin in healthy humans: A double-blind, placebo-controlled dose effect study. *Psychopharmacology* 172:145–56.

Huxley, A. 1977. *Moksha: Writings on psychedelics and the visionary experience.* New York: J.P. Tarcher.

Kast, E.C. 1962. The measurement of pain, a new approach to an old problem. *Journal of New Drugs* 2:344.

Kast, E.C. 1966a. Pain and LSD-25: A theory of attenuation of anticipation. In *LSD: The consciousness-expanding drug,* ed. D. Solomon, 239–54. New York: G.P. Putnam's.

Kast, E.C. 1966b. LSD and the dying patient. *Chicago Medical School Quarterly* 26:80–7.

Kast, E.C. 1970. A concept of death. In *Psychedelics: The uses and implications of hallucinogenic drugs,* ed. B. Aronson and H. Osmond, pp. 366–81. Garden City, NY: Anchor Books.

Kast, E.C., and V.J. Collins. 1964. Lysergic acid diethylamide as an analgesic agent. *Anesthesia and Analgesia* 43:285–91.

Metzner, R., ed. 2004. *Teonanacatl: Sacred mushroom of visions.* El Verano, CA: Four Trees Press.

Moreno, F.A., Wiegand, C.B., Taitano, K., and Delgado, P.L. 2006. Safety, tolerability and efficacy of psilocybin in patients with obsessive-compulsive disorder. *Journal of Clinical Psychiatry* 67 (11):1735–40.

Pahnke, W.N. 1969. The psychedelic mystical experience in the human encounter with death. *Harvard Theological Review* 62:1–21.

Presti, D., and Nichols, D. 2004. Biochemistry and neuropharmacology of psilocybin mushrooms. In *Teonanacatl: Sacred mushroom of vision,* ed. R. Metzner, pp. 89–108. El Verano, CA: Four Trees Press.

Riedlinger, T.J., ed. 1990. *The sacred mushroom seeker: Essays for R. Gordon Wasson.* Portland, OR: Dioscorides Press.

Rousseau, P. 2000. Spirituality and the dying patient. *Journal of Clinical Oncology* 18:2000–2.

Vollenweider, F.X., K.L. Leenders, C. Scharfetter, P. Maguire, O. Stadelmann, and J. Angst. 1997. Positron emission tomography and fluorodeoxyglucose studies of metabolic hyperfrontality and psychopathology in the psilocybin model of psychosis. *Neuropsychopharmacology* 16:357–72.

Walsh, R., and C.S. Grob, eds. 2005. *Higher wisdom: Eminent elders explore the continuing impact of psychedelics.* Albany, NY: State University of New York Press.

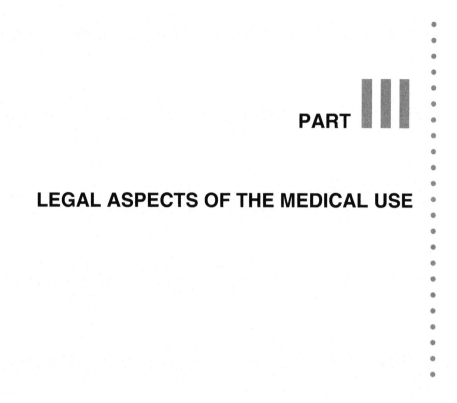

PART III

LEGAL ASPECTS OF THE MEDICAL USE

12

PSYCHEDELIC MEDICINE AND THE LAW

RICHARD GLEN BOIRE

Anyone who has ever had the dark cloud of serious illness descend into his or her life knows well the associated mental disease. To be struck with a grave physical illness is to be simultaneously enwrapped in dread, fear, and depression. The effect on the body cannot be separated from the effect on the mind, and the two feedback upon one another in complex patterns that will probably never be fully understood. Here in the West, medical doctors are just beginning to recognize the profound relationship between the mind and the body—a union long acknowledged by healers in other cultures. Eastern healers, for example, have long prescribed meditation with medication, and shamans, curanderas, and medicine people have, for millennia, utilized psychoactive plants and potions as primary healing tools.

Psychedelic medicines, those both ancient and modern, are unique in their ability to reliably access the mind–body interface. They hold out hope for healing where none might otherwise exist (for instance, in the case of cluster headaches as discussed by Halpern and Sewell in this volume). In those horrible cases when all hope has been lost, they may provide the only means of quickly coming to terms with impending death, and reducing emotional and physical suffering.

DOCTORS V. COPS: WHO SHOULD CONTROL MEDICINE?

As part-and-parcel of our nation's modern drug war policy, government politicians and federal law enforcement agents have stationed themselves in the middle of what was has historically been a private personal decision, perhaps made in conjunction with a physician or pharmacist.

As explained by historian Wallace F. Janssen, in "colonial days, and long afterward, consumers...were their own food and drug inspectors," "there was a striking absence of statutes dealing with drugs," (Janssen 1981, 422–5) and, although there were food inspection laws and standards for weights and measures, "drug laws were virtually non-existent" (Janssen 1975, 671).

Significant drug regulation in the United States did not begin until 1906. In that year, Congress enacted the Pure Food and Drug Act, which was premised on Congress's Commerce Clause powers to regulate interstate commerce and activities that "substantially affect" interstate commerce.[1] The 1906 Act barred misbranded and adulterated foods or drugs from entering interstate commerce, and prohibited false and misleading labeling.[2] Since 1906, there has been a steady march of more and more federal government control over drugs.

In 1909, the Smoking Opium Exclusion Act prohibited the importation, possession, and nonmedical use of opium.[3] Like the 1906 Act, this Act was premised on Congress' power to regulate interstate commerce.

In 1914, Congress used its taxation power to pass the Harrison Narcotics Act, which taxed those who produced, imported, or distributed opiates or cocaine derivatives, and set restrictions on possession.[4]

In 1917, the Senate passed the 18th Amendment, which took effect on January 16, 1920, prohibiting the manufacture, sale, and transportation of "intoxicating liquors." The 18th Amendment was enforced by passage of the National Prohibition Act of 1919[5] (also known as the Volstead Act), which also prohibited the possession of intoxicating liquors, but specifically recognized exceptions for religious use and medical use.[6] Alcohol prohibition was repealed on December 5, 1933, when the 21st Amendment was ratified.

In 1937, Congress passed the Marijuana Tax Act, which taxed any exchange or distribution of marijuana.[7] And, one year later, Congress passed the Food, Drug, and Cosmetic Act of 1938, which among other things required that new drugs be proven safe before marketing.[8]

With the exception of marijuana, it was not until 1965 that federal law directly targeted psychedelic drugs, thus beginning a significant slowdown in psychedelic research. In the previous 16 years (1950–1965), the potential of certain psychedelics to serve as revolutionary medicines was enthusiastically studied, producing over 1,000 published clinical papers documenting psychedelic treatment with 40,000 patients (Grinspoon and Bakalar 1997). In the 1950s and early 1960s, a cancer patient using LSD (lysergic acid diethylamide) as an adjunct to chemotherapy did not fear that his or her hospital bed would be transformed into a jail cot, nor did a doctor feel handcuffed in his or her choice of treatment options. In 1965, Congress acting under its Commerce Clause powers passed the Drug Abuse Control Amendments, which targeted stimulants and depressants, and for the first time, substances having a "hallucinogenic effect" on the central nervous system. This law was primarily aimed at regulating those who manufactured or dispensed such drugs, specifically exempting from its reach anyone who possessed such drugs for his or her personal use.[9]

It was not until 1968 that the personal possession of LSD became a federal offense. On October 5, 1968, President Lyndon Johnson signed into law an amendment to the 1965 Act,[10] stating, "under this bill the illegal manufacture, sale or distribution of LSD and similar drugs is made a felony, punishable by 5 years in prison and a $10,000 fine. The illegal possession of such a drug is made a misdemeanor punishable by up to 1 year in prison and a $1,000 fine."[11]

While the personal possession of LSD was federally prohibited in 1968, it took two more years before federal drug control policy was consolidated with the enactment of the Comprehensive Drug Abuse Prevention and Control Act of 1970.[12] Title II of the 1970 Act is popularly known as the Controlled Substances Act. In the Controlled Substances Act, Congress established a five-schedule scheme for regulating various substances. Schedule I includes the most tightly controlled drugs. Under federal law, to be placed in Schedule I a drug must be unsafe for use even under medical supervision, have a high potential for abuse, and have no currently accepted medical use. On the other end of the schedule spectrum is Schedule V, which contains those substances thought to have a low potential for abuse, relatively slight potential for physical or psychological dependence, and a currently accepted medical use.[13]

In 1970, Congress initially allocated various substances to particular schedules, but then authorized the Attorney General to schedule, transfer between schedules, or remove a substance from a schedule.[14] When enacted in 1970, Schedule I was populated with 17 psychedelic substances, denoted as "hallucinogens."[15] The list currently includes 34 substances.[16] With the primary exception of ketamine, nearly every psychedelic substance currently controlled under federal law has been placed in Schedule I, thereby legislating that they have "no accepted medical use" and are "unsafe even under medical supervision." Because physicians are prohibited from prescribing Schedule I substances, it is all but impossible for medical doctors and psychiatrists to utilize these potentially beneficial substances in treating their patients. Indeed, merely possessing a drug placed in Schedule I is a federal crime punishable by imprisonment and fines.

Dr. Thomas Szasz, professor emeritus of psychiatry at the State University of New York, Syracuse, has forcefully argued that since 1938, when federal prescription laws were first enacted,[17] physicians have been "parentified" and now act as "agents of the therapeutic state" (Szasz 1992).[18] As described by Dr. Szasz, under the 1938 law:

[g]overnment bureaucrats became the final arbiters of what counted as a therapeutic drug and as legitimate medical treatment in general. As a result, the patient lost his

right to drugs traditionally available in the free market; the doctor lost his freedom to medicate his patient as he saw fit, subject only to his patient's consent; and the medical profession lost its integrity as an organization independent of the political vagaries of politics.[19]

Regardless of whether one agrees with Dr. Szasz that prescription requirements are an affront to the autonomy of patients and doctors, it is impossible to dispute that in 2006 law enforcement agents, rather than medical professionals (or patients), often had more of a say in the treatment options available for some seriously ill and suffering patients.

Under federal law, ultimate authority over the scheduling of drugs (and hence over the determination of which drugs doctors can prescribe and which they cannot) is vested not in a medical organization but rather in the Attorney General of the United States. In 1973, shortly after the DEA (Drug Enforcement Administration) was created by President Nixon, the Attorney General delegated his scheduling powers to the Administrator of the DEA.[20] In making the required findings for scheduling any given drug, federal law requires that the Administrator consider the following eight factors:

1. The drug's actual or relative potential for abuse;
2. Scientific evidence of the drug's pharmacological effect, if known;
3. The state of current scientific knowledge regarding the drug or other substance;
4. The drug's history and current pattern of abuse;
5. The scope, duration, and significance of abuse;
6. What, if any, risk there is to the public health;
7. The drug's psychic or psychological dependence liability; and
8. Whether the drug is an immediate precursor of another controlled substance.[21]

The DEA is a law enforcement agency, not a medical body. In its thirty-year history, the DEA has been led by former police officers, military officers, and prosecutors with no training or experience in medicine. Yet, because the DEA is the federal agency that determines whether to place a drug in Schedule I, it is the DEA that ultimately holds the control over which drugs can or cannot be prescribed by physicians. Under federal law, the DEA Administrator's scheduling power is theoretically checked by the Secretary of HHS (Health and Human Services), who must approve the Administrator's intention to schedule a particular drug. In practice, however, the Secretary's "check" is likely to be a rubber stamp, approving whatever the Administrator recommends. For example, in the *Grinspoon* case (discussed, *post*), the U.S. Court of Appeals for the First Circuit criticized the HHS Secretary for just such a rubber stamp approval with respect to MDMA (methylenedioxymethamphetamine), commenting:

The record...reveals that the HHS performed in a less than admirable fashion in making its recommendation to the Administrator. The record indicates that HHS failed to look beyond its files upon receiving the Administrator's...request for a scientific and medical evaluation; neglected to consult any organization of medical professionals or even the FDA's own panel of experts, the Drug Abuse Advisory Committee; and simply rubber stamped the Administrator's conclusion by adopting the...analysis already performed by the DEA.[22]

Once the DEA Administrator has placed a substance in Schedule I, the drug is not available as medicine and possession of it for any reason except as authorized by federal agencies for research is a federal crime. Because of the extremist nature of the war on drugs, there is no federal exception for seriously sick or dying people. This, of course, includes medical use of marijuana. While increasing numbers of states are exempting medical users of marijuana from the state's marijuana prohibitions, these exemptions are limited to prosecutions that take place in *state* courts, not in *federal* court (and are limited to marijuana). In 2005, the U.S. Supreme Court made clear that even if a medical user of marijuana never crosses a state border, and obtains and uses his or her marijuana completely within a state with a medical protection, the federal government retains the power to prosecute that person for violating the *federal* marijuana prohibition.[23]

As things currently stand, the urgent therapeutic needs of such patients are forced to take back seat to the government's concerns about recreational drug use by healthy persons. Hence, a terminal cancer patient using marijuana, LSD, or MDMA, or psilocybian mushrooms, to aid his or her preparation for death, is treated no differently under federal law than a wild-eyed user of crack cocaine. In fact, crack cocaine (a.k.a., cocaine base) is acknowledged to have accepted medicinal applications and has been placed in Schedule II, whereas all medical properties of the psychedelic substances are denied.[24]

THE POLITICS OF MEDICINE: THE SCHEDULING OF MDMA

"The first casualty of war is truth" wrote the Greek playwright and poet Aeschylus around 500 BC. In the war on drugs, Aeschylus' proposition is surely realized. Drugs that patients and medical professionals have found beneficial are decreed to have "no accepted medical use" by the nation's top drug cop— the Administrator of the DEA—and are declared off-limits for use in treatment of any kind. This ugly politicized process is clearly illustrated by the history surrounding the scheduling of the drug MDMA.

First synthesized by the Merck pharmaceutical firm in 1912, but never marketed by the company, MDMA resurfaced in the early 1970s. With its short duration and unique characteristic for reliably heightening the capacity for introspection and self-acceptance, coupled with the easing of communication anxieties, MDMA soon caught the ear of psychotherapists who quietly began using the drug as an adjunct to therapy.

One such psychiatrist was Dr. George Greer. Colleagues of Dr. Greer discovered that MDMA facilitated the therapeutic process (see Chapter 7 by Greer and Tolbert in this volume). After spending a few months researching the laws and regulations, Dr. Greer concluded that if he manufactured the MDMA himself, and had peer review and informed consent, he could legally administer MDMA to his patients. He proceeded to synthesize a batch of MDMA with the assistance of Dr. Alexander Shulgin, Ph.D., and administered it to about 80 people over a five-year period (Greer and Tolbert 1990).

Although none of the patients to whom Dr. Greer administered MDMA suffered from disabling psychiatric conditions (Dr. Greer excluded such patients for safety reasons), well over 90% reported benefits that they considered significant. These included improvement of communication and intimacy during the sessions with spouses, and a general decrease in psychological problems afterward. Interpersonal relationships, self-esteem, and mood also generally improved. Many patients reported that these improvements in their lives lasted from weeks to years, even after only one or two sessions utilizing MDMA.

At the same time that Dr. Greer and a growing number of other psychotherapists were finding MDMA useful as an adjunct to therapy, recreational use of the drug was growing. In 1981, an underground manufacturer of MDMA gave it the marketing moniker "ecstasy," and its recreational use ballooned. Word of MDMA soon reached the DEA, which, in 1982, opened a file on the drug.

In the July 27, 1984, issue of the *Federal Register,* the DEA announced that it was moving to add MDMA to the list of Schedule I substances. The notice stated that MDMA had no legitimate medical use or manufacturer in the United States, was responsible for an undisclosed number of trips to emergency rooms, and had a high potential for abuse.[25]

Dr. Greer and other psychiatrists who were successfully using MDMA in therapy were alarmed when they learned of the DEA's intention to place MDMA in Schedule I. Dr. Greer and fifteen other medical professionals wrote the DEA explaining that in their professional experiences, MDMA had proven to be a tremendous aid to therapy, and could be used safely under medical supervision. Placing MDMA in Schedule I would make it all but impossible for anyone—medical professionals included—to use the substance in therapy. Not one person wrote to support the DEA's intention to place MDMA in Schedule I.

As a result of the doctors' letters, the DEA was forced to hold hearings on the matter of MDMA's proposed scheduling. Nine days of hearings were held in three cities during 1985. At the hearings, thirty-three witnesses testified and ninety-five exhibits were received into evidence. Psychiatrists testified that the drug was an invaluable therapeutic adjunct that was safe when used under professional supervision. Witnesses for the DEA countered that the psychiatrists were basing their testimony on nothing but anecdotes—that no controlled scientific studies existed to support their claims.

Shortly before the first hearing date, then-President Reagan appointed a new Administrator of the DEA. The appointee, John Lawn, had a long history as an upper-level special agent in the FBI but, like all other DEA administrators to date, absolutely no medical training or experience. In a remarkably unabashed affront to the hearing process that was already underway, the new Administrator, acting under emergency scheduling powers, unilaterally decreed that effective July 1, 1985, MDMA would be a Schedule I drug. The emergency scheduling provision allows the Attorney General to act without holding a hearing by asserting that there is an "imminent hazard to the public safety."[26] Administrator Lawn stated that notwithstanding the ongoing hearing on the issue of MDMA's appropriate status, emergency scheduling was "necessary to avoid an imminent hazard to the public safety." In particular, Administrator Lawn offered the following reasons for his decision to invoke the emergency scheduling provision:

Unapproved, so-called therapeutic use of MDMA continues in many sections of the country. Clandestine production, distribution and abuse of MDMA is occurring nationwide and appears to be escalating. The open promotion of MDMA as a legal euphoriant through fliers, circulars and promotional parties has recently surfaced in some areas. DEA agents estimate that 30,000 dosage units of MDMA are distributed each month in one Texas city. Drug abuse treatment programs have reported that they are seeing individuals seeking treatment who have taken multiple doses of MDMA. ...Of immediate concern to DEA in terms of hazard to public safety is a very recent research finding which suggests that MDMA has neurotoxic properties. A paper entitled "Hallucinogenic Amphetamine Selectively Destroys Brain Serotonin Nerve Terminals: Neurochemical and Anatomical Evidence" by G. Ricaurte, G. Bryan, L. Straus, L. Seiden and C. Schuster [(Ricaurte, 1985)], describes studies which show that single or multiple doses of MDA selectively destroy serotonergic nerve terminals in the rat brain....Experts have concluded that because of the neurotoxic effects of closely related structural analogs of MDMA (MDA, amphetamine and methamphetamine) and because both MDA and MDMA cause the release of endogenous serotonin, it is likely that MDMA will produce similar nuerotoxic [sic] effects to those of MDA.[27]

In a subsequent case, the federal convictions of several defendants for distributing and conspiring to distribute MDMA were reversed by the Ninth Circuit Court of Appeals, which found that Administrator Lawn overstepped his powers. The court held that the Attorney General never properly delegated to the DEA Administrator the *emergency power* to temporarily schedule controlled substances.[28]

Over the next ten months, however, the facts about MDMA were heard by Judge Francis Young, who presided over the hearings. After receiving and considering all the evidence admitted during the hearings, Judge Young issued his findings and recommendation on May 22, 1986. In a comprehensive opinion, Judge Young found that MDMA did *not meet a single one of the three criteria necessary for placement in Schedule I.* Judge Young reported that MDMA had a safe and accepted medical use in the United States under medical supervision. Furthermore, he found that the evidence failed to establish that MDMA had a high potential for abuse. Based on his thorough examination of the evidence, Judge Young recommended that MDMA be placed in Schedule III, which would allow doctors to use it in therapy and prescribe it, while still keeping it unavailable to the public at large.

Administrator Lawn refused to accept Judge Young's recommendation. In Administrator Lawn's opinion, because MDMA was not an FDA-approved drug, it *ipso facto* lacked both any currently accepted medical use in treatment and an accepted safety for use under medical supervision. Administrator Lawn also averred that Judge Young gave too much weight to the testimony and evidence of doctors and patients, and not enough consideration to studies on rats, or the lack of FDA approval. In a flat rejection of Judge Young's recommendation, Administrator Lawn decreed that effective November 13, 1986, MDMA would be permanently placed in Schedule I, not Schedule III.[29]

The medical community fired back. Lester Grinspoon, an associate professor of Psychiatry at Harvard Medical School, sued the DEA, seeking to invalidate MDMA's Schedule I status.[30] The federal circuit court that heard the case succinctly summarized the competing arguments: "The [DEA] Administrator reads 'accepted [medical use]' to mean that *the FDA* must have approved the drug for interstate marketing. Dr. Grinspoon, on the other hand, prefers to interpret "accepted" as meaning that the *medical community* generally agrees that the drug has a medical use and can be used safely under medical supervision."[31]

Calling Administrator Lawn's argument "strained" and "unpersuasive," the federal court rejected Lawn's argument and sided with Dr. Grinspoon.[32] The court vacated MDMA's Schedule I status and remanded the case to the DEA for reconsideration—prohibiting Administrator Lawn from making the lack of FDA approval the basis for his decision.[33] Forced to do so by the federal circuit court's ruling, the DEA on January 27, 1988, deleted MDMA from Schedule I, pending the Administrator Lawn's reconsideration of the evidence and Judge Young's recommendation.

Remarkably, in a perfunctory final rule decreed less than a month later, Administrator Lawn claimed that he had reconsidered the evidence and once again concluded that MDMA belonged in Schedule I.[34] In his published ruling, Administrator Lawn paradoxically gave greater weight to the *absence* of certain evidence than to the actual evidence admitted during the hearing. Evidence that psychiatrists had administered MDMA to approximately 200 patients with positive effects was summarily dismissed by Administrator Lawn, as "merely anecdotal," simply because it was not published. According to Administrator Lawn: [t]he published literature contains no references to the clinical use of MDMA nor animal studies to indicate such a clinical use. Recognized texts, reference books and pharmacopoeia contain no references to the therapeutic use of MDMA. The two unpublished studies supporting the therapeutic use of MDMA which were presented during the hearings, do not contain any data which can be assessed by scientific review to draw a conclusion that MDMA has a therapeutic use.[35]

Thirty days later (on March 23, 1998), in spite of clear evidence showing MDMA's promise in treating mentally suffering people, MDMA became a Schedule I "hallucinogen." Possession of the drug, for any reason except for authorized research studies, remains a federal offense.

CRIMINALIZING THE SICK

As the laws stand today, patients who use psychedelic medicines face the constantly looming threat that their medical problems will be compounded by legal problems. For many patients, the fear and social stigma engendered by the fact that psychedelic treatment makes them federal criminals is too much to bear, and they reluctantly forgo potentially beneficial treatment. For those who decide to go forward with psychedelic treatment despite its outlawed status, the treatment's medical benefits can be compromised by the incumbent stress inherent in the patient's suddenly precarious legal status.

For other patients, the dire need for relief from suffering, or the fact that death may loom near, can make the federal law nothing but a nuisance—outrageous nonetheless—but not something that will deter them. The testimony of an AIDS patient during the battle for an exemption that would allow terminally ill patients to use unapproved (but unscheduled) drugs speaks to the situation currently confronting seriously suffering or terminally ill patients who seek to use Schedule I psychedelic medications:

> [It's like being] in a disabled airplane, speeding downward out of control...[seeing] a parachute hanging on the cabin wall, one small moment of hope...[trying] to strap it on when a government employee reaches out and tears it off [your] back, admonishing, "You can't use that! It doesn't have a Federal Aviation Administration sticker on it. We don't know if it will work." (Delaney 1989)

Who would not snatch the parachute under such circumstances?

Physicians' Roles in Psychedelic Medicine Use

A medical doctor or psychologist convinced that treatment or therapy with a particular Schedule I psychedelic drug may benefit a patient confronts a number of difficult issues. Can a doctor or psychologist discuss treatment of a patient with an illegal psychedelic? What role, if any, can a doctor play if a patient is determined to use an illegal psychedelic for its physical and/or mental healing properties?

The answer to the first question is easy. Discussing of the healing potentials of a legal or illegal psychedelic substance with a patient is protected by the First Amendment.[36] The only exception is for speech that instructs a patient where or how to obtain an outlawed psychedelic, or somehow involves the doctor in a conspiracy with the patient to obtain the drug. Short of those limits, a doctor is well within the law to speak openly about the pros and cons of alternative treatment methods, including a patient's medical use of a particular outlawed psychedelic. Again, so long as the doctor does not provide information on how or where to obtain an outlawed drug, the First Amendment bars the government from dictating the content of a doctor's conversion with a patient. As a result, a doctor commits no crime by recommending particular books for the patient to read, or by conducting a search of Medline® or similar electronic databases for information on a psychedelic and then providing the fruits of his or her research to the patient.

If a patient decides to avail him or herself to a psychedelic in an attempt at physical or mental healing, the medical professional must be careful with respect to his or her role. A physician who provides a Schedule I psychedelic to a patient—even as part of a thoughtful treatment plan—is treated no better than a street corner crack dealer. Both the doctor and the crack dealer are distributing an outlawed drug in violation of federal and state law. The crime of distribution does not require multiple sales, or any sales at all. Simply giving away the drug can be sufficient for conviction.

A doctor who *assists* a patient in obtaining a Schedule I substance also commits a crime: namely, aiding and abetting the unlawful possession of a controlled substance. In most jurisdictions, this crime is punished just as harshly as if the doctor, him or herself, were the person who acquired and possessed the outlawed drug. Aiding and abetting is not only accomplished by physically procuring a Schedule I drug for a patient; the crime can also be committed by nothing more than speech. It is unlawful aiding and abetting, for example, if a physician tells a patient the name of a person who sells a Schedule I psychedelic, or arranges a meeting between the patient and a supplier of the drug. The First Amendment's protections for speech do *not* protect these sorts of actions.

With these legal concerns in mind, a physician who is asked by a patient for assistance in obtaining a Schedule I psychedelic is well-advised to explain to the patient that even if the doctor is sympathetic to the patient's plight, and believes that psychedelic therapy could well be of benefit, the physician will not provide *any* assistance in obtaining such a drug. On this point, the physician should not waver.

What is the potential criminal liability, as opposed to civil liability, of a medical professional who is present when a patient self-medicates with a Schedule I medication? As should be clear from the discussion above, a doctor commits a crime if he or she procures an outlawed psychedelic for a patient, stores an outlawed psychedelic, or gives an outlawed psychedelic to a patient. But, beyond such a clear violation of the law, criminal liability for a doctor falls into a gray area. For example, imagine a patient who arrives at a psychologist's office for a therapy session and ingests a psychedelic prior to entering the office. An isolated incident of this sort presents little worry of criminal liability for the psychologist. The psychologist would be ill-advised, however, to build an entire practice around such a scenario, or to promote such services. Most states have laws that prohibit so-called "drug houses," premises where "drug activity" occurs. In 1986,

Congress passed the "Crack House Statute,"[37] which was intended to "outlaw operation of houses or buildings, so called 'crack houses,' where 'crack,' cocaine and other drugs are manufactured of used."[38] In 2001, however, federal prosecutors indicted a promoter of rave dance parties and two venue managers, alleging that the men knew that attendees of the raves would be using MDMA during the all-night events.[39] The case was settled with a negotiated plea, which required the managers to pay a fine of $100,000 and placed them on five years probation.[40]

Another imaginable scenario is one in which a patient, independent of the professional's direct assistance, ingests MDMA, or some psychedelic medicine, and then calls the psychologist for advice or counseling. A psychologist in such a situation commits no criminal conduct by speaking with the patient over the phone, or by making a house call. Likewise, a psychologist who is merely present at an event where people have used a psychedelic medicine, violates no criminal law by providing medical assistance or counseling to those who seek his or her assistance or guidance.

The Medical Necessity Defense

For patients who decide to violate the criminal laws outlawing possession of Schedule I psychedelics, arrest is always a possibility. Plainly, an arrest for criminal drug possession, with its likely attendant jail time prior to bail, and the ongoing anxiety associated with defending oneself against criminal charges will add an immense amount of stress to any patient's life. Fortunately, in many states, a seriously ill patient who has been charged with possessing a small amount of an outlawed psychedelic medication will likely be treated relatively leniently by a court. There are few criminal defendants more sympathetic than an otherwise law-abiding citizen who has been struck with a serious or terminal illness.

The goal at any trial involving a medical user of a Schedule I psychedelic is twofold: (1) to obtain an acquittal based on a "medical necessity defense"; or, failing that (2) to educate the judge with respect to the medical use of the outlawed psychedelic and to the defendant's serious medical condition. The hope is that even in the event of conviction a fully informed judge will be lenient in imposing a sentence.

The general defense of "necessity" to charges of criminal conduct is centuries old. As a British court succinctly explained in a case decided in 1551, "where the words of [a law] are broken to avoid greater inconvenience, or through necessity, or by compulsion," the law has not been broken.[41] In essence, the necessity defense protects a person who has been forced to chose between the lesser of two evils, and in doing so was compelled to break the law. For social policy reasons, if the harm that is likely to result from compliance with a law is greater than that which will result from violating the law, a person is, by virtue of the legal defense of necessity, justified in breaking the law. Paradigmatic examples are a prisoner escaping from a burning jail, or a person who steals food from a cabin after being lost in the woods for a week. However, some states bar necessity defenses to criminal acts. Consequently, a patient who is considering a medical defense in the event that he or she is arrested for medical use of a psychedelic is well advised to research the law of his or her state or consult with an attorney to learn whether such a defense is viable.

The *medical* necessity defense is a particularized type of necessity defense, one in which the defendant asserts that the harm done by using an illegal drug was less than would have resulted by obeying the law and foregoing the ostensibly illegal treatment. More specifically, a patient who possesses a Schedule I psychedelic exclusively to treat his or her own serious illness must establish the following elements in order to present the medical necessity defense to a jury:

1. the patent's illness is not a fabrication and his or her suffering is severe;
2. lawful medical treatment was tried and found ineffective;
3. treatment with the particular Schedule I psychedelic reduces the patient's severe suffering and does not disproportionately cause other harm to the patient, to other people, or to the State's interest in otherwise controlling drugs.[42]

A physician can play a central role in assisting a patient in preparing a medical necessity defense. Indeed, aside from the patient's own testimony at trial concerning his or her illness and how the use of the Schedule I psychedelic helped to alleviate suffering, testimony by the patient's physician or therapist is likely to be the most important and compelling testimony presented at the trial.

Preparation for a medical necessity defense should begin long before any arrest. The doctor's files should describe the severity of the patient's suffering and the course of conventional treatment that was tried and found inadequate. Any legal medication that might possibly be a "substitute" for a Schedule I medicine should be tried, and any unsatisfactory results documented in detail.

In the event that a patient is arrested and the medical professional is called upon to testify at trial, the professional should explain to the jury the patient's extreme medical situation and difficult course of treatment. Next, the professional should testify to the unique benefit derived (actual or potential) by the patient's use of the psychedelic. This explanation should be based on at least three considerations: (1) the patient's self-report to the physician of the treatment's benefits; (2) the physician's examination of the patient, which corroborates the patient's apparent benefit from using the drug; and (3) the scientific, historic, and anthropological literature speaking to the medical use of the drug. Finally, the doctor may wish to testify that were it possible to legally prescribe the psychedelic medication for the patient, the doctor would do so given the unique needs of the patient and the lack of alternative conventional medications.

PRISONS OR HOSPITALS? THE FUTURE OF PSYCHEDELIC MEDICINE

Americans have respect for medical professionals and deep compassion for sick, diseased, or dying patients. A carefully restricted medical accommodation would reduce needless suffering and stress, while maintaining an otherwise strict drug control policy. Yet, the current laws, which outlaw *any* use of Schedule I psychedelic substances (with the exception of a few states, which have permitted the use of medical marijuana), place police concerns above medical needs. To a large extent this may be due to a silence from professional medical organizations and patient advocacy groups, both of which have made little effort to seek a legislative accommodation that would permit the lawful use of Schedule I psychedelic medicines under certain circumstances and under the supervision of a medical professional.

A statutory exemption permits members of the Native American Church to use peyote (a Schedule I psychedelic substance) in their religious ceremonies.[43] This has not led to abuse, nor has it resulted in members of the general public obtaining peyote for recreational use. There is no rational reason why a similar exemption, but restricted to *medical* use of Schedule I psychedelic medications, under the supervision of a medical doctor, could not be enacted to accommodate seriously ill or dying patients whose health or life may depend upon the potential healing evoked by a psychedelic medicine. Currently, limited amounts of almost all the Schedule I psychedelic medicines are being manufactured by pharmaceutical companies under federal authorization,[44] and a strenuous procedure already exists for tracking and regulating the manufacture and distribution of pharmaceutically manufactured controlled substances, including those in Schedule I.[45] Permitting seriously ill or terminal patients to lawfully use a Schedule I psychedelic substances when their doctors believe it is the last best hope would require only a slight modification of the law. The problem, of course, is not one of practicality, but rather one of politics.

With the recent wave of state laws permitting the medical use of marijuana, perhaps the political tide is turning. A truce in the drug war may not yet be possible, but more and more people agree that the wounded should be removed from the battlefield. Hopefully, the politicians will start listening.

NOTES

1. For a discussion of Congress' powers to legislate under the commerce clause, see *United States v. Lopez* (1995) 514 U.S. 549 [131 L. Ed. 2d 626, 115 S. Ct. 1624]; *Gonzales v. Raich* (2005) 545 U.S. 1 [125 S.Ct. 2195, 162 L.Ed.2d 1].

2. Pure Food and Drug Act, Pub. L. No. 59-384, 34 Stat. 768 (repealed 1938).

3. Opium Smoking Act, Pub. L. No. 221, 60th Cong., 35 Stat. 614 (February 9, 1909).

4. Harrison Narcotics Act, c. 1, 38 Stat. 785 (December 17, 1914).

5. National Prohibition Act, ch. 85, 41 Stat. 305.

6. *Id.,* Title II, §§ 6 and 7.

7. Marijuana Tax Act 1937, Pub. L. No. 238, 75th Cong. (1937).

8. Food Drug and Cosmetic Act of 1938, Pub. L. No. 75-717, 52 Stat. 1040 (1938), as amended 21 U.S.C. §§ 301 *et. seq.*

9. Drug Control Abuse Amendments of 1965, Pub. L. No. 89-74, § 2, 79 Stat. 226 (1965).

10. Drug Abuse Control Amendments of 1968, Pub. L. No. 90-639, 82 Stat. 1361 (1968).

11. "Statement by the President Upon Signing Bill Relating to Traffic in or Possession of Drugs Such as LSD," (October 25th, 1968) Online at http://www.presidency.ucsb.edu/ws/index.php?pid=29206.

12. 21 U.S.C. § 801 *et. seq.*

13. 21 U.S.C. § 812.

14. 21 U.S.C. § 811(a).

15. As initially enacted, subdivision (c) of Schedule I (21 U.S.C. § 812) stated: Unless specifically excepted or unless listed in another schedule, any material, compound, mixture, or preparation, which contains any quantity of the following hallucinogenic substances, or which contains any of their salts, isomers, and salts of isomers whenever the existence of such salts, isomers, and salts of isomers is possible within the specific chemical designation:

1. 3, 4-Methylenedioxy amphetamine.

2. 5-Methoxy-3, 4-methylenedioxy amphetamine.

3. 3, 4, 5-Trimethoxy amphetamine.

4. Bufotenine.

5. Diethyltryptamine.

6. Dimethyltryptamine.

7. 4-Methyl-2, 5-dimethoxyamphetamine.

8. Ibogaine.

9. Lysergic acid diethylamide.

10. Marihuana.

11. Mescaline.

12. Peyote.

13. *N*-Ethyl-3-piperidyl benzilate.

14. *N*-Methyl-3-piperidyl benzilate.

15. Psilocybin.

16. Psilocyn.

17. Tetrahydrocannabinols.

16. 21 CFR § 1308.11, subd. (d) (May, 2006).

17. Federal Food, Drug and Cosmetic Act of 1938, see endnote 2, *supra.*

18. For an excellent discussion of the early federal laws controlling drugs, see P. Temin, "The Origin of Compulsory Drug Prescriptions," *Jnl. of Law and Econ.* 22 (1):91–105 (April 1979).

19. *Id.* at p. 52.

20. 28 CFR 0.100(b) (1986).

21. 21 U.S.C. § 811 (c).

22. *Grinspoon v. DEA* (1st Cir. 1987) 828 F.2d 881, 897.

23. *Gonzales v Raich* (2005) 162 L.Ed.2d 1 [125 S.Ct. 2195].

24. See 21 U.S.C. § 812(c)(II)(a)(4).

25. 49 Fed. Reg. 30210-30212, July 27, 1984.

26. 21 U.S.C. Sec. 811 (h).

27. 50 Fed. Reg. 23118-23119, May 31, 1985.

28. [*U.S. v. Emerson* (9th Cir. 1988) 846 F.2d 541; accord, *U.S. v. Spain* (10th Cir. 1987) 825 F.2d 1426, 1429.]

29. *Ibid.*

30. *Grinspoon v. DEA, supra,* 828 F.2d 881.

31. *Id.* at p. 886.

32. *Ibid.*

33. *Id.* at p. 891.

34. 53 Fed. Reg. 5156-5159 (February 22, 1988).

35. *Ibid.*

36. *Conant v. Walters* (2002) 309 F.3d 62.

37. 21 U.S.C. § 856.

38. 132 Cong. Rec. 26, 474 (1986) (excerpt of Senate Amendment No. 3034 to H.R. 5484).

39. *McClure v. Ashcroft* (2003) 335 F.3d 404.

40. *Id.*

41. *Reninger v. Fagossa* (1551) 1 Plowd. 1, 19, 75 Eng. Rep. 1, 29-30.

42. See, for example, *Idaho v. Hastings* (Idaho 1990) 801 P.2d 563 [outlining elements of a necessity defense in a medical marijuana case]; Benjamin Reeve, *Necessity: A Recognized Defense,* 21 NEW ENG. L. REV. 779, 781 (1986).

43. 21 C.F.R. § 1307.31; 21 C.F.R. § 16(c) (1967).

44. Under the 2005 controlled substance production quotas, specified pharmaceutical companies are authorized to manufacture: 17 g of MDMA, 15 g of MDA, 2 g of psilocybin, 7 g of psilocin, and a whopping 61 g of LSD. (See "Controlled Substances: Revised Aggregate Production Quotas for 2005" 70 *Fed. Reg.* 68087-68089.) (Nov. 9, 2005); 21 U.S.C. § 826.

45. See 21 U.S.C. §§ 821–829.

REFERENCES

Delaney, M. 1989. The case for patient access to experimental therapy. *Journal of Infectious Diseases* 159 (3):416–9. Originally presented at 26th Annual Meeting of the Infectious Disease Society of America, October 27–28, 1988.

Greer, G., and R. Tolbert. 1990. *The therapeutic use of MDMA.* In *Ecstasy: The clinical, pharmacological and neurotoxicological effects of the drug MDMA,* ed. S. J. Peroutka, 21–36. Boston: Kluwer Academic Publishers.

Grinspoon, L., and J. Bakalar. 1997. *Psychedelic drugs reconsidered*. New York: The Lindesmith Center.

Janssen, W. 1975. America's first food and drug laws. *Food Drug Cosmetics Law Journal* 30:665–72.

Janssen, W. 1981. Outline of the history of U.S. drug regulation and labeling. *Food Drug Cosmetics Law Journal* 36:420–5.

Ricaurte, G.G., L. Bryan, L. Strauss, L. Seiden, and C. Schuster. 1985. Hallucinogenic amphetamine selectively destroys brain serotonin nerve terminals. *Science* 229 (4717):986–8.

Szasz, T. 1992. *Our right to drugs: The case for a free market*. Syracuse, NY: Syracuse University Press.

13

THE LEGAL BASES FOR RELIGIOUS PEYOTE USE

KEVIN FEENEY

While religious peyote use dates back several millennia (Schultes and Hofmann 1992), the practice of peyotism in the United States is a relatively recent phenomenon. The rise of peyotism, which was traditionally limited to Mexico, Texas, and the Southwest, was intrinsically tied to the rapid and widespread destruction of Native American cultures across the continent in the 19th century (Long 2000). During this period, tribes[1] from across the country were forced off their lands onto small reservations, which they often shared with other tribes who spoke different languages, had different cultures, and came from very different parts of the United States. While peyotism was unknown to most tribal groups in the early part of the 19th century, the removal of so many disparate tribes to isolated reservations produced circumstances where once remote practices and traditions could be shared and rapidly dispersed among numerous tribal groups. At this critical juncture, when many tribes were facing the loss of land, traditions, and way of life, peyotism surfaced as a way to create social and tribal solidarity among the diverse tribes that had been forced together, and at the same time preserve aspects of Indian culture (Long 2000). The peyote ritual, just as the Ghost Dance, became a symbol of resistance and helped form the foundation of a pan-Indian movement, a movement that would help create unity among American tribes against the cultural devastation wrought by European settlers.

The objective of this chapter is to explore and explain the legal bases that currently support the limited religious use of peyote. This chapter consists of four parts. The first part considers the history of peyote prohibition, religious exemptions, and the failed constitutional challenge that led to the current federal exemption; the second focuses on the parameters of the current federal exemption, as laid out in the AIRFA (American Indian Religious Freedom Act Amendments) of 1994, including who is protected and whether nonrecognized Indians may have an Equal Protection claim protecting their religious practices; the third concerns the RFRA (Religious Freedom Restoration Act) of 1993 and examines what the 2006 Supreme Court decision in *Gonzalez v. O Centro Espirita Beneficiente Uniao Do Vegetal* (*Gonzalez v. UDV*) means for non-Indian members of the NAC (Native American Church) and other peyotist traditions; and finally, the fourth part explores whether the protections offered by AIRFA and RFRA extend to the state level, and if so, to what degree. While the current federal exemption is limited to Indian practitioners of traditional Indian religions, it is my aim to demonstrate that nonrecognized Indians[2] might successfully seek protection under the statute by bringing an Equal Protection claim, and that all sincere practitioners, Indian and non-Indian alike, should find federal protection to practice traditional Indian religions under RFRA.

A BRIEF LEGAL HISTORY

The controversy surrounding ceremonial peyote use dates back several centuries, and stems from the belief of colonialists and missionaries that its use was an affront to God. In 1620, the Roman Catholic Church outlawed the use of peyote by indigenous peoples in Mexico (Beltran 1952). When peyotism later spread to the United States in the 19th century, Christian missionaries worked with the BIA (Bureau of Indian Affairs) to eradicate its use (Long 2000). Apart from the belief that peyote use was sinful, the use of peyote by Indians was hindering attempts to convert them to Christianity and assimilate them into American society.

As attempts to eradicate peyote use failed, those opposing its use looked to Congress. In 1918, the same year the NAC was incorporated, the U.S. House of Representatives passed a bill prohibiting peyote use (Long 2000). The bill did not advance further, and attempts to prohibit peyote at the federal level did not resume until the mid-1960s.

While peyote was rarely used recreationally, it was peyote's association with lysergic acid diethylamide and the 1960s counterculture that finally prompted Congress to outlaw peyote in 1965. This first piece of legislation, known as the Drug Abuse Control Amendments of 1965, was passed with the understanding that religious peyote use would be protected (Olson 1981). Shortly thereafter, a regulatory exemption was passed by the Department of HEW (Health,

Education, and Welfare) to allow the religious use of peyote by the NAC. The Act was soon replaced by the CSA (Controlled Substances Act) in 1970, which also lacked a statutory exemption for religious peyote use. The CSA, however, was passed with assurances by the newly formed BNDD (Bureau of Narcotics and Dangerous Drugs) that it would adopt a regulatory exemption similar to the previous exemption approved by HEW (Olson 1981). This exemption would allow "the nondrug use of peyote in bona fide religious ceremonies of the Native American Church" (Drug Enforcement Administration 1971).

Employment Division v. Smith: **The Free Exercise Challenge**

Despite the regulatory exemption promulgated by the BNDD, individual state governments were not bound to honor the exemption, and many states prohibited all uses of peyote, including use in traditional Indian religions. As a result, the limited federal exemption proved useless to many Indian peyotists who then faced state-level prohibitions to their religious practices. One of these individuals was a Klamath Indian by the name of Al Smith, a recovering alcoholic who worked as a substance abuse counselor in Roseburg, Oregon. After a dispute with his employer over his religious peyote use, Smith was fired for allegedly abusing an illegal substance. Smith applied for unemployment with the State of Oregon and was denied on the basis that he had been fired for "misconduct" (Epps 2001).

Smith brought a suit challenging the decision of the Employment Division to deny him unemployment benefits as a violation of his right to free exercise of religion under the First Amendment. The result was a landmark decision by the Supreme Court that reduced the once deferential Free Exercise Clause to a mere constitutional footnote, concerned only with the most blatant forms of religious discrimination (*Employment Division v. Smith* 1990).

Prior to the Supreme Court's decision in *Employment Division v. Smith* (1990), a three-part balancing test known as the *Sherbert* test was used to determine whether a law unconstitutionally burdened an individual's free exercise rights. Under the *Sherbert* test, the individual must first show that the law in question substantially burdens his free exercise of religion. In response, the government must show that the law serves a compelling government interest, and that the government interest cannot be advanced by any less intrusive means (*Sherbert v. Verner* 1963). The Supreme Court in *Smith* overturned this test in favor of a neutrality test. Under the court created neutrality test, the government would no longer need a compelling interest to burden religion but could burden religious practices so long as the law in question treated all people similarly. For Al Smith, this meant that Oregon's law prohibiting peyote use was valid because it prohibited peyote use by all people and was not specifically targeting the religious use of peyote by the NAC. The foreseeable impact of the law on the practices of the NAC was deemed unimportant.

The Aftermath of *Smith*

The fallout from *Employment Division v. Smith* (1990) was considerable, causing a universal outcry among religious groups across the country. These groups formed an unlikely political coalition, including groups as diametrically opposed to Pat Robertson's American Center for Law and Justice and the American Civil Liberties Union (Epps 2001). These groups converged for the purpose of pushing Congress to overturn the *Smith* decision by legislatively reinstating the *Sherbert* balancing test. Congress responded and passed the RFRA in 1993, which restored the *Sherbert* test used prior to *Smith*.[3]

While the movement to restore the *Sherbert* test was widely supported, American Indians were apprehensive about the proposed legislation's ability to effectively protect their rights to practice their religion. After all, Justice Sandra Day O'Connor, who did not support overturning *Sherbert,* joined the majority based on her view that religious peyote use would not have been protected by the Free Exercise Clause had the *Sherbert* balancing test been applied (*Employment Division v. Smith* 1990). In light of O'Connor's opinion, a request was made by a prominent Road man,[4] Reuben Snake, that the coalition adopts (as one of its objectives) protections for religious peyote use. This request was rejected by the coalition, which worried that such an objective was too controversial and would fragment their fragile coalition (Epps 2001).

Having recently suffered a tremendous loss at the Supreme Court, American Indian peyotists were hesitant to settle for a simple reinstatement of the *Sherbert* test, a test which in no way guaranteed protection for religious peyote use. The peyotists continued to lobby Congress. Finally, in 1994, Congress passed an amendment to the AIRFA recognizing that "the traditional ceremonial use of the peyote cactus as a religious sacrament has for centuries been integral to a way of life, and significant in perpetuating Indian tribes and cultures" and exempting Indian practitioners from the criminal prohibitions on peyote (AIRFA 1994).

A NEW EXEMPTION

AIRFA exempts the use of peyote by Indians, identified as members of federally recognized tribes, for "bona fide traditional ceremonial purposes in connection with the practice of a traditional Indian religion" (AIRFA 1994). Under this new exemption, mere NAC membership is insufficient; one must also be part of a federally recognized tribe. The removal of any reference to the NAC in the exemption acts to make the law more constitutionally palatable[5] and may also have been meant to narrow the exemption by excluding non-Indian peyotists.[6] This wording allows peyote use by practitioners of other Indian peyote religions, separate from the NAC, and recognizes the diversity of religious traditions that have developed around ceremonial peyote use.

To understand the scope of this new exemption, several issues need to be explored. First, who is an "Indian" for purposes of this Act, and what does it mean to be part of a federally recognized tribe? Second, what is the basis for allowing this select group of "Indians" to practice their traditional beliefs and for excluding "non-recognized Indians," as well as non-Indians who may also subscribe to these beliefs and practices? These questions are the subjects of the sections that follow.

Who Is an "Indian?"

Under the exemption, an Indian is defined as a member of a tribe "which is recognized as eligible for the special programs and services provided by the United States to Indians because of their status as Indians" (AIRFA 1994). This definition has two parts: (1) to qualify as an Indian under the exemption, one must be an enrolled member of a tribe, and (2) the tribe to which the individual belongs must be one that is recognized by the federal government (AIRFA 1994).

The fact that the statute exempts members of federally recognized tribes is important. As will be explored later, the federal government has a lot of flexibility in how it chooses to define the term "Indian" when passing legislation that provides services to or directly affects "Indians." Other than federal tribal recognition, elements used to define who is an Indian include treaty rights, whether an individual lives on or off a reservation, and the percentage of Indian blood an individual can claim through ancestry. Limitations on blood quantum (ancestry) can be particularly limiting and may serve to exclude non-Indian spouses or mixed race children from protections or benefits otherwise offered by the law. By choosing not to define the term "Indian" by blood quantum, the government has left the extent of the protections offered by the peyote exemption to be determined by individual tribes through tribal enrollment practices.

A tribe's right to define its own membership and enrollment criteria has been recognized by the Supreme Court as central to the tribe's "existence as an independent political community," and to the preservation of its traditions and culture (*Santa Clara Pueblo v. Martinez* 1978, p. 72 n. 32). Some tribes choose to require a minimum blood quantum,[7] while others will recognize mixed race children of any blood quantum so long as they are a child of a tribal member.[8] Thus the criterion for tribal enrollment often fluctuates from tribe to tribe.

Being enrolled in a tribe is not sufficient, however, to qualify for the peyote exemption. The tribe to which one is enrolled must be federally recognized, a limitation that ultimately excludes many ancestral Indians from legal protection, even when peyotism is a traditional religious practice. There are many tribes that never developed a government-to-government relationship with the United States and so have never been recognized; others have had the misfortune to lose their federally recognized status because of the Allotment Act, passed in 1887, or of unilateral termination of federally recognized status by the federal government. In the wake of the Allotment Act, many tribes were coerced into trading their sovereign rights, and thus federal recognition, for small parcels of land. Later, in the 1950s, more than one hundred tribes had their federally recognized status revoked in accordance with the termination policy of that era.[9] These policies left many tribes without a land base, without a recognized governing body, and generally ineligible for federal benefits and protections, which include the current peyote exemption.

This narrow definition of the term "Indian" excludes many who are Indians by race and heritage from claiming the peyote exemption and thus prohibits them from legally practicing their religious traditions. By limiting the exemption to members of federally recognized tribes, the exemption fails to recognize the pan-Indian nature of many peyote religions such as the NAC, which are not tribally based or tribe-specific religions. Whenever the federal government creates a classification of people for different treatment under the law, as it has done with the peyote exemption, it subjects itself to scrutiny under the equal protection guarantees of the Due Process Clause of the Fifth Amendment to the Constitution.

Equal Protection of Indians from Nonrecognized Tribes

The level of scrutiny applied under the Due Process Clause depends on the nature of the classification assigned. The law requires application of the highest level of scrutiny (strict scrutiny) when classifications are based on race.[10] Intermediate levels of scrutiny are applied to classifications based on sex, child illegitimacy, or alienage.[11] All other classifications are generally subject to the lowest level of scrutiny, usually referred to as rational basis review, which requires that the law in question be rationally related to a legitimate government interest. Although the protections offered by the peyote exemption appear to be based on a racial classification, thus requiring application of strict scrutiny, the Supreme Court has determined that, because the federal government has a special trust responsibility to protect and preserve Indian tribes and cultures, the laws singling out Indians for special protection fall within this responsibility and do not constitute racial classifications (*Morton v. Mancari* 1974).

The following section will explore what the trust responsibility means in terms of equal protection claims and whether the exemption may be extended to nonrecognized Indians. This section will also consider several alternative interests that may exclude nonrecognized Indians from the exemption, as well as any risks an expansion of the exemption may pose.

The Trust Responsibility

In 1974, the Supreme Court addressed the problems raised by the convergence of the government's trust responsibility with its duties under the Due Process Clause in a case called *Morton v. Mancari*. At issue in *Morton* was a federal law mandating employment preferences for Indians within the BIA. Non-Indian employees of the BIA alleged that the employment preference constituted racial discrimination in violation of Due Process.

Instead of simply finding that the law was based on a racial classification, the court set forth a test based on the trust responsibility for determining whether statutory preferences for Indians are Constitutional. The test can be stated as follows: where special treatment for Indians can be rationally tied to the fulfillment of Congress' unique trust obligation, which establishes a governmental duty to protect and preserve Indian tribes and cultures,[12] such preferences will be upheld as constitutional (*Morton v. Mancari* 1974, p. 555). This test can be broken down into two parts: first, the goal behind the classification must be within the purview of Congress' trust responsibility; second, the classification must be reasonable and rationally designed to further that goal. The court explained that classifications that pass this test would be considered political rather than racial classifications and would be subject only to rational basis review, the lowest level of scrutiny (*Morton v. Mancari* 1974).

In *Morton* (1974), the Court found that the purpose of the employment preference was to "further Indian self-government" (p. 555), a goal that falls within the purview of the government's trust obligation. The Court also found that the preference was reasonable and rationally designed to further that goal. The Court based these findings on the fact that the BIA only serves federally recognized tribes and only members of federally recognized tribes are eligible for the employment preference. This classification is reasonable because the BIA does not offer services to nonrecognized tribes and is rationally tied to the goal of furthering Indian self-government because it allows members of federally recognized tribes to have more say in the agency that governs their activities. Had the classification been extended to Indians from nonrecognized tribes, the preference becomes overly broad and is no longer clearly related to the goal of advancing Indian self-government. Under the latter circumstances, the law would have been more likely to fail as a racially based classification because extending the preference to Indians from nonrecognized tribes does not further the government's purposes of advancing Indian self-government and appears to be a simple racial classification.

After *Morton* (1974), it became clear that legislative preferences for Indians would not be subject to the strict scrutiny standards usually applied to racial classifications under the Fifth and Fourteenth Amendments, and that such preferences would be upheld so long as they were rationally related to the trust obligation. While the trust responsibility has generally been limited to issues regarding property or fiduciary rights held by recognized tribes or by treaty right, several court decisions have interpreted the trust responsibility as including a duty to preserve Indian culture and religion.

The Fifth Circuit, in the case of *Peyote Way Church of God v. Thornburgh* (1991), was one of the first courts to recognize preservation of Indian cultures and religions as "fundamental to the federal government's trust relationship with

Tribal Native Americans" (p. 1216). The First Circuit, relying partially on the decision in *Peyote Way,* also found that the government's trust responsibility extended to the preservation of Indian culture and therefore justified exemptions for the religious use of eagle feathers by Indians while denying the same rights to non-Indians (*Rupert v. Director, U.S. Fish and Wildlife Serv.* 1992). Some may argue that these courts are breaking new ground, but the inclusion of cultural and religious preservation as part of the government's trust responsibility is in keeping with the historical foundation of this unique relationship with American Indians.

The foundations of this relationship are based on the historical subjugation of Indian peoples by the U.S. government. As the Supreme Court has explained, this relationship arose because:

> the United States overcame the Indians and took possession of their lands, sometimes by force, leaving them an uneducated, helpless and dependent people, needing protection against the selfishness of others and their own improvidence. Of necessity, the United States assumed the duty of furnishing that protection. (*Board of County Comm'rs v. Seber* 1943, p. 715)

As the Supreme Court suggests, the foundations for the trust responsibility do not arise because certain tribes are federally recognized, or because they entered treaties with the United States, but because of actions by the U.S. government resulting in the decline of all American Indian cultures and societies.

While the government may be able to provide a rational basis for limiting some rights and protections to federally recognized tribes, such as employment preferences with the BIA that advance the goals of Indian self-government, protections for the preservation of Indian culture and religion cannot rationally exclude Indians who share in the same cultural and religious traditions.

THE TRUST RESPONSIBILITY AS A MEANS TO PRESERVE INDIAN RELIGIONS

In *Peyote Way* (1991), the Peyote Way Church of God, a non-Indian peyotist church, challenged the original peyote exemption alleging that the exemption was based on a racial classification in violation of equal protection. The Fifth Circuit, following the Supreme Court's lead in *Morton* (1974), sought to establish whether the classification was racial or political in nature. The Fifth Circuit, however, seems to have misunderstood the ruling in *Morton,* believing the Supreme Court had "characterized the BIA employment preference as a political rather than racial classification because the BIA regulations implementing the preference limit eligibility to members of federally recognized tribes who have at least 25% Native American blood" (*Peyote Way v. Thornburgh* 1991, p. 1215). Assuming that the exemption would only be acceptable as a political classification under *Morton* if it were limited to members of federally recognized tribes with at least 25% Indian heritage, the Fifth Circuit set out to "determine whether

NAC membership presupposes tribal affiliation and Native American ancestry, and thus effects a political classification under *Morton*" (p. 1215).

The Fifth Circuit, following this logic, determined that the peyote exemption was a political classification limited to members of federally recognized tribes with 25% Indian heritage (*Peyote Way v. Thornburgh* 1991). The court's finding was based on the testimony of Emerson Jackson, president of the NACNA (Native American Church of North America), one of over a hundred denominations of the NAC (Fikes 2002), who testified that these were the membership requirements of the NAC. The NACNA, unlike other congregations of the NAC, restricts membership to members of federally recognized tribes with 25% Indian heritage, a requirement that was adopted in 1982 (Stewart 1987). While each congregation of the NAC makes its own rules, and most accept non-Indians so long as they are seriously interested (Stewart 1987), the court did not hear this testimony and established the membership protocol for the NACNA as the standard for all congregations of the Church.[13] As a result, the Fifth Circuit's ruling in *Peyote Way* is premised not only on a misunderstanding of the holding in *Morton* (1974) but also on a misunderstanding of the NAC as well.

While Indian self-government was at issue in *Morton* (1974), the government interest behind the peyote exemption is not self-government but the preservation of traditional Indian religions. While self-government is unique to federally recognized tribes, and employment preferences for members of these tribes is rationally related to promoting self-government, Indian religion and culture are not unique to federally recognized tribes.

The NAC, first established in 1918, is not the product of one Indian Nation, and has never been tribe specific (Bannon 1998). In fact, "in 1918, when tribal leaders decided to incorporate and to choose a name, they chose the name "Native American Church" to emphasize...intertribal solidarity" (p. 478). By limiting the peyote exemption to federally recognized tribes, the Fifth Circuit failed to recognize the nature and history of the church and instead perpetuated the assimilationist measures used against Indian peoples that ultimately brought the NAC into existence. Indian religions, particularly peyotism, cross tribal lines and thus restricting the exemption to members of federally recognized tribes—as done by the Fifth Circuit and later by AIRFA—does not appear to have a rational basis. There may be, of course, other unarticulated reasons for restricting the classification under AIRFA.

OTHER GOVERNMENT INTERESTS

Although rational basis review is not a difficult standard to satisfy, it is not a green light for the government to do whatever it wants (*Romer v. Evans* 1996). While it is reasonable for the government to seek to preserve the religious practices of Indians, there appears to be little rationale in excluding Indians who are not federally recognized when they share a common religious tradition. Nevertheless, the government may have other interests in allowing only a narrow exemption to criminal drug laws.

One interest often advanced in cases of religious drug use is in protecting the health of the religious practitioner.[14] This interest is unlikely to succeed, however, particularly in light of the existing exemption. In the case of *Kennedy v. Bureau of Narcotics and Dangerous Drugs* (1972), a non-Indian religious group calling itself the "Church of the Awakening" sought an exemption for the religious use of peyote. The sole interest asserted by the government in denying the Church's petition was in protecting the health of the Church members. It was not surprising that the *Kennedy* court dismissed this interest. Citing the peyote exemption, the court found that the government had no "lesser or different interest in protecting the health of the Indians than it has in protecting the health of non-Indians" (p. 417).

Another interest cited in cases of religious drug use is in preventing the diversion of drugs used for religious purposes to the black market. To legitimately exclude nonrecognized Indians from the peyote exemption, the government would have to show that the exclusion is rationally related to the goal of preventing diversion of peyote. The problem with this argument is that peyote is a relatively obscure drug which has rarely appeared on the black market. The DEA (Drug Enforcement Administration) argued, in a case called *Olsen v. DEA* (1989),that the differences between illicit use and availability of peyote justified allowing an exemption for religious peyote use while simultaneously denying an exemption for religious marijuana use. The DEA explained:

> [T]he actual abuse and availability of marijuana in the United States is many times more pervasive...than that of peyote....The amount of peyote seized and analyzed by the DEA between 1980 and 1987 was 19.4 pounds. The amount of marijuana seized and analyzed by the DEA between 1980 and 1987 was 15,302,468.7 pounds. This overwhelming difference explains why an accommodation can be made for a religious organization which uses peyote in circumscribed ceremonies, and not for a religion which espouses continual use of marijuana. (p. 1463)

Because of the extremely limited availability of peyote, it is unlikely that expanding the exemption to include all Indian peyotists would increase the risk of diversion to the black market. This is a reality that is compounded by the severely depleted populations of peyote in its natural habitat, a depletion that is marked by the decreasing size of available peyote buttons[15] and the increasing difficulty in obtaining peyote among peyotists for religious purposes (Anderson 1995). While the annual peyote harvest brings in nearly two million peyote buttons, this is far short of the annual demand by the NAC, which approaches 5 to 10 million buttons a year (Anderson 1995). While peyote has yet to be listed as an endangered species, the increasing scarcity of the sacred cactus mitigates the argument that expanding the exemption would increase diversion to the black market.

RISKS OF AN EXPANDING EXEMPTION

Given an expanded understanding of the trust obligation, the peyote exemption would not likely survive an equal protection challenge by an NAC adherent from a nonrecognized tribe. There are those who worry, however, that such a challenge would put the survival of the peyote exemption in danger. John Thomas Bannon, Jr., senior counsel for the Department of Justice in the *Peyote Way* case, warns that:

> a decision holding the federal exemption unconstitutional would have been yet another blow to Native American culture and religion....Because it is unlikely that Congress would expand the exemption to include non-Indians...given the considerable potential for abuse such an expansion would provide. (Bannon 1998, p. 476)

Bannon's perception of the exemption is misguided. The case in *Peyote Way* was brought by a non-Indian church, and Bannon feared that ruling the exemption unconstitutional would require Congress to either exempt everyone who claims to use peyote religiously or eliminate the exemption. However, by invoking the trust obligation, the government may restrict the exemption to Indian religious practitioners. Such a limitation would be rationally related to the government's interest in preserving Indian culture and traditions. The government, however, does not have a trust obligation to the Peyote Way Church of God nor to the Church of the Awakening for that matter, and equal protection does not compel an extension of the exemption to them.

While Bannon (1998) argues that the exemption must be limited to members of federally recognized tribes, this position is irreconcilable with his exceptional historical account of the NAC. Bannon acknowledges that peyote "was instrumental in bringing stability to life on the reservations" when so many "different Indian peoples, different Indian cultures, and different Indian religions were thrown together" (p. 477). He calls the NAC "the most important pan-Indian institution in America" (p. 477), and yet calls for the preservation of an exemption that divides the church along tribal lines and strikes at the pan-Indian foundation of the NAC.

Limiting the exemption to recognized tribes arbitrarily excludes thousands of NAC members and peyotists, and cannot be said to be rationally related to preserving this pan-Indian religion. Without sheltering all purported "religious claimants," the 1994 peyote exemption can be expanded to protect all Indian people, regardless of tribal affiliation, and avoid equal protection violations by properly fulfilling the government's goal of preserving Indian religion pursuant to the trust obligation.

This interpretation of the trust obligation as applied to traditional religious use of peyote, however, may be a nonissue in light of the passage of the RFRA in 1993 and the 2006 ruling of the Supreme Court in *Gonzalez v. UDV*. Under the ruling in *Gonzalez,* nonrecognized Indians as well as non-Indians will likely be protected from the criminal peyote laws if they are practicing traditional Indian peyote religions.

THE RFRA

While the 1993 RFRA was originally regarded by Indian peyotists with skepticism, it may ultimately prove to be more effective than the 1994 AIRFA exemption. The original cynicism towards RFRA was based on Justice O'Connor's concurrence in *Employment Division v. Smith* (1990). O'Connor argued that under the *Sherbert* test, the government's interest in prohibiting a controlled substance would always exceed the interests of religious groups who used the substance as a sacrament. However, the recent Supreme Court decision in *Gonzalez v. UDV* (2006) rejected this view.

The case of *Gonzalez v. UDV* (2006) concerned a small religious sect, with origins in the Amazon Rainforest, who consume a sacramental tea brewed from plants indigenous to the Amazon. The tea, called 'hoasca,' contains DMT (dimethyltryptamine), a federally controlled substance. In 1999, three drums of hoasca headed from the Amazon to the American branch of the UDV Church were intercepted and confiscated by U.S. Customs inspectors. The UDV was subsequently threatened with prosecution.

In response, the UDV filed suit in Federal District Court seeking an injunction against application of the CSA to their religious use of hoasca. In their suit, the UDV argued that application of the CSA to their religious use of hoasca was a violation of their religious practices, as protected by RFRA. The Supreme Court agreed (*Gonzalez v. UDV* 2006).

Under RFRA, the *Sherbert* test is applied to determine whether a law violates an individual's religious freedom (*Callahan v. Woods* 1984). Under the *Sherbert* test, the individual must first show that the law in question substantially burdens his free exercise of religion. In response, the government must show that the law serves a compelling government interest and that the stated interest cannot be advanced by any less intrusive means (*Callahan v. Woods* 1984).

In *Gonzalez* (2006), the government conceded the first element of the analysis, that use of hoasca by the UDV was an important component of their religious practices, and that application of the CSA would substantially interfere with this practice. On appeal to the Supreme Court, the government argued that uniform application of the CSA itself constituted a compelling interest and that any exceptions to the Act would undermine this interest. The Court found that the mere placement of DMT into Schedule I[16] of the CSA by Congress could not relieve the government of its duty to meet its burden under RFRA. In support of its position, the Court cited both the statutory and the regulatory exemptions that have permitted limited religious use of peyote, a Schedule I controlled substance, for the last thirty-five years. The Court reasoned that if the government could make an exemption for peyote use in native religious traditions without undermining the goals of the CSA, then it could certainly make an exemption for the religious use of hoasca by the UDV (*Gonzalez v. UDV* 2006).

The Supreme Court's ruling means that the mere placement of a substance in Schedule I of the CSA is not a sufficiently compelling reason to permit the government to substantially burden a sincere religious practice without accommodation. As a result, the government must put forth a specific interest when burdening religious practices. The government must demonstrate the compelling nature of the asserted interest and must prove that the law cannot be tailored to accommodate the religious practice without undermining the stated interest.

Before reaching the Supreme Court, the government had argued that uniform enforcement of the CSA was the least restrictive means of advancing three such governmental interests. These articulated interests included "protecting the health and safety of UDV members, preventing the diversion of hoasca from the church to recreational users, and, complying with the 1971 United Nations Convention on Psychotropic Substances" (*Gonzalez v. UDV* 2006, p. 4). Because the Supreme Court decision in *Gonzalez* requires the government to articulate a compelling interest and demonstrate that the interest cannot be affected by any less restrictive means, it is necessary to understand the likely interests the government will advance against the religious use of Schedule I substances.

In support of its first interest, the government offered evidence that DMT, the controlled substance in hoasca, "can cause psychotic reactions, cardiac irregularities, and adverse drug interactions" (*Gonzalez v. UDV* 2006, p. 5). The district court found this evidence evenly weighted with evidence put forth by the UDV, which cited "studies documenting the safety of its sacramental use of hoasca" and presented "evidence that minimized the likelihood of the health risks raised by the government" (p. 5). The court found the evidence to be in equipoise and determined that the government failed to demonstrate that the health risks associated with the sacramental use of hoasca were sufficiently compelling to justify the substantial burden on the UDV's religious practices (*Gonzalez v. UDV* 2006).

In support of its second interest, the government "cited interest in the illegal use of DMT and hoasca in particular" and pointed to evidence of "a general rise in the illicit use of hallucinogens" (*Gonzalez v. UDV* 2006, p. 5) to support its contention that hoasca would be diverted to the black market. The UDV countered that given the small amounts of hoasca used by the church, the absence of any previous diversion problems, and the lack of any substantial illicit market for hoasca, the risk of diversion of hoasca to recreational users was too minimal to justify a substantial burden on their religious practices. The district court, finding the evidence on diversion to be "virtually balanced" (p. 5), determined that the government had again failed to carry its burden of demonstrating a compelling interest justifying a substantial burden on the religious practices of the church.

The district court also rejected the government's asserted interest in complying with the 1971 Convention on Psychotropic Substances outright, finding that the Convention did not apply to hoasca.[17] While the government may argue that it has other compelling interests in future RFRA cases, the arguments for protecting the health of religious practitioners and preventing diversion of controlled substances to the black market are likely to be recurring governmental interests in strict application of the CSA.

Should a non-Indian member of the NAC, or some other peyotist tradition, be arrested for peyote possession, he or she will likely have a viable defense in RFRA (1993). To claim RFRA, the defendant must usually demonstrate that the law in question substantially interferes with his free exercise of religion. This usually means that the defendant must show that the activities burdened by the law constitute religious practices based on a sincere religious belief. Congress, through passage of the AIRFA Amendments of 1994, has already recognized that use of peyote plays a significant role in some traditional Indian practices, and that enforcement of the CSA in these circumstances would substantially burden these religious practices. This congressional recognition should be sufficient to establish substantial interference with the religious practices of peyotists.

In response, the government will be required to put forth a compelling reason for excluding the individual from the peyote exemption. As described above, two interests that the government is likely to advance include (1) protecting the health and safety of the individual and (2) preventing diversion of peyote to the black market. In addition, the government will have to show that these goals cannot be accomplished by less restrictive means that would still allow an exemption for peyote use by the religious claimant. This is a showing that will likely prove difficult in light of the current peyote exemption for "Indians."

The interests in protecting the health of the religious claimant and preventing diversion of peyote suffer from the same weaknesses discussed under the equal protection analysis discussed previously. As explained by the Ninth Circuit in *Kennedy,* the government has no "lesser or different interest in protecting the health of the Indians than it has in protecting the health of non-Indians" (*Kennedy v. BNDD* 1972, p. 417). Nor is the likelihood of diversion of this scarce cactus likely to increase should non-Indians be allowed to practice peyotism within the folds of the NAC, or any other Indian peyote religions. While other Indian peyote traditions may be different, the NAC is not a racially or tribally based religion, and it has frequently embraced non-Indian members (Stewart 1987). Unless the government can articulate some other compelling reason for restricting the peyote exemption to Indians, RFRA will very likely serve to protect all adherents of peyotism in accordance with the open and inclusive nature of those traditions.

STATE LEVEL PROTECTIONS

The AIRFA peyote exemption and RFRA are both federal laws. While both are written to provide protections at the federal and state levels, the Supreme Court, in *City of Boerne v. Flores* (1997), struck down RFRA as applied to the states for unconstitutionally violating the principles of federalism and separation of powers. This means that RFRA is only a defense to federal prosecution, unless legislatively adopted by the state in question. Since 1993, only eleven states have adopted state equivalents of RFRA.[18] The AIRFA Amendments of 1994 appear to suffer from the same unconstitutional quality. Although AIRFA has yet to be overturned as applied to the states, it is possible that a court will rule that the peyote exemption only applies to federal prosecutions. As a result, peyotists need to be aware of their state laws should they practice their religion away from federal reservation lands. Currently, twenty-eight states recognize the use and possession of peyote for religious purposes,[19] of which fifteen have explicit legislative exemptions,[20] and two of which allow religious use of peyote as a legal defense.[21]

CONCLUSION

Since *Employment Division v. Smith* (1990), the legal foundations for the religious use of peyote have regained solid footing with the passage of both the AIRFA Amendments of 1994 and the RFRA in 1993. While AIRFA explicitly exempts the use of peyote in traditional Indian religions by members of federally recognized tribes, the RFRA, as interpreted by the Supreme Court in *Gonzalez v. UDV* (2006), appears to protect the religious use of peyote by all individuals who sincerely practice traditional Indian peyote religions. There is also a strong argument that the federal trust obligation requires the peyote exemption under AIRFA to be expanded to encompass all Indian peoples whether federally recognized or not. While the trust obligation is based on a government-to-government relationship between tribes and the federal government, it has been interpreted as encompassing a duty to protect and preserve traditional Indian culture (*Peyote Way v. Thornburgh* 1991; *Rupert v. Director, U.S. Fish and Wildlife Serv.* 1992). Indian culture and religion, such as the pan-Indian NAC, cross tribal boundaries and it is unlikely that any rational basis exists for restricting the federal government's duty of preservation of culture and religion to federally recognized tribes, to the exclusion of all other Indian peoples.

While the protections for religious peyote use currently stand on the strongest legal foundation they ever have, the peyote religions currently face a much greater threat than criminal prohibition. Due to land and economic developments in southern Texas where peyote is harvested commercially, and due to the harmful harvesting practices of some Indians and licensed peyote distributors, concern is mounting that peyote may soon become endangered (Anderson 1995; Sahagun 1994; Terry 2003; Trout 2002). While appropriate legal protections are finally in place for religious use of peyote, practitioners of traditional peyote religions now face a graver concern—preservation of their sacrament.

NOTES

1. The federal government has long used the term "Indian tribe" as an all encompassing designation that includes tribes, bands, nations, pueblos, and all other organized groups or communities of American Indians. While the term may not be a technically correct usage in an anthropological or scientific sense, the term is rooted in the law and is used here to maintain consistency with the usage of the term in a legal context.

2. "Non-recognized Indian" is a term I will use throughout this chapter to refer to individuals who are Indian by heritage, but who are excluded from the legal definition of "Indian" for purposes of the peyote exemption under AIRFA (1994).

3. It should be noted that RFRA reinstates the *Sherbert* test as a statutory protection only. It does not expand the constitutional protections for free exercise of religion, which were diminished by *Employment Division v. Smith*.

4. The term "Road Man" generally refers to an individual who leads peyote ceremonies.

5. The Ninth Circuit, in *Kennedy v. Board of Narcotics & Dangerous Drugs* (1972), accepted the argument that limiting the peyote exemption to the NAC was unconstitutional but declined to expand the exemption to the Church of the Awakening, which sought to be included in the exemption, because expanding "the regulation to include the Church of the Awakening...suffers the same constitutional infirmity as the present regulation" (p. 417).

6. For most of the history of the NAC, non-Indians have been allowed to participate in NAC ceremonies and also to become NAC members (Stewart 1987).

7. For example, the Ute require a 5/8 blood quantum for tribal membership, the Mississippi Choctaw require 1/2, and the Mashantucket Pequot of Connecticut require 1/16 tribal blood quantum. Of tribes that retain blood quantum eligibility rules, 1/4 blood is the most commonly required quantum.

8. Tribes in the East and Midwest generally use the criteria of descent rather than blood quantum to determine enrollment. Conceivably this means a child could be enrolled with a blood quantum as low as 1/100, so long as it is a descendant of a tribal member.

9. Termination was implemented as a policy in the 1950s with the goal of eliminating tribal self-government and of integrating Indians into the general population. During this period, a series of Acts were passed by Congress eliminating the governmental status and federal recognition of approximately 109 different tribes.

10. To pass muster under strict scrutiny, the law must be based on a compelling government interest and there must be no less restrictive means of achieving that interest. The *Sherbert* test, discussed earlier, requires application of strict scrutiny to laws which substantially burden religious practices.

11. Intermediate scrutiny requires that the law in question bear a substantial relationship to an important government interest which that law seeks to advance.

12. The trust responsibility is generally traced back to two early Supreme Court cases: *Cherokee Nation v. Georgia* (1831), and *Worcester v. Georgia* (1832).

13. The *Peyote Way* case is not the first time Emerson Jackson had asserted that the NACNA's strict membership requirements extended to all congregations of the NAC. In 1984, Jackson informed the FBI that a Mr. and Mrs. John D. Warner, peyote custodians for the NAC of Tokio, North Dakota, were not members of the NAC. Jackson testified that "they were not bona fide members of the NAC because they were not Indians" and were therefore in illegal possession of peyote (Stewart 1987, p. 333). The jury found the couple

innocent after they were able to prove that the Tokio congregation considered them bona fide members of the NAC (Stewart 1987).

14. See *Employment Division v. Smith* (1990). See also, *United States v. Kuch* (1968), *Kennedy v. Bureau of Narcotics & Dangerous Drugs* (1972), and *State v. Whittingham* (1973).

15. The term "peyote button" refers to the harvested top of the peyote cactus which is consumed either fresh or dried in religious peyote ceremonies.

16. A Schedule I drug is one that has been determined to have no medical value and a high potential for abuse.

17. The Supreme Court rejected the district court's contention that hoasca was not covered by the Convention but found that this fact was not an automatic demonstration of a compelling government interest in applying the CSA (*Gonzalez v. UDV* 2006).

18. Alabama, Arizona, Connecticut, Florida, Idaho, Illinois, New Mexico, Oklahoma, Rhode Island, South Carolina, and Texas.

19. Alaska, Arizona, California, Colorado, Idaho (reservation use only), Iowa, Kansas, Maryland, Minnesota, Mississippi, Montana, New Jersey, Nevada, New Mexico, North Carolina, North Dakota, Oklahoma, Oregon, Rhode Island, South Dakota, Tennessee, Texas (limited to 25% Indian blood quantum), Utah (reservation use only), Virginia, Washington, West Virginia, Wisconsin, and Wyoming.

20. Alaska, Arizona, Colorado, Idaho, Iowa, Kansas, Minnesota, Nevada, New Mexico, Oklahoma, Oregon, South Dakota, Texas, Wisconsin, and Wyoming.

21. Arizona and Oregon.

REFERENCES

Allotment Act, 25 U.S.C.A. § 331 (1887).

American Indian Religious Freedom Act Amendments of 1994, 42 U.S.C. § 1996a(1) (1994).

Anderson, E.F. 1995. The peyote gardens of south Texas: A conservation crisis. *Cactus and Succulent Journal* 67:67–73.

Bannon, J.T., Jr. 1998. The legality of the religious use of peyote by the Native American Church: A commentary on the free exercise, equal protection, and establishment issues raised by the Peyote Way Church of God case. *American Indian Law Review* 22 (2):475–507.

Beltran, G.A. 1952. La magia del peyotl. *Organo Oficial de la Universidad Nacional Autonoma de Mexico* 68 (6):2–4.

Board of County Comm'rs v. Seber, 318 U.S. 705 (1943).

Callahan v. Woods, 736 F.2d 1269 (9th Cir. 1984), *citing* Wisconsin v. Yoder, 406 U.S. 205 (1972), *and* Sherbert v. Verner, 374 U.S. 398 (1963).

Cherokee Nation v. Georgia, 30 U.S. 1 (1831).

City of Boerne v. Flores, 521 U.S. 507 (1997).

Controlled Substances Act, 21 U.S.C. § 801 (1970).

Drug Abuse Control Amendments of 1965, Pub. L. No. 89–74, 79 Stat. 226 (1965).

Drug Enforcement Administration, Department of Justice, 21 C.F.R. § 1307.31 (1971).

Employment Division v. Smith, 494 U.S. 872 (1990).

Epps, G. 2001. *To an unknown god.* New York, NY: St. Martin's Press.

Fikes, J. 2002. Peyote religion: Opening doors to the creator's heart. *Entheos: The Journal of Psychedelic Spirituality* 1 (2):75–82.

Gonzalez v. O Centro Espirita Beneficiente Uniao Do Vegetal, No. 04-1084 (2006).

Kennedy v. Bureau of Narcotics and Dangerous Drugs, 459 F.2d 415 (9th Cir. 1972).

Long, C. 2000. *Religious freedom and Indian rights.* Lawrence, KS: University Press of Kansas.

Morton v. Mancari, 417 U.S. 535 (1974).

Olsen v. Drug Enforcement Administration, 878 F.2d 1458 (D.C. Cir. 1989).

Olson, T. 1981. Peyote exemption for Native American Church. 5 Op. Off. Legal Counsel 403.

Peyote Way Church of God v. Thornburgh, 922 F.2d 1210 (5th Cir. 1991).

Religious Freedom Restoration Act, 42 U.S.C. § 2000bb (1993).

Romer v. Evans, 517 U.S. 620 (1996).

Rupert v. Director, U.S. Fish and Wildlife Serv., 957 F.2d 32 (1st Cir. 1992).

Sahagun, L. 1994. Peyote harvesters face supply-side problem; Scarce cropland and rising demand from Native Americans pits Texas ranchers against those looking to gather the flesh of god. *The L.A. Times* June 13, p. A5.

Santa Clara Pueblo v. Martinez, 436 U.S. 49 (1978).

Schultes, R. E., and A. Hofmann. 1992. *Plants of the gods: Their sacred, healing and hallucinogenic powers.* Rochester, VT: Healing Arts Press.

Sherbert v. Verner, 374 U.S. 398 (1963).

State v. Whittingham, 504 P.2d 950 (Ariz. Ct. App. 1973).

Stewart, O.C. 1987. *Peyote religion.* Norman, OK: University of Oklahoma Press.

Terry, M. 2003. Peyote population genetics study. *MAPS* xiii (1):21–22.

Trout, K. 2002. Faith, belief, and the peyote crisis. *Entheos: The Journal of Psychedelic Spirituality* 1 (2):83–6.

United States v. Kuch, 288 F.Supp. 439 (Dist. D.C. 1968).

Worcester v. Georgia, 31 U.S. 515 (1832).

14

AYAHUASCA, THE U.S. SUPREME COURT, AND THE UDV–U.S. GOVERNMENT CASE: CULTURE, RELIGION, AND IMPLICATIONS OF A LEGAL DISPUTE

ALBERTO GROISMAN AND MARLENE DOBKIN DE RIOS

INTRODUCTION

The effects of ayahuasca in human beings have been regarded by researchers, shamans, followers of religious groups, occasional users, and even by governmental authorities as having "religious," "therapeutic," "spiritual," and "constructive" qualities. Ayahuasca has also been called a "sacrament" and considered by indigenous populations to comprise "plant teachers." It has been considered harmful only in peculiar and extreme situations, such as when ingested in excessive quantities, or when used in combination with other substances, such as monoamine oxidase inhibitors like Prozac and dairy products. These properties led at the end of the 1990s to the award of a patent for an Ecuadorian specimen of the ayahuasca plant in the United States.

On another hand, in North America and European countries, the effects of ayahuasca are presumed to primarily reflect one of its compounds, DMT (5,5-N, N-dimethyltryptamine), classified as a "Schedule I" drug. This is construed as making ayahuasca illegal, reflecting and stimulating a repressive attitude that has characterized 20th century drug laws, and especially in the last decades in what has been called the "Drug War" (see Chapter 12, this volume). This resulted in the late 1990s in arrests of religious adherents and of the seizure of the ayahuasca preparation in Europe and the United States.

In contrast to this generally repressive attitude, and reaffirming the general treatment which has been granted to the ritual-religious use of peyote in the United States (also see Chapter 13, this volume), the U.S. Supreme Court in *Gonzalez v. O Centro Espirita Beneficente Uniao do Vegetal,* 546 U.S. (2006), ruled that the Brazilian religious organization with a branch in the United States would be allowed to ingest ayahuasca, even though it contains DMT. The tea—hoasca—is used by the UDV (União do Vegetal) as a sacrament in its religious rituals and has a legally protected status in Brazil.

In the case that is the focus of this chapter, the U.S. government initially refused to allow the ayahuasca through customs, seizing and threatening to destroy it. As a result, the UDV filed a federal lawsuit against the Attorney General to compel the government to return the hoasca and allow the UDV to import and use the tea in their religious ceremonies; subsequently, in 2002 the District Court of New Mexico granted a preliminary injunction to the UDV. We examine from various perspectives the process and reasoning of the Supreme Court Justices in allowing this psychedelic brew to have legitimate and protected religious use, a phenomenon with important precedents for the future use of sacramental psychoactives. The Supreme Court's decision has been one with potentially important significance for minority groups and individuals in America whose religious or spiritualist practices clash with the nation's drug laws. This chapter shows how these activities may be afforded protection from government oppression under statutes protecting religious liberty. We examine the context of ayahuasca use in Brazil, as it progressed from indigenous Amazonian use for healing and shamanic activities to sacramental use among religious groups in that country. We also provide a broader examination of the context in which the decisions of the U.S. Supreme Court are involved and the interpretive approach to the implications of its deliberations.

AYAHUASCA AND RELIGION IN BRAZILIAN SOCIETY

The legal status of substances such as ayahuasca is becoming increasingly important as the high court's positioning may establish borders between what is and what is not acceptable legally, and as perhaps a consequence, socially and culturally acceptable. An acceptance criterion was established for social and legal status of ayahuasca use in Brazil and therefore for the ayahuasca religions originating in Brazil over the last decades. Based on the claims of followers of the so-called "Ayahuasca Religions," ayahuasca is associated with religious, spirituality-focused, therapeutic, and socially constructive experiences. Therefore, the history of the incorporation of ayahuasca into Brazilian society is useful for understanding the UDV conviction to fight for its acceptance in the United States.

In the Brazilian Amazon, ayahuasca has been traditionally used in the context of Indian societies and also among the nonindigenous population, generally in locations remote from urban areas. Ayahuasca use has been configured by particular cosmologies and practices, most of them regarded as ritual or religious, which were based primarily on shamanistic knowledge about the use of plants. In this context, the knowledge and the prerogative of the ritual administration, and in some cases the use of ayahuasca itself, was reserved for experts alone. The best-known area where the nonindigenous organized religious use of ayahuasca emerged in Brazil is the state of Acre, in southwest Amazonia, at the border of Bolivia and Peru. In the populated area of Rio Branco, the capital of Acre, ayahuasca use has been highly influenced by "institutionalizing" religious ideologies, such as Christianity and particularly initiation-focused spiritualist traditions such as Esoterism and *Kardecismo* (see Hess 1991).

The Brazilian religious systems that use ayahuasca and emerged since the beginning of the 20th century have been called *Brazilian Ayahuasca Religions* (Labate and Araújo 2004; Goulart 2004). In this sense, the expression of Brazilian Ayahuasca Religions has been widely used to identify groups of people/religious organizations primordially set in Brazilian territory, which use a ritual preparation of the plants *Banisteriopsis caapi* and *Psychotria viridis* in rituals. The most widely known identification of the beverage is *ayahuasca,* although these groups have for cosmo-ideological reasons adopted names such as daime, hoasca, and vegetal.

One of the more visible ayahuasca-using religious systems which emerged in Brazil in the early 20th century is recognized today as *Alto Santo*. This original church established by Raimundo Irineu Serra between 1920 and 1930 is still active under the leadership of his widow, Peregrina Gomes Serra (Silva 1982). Another known as *Barquinha* was established by Daniel Pereira de Mattos in the 1950s, from experiences with his uncle (Irineu Serra) that inspired him to start his own group (Araújo 1999). The UDV was founded in the early 1960s by José Gabriel da Costa, who, according to his followers, had learned to use ayahuasca alone and among the *caboclo* population at the borders with Bolivia and Peru (Henman 1985; Brissac 1999). Santo Daime-CEFLURIS was organized in the 1970s under the leadership of Sebastião Mota de Melo, also a disciple of Irineu Serra; today this is the group that has had the most visible international expansion (Soibelman 1995; Groisman 2000).

The trajectory of these religious organizations throughout history has been characterized as having been set up by a struggle for distinction (differentiation) (Goulart 2004). One can argue that these groups' trajectory of development, by means of personal or institutional affiliation, significantly influenced the shift from a small-scale individually organized sessions that characterized mestizo use in Peru and Bolivia (Dobkin de Rios 1972; Luna 1986) to a collective institutional-focused organization of ayahuasca-using groups in Brazil.

Since the 1980s, there are also religious and nonreligious ayahuasca-using based groups in both rural and urban zones that are influenced by the so-called New Age Movement style of spirituality (Heelas 1996; Labate 2000; Rose 2005). Their forms of organization may be seen as ideologically connected to a phenomenon that has been called "new religious consciousness" (Soares 1990), which in addition to spiritualism, includes also environmentalism as its more substantial ideological appeal. The followers in the urban areas are in general middle-class civil servants, therapists, microentrepreneurs, military personnel, and intellectuals, mainly in groups such as Santo Daime-CEFLURIS, UDV, and Barquinha. In these settings, psychotherapeutic and spiritualist approaches are combined with doctrinaire principles in a more specific and pragmatic form. This can involve, for example, middle-class people searching for spiritual development or self-knowledge, or/and drug addicts in search of treatment with ayahuasca, an increasing trend since the end of the 1990s (Rose 2005).

In sum, although cosmological systems motivated by ayahuasca experience have general religious significance in South America, in Brazil the religious character of the experience is emphasized. Perhaps it would be more precise to say that it was in the Brazilian context that "religious use" became a "native" form of the definition of ayahuasca experience and an important element for the construction of the identity of Brazilian ayahuasqueros (healers and others who are regular ayahuasca users). Moreover, it is the religiously motivated approach which has been an effective basis for legitimization, establishing a sort of "social control" on ayahuasca use through an informal assumption that nonreligious use may not be authentically sacramental.

The Brazilian Religious Context

An approach to the religious panorama in Brazil is useful for understanding the form in which religious groups emerge and develop in the Brazilian religious context. In fact, a definition of what we may call the "Brazilian religious context" has been a challenge for researchers. Hess (1995, p. 80), for example, considered Brazil a

> laboratory of religious complexity...[which has]...two major poles—one represented by the Catholic church and the other by the popular religions of African origin-with a number of other positions in between...the two poles are the product of Brazil's colonial legacy of racism and slavery, and in this sense the religious playing field is already structured by a more general and historically rooted hegemony.

The Catholicism brought by the Portuguese colonialists to Brazil became a dominant and hegemonic religion, cultivated by powerful landlords, and later by economic elites, as the "official" religion. In this way, Catholicism was ideologically legitimized as a religion and as a space where social differences did not exist, where "the poor could share with the rich" and where "in the eyes of God everyone is equal." The utopia of such an open religious path is regarded as responsible for establishing a basis for the emergence of what has been called a different "Brazilian styles of spirituality" (Carvalho 1994).

The hegemony of the "official" Roman Catholic Church established in colonial times is still evident, but over time a significant place was granted in the socio-cultural and political context to Popular Catholicism (a sort of reaction to Institutionalized Catholicism) and to the emerging Protestantism (basically for the so-called Neo-Pentecostal religions). In this dynamic, "local" interpretations and practices of Christianity increasingly developed in many regions of the country.

Beyond this process of reinterpretation, Carpenter and Roof (1995) noted, for example, that in the 1980s a significant decline in the Brazilian Catholic population was detected. The situation was characterized by what the authors define as a "Roman Catholic Center with an Effervescent Periphery" (1995, p. 47). At the end of the 1990s, this "periphery" was more than "effervescent," and those that significantly increased their presence in the Brazilian religious context included Evangelical Protestant churches, best known as *Neo-pentecostalismo*; the European—but locally adapted *Kardecismo*; and the Afro-Brazilian religions. In sum, a "religious way of life" is an important part of Brazilian context and identity construction. As Bastide (1978) had described, the pluralistic religious scene is occupied by different and "interpenetrated" forms of religiosity.

In characterizing further the context, Hess and DaMatta (1995) points out that Brazil can be compared only with the United States and Canada in terms of its continental proportions, regional contrasts, demographic diversity, and economic divisions. Thus locality and diversity are important conditions for religious choice. Catholicism is included in what Hess calls an "ideological arena" (Hess 1991), in which religion, science, medicine, social science, and political ideology, at both the national and the international levels, struggle to construct hegemony. In this context, different religious systems also dispute the interest of potential members and more than faith is relevant to maintaining prestige and social acceptance. Therefore the other levels of social relations have to be addressed by religious institutions to construct a legitimized place in the society.

This social–political dynamic had also triggered another phenomenon which has been called by Brazilian religious context researchers as *trânsito religioso* (literally "religious transit"). The expression synthesizes the phenomenon of the almost freely accepted movement among different religious systems that a Brazilian citizen can be involved in simultaneously. In discussing what may be the fundamental cultural background for this sort of religious transit, Brandão (1994) points out that in Brazil, each religious institution or system that produces religious significance does not want to claim to have the whole truth. They all may focus on a "meaning exchange." Therefore, despite the fact that the Catholic church is hegemonic, there is an intense movement of followers between different religious systems. In this sense, it is possible to see a person from a Catholic background, who one day attends a mass with the family, praying to God to give him health and prosperity, and who on the next day may attend an Umbanda ritual, dancing under the control of an African divinity, or incorporating a spirit of a Caboclo or Pomba-Gira or Preto Velho (spiritual entities related to the

Afro-Brazilian religion Umbanda), and obtaining spiritual advice for finding a lover or money.

The Brazilian Cultural Context and the UDV

The UDV, founded in 1962 by José Gabriel da Costa, is characterized by Sérgio Brissac (1999) as part of the Brazilian religious panorama, ritualizing the frontiers between personal/daily life and the individuals' experience with ayahuasca. An extensive study of the historical trajectories of the so-called Brazilian Ayahuasca Religions shows this religious trend of encapsulating the states of mind and body provided by the substance as part of a "religious experience" as opposed to simply "getting high." A brief review of the Brazilian forms of religious expression illustrates that the ayahuasca-using organized groups formulated a variety of ritual and theological systems in developing their activities as part of this religious panorama. Since its earliest introduction to nonindigenous settings, ayahuasca use was associated with the cosmological ideologies based on foreign spiritualist traditions such as Christianity, Kardecism, Theosophy, and Afro-Brazilian religions.

The Brazilian anthropologist, Roberto Da Matta has argued that "cultural consistency" in the form of an aggregating ideological force was applied to diverse migratory groups in an extensive territorial occupation, since all of Brazil was colonized initially by the Portuguese. In that sense, Portuguese colonialist ideology was mainly focused on the "transfer" and reproduction of social–cultural controlling features from the host country to the colony. As DaMatta showed (1974), as soon as the Portuguese invaded what was to be Brazilian territory, they consistently tried to make it an "Immense Portugal." Therefore, Portuguese social and legal structures were applied by colonial administrators to the colony. Throughout history, a highly hierarchical society was constituted, based on an extensive and extended chain, in which even the personal treatment of a common citizen provided to, or by, a state authority was regulated and bureaucratically established. Although today the imported social structure is no longer central to the Brazilian elites, its cultural effects have been reported as far as it concerns the reaction of oppressed populations. Therefore, the reaction to this system was configured by a permanent motivation to transgress limits and regulations which were considered to characterize the Brazilian cultural context, an expression of a constant "dyonisian" character in a changing social–cultural environment. In addition, if we transpose this argument to religious life in Brazil, actually it is possible to find elements in many of the Brazilian religious systems that refer to "paths" and "beings" who are in mediatory and transitive status. This suggests that in daily life typical of highly hierarchical structured society, the oppressed may seek "another place" to work out mediation, ambiguity, and fundamentally, existential negotiation. And this place may be called a "spiritual plane," "spiritual world," or "world of spirits."

This evaluation of a permanently changing/mediating cultural conduct may be actually challenged and shared by what we can find on "the other side of the coin," or in the rigid and conservative style found among some segments of Brazilian society. In an ambiguous way, the life styles that originated from populations with so-called middle-class background incorporate—at least in the members' discourses—the idea of "order and hierarchy."

In fact, this reflects the colonizers' expectation on how the colonial population should behave. Among this segment of the Brazilian population, conservative values and hierarchical structures are highly regarded and military organization is adopted, even regarding how a psychoactive substance is to be used by a religious group. The UDV therefore has appropriated conservative values which emphasize a general "State-enforcing" attitude configured in political investment in legalization and public acceptance of their own religious practices. In addition, and as an example of this conservative attitude, the UDV publicly accuses another Brazilian ayahuasca religion for using "illegal" drugs, as in the case of the Santo Daime group, which has traditionally included cannabis as a sacramental plant along with ayahuasca in its pantheon. It was this general conservative attitude of the UDV which stimulated Anthony Henman (1985) in one of the first academic works published about UDV outside Brazil to call the organization "authoritarian."

In summary, we can think about the Brazilian cultural context as sympathetic to both innovative and conservative forms of religion, including those that use psychoactive substances basically as a cultural strategy to provide ways to prevent unilateral dominance, to explore human possibilities, and furthermore, to be efficacious in meeting the needs of their adherents.

The Legal Status of Ayahuasca and Its Derivatives in Brazil

The use of ayahuasca is not completely legal in Brazil. Similar to what has happened in the United States, official permission was granted by Brazilian governmental agencies exclusively for the ritual-religious use of this substance. Historically, the process of establishing the legal status of ayahuasca in Brazil was strongly influenced by the existence of active ritual-religious ayahuasca-using groups. In the 1970s and 1980s, after a long-term informal tolerance of local ayahuasca-using groups, Brazilian authorities, reacting in part against the national expansion of these groups, started a campaign to include ayahuasca and the plants with which it is combined in controlled drugs list established by the DIMED (Divisão Nacional de Vigilância Sanitária, Ministério da saúde—The National Division of Health Vigilance, Minister of Health, the national drug control agency), the agency for the control (production, distribution, and consumption) of drugs in general in Brazilian territory. The authorities' claims went to the CONFEN (Conselho Federal de Entorpecentes) (later replaced by the Conselho Nacional de Drogas—CONAD), the governmental agency responsible for controlling the production, distribution, and consumption of drugs in Brazil. The agency placed the plants on the list, but after reactions from religious groups, they appointed several expert commissions. The first, in 1986, reported its conclusions, recommending the exclusion of the plants from the list, which was established by the *Resolução do Conselho Federal de Entorpecentes— CONFEN,* n° 06, de 04.02.1986. The two other commissions, in 1987 and 1992, confirmed the decision. In 2004, the Resolução n° 5, do CONAD (of 11.04.2004) consolidated the previous decisions and established the procedures for the permanent legalization of the ritual-religious use of ayahuasca in Brazil.

RELIGION AND THE U.S. SUPREME COURT

A controversial issue, the theme of religious freedom has been central in the debate about the U.S. Constitution's regulations in the U.S. Supreme Court. In examining the text of the U.S. Constitution First Amendment, researchers have pointed out that its writers were concerned with controlling the elites' power— represented by the State—to rule the consciousness of others. This concern was fundamentally derived from a reaction to centuries of religious-based oppression and political domination. The concern with the controlling power of the state and its agents to rule individual consciousness is clear. However, in searching for the implications of the text itself, its contents suggest that it intends to establish a circumstantial "accommodation" in case of divergence and dispute. In sum, the motivations of governmental politics and agendas may first attempt to prevent controversies but finally, to create given facts for a subsequent court dispute.

Pohlman's (2004, p. 249) compilation of cases concerning constitutional debates in the United States points out that: "religious freedom in the United States is based upon two constitutional principles that pose difficult problems of interpretation because they are in tension with one another. The First Amendment prohibits the federal government from promulgating any law 'respecting an establishment of religion' or 'prohibiting the free exercise thereof." In this context, the author asks: "Is a tax on church property an illegitimate burden upon religion prohibited by the 'free exercise' clause or is a religious exemption from the tax an illegitimate 'establishment' of religion?" (Ibid.).

In this simple question, Pohlman summarizes the problem of legal text interpretations and decisions, when a lack of or a negligence about self-evidence can be observed in legal systems. He also addresses the semantic tensions raised by different interpretations of the text of laws. Interestingly, the dynamics of law or of legal judgment processes meets the same problems generated by religious practices throughout history. In sum, as in theological discussion, judicial debate is also concerned with the best meanings for the adoption of regulatory texts, such as constitutional ones. An eloquent example of this tension can be found in the First Amendment text itself, from which one may ask: "what does it mean for government to 'abridge' free speech?"

Another researcher who also has analyzed the U.S. Supreme Court approach to the religious freedom disputes was Carolyn N. Long (2000), who examined perspectives of the controversial peyote-related legal case *Employment Division of Oregon v. Smith,* 494 VS. 872 (1990). Long (2000, p. 52) takes as a principle that: "during the sixty years of the Supreme Court's free exercise (of religion) jurisprudence, the definition and application of the free exercise clause as a protector of religious conduct had not progressed a great deal." In the following, Long discusses relevant issues from the First Amendment–related decisions of the U.S. Supreme Court involving similar cases in light of the fact that when more than one constitutional issue is articulated the court may pronounce itself in more favorable terms. Interestingly, the manner in which the case was appealed to the Court had a direct effect on how the Supreme Court framed the First Amendment issue in each case and the outcome of the decision: "Cases involving multiple First Amendment guarantees were successful, and those appealed only under the free exercise clause were unsuccessful" (Long 2000, p. 51).

Analyzing the Supreme Court decisions in its historical trajectory, Long observes that the attorneys' strategies in cases involving the First Amendment on the religion-free exercise appeal were consistently more successful when articulating the argument with other constitutional guarantees. Another relevant issue is the compelling interest test created to establish a parameter of evidence on the consistency of governmental claims on disputes associated with religious freedom. As Long (2000, p. p. 52) reported: "the contemporary treatment of religious related clauses was set up by the constitutional standard promulgated in the case known as Sherbert v. Verner, in 1963, when the U.S. Supreme Court adopted definitively the application of a compelling interest." However, the uniqueness of each of the cases implied evaluating each one to see if application of the compelling interest test was warranted. This became a controversial issue.

U.S. Supreme Court Deliberation in Gonzalez v. O Centro Espirita Beneficente Uniao do Vegetal

In this section, we do not provide a full legal analysis but rather look at key issues. The U.S. government accepted that the UDV was a genuine religious organization with a sincere use of hoasca for religious purposes. Evidence was marshaled by the UDV lawyers to show long-term religious use of ayahuasca in the Amazon region for millennia. The U.S. government's concern, rather, was that the tea used as a sacrament has as one of its constituents, DMT, a Schedule I drug. This was prohibited by the Federal Controlled Substances Act and considered to constitute a harm/danger that overrides individual religious rights. The UDV countered with their argument that the RFRA (Religious Freedom Restoration Act) of 1993 allowed them to use the hoasca because it was an essential sacrament in their religious rituals and that the seizure of 30 kg. of the hoasca tea was a violation of the religious rights of the UDV members.

There were two appeals by the government after the UDV obtained favorable rulings of the preliminary injunction. First, the U.S. government was given an emergency stay while their request was reviewed; then it was followed by an appeal to the U.S. Supreme Court. In March 2005, the Supreme Court heard arguments by both sides. On February 21, 2006, in an unanimous opinion authored by the new Chief Justice Roberts, the court ruled in favor of the UDV. The reasoning was that the RFRA passed by Congress allowed the federal courts to determine on a case-by-case basis if a federal law placed a burden on a religious practice. The drug property of the mixture was not itself sufficient grounds to deny the UDV's religious practices. The burden fell on the government to prove that the UDV's religious use of hoasca was outweighed by the danger of the DMT. The government made three arguments to ban all use of hoasca, including UDV religious use. First, they argued that it was necessary to protect the health and safety of the UDV members, 130 of them in New Mexico. Secondly, they argued that the ban was necessary to prevent the illegal diversion of ayahuasca outside of the UDV church. They finally cited the international drug control treaty, the 1971 Convention of Psychotropic Substances, which required the United States to prohibit all use of DMT, even the trace amounts found in the hoasca tea used by the UDV (see Chapter 12, this volume).

The first two interests—health of UDV members and the prevention of diversion—were seen to be a "wash" with both sides' arguments canceling each other out. The government argued that DMT was unsafe and that hoasca could be diverted. The UDV on the other hand had evidence to show that the tea was quite safe and no actual diversion had occurred in the past. Evidence from the Native American Church's safe use of peyote, also a Schedule I drug, was introduced and the hundreds of thousands of individuals who took the substance in a religious setting without problems was cited. Thus, the government did not meet its burden of proof to justify the specific harm entailed.

Finally, in reference to the 1971 Convention of Psychotropic Substances that required the United States to ban all use and importation of DMT, the UDV argued that it did not apply since the DMT was in plant form, which was not covered by the convention. The Supreme Court found the argument to be spurious because while the method of preparation may not be advanced, consisting only of a simmering brew, the tea nonetheless qualified as a preparation under the Convention. But in ruling in favor of the UDV, the Court argued that the government failed to present any evidence to show how that exemption for the UDV would frustrate the government's international duties under the Convention. The Court noted that the UDV, as a religious organization, uses its hoasca sacraments very carefully. It monitors its members health and there is a very small number of adherents in the United States. As Boire (Chapter 12, this volume) points out, this is the first entheogen case to reach the Supreme Court after the findings in the *Department of Human Resources of Oregon v. Smith,* when the Court found that the First Amendment's free exercise clause did not protect the use of peyote by the Native American Church. Subsequently, Congress has reiterated the importance of the free exercise of religion when it enacted the RFRA. In the future, the RFRA will have to be applied to relevant situations on a case-by-case basis, as specifics of religious practices involved will be examined, along with the details of the entheogen in question and particular reasons and evidence the U.S. government presents regarding why no accommodation is possible.

Jeffrey Bronfman, the chief Mestre or religious leader of the UDV in the United States, has argued that the case is unique in many respects because it involves a clash between two federal statues: one based in the First Amendment to the Constitution and protecting an individual's free exercise of religion, and the other serving the important governmental and public interests of protecting society against the abuse of drugs. Richey, in an article for the Christian Science Monitor (2006), wrote that the RFRA requires the federal government to justify any measure that substantially burdens a person's ability to practice his/her religion. This finding is a robust defense of religious freedom and the individual's ability to practice his/her faith free of government interference. It supports the use of drugs or any other material substances as an aid or pathway to spirituality or a greater understanding of the divine.

Legal Decisions as Cultural Devices

The contents and forms of UDV–USA legal case arguments and their relationships with empirical knowledge reveal and situate political aspirations, expectations, and subjective concerns held by representative agents of the State, of the groups involved, and of other interested parties to the UDV–USA case. These include the U.S. Supreme Court magistrates, regarding: (1) what they think about the accepted knowledge on the effects of the use of psychoactive substances for individuals and groups; (2) how these agents in the context of the disputes evaluate the consequences of the regulatory texts in face of empirical knowledge produced by researchers; and (3) which may be the parameters established for understanding the mechanisms used as fundamentals to assure the rights, the integrity, and the well-being of users associated with the ceremonial religious ingestion of psychoactive substances.

Analysis of the legal debate regarding the religious use of psychoactive substances in the UDV–USA case reveals the influence the State may have in configuring religious practices. When legal concerns are added to the general attitude among religious followers, it is of considerable importance that adherents may modify routines to satisfy the new requirements. This includes, for example, to limiting access to those who would be able to use the ayahuasca for therapeutic purposes. Or it might include limiting the religious use to those for whom it is "medically safe," even though it is a sacrament to be generally used by religious adherents.

In the same route, a religious group that uses a sacramental-divinatory psychoactive substance necessarily implies expression of self and models of being that are negotiated with followers. In this aspect, forms and processes of negotiation are triggered by the trial itself. The negotiation, and its implications, when lacking fruition may provoke conflict. The contents of this conflict, when motivated by inconsistent governmental action, are based mainly in an emphasis on the role of the state as a simple regulatory agency, e.g., the state agents, as drugs control agencies, or repressive agencies, and are activated by a superficial or narrow conception of the related phenomena. In other words, the investigation may be carried out only to produce evidence of preconceived "potential" and even hypothetical harm.

The cases of peyote and ayahuasca in the United States appear to be good examples of a conflictive attitude in this matter. An examination of the implications of permission and/or prohibition contributes to the competence of the State in preparing and substantiating itself for deliberate action on the legality and the legitimacy of these religious practices. Both the explicit and the implicit visions expressed in the texts of official agents concerning the use of these psychoactive substances to modify states of consciousness have been motivated mainly by a narrow view that mechanically associates drugs with crime and illness. This produces and infuses an existent semantic field as Umberto Eco (1976) has called a specific and historically configured articulation of ideas and keywords which may constitute a supposedly logical framework to provide sense to thought and attitude.

This framework as applied by the social actors involved may consequently produce expressions of rejection and conflict. In cases such as those related to the so-called drug abuse, relations of conflict have been contemporarily established at a generalized level. Authorities have been motivated by quantitative data, with a strong "medicalized" influence from epidemiology. Therefore, the evidence to sustain a recommendation for the proscription of substances is produced in clinical/hospital-like contexts, with synthesized samples of the substances. The empirical basis for the U.S. government's argument against the use of ayahuasca from DMTs focused on research that is typical and paradigmatic to understand the issue we raise here.

In the semantic field created by previously defined and repressive attitude, ayahuasca—called by religious users a sacrament—may be called "drug"; its transportation from where it is prepared to where it will be use in worship may be called "trafficking"; and, its effects—recognized by adepts as divinatory, therapeutic, or oracular—may be regarded as "hallucinatory," risky, and/or harmful to health. Therefore, in a context of arguments regarding the supposedly and potentially harmful effects of ayahuasca, an eventual permission to use the substance might be associated automatically with anti-drugs policies. It is likely that this attitude may prevent the expansion of the knowledge about social and cultural effects of the use of these kind of substances, at least in a religious-ritually controlled context.

IMPLICATIONS OF THE UDV–USA CASE

The UDV–USA case has opened a very significant space for the debate on the so-called constructive, beneficial, or ritually controlled use of psychoactive substances in nonmedical contexts. Furthermore, the U.S. Supreme Court decision on February 21, 2006, shows that it considered seriously recommendations like those made by Calabrese in his analysis of the outcomes of already-mentioned *Employment Division of Oregon v. Smith,* 494 VS. 872 (1990) peyote use related case; this was fundamentally to treat consistently, and not ethnocentrically, such legal disputes (Calabrese 2001). The serious consideration by the U.S. Supreme Court justices was demonstrated in a very cautious and skeptical position when confronted with superficial arguments not very well sustained by evidence. In the UDV case, there was a slightly different attitude in which the justices demonstrated care in accepting official arguments.

The most visible impact of the U.S. Supreme Court's decision is its referendum on the historically controversial permission for the use of peyote in a ritual-religious setting within the Native American Church. While having avoided establishing a definitive permissive status for any religious use of psychoactive substances, the Supreme Court may have sealed its position about inconsistent arguments on the "risk and prejudice" of using any kind or quantity of a psychoactive substance. The following sections analyzes some of the cultural, legal, and political implications of the *Gonzalez v. O Centro Espirita Beneficente Uniao do Vegetal,* 546 U.S. case and U.S. Supreme Court decision which go beyond those already mentioned by Boire (Chapter 12, this volume).

Culture and Sovereignty

Theories of cultural "modeling" (Geertz 1973) and/or cultural-focused phenomenology (Winkelman 1996; Csordas 1994) have had a fundamental place in the debate on the relationships between humans and humans, and humans and planetary "natural" resources, among which are included psychoactive plants. Therefore it is relevant here to note the remark made by Boire (2006, p. 20) that

> the Supreme Court rejected the finding by the District Court, explaining, Hoasca is a solution or mixture containing DMT; the fact that it is made by the simple process of brewing plants in water, as opposed to some more advanced method, does not change that. The tea plainly qualifies as a preparation under the Convention.

This quote by Boire from the Supreme Court decision text implies a culture theory discussion which shows a lack of consideration to what classic sociologists[1] have pointed systematically out—namely, that ritual is a form of social–cultural saturation or structuring of social life, people and things, and also contemporary researchers, like Norman Zinberg (1984), for example, and his set and setting analysis model have also affirmed.

Therefore, if the "preparation" here would simply be to put the plants together and simmer them, a "structuring" property may not be applied. However, if we consider from a sociological as well as phenomenological positions that a "religious" use and context is justified and applied (as was granted in the decision concerning peyote ritual religious use by Native American Church participants), it is consequent to accept that a "ritual-religious" preparation may also "socially and culturally saturate the substance," structuring the experience and potentially establishing well-being and social constructive relationships (Groisman and Sell 1996).[2]

The legal debate in the UDV–USA case shows how cultural concerns may have a profound impact in establishing limits and permissions for accepted social practices as they emerge in an urban-industrial society and are "globalized" and regulated by written laws. In this sense, a great deal of discussion was carried out between judges and attorneys to figure out the acceptable extensions of the limits of sovereignty established by the International Treaties signed by U.S. government across time and Constitutional valid legislation. In addition, the Supreme Court Justices duly considered the precedence between the 1976 and the 1987 international treaties on control of drugs and the legislation triggered by the First Amendment, which was in 1994 consolidated by the RFRA.

The concept of sovereignty was also called upon when the U.S. attorney argued that if ayahuasca religions come from another country, that country's government should be responsible for and called upon to control its expansion. These debates became so intense in the hearing of November 2005 that in more than one passage, the U.S. government attorney mentioned the intention of proposing to "other countries" to change their general attitude in relation to drugs, suggesting that there may be initiatives from the U.S. government to press the Brazilian government to block ayahuasca exportation. It is relevant to report that in the months after the U.S. Supreme Court decision, the Brazilian government formed a high profile "task force" for monitoring and establishing rules and legislation for the ritual use of ayahuasca.

Finally, in the hearing of November, 1, 2005, one of the main discussions was based on the historic and doctrinaire trajectory of the U.S. Supreme Court decisions on the issue of "Religious Freedom." The implicit "tradition" of the court decisions suggested an "internal" debate among Justices, and on the other hand, updating their approach to analyzing which forms of cultural life would be acceptable. The case debate evidences the weight that the jurisprudential tradition of U.S. law has in defining what can be called "legally acceptable." This may become at last highly influential on the social or cultural acceptance and/or social or cultural "tolerance of practices," implying relationships of law and politics with religion.

Religion, Law, and Politics

Associated with the legal dynamics of the UDV–USA as well as with Western legal tradition are other issues raised eloquently about the forms of communication established by the legal debate. The secularized and simplifying "idiom" of the legal system and the National state is the communication form established as the basis for the unfolding debate. In this sense, a religious group might have to reject its own particularly divinatory language, as well as sometimes its native, traditional, cosmological points of view, in order to have its arguments accepted or at least interpreted by the Court protagonists, including their own legal representatives. This establishes a very tricky paradox if we consider that a religious group or a citizen has the right to believe and practice their religion.

When referring to it, however, a secular translation may apply in order to establish appropriate legal communication. This is what happened in Brazil in the 1980s (Groisman 2000), when Santo Daime and UDV were subject to a governmental investigation. As already mentioned, the Brazilian government appointed a high-profile experts' commission, including military, psychological, anthropological, and sociological professionals to visit ayahuasca religious centers *in situ*. Some of the participants of the commission participated in rituals and also ingested the substance, some of them reported officially their view on its "personal and social beneficial effects." This procedure involved a different approach, and at least, a culturally influenced style of conducting arguments, as the commission appointment was a result of requests from the religious groups themselves.

Actually, most of the contents of the legal debate may appear inconsequential to those who have ingested the beverage in a ritual context and are hopeless to think about the experience exclusively from a "legal" point of view, as so many complex aspects of human life may be involved in the event. It is perhaps this complexity which may have challenged and also confused public authorities, stimulating them to reify the impact of the ritual-religious use of ayahuasca—as well as of other similar substances such as peyote—as "drug abuse." It is not new in human history to reduce to "superstition" or "savagery" those qualities which Western culture is not able to comprehend or it is resistant to accept. The special political status which was granted to Native American Church members was another issue raised by the Supreme Court decision. Why was it not applied to UDV members? To say that Indian background justifies an exception may be paradoxical if we consider any arguments based on biochemical grounds.

Finally, we may notice that some issues may still remain obscure in the trial debate on the UDV–USA case. In many passages, it is not clear who is the "defendant"—whether it is a human being who was involved with an alleged criminal act, or if the "defendant" is actually the substance itself (which appears to be in the discourse), as having a sort of uncontrolled power to harm. The implication of this aspect of the debate is that it implicitly does not recognize any harmful effects of a substance (at least in most of the substances used by human beings) as a consequence of the form in which is used.

CONCLUSIONS

In this work, we have laid out for the reader a most important legal finding by the U.S. Supreme Court, permitting a religious group originating in Brazil but located as well in the United States—the UDV—to use ayahuasca as a sacrament in its religious rituals. The plant-made sacrament is derived from the Amazon, having a long history of spiritual and religious use among indigenous peoples, of therapeutic and oracular use among mestizo healers throughout the Amazonian countries of Brazil, Peru, Colombia, and Bolivia, and since the 1920s, among new religions, and since the 1960s by UDV, in institutional religious context.

We trace this process of change historically, anthropologically, and linguistically and provide a vision of the future where we anticipate that the principles of religious freedom will trump those of political definitions of illicit acts and substances. "Hallucinogenic" use to access spiritual realms must be distinguished from the use of substances to deaden pain and anguish or to provide hedonistic experiences.

Finally it is relevant to affirm that our account tried to show that a reified attitude, limited by preconceptions, or even by an exclusively focused legislatorial debate, might prevent Western cultures from establishing a constructive dialogue with those with whom we are actually producing a consistent and genuine knowledge on a remarkable and still little known psycho (soul) pharmaco (medicine).

ACKNOWLEDGMENTS

Our special thanks to the editor of this volume for the opportunity of reflection and dialogue, specially to Michael Winkelman for time and trouble in reading the manuscript and making so relevant suggestions. We would also like to thank Gelci T. Galera, who made a final text revision, the *Coordenação de Aperfeiçoamento do Pessoal do Ensino Superior*—CAPES—Brazil, and colleagues at the *Departamento de Antropologia*—UFSC for their support.

NOTE

1. For example, Durkheim [1965 (1915)], and more contemporarily anthropologists such as Mary Douglas [1970 (1966)].

2. For additional sources on these issues, also see Engle (2001), Epps (2001), Feldman (2000), Antieau et al. (1965), Finkelman (2000), Kurland (1962), Perry (2006), Post and Frazier (1998), Smith and Snake (1996), and Sullivan (1995).

REFERENCES

Antieau, J.C., P.M. Carroll, and T.C. Burke. 1965. *Religion under the state constitutions.* New York: Institute for Church-State Law/Alpert.

Araújo, W.S. 1999. *Navegando sobre as ondas do Santo Daime: História, Cosmologia e Ritual da Barquinha*. Campinas: Unicamp.

Bastide, R. 1978. The African religions of Brazil: Toward a Sociology of the interpenetrations of civilizations. Baltimore, London: The John Hopkins University Press.

Boire, R.G. 2006. RGB on UDV vs USA: Notes on the hoasca supreme court decision. *Multidisciplinary Association of Psychedelic Studies Bulletin* XVI (1): 19–21.

Brandão, C.R. 1994. A crise das instituições tradicionais produtoras de sentido. In *Misticismo e Novas Religiões*, ed. A. Moreira and Renée Zicman. Petrópolis: Vozes.

Brissac, S. 1999. Alcançar o Alto das Cordilheiras: A vivência mística de discípulos urbanos da União do Vegetal. Paper presented to the *IX Jornadas sobre Alternativas Religiosas na America Latina*, Rio de Janeiro, set/1999 (manuscript).

Calabrese, J.D. 2001. The Supreme Court versus peyote: Consciousness alteration, cultural psychiatry and the dilemma of contemporary subcultures. *Anthropology of Consciousness* 14 (2):4–18.

Carpenter, R.T., and W.C. Roof. 1995. The transplanting of Seicho-No-Ie from Japan to Brazil: Moving beyond the ethnic enclave. *Journal of Contemporary Religion* X (1):41–54.

Carvalho, J.J. 1994. O Encontro de Velhas e Novas Religiões: Esboço de uma Teoria dos Estilos de Espiritualidade. In *Misticismo e Novas Religiões,* ed. A. Moreira and R. e Zicman. Petrópolis: Vozes.

Csordas, T.J. 1994. *The sacred self: A cultural phenomenology of charismatic healing.* Berkeley: University of California Press.

DaMatta, R. 1974. *Relativizando: Uma introdução à antropologia social.* S. Paulo: Vozes.

Dobkin de Rios, M. 1972. *Visionary vine: Psychedelic healing in the Peruvian Amazon.* San Francisco: Chandler.

Douglas, M. 1970 (1966). *Purity and danger: An analysis of concepts of pollution and taboo.* London: Routledge and Kegan.

Durkheim, E. 1965 (1915). *The elementary forms of the religious life.* New York: Free Press.

Eco, U. 1976. *A theory of semiotics.* Bloomington: University of Indiana Press.

Engle, K. 2001. From skepticism to embrace: Human rights and the American Anthropological Association from 1947-1999. *Human Rights Quarterly* 23:536–59.

Epps, G. 2001. *To an religious unknown freedom. God on Trial.* New York: St. Martin Press.

Feldman, S., ed. 2000. *Law and religion: A critical anthology.* New York and London: New York University Press.

Finkelman, P. 2000. *Religion and American law: An encyclopedia.* New York and London: Garland.

Geertz, C. 1973. *The interpretation of cultures.* New York: Basic Books.

Goulart, S. 2004. Contrastes e continuidades em uma tradição Amazônica: As religiões da ayahuasca. Doctorate thesis. PPGCS, Campinas: Unicamp.

Groisman, A. 1999. *Eu venho da Floresta: Um estudo sobre o contexto simbólico do uso do Santo Daime.* Florianópolis: EdUFSC.

Groisman, A. 2000. *Santo Daime in the Netherlands: An anthropological study of a New World religion in a European setting.* PhD Thesis, University of London.

Groisman, A., and A.B. Sell. 1996. Healing power: Neurophenomenology, culture and therapy of "Santo Daime." In *1995—Yearbook of Cross-Cultural Medicine and*

Psychotherapy-V.5. Sacred plants, consciousness and healing, ed. M. Winkelman and W. Andritzky. Berlin: Verlag.

Heelas, P. 1996. *The new age movement: The celebration of the self and the sacralization of modernity.* London, Blackwell.

Henman, A. 1985. Ayahuasca use in an authoritarian context: The case of the União do Vegetal. Paper presented to the *45th Congreso Internacional of Americanistas,* Bogotá, Colombia [published in Spanish, as: Uso del ayahuasca en un contexto autoritario. El caso de la União do Vegetal en Brasil. *América Indígena* 46 (1):219–234, 1986].

Hess, D. 1991. *Spirits and scientists: Ideology, spiritism, and Brazilian culture.* Pennsylvania: Pennsylvania State University.

Hess, D., and R. DaMatta. 1995. *The Brazilian puzzle: Culture on the borderlands of the Western World.* New York: Columbia University Press.

Kurland, P.B. 1962. *Religion and the law: Of church and state and the supreme court.* Chicago: Aldine.

Labate, B.C. 2000. *A Reinvenção do uso da ayahuasca nos centros urbanos.* Master dissertation. Campinas, IFCH- Unicamp.

Labate, B.C., and Wladimir Sena Araújo, eds. 2004. *O uso ritual da ayahuasca.* Campinas: Mercado das Letras/FAPESP.

Long, C.N. 2000. *Religious freedom and Indian rights: The case of Oregon vs. Smith.* Lawrence: University Press of Kansas.

Luna, L.E. 1986. *Vegetalismo: Shamanism among the mestizo population of the Peruvian Amazon.* Stockholm:Almqvist & Wiksell.

Perry, R.W. 2006. Native American tribal gaming as crime against nature: Environment, sovereignty, globalization. *Political and Legal Anthropology Review* 29 (1): 110–31.

Pohlman, H.L. 2004. *Constitutional debate in action: Civil rights & liberties.* Lanham, Boulder, NY, Toronto and Oxford: Rowman & Littlefield.

Post, R.C., and R. Frazier, eds. 1998. *Censorship and silencing: Practices of cultural regulation.* Los Angeles: The Getty Research Institute for the History of Art and the Humanities.

Richey, W. 2006. The Supreme Court takes up a case involving a New Mexico sect that could be important for other minority religions. Christian Science Monitor. Retrieved from www.csmonitor.com/2005/0419//index.html (June 06, 2005).

Rose, I.S. de. 2005. Espiritualidade, terapia e cura: um estudo sobre a expressão da experiência no Santo Daime. Master dissertation, Florianópolis: PPGAS-UFSC.

Silva, C.M. 1983. O Palácio Juramidan. Santo Daime: Um Ritual de Transcendência e Despoluição (Master dissertation), Universidade Federal de Pernambuco, Recife-Brazil.

Smith, H., and Reuben Snake, eds. 1996. *One nation under god: The triumph of the Native American Church.* Santa Fe: Clear Light.

Soares, L.E. 1990. O Santo Daime no contexto da nova consciência religiosa. *Cadernos do ISER 23.* Rio, ISER.

Soilbelman, T. 1995. My father and my mother, show me your beauty: Ritual use of ayahuasca in Rio de Janeiro. Master dissertation, The California Institute of Integral Studies.

Sullivan, W.F. 1995. *Paying the words extra: Religious discourse in the Supreme Court of the United States.* Cambridge, MA: Harvard University Press.

Winkelman, M. 1996. Psychointegrator plants: Their roles in human culture and health. In *Sacred plants, consciousness and healing. Yearbook of cross-cultural medicine and psychotherapy,* ed. M. Winkelman and W. Andritzky, Vol. 6, 9–53. Verlag: Berlin.

Zinberg, N. 1984. *Drug, set, and setting The basis for controlled intoxicant use.* Cumberland: Yale University Press.

15

CONCLUSIONS: GUIDELINES FOR IMPLEMENTING THE USE OF PSYCHEDELIC MEDICINES

MICHAEL J. WINKELMAN AND THOMAS B. ROBERTS

The authors of our chapters have tempered their encouraging results from preliminary studies with reminders that psychedelic medicine has not yet met the criteria of establishing medical safety and efficacy with DBCS (double-blind clinical studies) and the full phases of evaluation. To what extent have psychedelic medicines passed the standards of clinical medicine or biomedical science? To what extent are these standards necessary and appropriate? What uses of psychedelic medicines are justified in terms of the currently available evidence? And how might one avail themselves of these resources? These questions are addressed in this chapter.

SCIENTIFIC EVALUATION OF PSYCHEDELIC MEDICINES[1]

Where does the field of psychedelic medicine stand with respect to scientific and clinical evaluation? In order to assess this question of where the field of psychedelic medicine stands as an established set of treatment tools with potential for the future, we employ the standard model of different phases of evaluation, briefly outlined by Frecska (Chapter 4, this volume). This involves:

Phase I studies which are primarily intended to evaluate safety (toxicity), side effects, and safe dosage range, normally using small groups of healthy subjects;

Phase II trials which use small groups of strictly selected patients to further evaluate safety and to determine effectiveness and ideal doses for targeted illnesses;

Phase III trials which use randomized clinical trials with large groups of patients, who may have diverse comorbid conditions, to confirm effectiveness, monitor adverse drug effects and interactions, and compare the effects of the new substances with commonly used treatments; and

Phase IV trials take treatments that have been shown as effective for a condition and use additional controlled trials to determine additional information regarding side effects, safety, long term risks, and benefits, and to perform comparisons with other procedures for the same condition.

Because of prohibition over the last 35 years, there have been difficulties in achieving these phases of evaluation for the psychedelic medicines. Consequently, our approach to assessing the evaluation of these medicines has to be broader, and at times retrospective (in contrast to the prospective design of the premarketing trials of the legal drugs) specifically:

Phase I studies relying on *patient* populations that have the possibility of showing risks (adverse reactions) where none would exist in normal populations; and *Phase II* studies that evaluate outcomes in patient populations, but not always with the benefit of the double-blind studies. This leaves open the possibility of placebo effects, but for reasons discussed below, this may be viewed as an acceptable part of a *complementary* treatment that relies on set and setting effects as basic to psychedelic therapeutic processes. We characterize Phase II evidence as "limited" when lacking certain features such as the benefit of double-blind controls or having been carried out with nonstandard patient populations.

Table 15.1 summarizes the data that has been presented by the authors of the chapters here in this volume and Volume 2. We suggest that this indicates a generally well-established safety in studies to be considered here as Phase I. To the extent that there are Phase II trials, many reflect the practices of the 1960s and consequently have lacked the standards of DBCS expected in today's more rigorous methodological climate.

Nonetheless, these less than ideal earlier studies, combined with a variety of case studies and user reports and epidemiological studies, substantiate that the broad range of psychedelic medicines are safe and apparently effective adjuncts for a range of conditions, particularly the addictions (also see Volume 2). However, because of the lack of open research possibilities, we do not have the full range of studies normally done to evaluate toxicity, nor effective trials for Phase II and beyond for most of these substances.

While the double-blind clinical trials are limited, other forms of evidence can be used. As Frecska (Chapter 4, this volume) indicates, even when we include the statistics on *abuse* as opposed to responsible use, there is evidence of little

Table 15.1   Phases of Evaluation of Psychedelic Medicines

Psychedelic	Phase 1	Phase II	Phase III	Phase IV
LSD	Yes	Limited[2]		
MDMA	Yes	Currently		
DMT[3]	Yes	No		
Ayahuasca[4]	Yes	Limited		
Psilocybin[5]	Yes	Yes		
Mescaline/peyote[6]	Limited	Limited	De Facto	
Ketamine[7]	Yes	Yes	Yes	Current
Ibogaine[8]	Yes	Yes		
Marijuana[9]	Yes	Yes		

physical harm from psychedelic medicines (Strassman 1984, 1994; Nichols 2004). Other epidemiological approaches such as the use of cross-sectional (e.g., comparing uses and nonusers) as well as retrospective (i.e., life history studies of users) and longitudinal data can help reveal risks—or lack thereof. Such study methods can be applied to cohorts of psychedelic medicine users and when compared to appropriate matched control groups or population norms, can provide a basis for asserting scientific evidence of safety.

As McKenna points out (this volume) with respect to ayahuasca, while we lack controlled clinical trials, evaluations based on clinical judgments of experienced practitioners point out that there is substantial evidence that the psychedelic medicines are effective in the treatment of a range of conditions. As Alper and Lotsof (Chapter 4, Volume 2) point out in their assessment of ibogaine, we can begin to employ more complex, albeit less traditional, forms of validation through a "triangulation" that combined data derived from animal research, the numerous medical case studies and personal accounts of those who have received these substances as treatments, and limited published case series. This would constitute what we discuss here as "limited" evidence. Other criteria of the effectiveness of medicines would include clinical judgment based on extensive experiences (e.g., Grof 1979; also see Volume 2, Chapters 9–11 and 13 by Grof, Merkur, House, and Walsh and Grob; similar cross-cultural uses and alleged effects (independent invention/discovery); patient satisfaction and enhanced ability to engage activities of daily living and lifestyle; and pharmacological studies indicating biological mechanisms of action of active ingredients.

Ketamine: An exception to these generally cautious assessments of the evaluation of these psychedelic medicines is ketamine (see Krupitsky and Kolp, Chapter 5, Volume 2), which has received FDA (Food and Drug Administration) approval for other uses and has been widely employed for the treatment of addictions in Russia. These applications of ketamine were primarily as a *research* activity and were NOT officially registered with the Russian Ministry of Health for approval as adjunct in the therapeutic treatment of addictions. Nonetheless based on his assessment of the rules of the FDA, Kolp (pers. comm.)

characterizes the research of Krupitzky and his colleagues as constituting the completion of Phase I, Phase II, and Phase III clinical trials in the ketamine psychedelic psychotherapeutic treatment of alcoholism and opioid dependence. Currently, their research constitutes the beginning of Phase IV in the United States as Kolp and colleagues are initiating multicenter, randomized, double-blind studies of the ketamine psychedelic psychotherapy. Krupitzky and colleagues are similarly at this phase, currently treating in excess of 1,000 patients with ketamine psychedelic psychotherapy (Kolp, pers. comm.; see Krupitsky and Kolp, Chapter 5, Volume 2). Ketamine constitutes a special case among the psychedelic medicines since it was already an FDA-approved drug for more then 35 years ago. The FDA does not requires the same registration procedures for a new ("off-label") treatment as it does for a new drug. Since its initial approval, research has been conducted on ketamine off-label uses in the treatment of a variety of conditions including chronic pain disorder, intractable seizure, strokes and heart attacks (Kolp, pers. comm.).

Are Double-Blind Studies Appropriate Criteria for Psychedelic Medicines?

The authors of our chapters have tempered their encouraging results from preliminary studies with reminders that psychedelic medicine has not yet met the criteria of establishing medical safety and efficacy with DBCS. This "gold standard" of biomedicine might seem to be the appropriate response from a profession (and society) that prides itself on the use of science to make decisions regarding health resources. But is this in fact what happens? Does biomedicine itself rely on the gold standard of DBCS to determine what treatments we can receive? Or is the "gold standard" a kind of "double standard," an ethnocentric judgment applied more to others' medicines rather than one's own?

A variety of studies realized by agencies of the U.S. government have found that only about 20–30% of commonly used biomedical procedures had actually been tested with double-blind clinical procedures (see Cassiday 1996; McKee 1988 for references and discussion). Most of biomedicine's common daily practices are not substantiated by the strictest criteria of medical science. No DBCS are carried out on the use of multiple medications simultaneously, a common aspect of biomedicine that causes drug interaction effects that constitute a major cause of death in the United States.

The reasons why biomedicine does not rely strictly on DBCS are legion—the difficulties with control conditions and blinds (e.g., what is involved in a double-blind procedure for cardiac bypass surgery?); the ethical problems produced by withholding a potentially effective treatment from someone who needs it in the interest of a scientific study; and the funding sources and research priorities of drug companies.

Biomedicine and the other ethnomedical traditions of the world rely on many forms of evidence to establish some degree of certainty about the efficacy of their procedures. What should be the standards held for the use of psychedelic medicines? This depends on the specific medicines, patients, and conditions.

But in spite of limited scientific studies of psychedelic medicines, most have passed Phase I evaluations as generally safe, providing evidence that supports the widespread application of psychedelic medicines, reclassified as Schedule II. The range of conditions for which psychedelic medicines have been used are limited, but given the wide range of uses found cross-culturally (e.g., see Schultes and Winkelman 1996; Schultes and Hofmann 1979; Winkelman, Chapter 8, Volume 2), they ought to be evaluated for a wide range of supervised uses for many different conditions including physical diseases and psychosocial and cultural-bound illnesses.

The DBCS must be understood in the context of the effort to separate the placebo effect from the pharmacological action. These placebo effects are part of the well-recognized powerful set and setting effects that determine the major outcomes from use of psychedelic medicines. One of the challenges of psyche-delic studies is the notorious difficulty in maintaining a double blind in it, as the powerful effects become quickly apparent to patients and clinicians. Furthermore, the scientific necessity for control of the placebo effect is at odds with the intent of many applications of psychedelic therapies, where the medicines are used to amplify the set and setting effects through intention and focus of attention and interactions with others. The placebo effects of set and setting are so powerful in the case of psychedelic medicines as to have produced three major paradigms of the psychedelics' effects: psychomimetic, psycholytic and psychedelic (high dose) (Chapter 3, this volume; Yensen 1985, 1996; Bravo and Grob 1989; Grob and Bravo 1995)

The effects of psychedelic medicines are to a great degree dependent on the social dynamics and interpersonal relations of the sessions. This makes them amplifiers of other dynamics and enhancers of other processes. This illustrates that an important part of the mechanism of psychedelic medicines is the placebo-psychological effect in a very broad way. Psychedelic medicines seek to enhance placebo effects, and based on numerous self-reports they do. Control procedures designed to reduce placebo effects also counter the basic mechanisms affected by psychedelic medicines. If a basic premise of psychedelic medicine is to enhance set and setting effects, placebo effects need to be included with the treat-ment effect, not separated from it.

This notion of including the placebo may seem alien to medical researches steeped in the traditions of the DBCS. But such approaches are becoming a stan-dard in the context of *integrative* medicine, where the traditional biomedical treat-ments are being integrated/combined with the so called alternative medicines in a complementary fashion. The assessment methods in these approaches compare patients receiving the standard biomedical treatment alone with patients who receive standard biomedical treatment plus the "alternative/complementary" treatment. Such additive models are often advocated by supporters of psychedelic medicines, who see them as adjunctive to aspects of standard psychotherapeutic care.

A closing note on the appropriateness of double-blind studies for evaluation of psychedelic medicines should also consider the notorious difficulty in achieving this for medications that have such powerful effects. The ability of both patients and clinicians to break the blind in psychedelic studies is well known. The powerful effects of these substances make it difficult to come up with an appropriate control that evokes similar powerful experiences without compromising the uniqueness of the psychedelic medicine (but see Griffiths et al., Chapter 12, Volume 2). Consequently, the integrative open-label model may ultimately be the best model for evaluations of psychedelic medicines, assessing how their adjunctive use enhances the outcomes ordinarily achieved with standard biomedical practices. And if this includes in part a placebo effect, we should embrace this as a positive outcome to be enhanced with the psychedelic medicines.

USE OF ANALYTIC DESIGNS FROM EPIDEMIOLOGY FOR PSYCHEDELIC MEDICINE RESEARCH

The methods that epidemiologists use to identify risk factors associated with specific diseases can be used to assess risks for psychedelic medicine use (see Chapter 4, this volume) as well as the possible effectiveness of their use as treatments for specific diseases. Epidemiological methods such as case control and cohort studies (see Kelsey et al. 1996) can be used to examine at outcomes of psychedelic medicine treatments. For instance, in the case of Sewell and Halpern's research (this volume) on the effectiveness of psychedelic medicines in the treatment of cluster headaches, effectiveness can be assessed using methods such as case control studies. This involves comparisons of those psychedelic medicine "self-medicators" with a matched group that relied strictly on conventional medicine. Case control studies draw inferences by making comparisons of a target group (e.g., cluster headache patients who have experienced prolonged remission from psychedelic medicines) with a matched control group of cluster headache patients who have not them. Similarly, case control studies can make inferences about the level of effectiveness of ibogaine treatment of heroin addictions by making comparisons of the period of sobriety of heroin users who have taken ibogaine with a control group of heroin addicts in recovery who have not used ibogaine.

The relative ease of quick comparisons with case control studies can make them useful for initial screening of the effectiveness of psychedelic medicines in the treatment of new and intractable diseases or infrequent diseases. While there are disadvantages to case control methods because of lack of accurate information on risk factors and confounding variables, and recall bias, if the time sequence for disease and exposure to psychedelic medicines can be established, there is a better basis to infer cause and effect relationships. *Cross sectional (prevalence)* studies normally assess data from a relatively short period of time. These studies normally assess exposure and disease at the same time (e.g., hallucinogen use and cluster headache symptoms), and then assess the prevalence of the cluster headache condition in the different groups (psychedelic medicine users vs. nonusers). In epidemiology, it is routine to use cross-sectional methods to assess existing cases of disease and compares the rates for groups with and without exposure to specific factors. Cross-sectional studies are particularly suited for studying diseases that have a slow onset and long duration and are generally not identified and cared for until they have reached advanced stages. This makes it possible to see, for instance, if hallucinogen use may be preventive in some disease. *Retrospective (or historical) cohort studies* can use medical history interviews to determine the possible relationship of prior use of psychedelic medicines to the manifestations of disease conditions.

SUMMARY OF PSYCHEDELIC MEDICINE TREATMENT POTENTIALS

Halpern (Volume 2) makes the point that considering the limited efficacy of current treatments for drug addiction, a problem that is evidenced in the high rates of chronic relapse for these conditions, the use of psychedelic substances for treatment of drug dependence is an ethical responsibility of the medical field. Given the much greater safer safety profile of the psychedelics compared to major addictive drugs (see Frecska, this volume), even repeated use of psychedelic medicines as treatments is more ethical than professional maintenance/treatment programs employing drugs of high abuse or substitutes (e.g., methadone treatment or supervised application of heroin) because of their abuse and overdose potential.

Unfortunately, this option of safer and likely more effective treatment is generally precluded by the control exercised by administrative law. This makes it a moral responsibility of politicians to reverse this three and a half decade prohibition on the use of these valuable medicinal substances.

As Frecska summarizes in his chapter here, we have begun to see the use in well-controlled Phase II trials of several psychedelics such as ibogaine, marijuana, MDMA (3,4 methylenedioxymethamphetamine), and psilocybin. But because of the great cost of a Phase III studies, there is little hope that we will see these proceed without some changes in the government funding or industry approaches that will make these substantial investments. Goldsmith (Chapter 7, Volume 2) points to the need for changing the policies of bureaucracies, particularly at the level of the U.S. Department of Health and Human Services, where the bureaucracy resists drug policy and research changes even where permitted by law. This requires a public relations approach to changing public perceptions, which have as of yet been a failure for those who favor drug policy reform. Goldsmith outlines processes of moving from awareness of issues to a broad enough public interest to support changes in administrative policies that can lead to ultimately achieve approval of these medicines as legitimate and mainstream approaches. He points to a strategy of targeting people who are organizational levers and administrative decision makers who are key to the introduction to new programs and policy directions.

This will require strategic alignments with other interests, and Goldsmith points out that treatment of central social problems such as addictions is a good point at which to focus initial energies. Part I of Volume 2 attests to the wide range of successful applications of psychedelic medicines to addictions. But to change the political climate in the United States greater development of education and advocacy groups will be necessary. These are the functions of many organizations, including Drug Policy Foundation, DPA (Drug Policy Alliance), MAPS (Multidisciplinary Association for Psychedelic Studies), and the CCLE (Center for Cognitive Liberty and Ethics).

In the following sections we address four major interrelated approaches to enhancing responsible access to psychedelic medicines through:

- Utilizing currently available psychotherapeutic and religious resources;
- Altering social attitudes through education and the media;
- Changing administrative policies through public policy, judicial, and legislative approaches; and
- Inventing new approaches through a business or corporate model.

SELF-ADMINISTERED THERAPY

In Volume 2, a variety of our authors (e.g., Merkur, Goldsmith, and House) illustrate that a wide range of clinical knowledge has been developed regarding the safe and effective use of psychedelic medicines. It should be noted that therapeutic recommendations for the use of psychedelic medicine include the presence of qualified therapists. While there are uses of psychedelic medicines that focus on individual self-administration (see Chapter 8, Volume 2), even those are generally under the supervision of experienced healers. How does one get qualified supervision in the current legal context?

Foreign Sources

The general lack of legal access to psychedelic medicine in the United States suggests foreign treatment sources as a primary means of access. Foreign opportunities for loosely structured self-directed psychedelic therapy are found within the mestizo and new age ayahuasca and San Pedro traditions of Peru. More formal treatment protocols are available for the treatment of various addiction problems, as discussed in Chapters 4–6 by Mabit, Krupitsky and Kolp, and Alper and Lotsof in Volume 2.

The loosely self-administered therapeutic applications of ayahuasca manifested in the international "drug tourism" (Dobkin de Rios 1994) provide many North Americans and Europeans the therapeutic potentials of ayahuasca. Ayahuasca ceremonies are available in much of South America, particularly the Amazonian countries. Winkelman (2005) discovered that these people are in

search of the kinds of powerful personal and spiritual healing provoked by psychedelic medicines. Contrary to the search for hedonistic highs implied by the
characterization as "drug tourists," their principal motivations are characterized
by seeking spiritual relations and personal spiritual development; various forms
of emotional healing, particularly unresolved traumas; and the development of
personal self-awareness, including some sense of direct contact with a sacred
nature, God, spirits, and plant and natural energies produced by the ayahuasca.
Their motivations for their journeys and the perceived benefits that they report
both point to transpersonal concerns. The principal perceived benefits involve
increased self-awareness, personal insights, access to deeper levels of the self that
enhance personal development, and expressions of the higher self which provided
personal direction in life (Winkelman 2005).

Wasiwaska, a Research Centre for the Study of Psychointegrator Plants,
Visionary Arts, and Consciousness established by Luis Eduardo Luna, exemplifies a multifacted organization focused on the provision of private group therapy
with psychedelic medicines. Wasiwaska (the House of the Vine) is a legal Brazilian nonprofit organization located in Florianópolis, Santa Catarina, in southern
Brazil. This institute also promotes a variety of research projects on ayahuasca.

Domestic Adaptations to Prohibition

Eventually, there may also be several other approaches available to those
remaining in controlled areas through various forms of self-medication as
an adaptation of shamanism. These self-medication approaches may be both
solitary or interpersonal "recreational consumption," or could potentially occur
in professional settings that are integrated into a semi-structured group therapeutic setting with ritual activities and processing. Psychotherapists might be
protected in an occasional practice where clients self-administer psychedelics
in a group retreat setting (see relevant discussion in Boire, this volume). Therapists could probably find protection by disclaimers and the provision of other
natural altered state of consciousness induction practices as part of spiritual
healing practices (e.g., see Winkelman's Chapter 8 on shamanic guidelines
in Volume 2). Therapist could obtain greater protection from persecution by
providing "psychedelic retreats" managed by therapists and in which each
client brought their own preselected particular psychedelic medicine.

Some other psychedelic treatments may not require the group dynamics to
the same degrees, such as with the cluster headaches. As Boire discusses, such
people who find themselves driven to self-medicate with psychedelics might be
legally protected through documenting their medical needs and frustration with
conventional medicines.

It is imperative that we apply psychedelic medicines to the treatment of some
of the most ravaging social diseases of our times, the addictions to alcohol,
tobacco, and opiates and their synthetic derivatives. The generally acknowledge
success rate in the addictions treatment industry does not appear to be much

different from the spontaneous remission rate. And while Alcoholic Anonymous and its derivative organizations do provide some degree of treatment success, it is obviously not a successful venue for most addicts.

The range of psychedelic addiction treatments is truly impressive, as we will see in the chapters of Part II, Volume 2. Peyote, ibogaine, ayahuasca, LSD (lysergic acid diethylamide), and ketamine are among the psychedelic medicines for which we have substantial evidence of their effectiveness in addictions medicine.

Religious Therapies

The existing legal frameworks discussed by Fenney (Chapter 13, this volume), and Groisman and de Rios' (Chapter 14, this volume) discussion of the cultural contexts of the Brazilian Ayahuasca religions and the U.S. Supreme Court justices decisions, establish some broad parameters within which religious formation, conversion, and evangelism might extend the therapeutic applications of psychedelics as sacraments and entheogens. The ability to establish new U.S. -based local churches of the Brazilian Ayahuasca churches may be protected in the current judicial climate. Brazilian Ayahuasca religions coming to the United States are a likely possibility. In fact, they are here now. Existing American religious groups (e.g., Unitarian Universalists) could conceivably engage in ecumenical outreach to ayahuasca churches, inviting them to the United States to share their sacraments and expand religious/pastoral counseling through using psychedelic medicines as entheogens.

The broader range of spiritual applications are indicated by authors in Volume 2, particularly Chapters 8, 11, 13, and 14 by Grof, Walsh and Grob, Marsden and Lukoff, and Winkelman, who point to the transpersonal uses of these medicines. The potential applications of these substances as entheogens are among the most widely established in human history, although their place in modern medicine has yet to be determined. Yet the work of Griffith et al. (Volume 2) illustrates that these spiritual applications are reliably induced by psychedelic medicines, pointing to a relatively unexplored aspects of human well-being that are addressed by psychedelic medicines.

EDUCATION AND IMPROVING PUBLIC KNOWLEDGE

Education about the actual effects and potentials of psychedelic medicines and other drugs is a crucial aspect of increasing the use of these resources, backed by the knowledge of the parameters of their safe use and efficacious effects. A variety of policy organizations (see next section) have attempted to change the opportunities regarding drugs through an education approach that focuses on affecting public health policy. Their focus is to educate society, legislators, and administrators regarding regulation of drugs based in science, compassion, and activities that enhance health and protect human rights. Education is a central tool in addressing the misinformation, fears, and prejudices that contribute to the legal and administrative attitudes that waste resources in punitive activities and prohibition efforts that produce more problems than they solve. Many problems of addiction are caused by the drug war and oppressive judicial and administrative measures rather than the drugs. Through education we can best hope to advance drug policies that reduce harms of drug misuse as well as drug prohibition. The kinds of evidence our authors provide in these two volumes are a contribution to similar efforts. Two other educational venues merit special notice—schools and the media.

Schools

When things in my (Roberts) honors seminar "Foundations of Psychedelic Studies" start to drag a bit, I have found a topic that always enlivens the discussion—the DARE drug education program. Spiced by snickers, guffaws, and rolling eyes, the discussion heats up, and almost everyone in my class has a "horror story" about this futile program. Why is drug education in failing health, and how can it be revived? Truth is a powerful serum, but drug education programs are about "Keeping kids off drugs" not about telling the truth, the whole truth, and nothing but the truth.

Unfortunately, the biased and slanted information that my students report represents the general state of drug education and public knowledge, both formal education in schools and informal education in the news media. We hope these two volumes will be a segment of the whole truth. And, of course, we are presenting up-to-date ideas on some medical aspects of psychedelic drugs, while a full picture would be vast and include not only psychedelic drugs but also other psychoactive drugs, and it would stretch beyond medicine to the arts, sciences, religion, and elsewhere.

One reason our culture has such a difficult time thinking clearly about drugs is that our system of ideas is adapting only slowly to recognize that there are benefits of using other mindbody states (states of consciousness) in addition to our ordinary awake state (Roberts 2006). When the psychedelic 60s erupted decades ago, an interest in mindbody practices such as meditation, yoga, or breathing exercises were largely misinterpreted and mistrusted. Now churches teach mediation, park districts and schools offer yoga classes, and health professionals teach relaxation exercises; over the decades, our culture is becoming educated about the benefits of mindbody psychotechnologies and coming gradually to accept them. Also, during this time the number of prescribable, psychoactive medicines has—ahem—mushroomed. Culturally, we still have much to learn from some premodern societies about other mindbody states, ways to access them, and how to use them (Winkelman, Chapter 1, this volume, and Chapter 8, Volume 2).

From a scientific perspective, presenting partial information as if it were the whole story is little different from lying. Everything one says may be true, but if a biased selection of the information misrepresents the whole evidence, this is likely to lead to a misleading conclusion. This is the way lawyers work, not scientists: lawyers start with the conclusion and marshal evidence to support it. Along the way, they disregard conflicting information. (It may be no odd occurrence that most politicians, who set drug policy and fund drug education, are lawyers.) Scientists, on the other hand, will include all the information and ask: "What conclusions does this evidence require us to make?" Most drug education programs work in the lawyerly way: they start with the conclusion that all drug use is bad, then they collect the information that supports their prejudged conclusion.

This has a tragic downside: judging from my sample of college juniors, when we present biased information about drugs, students come to recognize this and throw out the realistic cautions because of the exaggerated fears. If anything they are taught is wrong or misleading, the baby of realistic warnings gets thrown out with the dirty waters of lies and exaggerations.

News Media as Educators

On a wider social scale, our educators are the news media, and with some notable exceptions, they are little better than DARE.

A DOZEN HANDY GUIDELINES FOR REPORTING ON DRUG RESEARCH

In 1997, a group of leading scientists, law enforcement specialists, and health policy experts proposed a 14-point *Principles for Practical Drug Policies* (Federation of American Scientists). Among the 14 policies they recommend as "a middle way" was a drug policy based on scientific evidence, civility toward those with different solutions, and honesty about facts, proposals, and motives. How might a responsible news media write fact-based news stories and educate people on psychedelics and other psychoactive drugs? The following questions will help reporters clarify drug issues, and readers judge the content of the stories they read.

When they receive information about drug studies or talk to officials, they can ask the following questions.

Was the drug used actually the same as the drug reported on? During the early press reports of MDMA (Ecstasy, X, and the rave drug), the press reported results of MDA (methylenedioxyamphetamine) research as MDMA research. Even a very slight change in a molecule can greatly change its biological and psychological effects.

Was the route of administration the usual route? The effects of a drug vary greatly according to the four S's—whether it is smoked, swallowed, snorted, or shot. For example, when a drug is swallowed, a great many biological events take place in the stomach and liver before the drug is generally circulated in the blood stream. Injections, which are usually used in animals, bypass this process. When a drug is smoked, some chemical structures are broken, and new chemicals can be formed.

Was the research in vitro (test tube) or in vivo (in living organisms)? Substances induce a cascade of biological events in living organisms, but this number is drastically diminished in a test tube. Some side effects (both desirable and undesirable) are missed in the test tube, and some effects that appear in the test tube would not occur in a living body, or would occur at a much diminished degree.

Was the dosage typical of common usage? It makes little sense to claim a drug has an affect if the dosage was extremely high or low. When a researcher reports that the dosage was, say, "x milligrams per kilogram of body weight," reporters and readers or TV viewers should ask, "What is the typical concentration in a typical user?" Researchers should compare the experimental dose with the typical use. It is helpful to think of street use in terms of a normal curve, which range from very low to very high doses, but with the majority in the middle. Where do the problems derive? From "normal" doses or the high extremes?

Was the research done on people or other animals? Reports of behavioral change by psychoactive drugs in animals are minimally generalizable to humans. Biological activity such as attachment at receptor sites is more applicable. The lack of generalizability is especially true for drugs which are taken primarily for their effect on thinking and emotions. What does it mean to say that a drug effects cognitive processes of a rat or gives a sense of well-being to a monkey?

Was an alleged drug actually the drug taken? This is especially a problem with "street drugs." A dealer who is out of a certain drug may substitute another, and the purchaser may attribute his/her experience to the wrong drug. This is also a problem with dosage and contamination. Information based on street drugs and research based on pure laboratory samples may or may not apply to each other.

How typical is an expert's report of a drug's effects on humans? Doctors, police officers, and mental health professionals are likely to see people who have had bad effects of drugs. Although their sample is skewed toward reporting ill effects, it probably is useful in answering the question, "What are the *possible dangers* of this drug?" Their experience is not accurate in answering, "What is a *typical effect* of this drug?" Asking most drug specialists about drugs is like asking a divorce lawyer about marriage.

Does "drug-related" mean "drug money related"? Most "drug related violence" does not come from using drugs but comes from fighting over the money associated with drugs—to obtain the money to buy drugs, fighting over the profits, intergang competition, debts, etc. Drug trafficking is a lucrative, tax-free business that is engaged in for profit.

What are the "set" and "setting"? In human subjects, major effects of psychoactive drugs result from the person's "set" (expectations, mood, and frame of mind) and "setting" (location). In psychoactive drugs, set and setting are primary influences. This applies less to drugs which are taken for somatic, bodily purposes; thus, when medical doctors think about the effect of a psychoactive drug, they may not recognize the primacy of its set and setting.

Why do people do this drug? Whenever a large number of people do something, it is worth assuming there are many reasons, and most people probably have a mixture of reasons. A way to test the expertise of an alleged "expert" is to probe to see if he or she recognizes multiple reasons why people like drugs. It is worth asking, "What benefits do people who use this drug think (rightly or wrongly) they are obtaining?" The more complex the answer, the greater the likelihood you have a well-informed "expert."

Talk to people who have actually taken the drug. The news stories I read seem to rely on third parties telling why they think people do the drug being reported on. "Peer pressure" and "to escape reality" are probably true some of the time, but if we want to write policies to affect people's behaviors, can we do so without knowing why they do those behaviors? Most people voluntarily take drugs because—rightly or wrongly—they think they benefit from doing so. What are these alleged benefits?

Why are you telling me this? Reporters and editors are taught to be skeptical, always to have the questions "Why are you telling me this?" and "What will you gain if I report this?" in the back of their minds. But for some reason, they naively switch off these questions for drug stories. They know that other governmental press releases, news conferences, and interviews are provided in order to get an agency's message across, and an implicit or explicit background theme for many such news events is we need more funding. Since the funding of drug war agencies depends on their ability to scare people about drugs, the bigger the scare, the greater the funding.

Unfortunately, much drug reporting is naive, divisive, sensationalistic, and simplistic. Reporters can educate the public and increase the accuracy of their stories by exercising the common skills of reportorial skepticism, and readers can understand drug news stories better by asking questions based on common sense.

PUBLIC HEALTH POLICY, JUDICIAL, AND LEGISLATIVE APPROACHES

There is a surprising large number of organizations supporting reform in drug policies and rational approaches based on both rational evidence and human caring.

Drug Policy Alliance[10]

The DPA (see www.drugpolicy.org) points out that it is the state legislatures which have traditionally been at the forefront of policy change on drug laws. Local context provides "laboratories" for experimenting with new ideas and potential solutions. This is exemplified in drug policy reform on issues such as drug sentencing, medical marijuana use, overdose prevention and treatment programs, and the expansion of drug treatment services. The "Drug Policy Reform: The State of the States, 1996–2002" (DPA, www.drugpolicy.org) summarizes many of these developments promoted by local voters and state governments who have enacted more than 150 significant drug policy reforms during the last decade. While the DPA's focus on education has focused on marijuana and other commonly used illicit drugs, it has provided a context within which to discuss alternatives to current drug policies and treatment alternatives to incarceration.

For example, the DPA organized voters in Oakland, CA, to support Medical Marijuana use through a ballot measure that established a framework for decriminalizing marijuana and making it the local police's lowest enforcement priority, instead focusing their resources to address violent crime. Although local ordinances have allowed for local use of some substances such as marijuana, there has been a constant battle with the federal authorities who feel that they are not limited by state initiatives.

A significant feature of the policy advocacy has been a focus on harm reduction strategies that attempt to reduce problems, particularly those associated with enforcement. The ideas of reducing harms can be expanded to appreciating potential benefits where substances have proven medicinal uses, maximizing potential benefits of psychedelic medicines through their judicious use. These possibilities for the broader use of psychedelic medicines have not yet been a significant focusing of the referendum process, the milder marijuana typically being the focus of the referendum process. Nonetheless the role of the DPA and similar activist organizations in supporting the development of legislative and referendum work at the state levels leaves open the possibility of legislated treatment programs in the same way that we have seen legislated needle exchange and methadone programs.

A significant feature of this multifaceted approach has been to include a continued and expanded resistant to the War on Drugs. The immense expenditure focused on the arrest, prosecution and incarceration of tens of thousands of persons each year for crimes associated with the possession and use of illegal drugs has led to an erosion of many constitutional rights. The War on Drugs is a war on public health that has been resisted by public health organizations such as the American Public Health Association, as well as other professional organizations such the American Society of Addiction Medicine, the National Association of Alcoholism and Drug Abuse Counselors, and the American College of Obstetricians and Gynecologists.

Center for Cognitive Liberty and Ethics[11]

Combined education and legal approaches have been emphasized by the CCLE (www.cognitiveliberty.org) as well. The CCLE is a network of scholars that address issues in the intersection of law and policy issues as they pertain to cognitive freedoms to use psychedelic medicines and other drugs.

Their educational and policy approach has addressed policies necessary to preserve the ethics of the freedom of thought regarding these substances.

The clinical applications of psychedelic medicines clearly move the concerns beyond the context of purely medical use and into the improvement and enhancement of cognitive abilities. They emphasize the importance of protecting personal freedoms involving the exploration of the capabilities of our own minds as a direct right as long as it does not directly harm others. There are many forms of resistance to the governments' efforts to limit and criminally prohibit forms of consciousness and cognitive enhancement. The CCLE has emphasized the importance of social impact litigation as a process for broadly advancing the potential to exercise our cognitive liberties, and has filed legal briefs on the topic of cognitive liberty in federal court. But central to their efforts is raising awareness of the emerging issues of cognitive liberty through outreach and education campaigns designed to provide people with the information necessary so that they can empower themselves to participate meaningfully in public discourse and affect relevant democratic processes.

Multidisciplinary Association for Psychedelic Studies[12]

The combined public education, research, and policy efforts necessary to change the political climate limiting the use of psychedelic medicines are exemplified in MAPS (see www.maps.org). MAPS is a membership-based nonprofit research and educational organization founded in response to increasing governmental control exemplified in the classification of MDMA as a Schedule 1 drug by the DEA (Drug Enforcement Administration). MAPS exemplifies the private sector organizations that take a multifaceted approach to changing the political climate through education, organization of local political efforts, lawsuits, and research funding. Its scope of activities range from a research mission engaged in sponsoring scientific researchers to spearheading efforts to obtain governmental approval for research projects, engaging in fund raising activities, and conducting and reporting on psychedelic research to make necessary information available to legislators, administrators, and the voting public.

MAPS programs exemplify the need to address these issues of personal consciousness and cognitive freedom, embodied in the conflicts of the politically and ideologically driven War on Drugs with personal and scientific freedoms. This negation of science has led to gross social problems, embodied in economic, civil, and social problems from drug enforcement rather than drug use. MAPS has played a significant role in pointing to the source of these conflictive societal dynamics in the deep-seated cultural traditions, and the collective and individual ambivalence about spiritual experiences. MAPS seeks to achieve a balance between adequate control of powerful psychedelic medicines and the rights of scientific researchers, clinicians, patients, and people with a nonmedical interest in the applications of these in spiritual, recreational, and creative contexts.

Through the funding of research, MAPS contributes to the development of beneficial applications of psychedelic medicines in psychotherapeutic practices and physiological research, as well as treatment of pain and addictions and exploration of spirituality, creativity research, shamanic healing, psychic abilities, and a range of research projects on brain physiology. It supports a range of projects (e.g., see chapters in this volume, such as Abrams'). Because of funding provided by organizations like MAPS, research teams are able to operate in other countries where restrictions are less onerous (e.g., Canada, Israel, Russia, and Switzerland).

The Federal government's administrative apparatus has proven to be a major impediment to research, imposing a range of administrative barriers that preclude access to needed medicines or approvals for studies (e.g., see Strassman 2001). MAPS has sponsored lawsuits against DEA for their refusal to issue the required permits for growing facilities, access to drugs and approvals for applications, a venue that will be increasingly necessary to fight against the arbitrary bureaucratic impediments to legitimate research and treatment (also see Doblin's [2001] doctoral dissertation "Regulation of the Medical Use of Psychedelics and Marijuana").

The need to act at the level of the election of sympathetic federal officials—including the president—is emphasized in the MAPS statement that "there will probably be no privately-funded medical marijuana research effort ever started until a more reasonable President is in office." Other venues of action for overcoming administrative and judicial impediments could include a campaign of pressure through letters of support from members of Congress to influence the DEA Administrator to make favorable recommendations. In the face of federal level opposition to research, the development of state-level reforms becomes even more significant.

But organizations such as MAPS depend on public support, which is limited and insufficient for the range of research projects currently awaiting support. MAPS uses private donations and other forms of fund raising to acquire resources to fund research for scientists to design studies, seek funding, and obtain necessary institutional and governmental approval for studies into the risks and benefits of psychedelic medicines. A specific focus of MAPS' mission has been to sponsor scientific research necessary to seek FDA-approval for the use of psychedelics and marijuana as prescription medicines. This also requires a public education approach to provide correct and honest information about the risks and benefits of psychedelic medicines.

MAPS educational mission is complemented in its operation as a nonprofit pharmaceutical company with the priority of researching the potential of MDMA (Ecstasy) and marijuana as FDA-approved prescription medicines. The formidable expenses normally involved are illustrated in the MAPS estimate of a $5 million cost for the five years of research necessary to meet FDA criteria for the safety and efficacy of a single psychedelic medicine for just one clinical indication. These costs make the idea of a business model—a corporate approach—an almost necessary avenue for exploration and development in the current political climate.

A CORPORATE SOLUTION

How might we use psychedelics most advantageously and at the same time limit their risks? As these two volumes of this book and especially this chapter and the concluding chapter of Volume 2 show, the diversity of psychedelics' possible uses leads to a diversity of ways to embed them in existing institutions and possibly new ones. In these concluding chapters, we regard only a few of them.

When I (Roberts) first considered a corporate answer to how to develop psychedelics safely and efficiently, I thought about writing an essay proposing such a company, but my thoughts kept leapfrogging from ordinary sentences and paragraphs to imagining what a prospectus for such a company would look like. How could these ideas make sense to Wall Street types? How might the City act? Rather than write a straightforward narrative essay and hope that some day the essay would inspire a startup company, my mind jumped immediately to a prospectus-as-essay.

Like science fiction, this part of our concluding chapter is business fiction. Scifi ideas often presage actual events and inventions. Similarly, this attempt at bizfi may foretell the future too. Here are selected ideas from that longer, fictional prospectus.

PRELIMINARY PROSPECTUS

Community Psychedelic Centers International, Inc.

Incorporated in the State of Delaware

An offering of 10,000,000 shares of common stock at $20 each

SUMMARY Community Psychedelic Centers International, Inc., ("CPC or "the company") anticipates offering 10,000,000 shares of common stock on or about (date forthcoming). This will be the initial public offer for the company and may represent special risks. The company expects to provide two types of services: (1) psychedelic-assisted psychotherapy and (2) and psychedelic-assisted professional development (See "The Company's Business" below). With the proceeds of this offering, the company expects to establish therapeutic centers and professional development centers. The therapeutic centers will consist of (1) free-standing, self-contained centers for referral patients and (2) on-grounds, in-house centers located at existing major mental health hospitals and centers. The Professional Development Centers will provide service for clients who wish to enhance religious experience, creativity, personal growth, academic and scholarly research, and similar non-therapeutic purposes.

The company believes it has already identified several potential drug candidates as investigational new drugs, and furthermore, that while additional studies may be required to firmly establish their safety and efficacy, preliminary studies support both their safety and efficacy.

The company will receive approximately 85% of the proceeds of this offering. The underwriters will receive approximately 1% for underwriting and miscellaneous fees, and approximately 14% will go to the individuals who comprised CPC Partners and are now the current stockholders.

Underwritten by

Hofmann & NiewKranium, Inc.
    Member of the Zurich, New York, and Amsterdam Stock Exchanges
HANDPRIK & TWIST, inc.
    Member of the Sausalito, La Honda, and Montauk Stock Exchanges

The Company

The CPC (Community Psychedelic Centers) Partnership was formed with 20 partners. This partnership organized CPC International, Inc. and incorporated it in the state of Delaware. CPC has applied to the FDA to commence clinical trials of several drugs which CPC believes offer advantages as adjuncts to psychotherapy. CPC also believes these drugs as used within the confines of the proposed sessions are effective methods of increasing professional development including, but not limited to, creativity and problem solving, providing insights of value to academic and scientific researchers, enhancing primary religious experience, stimulating artistic works, and exploring and developing the human mind. No assurance can be given that the candidate drugs will prove effective, and if they are, no assurance can be given that the FDA will approve their uses as anticipated by CPC.

CPC believes that these drugs should not be prescribed to patients in such a way that the patients can buy them and self-administer them, but that their proper use requires the presence of fully trained professionals. Patients may not take these substances home with them. An analogy might be anesthetics, which are administered only by properly prepared professionals.

TRADING SYMBOL

CPC International has applied to the NASDAQ (National Association of Securities Dealers Automated Quotation system) to trade CPC stock under the symbol *LSDD.*

CHARITABLE ALLOTMENT

An unusual feature of this offering is the "charitable allotment." Purchasers of these shares at the underwriting are required to donate half their purchases to a charity recognized as such by the U.S. Internal Revenue Service or by appropriate state, local, or national laws in the jurisdictions where purchasers reside. For example, if someone buys 200 shares, he or she must donate 100 shares to a recognized charity. These shares are fully registered and identical to all other units. CPC's tax consultants believe that such gifts may qualify as a charitable donation for Federal Income Tax purposes, but the Internal Revenue Service has not made a determination on this issue.

CHARITABLE CHOICE—PSYCHEDELIC FOUNDATION

Investors may select any charity or charities of their choice, such as a church, university, museum, community organization, or other legally recognized eleemosynary institution. CPC partners has established Psychedelic Foundation, Inc. to receive these and other donations if investor-donors so desire. Psychedelic Foundations is entirely separate from CPC, and its charter allows it to fund a wide variety of health-related, educational, religious, scientific, civic, and other *pro bono* projects. This includes, but is not limited to, paying fees for treatment and services for people who cannot afford to pay for CPC's services. Although CPC Partners hopes investors will contribute their charitable allotment so as to further psychedelic research, either through Psychedelic Foundation or through organizations such as the MAPS, the Albert Hofmann Foundation, or the Heffter Research Institute, the underwriters will not give preference because of the charity which is to receive the donor shares.

Services

Unlike pharmaceutical companies, whose business is the manufacture and sale of pharmaceuticals, CPC's primary business will not consist of drug sales but will consist of the service of providing professionally guided psychedelic "sessions." CPC may derive income from the manufacture and sale of its drugs, but this is expected to be incidental to the company's main business. The company's primary service will include screening and preparation for the sessions, conducting the session, and follow-up.

The company's structure consists of two divisions, the Psychedelic Therapy Division and the Psychedelic Professional Development Division. The company calls prospective purchasers of the services of the Psychedelic Therapy Division "patients" and calls prospective purchasers of the services of the Psychedelic Professional Development Division "clients."

Depending on regulatory and other matters, the two divisions and their centers may be located in the same state or in different states and in the same nation or in different nations. They may also be housed together or separately.

SESSIONS

Both therapeutic services and professional development services will consist of four phases: (1) screening, (2) preparation, (3) the session, and (4) post-session follow-up. Because these differ according to the nature of the patients and clients and the nature of the desired outcomes, the details of the procedures are only summarized here and are more fully described in *Manual of Procedures for Psychedelic Sessions,* which is incorporated herein by reference.

Screening consists of physical and psychological examinations to determine whether the applicant, clients, and patients are physically hardy enough to withstand possible stressful emotional and psychosomatic stress. Preparation consists of determining the client's/patient's personal preferences of setting and explaining to the client/patient the kinds of experiences he or she is likely to experience during the session, the activities which may occur (such as listening to music), and so forth. It will include establishing rapport with the guide or guides who will attend the patient/client during the session day. A typical session will take a full day. The client/patient will be accompanied throughout the session by at least one professional.

After a session, which may last 12 hours or more, clients and patients may stay overnight at the center or may be accompanied to their homes. In the case of patients who are residents at mental health treatment facilities, they will be returned to the custody of their institutions either the same day or they may stay overnight and return the next day. During the follow up, the session and its effects will be evaluated. In the case of patients, this activity will include consulting and/or reporting to the patient's doctor and/or therapist. In the case of clients, the client, as well as the sessions guide, will typically evaluate the outcome. Owing to the nature of psychedelic sessions, the follow-up evaluations may include unanticipated results as well as the intended ones.

THERAPY DIVISION

Psychedelic Therapy Centers will provide services only to clients who are referred by mental health professionals who are certified or licensed in the jurisdictions where the centers are located. In the United States, these will vary from state to state. Internationally, these will vary from country to country. Officially recognized competent authorities are likely to include, but not be limited to, psychiatrists, clinical psychologists, and others similarly licensed or certified.

At the present, CPC believes its proposed therapeutic services have been shown by preliminary studies to be safe and efficacious for the following indications: alcoholism, drug addiction, post-traumatic stress disorder, lost memory recovery, depression, autism, and selected neurotic and psychotic diagnoses recognized in the *Diagnostic and Statistical Manual—IV.* Regulatory approval will require additional studies to establish these claims.

As experience with these drugs and CPC's method of running sessions increases, CPC believes that other indications will emerge. Among these is the possibility that intense, overwhelming self-transcendent experiences may boost the immune system. CPC believes that to date existing studies suggest this may be the case, but that such evidence is not strong, and that additional studies may or may not confirm these leads.

Psychedelic Therapy Center's current plans call for some of its centers to be located in-house or on the grounds of existing mental health facilities such as state mental hospitals, private residential treatment centers, and similar locations. Other centers will be located as free-standing centers. CPC envisions free-standing centers located so as to serve the needs of several mental health facilities and professionals in an area.

CPC believes that psychedelic sessions also have value in the training of mental health professionals and will provide both preservice and in-service education for these groups. CPC plans to apply to appropriate governmental agencies and/or educational accrediting agencies for permission to offer Continuing Education Units, "CEU's." In some cases, these CEU's may be offered in conjunction with educational institutions such as medical schools, nursing schools, institutions of higher education, professional societies, and others. While CPC believes enough referrals will occur to make the Psychedelic Therapy Centers profitable, no assurance can be given that this will be the case.

PROFESSIONAL DEVELOPMENT DIVISION

Psychedelic Professional Development Centers will provide services for professional and vocational development in business, religion, education, scholarship, science, law, mental health, the arts, and related fields. Instead of being undertaken for the purpose of curing an existing mental health condition, sessions will be undertaken to work in these fields. CPC believes this division's proposed services have been shown to be safe and efficacious, but it makes no assurance that regulatory agencies will interpret the existing studies this way. A major barrier to regulatory approval is the assumption that psychoactive substances have appropriate use only in medicine and psychotherapy. CPC may have to undertake, or cause to be undertaken, additional studies to provide evidence of the usefulness of psychedelic sessions for nonmedical purposes.

Because the proposed activities of the PPDC are not medical or psychotherapeutic, it is not clear which governmental agencies, if any, have jurisdiction over these issues. This unresolved regulatory issue is especially acute for the religious, artistic, and educational uses because these areas have traditionally been outside U.S. government control. Pending the resolution of this issue, CPC may establish its first Professional Development Centers outside the United States.

Clients of the Professional Development Division must be certified as at low risk of aversive consequences from their sessions, and like the patients of the Psychedelic Therapy Centers, they will undergo screening, preparation, the session itself, and post-session follow-up.

Some Psychedelic Professional Develop Centers may be associated within one specific institution such as a major university, research facility, church, or monastery; others may serve consortia of institutions; and others may be associated with, or sponsored by, professional organizations.

DRUG DISCOVERY AND CANDIDATE DRUGS

While most pharmaceutical companies and drug discovery companies spend many years and much effort identifying new drug candidates, CPC believes it has already identified potentially successful investigational new drug candidates, including LSD, DPT (dipropyltryptamine), DMT (dimethyltryptamine), MDA, MDMA, psilocybin, ayahuasca, and mescaline. Other compounds may be added from time to time.

DRUG TESTING AND APPROVAL

Because appropriate Federal agencies in the United States and in selected foreign countries have already granted some of these drugs the status of Investigational New Drugs, CPC believes its applications for approvals as treatments will move expeditiously if additional scientific and medical studies are successful.

Investment Questions

How likely is this busfi idea to presage such a company and an initial public offering of its stock? Are there people who would invest in it? The chapters in these two volumes indicate a wide variety of possible medical and psycho-therapeutic applications, and the concluding chapter of Volume 2 describes nonmedical applications from creative problems solving and scientific insights to education and spiritual development. Many people already know of psyche-delics' positive uses, making them potential investors. Some potential investors have experienced psychedelic drugs themselves and believe they have benefited from them; others know people who have experienced psychedelic drugs and believe they have benefited from them; still others are familiar with the scientific and medical findings in pilot and preliminary studies.

PSYCHEDELICALLY INFORMED

Is there enough financial interest to organize such a company and offer its stock to the public? According to the 2002 National Survey on Drug Use and Health, 24,500,000 Americans have ever used LSD. The 2002 National Survey of Drug Use and Health estimates that 34,300,000 Americans have ever used some form of hallucinogens, with that number climbing every year. Here are another 10,000,000 people with some percentage wanting to invest in LSDD stock. If even 1% of the LSD number was likely investors that would be 245,000 people; of course, the actual number may be larger or smaller.

To start conservatively and consider only retirement accounts in the United States—IRA, 401(k), 403(b), and similar accounts—for only 1% of the former LSD users and assumed investments of $5,000 per person:

$$245,000 \times \$5,000 = \$1,225,000,000$$

Presumably, some investors would want to invest more than $5,000 per person.

LARGER RESERVOIRS OF MONEY

Individually controlled retirement funds are only a small slice of the overall equity investment pie, and other sources of funds exist. Mutual funds, banks, insurance companies, pension plans, and similar financial fiduciaries are bigger pools of funds. Could these numbers be doubled or more than doubled when we consider foreign investors? There are some very wealthy individuals and venture capitalists who realize the business potentials of psychedelics and know a good speculation when they see one. It is widely rumored that among the Silicon Valley multimillionaires and billionaires, there are many who use psychedelics or have used them in the past.

DUE DILIGENCE

But would professional investors want to take the risk of investing their clients' funds in LSDD? Exercising fiduciary responsibility requires them to carefully and thoroughly investigate possible investments for both their risks and for possible rewards. To do this for CPC, these financial intermediaries (people who handle other peoples' money) would have to acquaint themselves with the research such as the chapters in these two volumes and similar sources. While they probably wouldn't read the psychedelic research on their own, exercising "due diligence," as it's called, would inform them about psychedelics' potentials. An ironic side-benefit from a psychedelic stock offering is educating large and powerful groups about psychedelics' benefits. This benefit is not to be underestimated.

Another byproduct benefit of a psychedelic stock offering is that CPC would need medical and scientific research done. Just as happens with pharmaceutical and healthcare companies now, some of the funds raised would flow to universities and medical research institutes. Additionally, owners of LSDD could develop into a supporting constituency for supporting both CPC, specifically, and psychedelic research, in general. The charities that received their pro bono charitable allotments—churches, schools, universities, museums, hospitals, civic organizations, and so forth—would share an interest in psychedelics, learning about them and supporting further research. Again, the effect of this should not be underestimated.

In a broader framework, the chapters in these two volumes are about much more than curing specific illnesses; their implications go far beyond the field of medicine and healthcare. As this concluding chapter of this volume and its companion concluding chapter of Volume 2 propose, used carefully, psychedelics' benefits can extend to education, the arts, and religion (Roberts 2001, 2006) as well as medicine. As this section of the chapter shows, the business community can benefit from psychedelics and hasten these benefits for society.

CONCLUSIONS

The conclusions and recommendations we have considered here and the drug policy groups we have listed are only some of the ways and means of strengthening drug policy and appropriate medicinal applications. The Internet web sites we have given provide many links to other ways. We recommend you explore them and the chapters of Volume 2 where many other aspects of the applications of psychedelic medicines are explored.

NOTES

Thanks to our contributors for making these conclusions more apparent through their research and the reports provided here. These assessments of the therapeutic potentials need to be considered in light of the recommendations made in the previous chapters, especially Passie, Frecska and Greer, and Tolbert.

1. Thanks to Ede Frecska for his assistance in constructing this section, and the information provided by our contributors, especially Krupitsky and Kolp.

2. For Phase I, see Farber et al. (1998); Phase II for "limited" evidence, see Grof (1975; 1979); Halpern, Volume 2. We characterize Phase II evidence as "limited" when lacking the benefit of double-blind controls but strongly suggested from less rigorous forms of validation such as animal research, medical case studies, and personal accounts and case series.

3. MDMA has undergone several studies constituting Phase I trials, both in the United States and Europe, with hundreds of participants evaluated in controlled studies. For MDMA Phase I studies, see De la Torre et al. (2000); Grob et al. (1996); Liechti et al. (2000); Vollenweider et al. (1999); Gamma et al. (2000); Gouzoulis-Mayfrank and Daumann (2006); also see Mithoefer (2003); for current Phase II studies see Mithoefer, this volume.

4. For Phase I studies of DMT, see Strassman (2001).

5. For Phase I studies of Ayahuasca, see Grob et al. (1996); Callaway et al. (1999); for limited Phase II evidence, see McKenna, this volume, Mabit, Volume 2.

6. For Phase I and II evaluations of psilocybin, see Moreno and Delgado, Grob, this volume.

7. For Phase II evaluations, we have case studies of Peyote Church members (see Halpern 2004; Halpern et al. 2005 for reviews); for evidence of Phase III–approved therapeutic use, we have the practice of the Indian Health Service, a branch of the U.S. federal government, approving use of peyote for treatment of alcoholism among Native Americans (see Calabrese, Volume 2).

8. Ketamine is already classified as a Schedule III drug, with approved uses. Phase I, Phase II, and Phase III clinical trials in the ketamine psychedelic psychotherapeutic treatment of alcoholism and opioid dependence have been carried out, and currently there is research that constitutes the beginning of Phase IV (see Kolp and Krupitsky, Volume 2; Krupitsky et al. 2002).

9. The FDA-approved clinical trials of ibogaine were not, however, completed as NIDA withheld funding for the planned and approved Phase I and II protocols and subsequently ended its ibogaine evaluation project in 1995. Nonetheless, the continuing use of ibogaine for addictions treatment in the United States and around the world constitutes a "vast uncontrolled experiment," which when combined with the other kinds of studies (case reports, preclinical toxicological evaluation, and initial Phase I trials of safety pharmacokinetic; paraphrase from Alper and Lotosf, Volume 2), provides a substantial body of evidence constituting preclinical proof of concept (See Alper et al. 1999; Alper 2001; Mash et al. 1998, 2001; Alper and Lotosf, Volume 2).

10. Material in this section liberally adopted from www.drugpolicy.org.

11. Material in this section liberally adopted from www.cognitiveliberty.org.

12. Material in this section liberally adopted from www.maps.org.

REFERENCES

Alper, K.R. 2001. Ibogaine: A review. The alkaloids. *Chemistry and Biology* 56:1–38.

Alper, K.R., H.S. Lotsof, G.M. Frenken, D.J. Luciano, and J. Bastiaans. 1999. Treatment of acute opioid withdrawal with ibogaine. *American Journal of Addiction* 8 (3): 234–42.

Bravo, G., and C. Grob. 1989. Shamans, sacraments and psychiatrists. *Journal of Psychoactive Drugs* 21 (1):123–8.

Callaway, J.C., D.J. McKenna, C.S. Grob, G.S. Brito, L.P. Raymon, R.E. Poland, E.N. Andrade, E.O. Andrade, and D.C. Mash. 1999. Pharmacokinetics of hoasca alkaloids in healthy humans. *Journal of Ethnopharmacology* 65:243–56.

Cassiday, C. 1996. Cultural context of complementary and alternative medical systems. In *Fundamentals of complementary and alternative medicine,* ed. M. Micozzi, 9–34. New York: Churchill Livingstone.

De La Torre, R., M. Farre, P.N. Roset, C. Hernandez Lopez, M. Mas, J. Ortuno, E. Menoyo, N. Pizarro, J. Segura, and J. Cami. 2000. Pharmacology of MDMA in humans. *Annals of the New York Academy of Sciences* 914:225–37.

Doblin, R. 2001. Regulation of the medical use of psychedelics and marijuana. Doctoral dissertation, Harvard University.

Dobkin de Rios, M. 1994. Drug tourism in the Amazon. *Anthropology of Consciousness* 5 (1):16–9.

Farber, N.B., J. Hanslick, C. Kirby, L. McWilliams, and J.W. Olney. 1998. Serotonergic agents that activate 5HT2A receptors prevent NMDA antagonist neurotoxicity. *Neuropsychopharmacology* 18:57–62.

Federation of American Scientists. 1997. *Principles for practical drug policies,* http://www.fas.org/drugs/Principles.htm.

Gamma, A., E. Frei, D. Lehmann, R.D. Pascual-Marqui, D. Hell, and F.X. Vollenweider. 2000. Mood state and brain electric activity in ecstasy users. *Neuroreport* 11: 157–62.

Gouzoulis-Mayfrank, E., and J. Daumann. 2006. Neurotoxicity of methylenedioxyamphetamines (MDMA; ecstasy) in humans: How strong is the evidence for persistent brain damage? *Addiction* 101:348–61.

Grob, C., and G.L. Bravo. 1995. Human research with hallucinogens: Past lessons and current trends. *Yearbook of Transcultural Medicine and Psychotherapy,* 129–142.

Grob, C.S., D.J. McKenna, J.C. Callaway, G.S. Brito, E.S. Neves, G. Oberlaender, O.L. Saide, E. Labigalini, C. Tacla, C.T. Miranda, R.J. Strassman, and K.B. Boone. 1996. Human psychopharmacology of hoasca, a plant hallucinogen used in ritual context in Brazil. *The Journal of Nervous and Mental Disease* 184:86–94.

Grof, S. 1975. *Realms of the unconscious: Observations from LSD research.* New York: Viking Press.

Grof, S. 1979. *LSD psychotherapy.* Pomona, CA: Hunter House.

Halpern, J.H. 2004. Hallucinogens and dissociative agents naturally growing in the United States. *Pharmacology and Therapeutics* 102 (2):131–8.

Halpern, J.H., A.R. Sherwood, J.I. Hudson, D. Yurgelun-Todd, and H.G. Pope Jr. 2005. Psychological and cognitive effects of long-term peyote use among Native Americans. *Biological Psychiatry* 58 (8):624–31.

Kelsey, J., A. Whittemore, A. Evans, and W.D. Thompson. 1996. *Methods in observational epidemiology.* New York: Oxford University Press.

Krupitsky, E., A. Burakov, T. Romanova, I. Dunaevsky, R. Strassman, and A. Grinenko. 2002. Ketamine psychotherapy for heroin addiction: Immediate effects and two-year follow-up. *Journal of Substance Abuse Treatment* 23 (4):273–83.

Liechti, M.E., and F.X. Vollenweider. 2000. Acute psychological and physiological effects of MDMA ("Ecstasy") after haloperidol pretreatment in healthy humans. *European Neuropsychopharmacology: The Journal of the European College of Neuropsychopharmacology* 10:289–95.

Lintzeris, N., J. Strang, N. Metrebian, S. Byford, S. Lee, C. Hallam, and D. Zador. 2006. Methodology for the Randomised Injecting Opioid Treatment Trial (RIOTT): Evaluating injectable methadone and injectable heroin treatment versus optimised oral methadone treatment in the UK. *Journal of Harm Reduction* 3:28.

Mash, D.C., C.A. Kovera, B.E. Buch, M.D. Norenberg, P. Shapshak, W.L. Hearn, and J. Sanchz. 1998. Medication development of ibogaine as a pharmacotherapy for drug dependence. *Annals of the New York Academy of Sciences* 844:274–92.

Mash, D.C., C.A. Kovera, J. Pablo, R. Tyndale, F.R. Ervin, J.D. Kamlet, and W. Hearn. 2001. Ibogaine in the treatment of heroin withdrawal. *Alkaloids Chemistry Biology* 56:155–71.

McKee, J. 1988. Holistic health and the critique of Western Medicine. *Social Science and Medicine* 269:775–84.

Mithoefer, M.C. 2003, Revised 2005. Study Protocol Phase II clinical trial testing the safety and efficacy of 3,4methylenedioxymethamphetamine (MDMA)-assisted psychotherapy in subjects with chronic posttraumatic stress disorder. Study # 63-384, http://www.maps.org/research/mdma/ptsd_study/protocol/protocol030605.html.

Nichols, D.E. 2004. Hallucinogens. *Pharmacology and Therapeutics* 101 (2):131–81.

Roberts, T.B. 2006. *Psychedelic horizons: Snow White, immune system, multistate mind, enlarging education.* Exeter, U.K.: Imprint Academic.

Schultes, R., and A. Hofmann. 1979. *Plants of the gods.* New York: McGraw Hill. Repr. Rochester, VT: Healing Arts Press, 1992.

Schultes, R., and M. Winkelman. 1996. The principal American hallucinogenic plants and their bioactive and therapeutic properties. In *Sacred plants, consciousness and healing, yearbook of cross-cultural medicine and psychotherapy,* ed. M. Winkelman and W. Andritzky, Vol. 6, 205–40. Verlag: Berlin.

Strassman, R. 1984. Adverse reactions to psychedelic drugs: A review of the literature. *Journal of Nervous and Mental Disease* 172 (10):77–595.

Strassman, R. 1994. Hallucinogenic drugs in psychiatric research and treatment. *Journal of Nervous and Mental Disease* 183 (3):127–37.

Strassman, R. 2001. *DMT the Spirit Molecule.* Rochester, VT: Park Street Press.

Vollenweider, F.X., A. Gamma, M. Liechti, and T. Huber. 1999. Is a single dose of MDMA harmless? *Neuropsychopharmacology* 21:598–600.

Winkelman, M. 2005. Drug tourism or spiritual healing? Ayahuasca seekers in Amazonia. *Journal of Psychoactive Drugs* 37 (2):209–18.

Yensen, R. 1985. LSD and psychotherapy. *Journal of Psychoactive Drugs* 17 (4):267–77.

Yensen, R. 1996. From shamans and mystics to scientists and psychotherapists: Interdisciplinary perspectives on the interaction of psychedelic drugs and human consciousness. In *Sacred plants, consciousness and healing, yearbook of cross-cultural medicine and psychotherapy,* ed. M. Winkelman and W. Andritzky, Vol. 5. Berlin: Verland und Vertrieb.

INDEX

ABOUT THE EDITORS AND CONTRIBUTORS

EDITORS

Michael J. Winkelman, PhD (University of California-Irvine), MPH (University of Arizona), is an Associate Professor in the School of Human Evolution and Social Change at Arizona State University and former Head of Sociocultural Anthropology. He has served as President of the Anthropology of Consciousness section of the American Anthropological Association and was the founding President of its Society for the Anthropology of Religion. He has engaged in cross-cultural and interdisciplinary research on shamanism for the past 30 years, focusing principally on the cross-cultural patterns of shamanism and identifying the associated biological bases of shamanic universals and altered states of consciousness. His principal publications on shamanism include *Shamans, Priests and Witches* (1992) and *Shamanism: The Neural Ecology of Consciousness and Healing* (2000). He has also addressed the role of psychedelic medicines in shamanism, developing neurophenomenological perspectives that link the experiences to the underlying physiological processes (e.g., his coedited *Sacred Plants, Consciousness and Healing* [1996]). He has also explored the applications of shamanism to contemporary health problems of addiction ("Alternative and Traditional Medicine Approaches for Substance Abuse Programs: A Shamanic Perspective," *International Journal of Drug Policy* 12:337–351, 2001). He is currently working on a book on the biology of religion. He can be contacted at michael.winkelman@asu.edu.

Thomas B. Roberts, PhD (AB Hamilton College, MA University of Connecticut, PhD Stanford), is a Professor Emeritus at Northern Illinois University, where he taught *Foundations of Psychedelic Studies* since 1982 (currently as an Honors Program Seminar). This is the first catalog-established psychedelics course. He co-organized an entheogen conference cosponsored by the Chicago Theological Seminary and the Council on Spiritual Practices resulting in *Psychoactive Sacramentals* (2001). His publications include *Psychedelic Horizons: Snow White, Immune System, Multistate Mind, Enlarging Learning* (2006), and the online archive *Religion and Psychoactive Sacraments* (1992–2001) www.csp.org/chrestomathy. He wrote the entheogen chapter for the three-volume set *Where God and Science Meet* (2006) and is expanding it into a book *Increasing Spiritual Intelligence—Chemical Input, Religious Output.* He is a founding member of the Multidisciplinary Association for Psychedelic Studies and of the International Transpersonal Association and a cofounder of the Council on Spiritual Practices. As the first of his retirement activities, he spent the fall of 2006 as a Visiting Scientist at the Johns Hopkins Department of Psychiatry and Human Sciences' Behavioral Biology Research Center chairing a weekly staff development discussion about psychedelics.

CONTRIBUTORS

Donald I. Abrams, MD, is Chief of Hematology-Oncology, San Francisco General Hospital and Professor of Clinical Medicine, UCSF (University of California San Francisco). He is a graduate of Brown University and received his MD from the Stanford University School of Medicine. His postdoctoral training was in Internal Medicine at the Kaiser Foundation Hospital in San Francisco followed by a fellowship in Hematology-Oncology at the UCSF. He has been involved in research on HIV medicine since 1981, serving for many years as the assistant director of the UCSF Positive Health Program at San Francisco General Hospital. He recently became the Director of Clinical Programs at the UCSF Osher Center for Integrative Medicine. Since 1993, he has received two grants from the National Institute on Drug Abuse and three from the University of California Center for Medicinal Cannabis Research to conduct clinical trials investigating the safety and effectiveness of smoked cannabis in order to generate evidence in an arena where science does not always supersede the politics. Results of his team's studies have been presented at numerous international conferences and published in the *Annals of Internal Medicine, AIDS,* and the *Journal of Clinical Pharmacology.* He is a member of the editorial board of the *Journal of the International Association for Cannabis as Medicine.*

Richard Glen Boire, JD, received his law degree in 1990 from UC Berkeley's School of Law (Boalt Hall). He is one of the world's leading legal authorities on visionary plants and substances. From 1993 to 1999, he was the publisher and editor of TELR (*The Entheogen Law Reporter*). He is also the author of the books *Marijuana Law* and *Sacred Mushrooms and the Law*, and translator of the *Salvia Divinorum Growers Guide*. He is coauthor of *Medical Marijuana Law*. He has written legal chapters for a variety of books, including Timothy Leary's *The Politics of Psychopharmacology*. He has also authored legal articles in several textbooks and has published many articles on drug law and policy. He has testified about Ecstasy before the U.S. Sentencing Commission in Washington, D.C., and before the California Public Safety Committee. In each case, his testimony helped produce lower penalties for ecstasy than those under consideration. Since January 2000, in addition to his private law practice, he has served as legal counsel for the Center for Cognitive Liberty & Ethics, a law and policy center devoted to protecting freedom of thought and the unlimited potential of the human mind. He is a member of the California Bar and has been admitted to practice before the Ninth Circuit Court of Appeals, as well as the U.S. Supreme Court. He is a member of the National Association of Criminal Defense Attorneys, the NORML Legal Committee, the American Bar Association, and the California Bar Association. He can be reached at rgb@cognitiveliberty.org.

Pedro L. Delgado, MD, is Dielmann Professor and Chairman of the Department of Psychiatry and Associate Dean for Faculty Development and Professionalism at the School of Medicine, The University of Texas Health Sciences Center at San Antonio. He earned an MD with election into AOA and an MA in pharmacology from the University of Texas in Galveston. His internship and residency in psychiatry were completed at Yale University after which he served for several years on the Yale faculty. Between 1992 and 2000, he served at the University of Arizona, where he was Professor, Associate Department Head, and Director of Research in the Department of Psychiatry. From 2000 to 2005, he served as the Douglas Bond Professor and Chairman of the Department of Psychiatry, Case Western Reserve University. He is an internationally renowned researcher and frequent lecturer on the neurobiology of major depression and the biological mechanisms underlying antidepressant action. He has had continuous Federal funding for over 14 years for his research on the biology and treatment of depression. He is a past President of the ASHP (American Society for Hispanic Psychiatry) and takes an active role in mentoring young physicians.

Marlene Dobkin de Rios, PhD, is an Associate Clinical Professor of Psychiatry and Human Behavior at the University of California, Irvine, where she teaches 1st, 2nd, and 3rd year psychiatric residents and fellows on medical anthropological concepts. She is Professor Emerita of Anthropology at California State University Fullerton, where she taught medical and psychological anthropology for more than 30 years. Author of 5 books and more than

300 articles and book chapters on hallucinogens and culture, she has been the recipient of several grants and contracts over the years, including a Fulbright Travel Award and a NIMH training grant. She was a health science administrator at the National Institute of Mental Health from 1980 to 1981, overseeing a budget in excess of nine million dollars. Currently she works as a licensed psychotherapist in California with Latino immigrant clients. Her most recent book in the area of hallucinogenic research is *LSD, Spirituality and the Creative Process* (2003), published by Inner Traditions.

Kevin Feeney, JD, is a graduate of the University of Oregon School of Law, where he studied public interest and civil rights law. As a law student in 2003, he was selected to be the Summer Fellow for the CCLE (Center for Cognitive Liberty & Ethics) in Davis, California. While a Summer Fellow, he assisted the CCLE in conducting legal research, including investigating the legal foundations for religious peyote use by American Indians. This research led to the development of an unpublished article examining the conflict between survival of peyotism as a religious tradition and of peyote as a species, and how the conflict might be resolved in a legal context through use of the Endangered Species Act and various legal protections for religious freedom. His other research interests include examining the legal barriers and the developing legal issues surrounding the medical use of marijuana. He has written extensively on this subject and is coauthor, with Richard Glen Boire, of the book *Medical Marijuana Law* (2007). He previously self-published the *Oregon Medical Marijuana Law Reporter* (2003–2006), a tri-annual law journal that tracked and examined changes and advances in marijuana law, both nationally and at the state level. He is currently working in the field of drug and alcohol treatment, and serves on the Board of Directors for the Compassion Center, a nonprofit organization serving medical marijuana patients in the state of Oregon.

Ede Frecska, MD, PhD, is Chief of Psychiatry at the National Institute of Psychiatry and Neurology in Budapest, Hungary. He received his medical degree in 1977 from the Semmelweis University in Hungary. He then earned qualifications as certified psychologist from the Department of Psychology at Lorand Eotvos University in Budapest. He completed his residency training in Psychiatry both in Hungary (1986) and in the United States (1992). He is a qualified psychopharmacologist (1987) of international merit with 15 years of clinical and research experience in the United States (Mount Sinai School of Medicine in New York; State University of New York at Stony Brook; University of Florida at Gainesville), where he reached the rank of Associate Professorship. He published more than 50 peer-reviewed scientific papers and book chapters as an invited contributor in research on schizophrenia and affective illness. In his recent experimental work, he is engaged in studies on psychointegrator drugs and techniques. He is specifically interested in the neurobiological mechanism of initiation ceremonies (published in Ethos, 1987) and healing rituals using ayahuasca preparation (published in *Journal of Psychoactive Drugs,* 2003 and *Psychopharmacology* [Berlin], 2004). He has been participating in several pharmaceutical industry sponsored Phase II and Phase III (drug safety and efficacy) trials. He is a member of several professional organizations (American Psychiatric Association, European College of Neuropsychopharmacology, and Collegium Internationale Neuro-Psychopharmacologicum) and has received grants and awards from a variety of sources (National Alliance for Research on Schizophrenia and Depression and National Institute of Alcohol Abuse). His recent principal publications include Neuro-ontological interpretation of spiritual experiences. *Neuropsychopharmacologia Hungarica* (2006); Frecska E, Csokli Z, Nagy A, Kulcsar Z. (2004). Neurophenomenological analysis of the therapeutic relationship in ritual healing. *Neuropsychopharmacologia Hungarica, 6,* 133–143; and Frecska E, White KD, Luna LE. (2004). Effects of ayahuasca on binocular rivalry with dichoptic stimulus alternation. *Psychopharmacology* (Berlin), *173,* 79–87.

George Greer, MD, is the Medical Director of the Heffter Research Institute, the only scientific institution devoted to psychedelic research, and a clinical psychiatrist in Santa Fe, NM. In 1984, he and other authors in these volumes petitioned the Drug Enforcement Administration and testified at hearings against placing MDMA in Schedule I, in an attempt to keep it available for medical practice. He received his MD from the University of Texas Medical Branch. He is a Past President of the Psychiatric Medical Association of New Mexico and a Distinguished Fellow of the American Psychiatric Association. He was Chief Psychiatrist and Clinical Director of Mental Health Services for the New Mexico Corrections Department from 1990 to 1998.

Charles S. Grob, MD, is Director of the Division of Child and Adolescent Psychiatry at Harbor-UCLA Medical Center and Professor of Psychiatry and Pediatrics at the UCLA School of Medicine. He did his undergraduate work at Oberlin College and Columbia University and obtained a BS from Columbia in 1975. He received his MD from the State University of New York, Downstate Medical Center in 1979. Prior to his appointment at UCLA, Grob held teaching and clinical positions at the University of California at Irvine, College of Medicine, and the Johns Hopkins University School of Medicine, Departments of Psychiatry and Pediatrics. He conducted the first U.S. government–approved psychobiological research study of MDMA and was the principal investigator of an international research project in the Brazilian Amazon studying the visionary plant brew, ayahuasca. He is currently conducting an approved research investigation on the safety and efficacy of psilocybin treatment in terminally ill patients with anxiety (www.canceranxietystudy.org). He is the editor of *Hallucinogens: A Reader,* published by Tarcher/Putnam in 2002, and the coeditor (with Roger Walsh) of *Higher Wisdom: Eminent Elders Explore the Continuing Impact of Psychedelics,* published by SUNY Press in 2005, and he has published numerous articles on psychedelics in medical and psychiatric journals and collected volumes. He is a founding member of the Heffter Research Institute, which is devoted to fostering and funding research on psychedelics.

Alberto Groisman, PhD (University of London), was born in Porto Alegre, Brazil. He is an anthropologist who carries out research and teaches in the Department of Anthropology at Universidade Federal de Santa Catarina, Brazil. He has investigated the ritual-religious use of psychoactive substances since the 1980s, with fieldwork among participants of the ayahuasca religion Santo Daime in the group's headquarters, Ceu do Mapia, in the interior of Amazonia. He is interested in studying the reverse of the traditional anthropological approaches to the routes of diffusion from the Northern Hemisphere to the Southern Hemisphere, carrying out studies in 1990s among Santo Daime participants in the Netherlands. A member of the Associacao Brasileira de Antropologia, and American Anthropological Association, his main research interests are related to Symbolic Anthropology, Anthropology of Religions, Anthropology of Health, and ethnographic knowledge and the law. He has specifically worked on the relationships between religion and health, the ritual-religious use of psychoactive substances, ritual and health in Brazil, and psychoactive substances users' life history. In 2006, he participated in a postdoctorate program at Arizona State University on the legal status and treatment of the religious use of ayahuasca in the United States and how ethnographic knowledge has been used in these cases.

John H. Halpern, MD, is Assistant Professor of Psychiatry, Harvard Medical School, Boston, MA, and is Associate Director of Substance Abuse Research, Biological Psychiatry Laboratory, McLean Hospital, Belmont, MA. He has published extensively on the effects of hallucinogens and continues to research the special hallucinogen issues of legitimate religious use, health consequences from illicit use, and the potential therapeutic applications for drug and alcohol addiction, cluster headache, and for vexing end-of-life issues faced by the terminally ill. He has received from the National Institutes of Health direct research support for his work including a Career Development Award.

Dennis J. McKenna, PhD (MA in botany from the University of Hawaii), received a doctorate in Botanical Sciences from the University of British Columbia. He is currently a senior lecturer for the Center for Spirituality and Healing in the Academic Health Center at the University of Minnesota; he also works as a senior research scientist at the Natural Health Products Research Group of the British Columbia Institute of Technology, Vancouver. He received postdoctoral research fellowships in the Laboratory of Clinical Pharmacology, National Institute of Mental Health, and in the Department of Neurology, Stanford University School of Medicine. In 1990, he joined Shaman Pharmaceuticals as Director of Ethnopharmacology. He relocated to Minnesota in 1993 to join the Aveda Corporation, a manufacturer of natural cosmetic products, as Senior Research

Pharmacognosist. For 25 years, McKenna has studied ethnopharmacology and plant hallucinogens. He is coauthor, with his brother Terence, of *The Invisible Landscape* (Seabury Press, 1975; Citadel Press, 1991), a philosophical and metaphysical exploration of the ontological implications of psychedelics. He serves on the Advisory Board of the American Botanical Council and on the Editorial Board of *Phytomedicine: International Journal of Phytotherapy and Phytopharmacology*. He is a founding board member and Vice-President of the Heffter Research Institute, a nonprofit scientific organization dedicated to the investigation of therapeutic applications for psychedelic plants and compounds. He was a primary organizer and key scientific collaborator for the Hoasca Project, an international biomedical study of Hoasca, a psychoactive drink used in ritual contexts by indigenous peoples and syncretic religious groups in Brazil. He has conducted extensive ethnobotanical fieldwork in the Peruvian, Colombian, and Brazilian Amazon. He is author or coauthor of over 40 scientific papers in peer-reviewed journals such as the *Journal of Ethnopharmacology, European Journal of Pharmacology, Brain Research, Journal of Neuroscience, Journal of Neurochemistry, Journal of Nervous and Mental Disease,* and *Economic Botany.*

Michael Mithoefer, MD, is a psychiatrist in private practice in Charleston, SC, and is principal investigator in the current U.S. study into the effectiveness of MDMA-assisted psychotherapy for chronic PTSD. He is Board Certified in Psychiatry, Internal Medicine, and Emergency Medicine and is a Grof Certified Holotropic Breathwork Facilitator. In addition to research, his clinical practice includes treating patients with PTSD using combinations of psychotherapy, medication, and experiential techniques such as EMDR, body centered emotional release work, and Holotropic Breathwork. Much of his work is done in partnership with his wife, Ann Mithoefer, BSN, who was also trained and certified as a Holotropic Breathwork Facilitator by Stanislav Grof, MD, and is co-therapist in the MDMA/PTSD study.

Michael Montagne, PhD, is Professor of Social Pharmacy and Associate Dean of Graduate Studies at the Massachusetts College of Pharmacy and Health Sciences and Adjunct Professor of International Health at Boston University's School of Public Health. Educated in pharmacy and sociology at the University of Minnesota, he then received postdoctoral training in psychiatric epidemiology at Johns Hopkins University. He has coauthored *Searching for Magic Bullets: Orphan Drugs, Consumer Activism, and Pharmaceutical Development* (1994), *Clinical Research in Pharmaceutical Development* (1996), and *Pharmacoepidemiology: Principles & Practice* (2001). For over 20 years, he has contributed articles on psychedelic drugs to publications as diverse as the *Journal of Psychedelic Drugs, International Journal of the Addictions, Integration,* the *MAPS Newsletter,* and *Psychedelic Monographs & Essays* and book chapters for Tom Lyttle's *Psychedelics* and Julie Holland's *Ecstasy: A Complete Guide.* He also has continuously researched the social and cultural aspects of antidepressant medications from the second-generation tetracyclics in the early 1980s to the current SSRIs. His primary research interests are the meaning of drug effects, the social pharmacology of drug-taking experiences, and the process by which knowledge about drugs and their effects is socially constructed.

Francisco A. Moreno, MD, is an Associate Professor of Psychiatry at the University of Arizona College of Medicine. He has been conducting research in biology and treatment of mood and anxiety disorders, geared to improve our understanding of the brain basis for mental illness and the underlying mechanism of action of antidepressants/anti-anxiety drugs, and treatment resistance. He is originally from Mexico where he obtained his MD at the University of Baja California, then completed his psychiatry residency and research training in Neuropsychopharmacology at the University of Arizona Health Sciences. Through his research collaborations, he utilizes various research methodologies such as molecular, biochemical, electrophysiological, pharmacological, and behavioral correlates of depression and anxiety disorders. His work is funded by grants from the National Institutes of Health, private foundations, and collaborations with industry. He has supervised and mentored a number of interdisciplinary students, psychiatry residents, research fellows, and junior faculty. His clinical interest and expertise include treatment-resistant mood and anxiety disorders. He has written extensively in these topics, which include several papers in the role of psychedelics, serotonin, and OCD. He recently conducted a promising clinical pilot study of oral psilocybin administration in patients with obsessive compulsive disorder at the University of Arizona. He serves often as a psychopharmacology consultant to government institutions, health insurances, and pharmaceutical/device industry.

Torsten Passie, MD, PhD, is currently an Assistant Professor for Consciousness Studies at Hannover Medical School, Department of Clinical Psychiatry and Psychotherapy. He studied philosophy, sociology, and medicine and wrote a medical dissertation focused on the existential philosophical aspects of psychiatric diseases. Due to his specific interest in unconventional healing practices, he extensively travelled through Mexico and Guatemala. He worked at the Psychiatric University Clinic Zürich on altered states of consciousness. For some years, he worked as the last research assistant of Professor Hanscarl Leuner (Göttingen), the leading European authority on therapeutic use of hallucinogens. His research activities center on the psychophysiology and conceptualization of altered states of consciousness, including clinical research with hallucinogenic drugs. Other areas of interest include psychotherapy research, consciousness, addiction, phenomenological psychiatry, and shamanism. He is the author of comprehensive overview of psycholytic and psychedelic therapy (*Psycholytic and Psychedelic Therapy Research 1931–1995: A Complete International Bibliography,*

Hannover: Laurentius, 1997), and has published other articles on psychedelic medicines in *Addiction Biology* and the *Journal of Psychopharmacology.*

R. Andrew Sewell, MD, is an Assistant Psychiatrist at McLean Hospital/Harvard Medical School, where he works at the Alcohol and Drug Abuse Research Center following a dual residency in neurology and psychiatry at the University of Massachusetts Medical School. He is a member of the Scientific Program Committee of the American Neuropsychiatric Association, and also the Headache and Facial Pain Section of the American Academy of Neurology, and a longtime supporter of the Multidisciplinary Association for Psychedelic Studies. He is particularly interested in frontal lobe disexecutive disorders, trigeminal autonomic cephalgias, and psychedelic drugs.

Requa Tolbert, RN, MSN, is a psychiatric nurse and artist. She received her Masters in Nursing from Duke University. She and Dr. Greer are married, and they conducted therapeutic sessions with MDMA from 1980 to 1985, before MDMA became a controlled substance. They have written the only published clinical study to date on the therapeutic use of MDMA.